POWER FACTOR
TRAINING
LOGBOOK

PETER SISCO AND JOHN LITTLE

AUTHORS OF *POWER FACTOR TRAINING*

CB
CONTEMPORARY BOOKS

Library of Congress Cataloging-in-Publication Data

Sisco, Peter.
    Power factor training logbook / Peter Sisco and John Little.
       p.   cm. — (Power factor training)
    ISBN 0-8092-2429-1
    1. Weight lifting—Training.   I. Little, John R., 1960–
    II. Title.   III. Series.

    RC1220.W44S574   2000
    613.7'13—dc21   99-56933
                                              CIP

This book is dedicated to every bodybuilder and athlete who has an inquiring, rational mind; to every person who can throw off the chains of comfortable habit and unproven premises and move in a new direction that is guided by reason and observational evidence, no matter where that direction takes him; to every person who tries a thing and immediately thinks, "How can I make this better?"; to every person who is unafraid to challenge the false beliefs of the herd and lead others out of the caves and into the light.

In the parlance of bodybuilding, it is the people with these "genetics" who are truly the greatest champions of the human race. To these people, not just in the science of human strength but in every science, we owe our enormous gratitude.

Cover design by Todd Petersen
Cover and interior photographs by Mitsuru Okabe
Interior design by Hespenheide Design

Published by Contemporary Books
A division of NTC/Contemporary Publishing Group, Inc.
4255 West Touhy Avenue, Lincolnwood (Chicago), Illinois 60712-1975 U.S.A.
Copyright © 2000 by Peter N. Sisco and John R. Little
All rights reserved. No part of this book may be reproduced, stored in a retrieval
system, or transmitted in any form or by any means, electronic, mechanical,
photocopying, recording, or otherwise, without the prior written permission of
NTC/Contemporary Publishing Group, Inc.
Printed in the United States of America
International Standard Book Number: 0-8092-2429-1
00 01 02 03 04 05 RRD 15 14 13 12 11 10 9 8 7 6 5 4 3 2 1

Caution: This program involves a systematic progression of muscular overload that leads to the lifting of extremely heavy weights. As a result, a proper warm-up of muscles, tendons, ligaments, and joints is mandatory at the beginning of every workout.

Warning: As this is a very intense program, it requires both a thorough knowledge of proper exercise form and a base level of strength fitness. Although exercise is very beneficial, the potential for injury does exist, especially if the trainee is not in good physical condition. Always consult with your physician before beginning any program of progressive weight training or exercise. If you feel any strain or pain when you are exercising, stop immediately and consult your physician.

Other Books in the Power Factor Training Series

Power Factor Specialization: Abs & Legs

Power Factor Specialization: Shoulders & Back

Power Factor Specialization: Chest & Arms

Power Factor Training: A Scientific Approach to Building Lean Muscle Mass

Contents

Introduction

This book is your key to uninterrupted progress.

Without comprehensive knowledge of the amount of work your muscles are presently engaged in, you will have no way of knowing where you stand, where you are going, or how you're going to get there.

With this *Power Factor Training Logbook*, you will be able to know—instantly—whether or not you have had sufficient time off or too much time off, whether the weights you have chosen for your exercises are too heavy or too light, and whether the exercises you are currently using to develop strength and size in a specific body part are actually accomplishing that objective or are really wasting your time and training energy.

When Peter Sisco and I developed the principles of Power Factor Training in 1992, we were confident that if bodybuilders and strength athletes were serious about making progress (which is what all training is supposed to be about), then they would require something more tangible than the "do as you please," "train to the point of discomfort," "instinctive training" methodology that was then all the rage. That our approach would be so popularly received— by both the scientific community and the great mass of dedicated strength trainees—was not something we could have predicted.

The fabulous gains in muscle strength and size that trainees of our Power Factor Training system experienced (and continue to experience), are not, however, the result of our books. They are the result of the efforts of individuals such as you who opted to exercise their individual intellect and train intelligently—"by the numbers," if you will. They did the work. They understood that each workout was something to be surpassed, and, by keeping track of their progress by using the log sheets from our book *Power Factor Training*, they were able to identify their optimal (and highly individual) training loads, training exercises, and frequency of workouts.

A training logbook is very much like making a map of a journey, whose destination is the fulfillment of your physical potential. The logbook allows you to see at a glance where you have strayed off course; what routes brought you to your destination quickest; and what impact extraneous factors such as diet, sleep, and other forms of exercise have had on hastening your journey.

The contents of a typical Power Factor trainee's gym bag did not simply contain the usual mix of weight-lifting belts, lifting chalk, wrist straps, and hooks, but also featured several new items: a stopwatch, a pen, a calculator, and, most important, photocopies of the log sheets in *Power Factor Training*.

The *Power Factor Training Logbook* reflects new developments (such as data from our popular Power Factor Specialization series of books). We have also included a brief overview of the Power Factor Training system and its key principles. In addition, there are four appendices, providing workout records for complete workouts, specialized body part routines, individual exercises, and progress graphs for each of the exercises and training sessions you will be performing in your Power Factor Training workouts.

Without such knowledge, you are a traveler without a destination, a sailboat captain without a tiller. Unable to chart your own way, you are left to the mercy of the winds of any passing fancy, which, in many instances, will end up taking you miles off course. And, in the case of bodybuilding and personal fitness, the damage that could be done to your body can often be fatal.

As always, be your own best coach and personal trainer. You will know if you are progressing or "doing the right thing," taking enough time off in between workouts, or even lifting the weights in the proper manner by one simple factor: your progress records. If the numbers are increasing with each workout, then you're on the right track. If they have plateaued or decreased, then you've made a wrong turn somewhere. It's that quick and that simple.

With the *Power Factor Training Logbook*, you hold in your hands the key you need to unlock the greatest muscular size and strength gains of your life. Train by the numbers and everything else will look after itself.

Both Peter and I would like to thank you for your unwavering support of our efforts to demystify the science of muscle growth and encourage you to explore the new frontiers of strength and size that await you within the journey of your training career.

As always, train smart!

John Little
Co-Developer, Power Factor Training

The Power Factor Measurement and Why You Need It

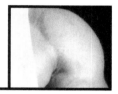

WHAT IS A POWER FACTOR?

We believe that there are two keys to stimulating muscle growth: (1) trigger growth by subjecting your muscles to an overload of "a great amount of work in a unit of time" and (2) make that overload progressively greater from workout to workout. Suppose you bench-press 150 pounds 30 times in 2 minutes today. And that's all you can do; you can't complete one more rep. Then you return to the gym next week and bench-press 150 pounds 30 times in 1.5 minutes, and that's all you can do; you can't get one more rep. Both days you lifted 150 pounds for 30 repetitions. But guess what? When you do it in 1.5 minutes, you are stronger than when you did it in 2 minutes.

If you don't believe us, ask Isaac Newton. It's a law of physics—the only way to lift the same amount of weight in a shorter amount of time is with a stronger "engine." If your muscles (the engine) are capable of lifting at a higher rate, then they must be stronger. With conventional weight training, however, the time it takes to perform the lifting is completely ignored. In the example we've just described, if you ignored time you would enter the same results for the two workouts in your logbook and promptly get discouraged that you are not making any progress.

THINKING IN POUNDS PER MINUTE

The Power Factor is a measurement of the total amount of weight you lift divided by the time it takes to lift it. It's measured in pounds per minute. Ask the average bodybuilder in a gym what he or she bench-presses and the reply might be, "I can bench 275." Ask a person who uses Power Factor Training the same question and the answer might be, "I can bench 5,300 pounds per minute." Because of the laws of physics and the law of muscle fiber recruitment, the latter is a much more comprehensive measurement. Once you begin to think in pounds per minute, your training objectives and progress become crystal clear.

Using Power Factor Training, you will be able to calculate a precise Power Factor and Power Index for each exercise you perform and for your entire workout. You will also be able to calculate ahead of time what workout you will be required to perform next time in order to meet your goals of increased size and strength. This means that every workout can pay off in gains. If it doesn't, you'll know exactly where and why you fell short.

You may, for example, find that your deadlift power went down 15 percent even when your leg press power went up 21 percent. This level of precision and isolation represents a revolution in strength training.

WHAT ABOUT DISTANCE?

At this point, you might be wondering why we haven't included the distance that the weight travels as part of the power calculation. There are two reasons that it is left out. First, as a practical matter it is difficult to measure precisely the movement of the bar when lifting, especially movements that involve an arc of motion, which require computations using pi (3.14159). Second, the length of your arms and legs isn't going to change over time, so all those distance measurements would just factor out of any comparisons that are made, leaving only differences in the weight lifted and the time. This is why we do not use horsepower or watts to measure the power that your muscles generate. A Power Factor is ideal because of its simplicity and ease of use.

DETERMINING YOUR POWER FACTOR

The purpose of calculating a Power Factor for each exercise you perform is to provide a precise numerical measurement of your muscular output. Once you have a numerical representation of your output, you can compare the overload and effectiveness of every workout that you perform. For example, examine the two workouts shown in Figures 1.1 and 1.2. (The time given for each total workout includes the time taken between exercises to rest and to set up the equipment. That's why the individual times do not add up to the total time.)

Of these two similar workouts, Workout 2 appears more rigorous because it involves a heavier weight in every exercise. It stimulates more growth, right? Wrong. Actually, Workout 1 has a Power Factor that is 38 percent higher than that of Workout 2 and involves lifting an additional 10,135 pounds of weight. Workout 1 represents more work in a unit of time—the key to muscle growth stimulation. It is virtually impossible to precisely gauge that difference by feel alone. With Power Factor Training, measuring by feel is obsolete.

Figure 1.1

WORKOUT 1

Exercise	Sets	Reps	Weight (lbs.)
Shoulder press	2	20	150
	2	20	180
	3	15	225
	Time to complete: 10 mins.		
Lat pulldown	2	30	80
	2	20	90
	2	15	100
	Time to complete: 11 mins.		
Barbell deadlift	2	30	135
	2	20	155
	2	15	175
	Time to complete: 14 mins.		
Total time to complete: 41 mins. *			

*includes 6 minutes to rest and set up equipment

Figure 1.2

WORKOUT 2

Exercise	Sets	Reps	Weight (lbs.)
Shoulder press	2	20	150
	2	12	190
	2	10	245
	1	3	260
	Time to complete: 13 mins.		
Lat pulldown	2	20	90
	2	15	100
	2	10	120
	Time to complete: 13 mins.		
Barbell deadlift	2	20	155
	2	20	175
	2	15	190
	Time to complete: 14 mins.		
Total time to complete: 46 mins. *			

*includes 6 minutes to rest and set up equipment

ANALYZING WITH THE POWER FACTOR

Let's use the Power Factor measurement to examine your shoulder press performance in Workouts 1 and 2 shown in Figure 1.1 and Figure 1.2.

In Workout 1, you begin by lifting 150 pounds 20 times and perform 2 sets for a total weight lifted of 6,000 pounds. Then you perform 2 sets of 20 repetitions with 180 pounds, which adds 7,200 pounds to the total. Finally, you increase the weight on the bar to 225 pounds and perform 3 sets of 15 reps to add an additional 10,125 pounds. This brings the total amount of weight you lift to 23,325 pounds. Since it takes you 10 minutes to lift all that weight, your rate of muscular output, or Power Factor, is 2,333 pounds per minute (23,325 pounds divided by 10 minutes).

In Workout 2, you start out by lifting the same 150 pounds 20 times for 2 sets for a total weight of 6,000 pounds Then, believing that simply adding weight alone will increase your muscular output, you increase the weight to 190 pounds and perform 2 sets of 12 reps for an additional 4,560 pounds. Pushing your limit further, you increase the weight to 245 pounds and perform 2 sets of 10 reps for an additional 4,900 pounds. Finally, still feeling strong, you increase the weight to 260 pounds and squeeze out 3 reps, bringing your total shoulder press weight to 16,240 pounds—exactly 7,085 pounds *less* than the same exercise in Workout 1! Further, since it takes 13 minutes to complete the shoulder press exercise, your Power Factor drops to a comparatively dismal 1,249. That's 1,084 pounds per minute less than Workout 1—a much lower intensity of lifting.

After the last rep on each of the shoulder press exercises, you are completely tired out. You are not able to complete another rep. You are "pumped," and by every sensory measure you feel that you have given your best effort to stimulate growth. But the fact is that by using the correct combinations of weight and repetitions, Workout 1 is 38 percent more effective at generating muscular overload and the growth stimulation that goes along with it.

The same calculations reveal similar results for both of the other exercises as well as for the overall workout.

Figure 1.3

POWER FACTORS FOR WORKOUTS 1 AND 2			
Exercise	Total Weight	Time	Power Factor
■ **WORKOUT 1**			
Shoulder press	23,325 lbs.	10 mins.	2,333 lbs./min.
Lat pulldown	11,400 lbs.	11 mins.	1,036 lbs./min.
Barbell deadlift	19,550 lbs.	14 mins.	1,396 lbs./min.
Total workout weight:	*54,275 lbs.*		
Total workout time:	*41 mins.**		
Overall workout Power Factor:	*1,324 lbs./min.*		
■ **WORKOUT 2**			
Shoulder press	16,240 lbs.	13 mins.	1,249 lbs./min.
Lat pulldown	9,000 lbs.	13 mins.	692 lbs./min.
Barbell deadlift	18,900 lbs.	14 mins.	1,350 lbs./min.
Total workout weight:	*44,140 lbs.*		
Total workout time:	*46 mins.**		
Overall workout Power Factor:	*960 lbs./min.*		

*includes rest and set-up time

FINDING YOUR "SWEET SPOT"

By all measures, Workout 1 is superior. The reason is that there is a relationship between the amount of weight that you put on the bar and the number of times you can lift it. It's obvious that if the weight is very light you can do many reps, but it takes a long time. If the weight is very heavy, you can only do a few reps, and the lifting will be completed quickly.

For example, suppose that you want to determine your muscular output at the two extreme ends of this spectrum. Using the bench press, first you select a very light weight, let's say 10 pounds, and you perform sets of 40 reps at a time. After 25 sets, you are completely fatigued and cannot perform another rep. All this takes 45 minutes. So, you lifted 10 pounds a total of 1,000 times for a total weight of 10,000 pounds. Since it took 45 minutes to lift all that weight, your Power Factor is 222 pounds per minute. That is a low Power Factor; our grandmothers could lift more than 222 pounds per minute.

Next, you test the other end of the spectrum by lifting the heaviest weight you possibly can. You put 300 pounds on the bar and, mustering all the strength you can, you perform 1 rep. You rest for a few seconds, and then try to get another rep, but you just can't; 300 pounds is your 1-rep maximum. This calculation is easy: 300 pounds in 1 minute is a Power Factor of 300 pounds per minute. It's also a very low Power Factor—a fraction of what you are capable of generating.

This example clearly illustrates a critically important element of strength training. If you lift too light a weight, you cannot generate a high Power Factor; yet if you lift too heavy a weight, you also cannot generate a high Power Factor. Somewhere in the middle lies your personal "sweet spot" where the perfect combination of weight, reps, and time yield your highest possible Power Factor. Finding that spot is the key to maximally efficient and productive workouts.

The optimal Power Factor varies considerably from person to person. Imagine that Jake and Enrico experiment to determine how the weight they are lifting affects the number of reps they can complete in a 2-minute period. Their results are shown in Figures 1.4, 1.5, and 1.6.

As you can see in Figure 1.5, Jake generates his highest Power Factor when he has 140 pounds on the bar. At that weight, he can get the best ratio of total weight lifted per unit of time. That is his sweet spot. Understanding this concept is the most critical element

Figure 1.4

Weight on Bar	JAKE			ENRICO		
	Total Reps	Total Weight (lbs.)	Power Factor (lbs./min.)	Total Reps	Total Weight (lbs.)	Power Factor (lbs./min.)
40	120	4,800	2,400	120	4,800	2,400
60	108	6,480	3,240	111	6,660	3,330
80	96	7,680	3,840	102	8,160	4,080
100	84	8,400	4,200	93	9,300	4,650
120	72	8,640	4,320	84	10,080	5,040
140	63	8,820	4,410	80	11,200	5,600
160	54	8,640	4,320	76	12,160	6,080
180	45	8,100	4,050	72	12,960	6,480
200	36	7,200	3,600	68	13,600	6,800
220	29	6,380	3,190	64	14,080	7,040
240	22	5,280	2,640	50	12,000	6,000
260	15	3,900	1,950	36	9,360	4,680
280	8	2,240	1,120	16	4,480	2,240
300	2	600	300	4	1,200	600

Figure 1.5

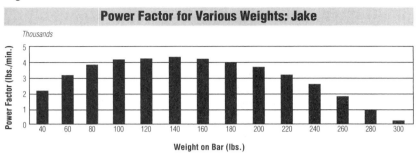

Figure 1.6

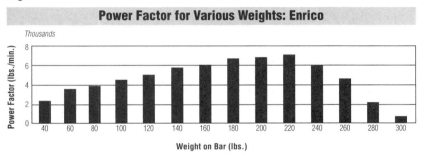

of Power Factor Training. Jake could put more weight on the bar. In fact, he can lift 300 pounds, but if he does, the total weight he can lift per minute is greatly decreased. Since human muscles grow stronger and larger only when taxed beyond their normal operating capacity, it is crucial to discover what your operating capacity is in the first place. Jake can lift 280 pounds 8 times in 2 minutes, and it will take everything he has to perform those reps, but it is nowhere near his muscles' full capacity for lifting. Therefore, while that routine might generate some adaptive response, it is very inefficient compared to Jake lifting 140 pounds 63 times in the same 2-minute period. This is a principle of physics. An engine that lifts 4,410 pounds per minute has to be more powerful than an engine that lifts 1,120 pounds per minute. Your muscle fibers are the engine; nothing else does the lifting.

Enrico has a different optimal Power Factor. His highest Power Factor is achieved when he has 220 pounds on the bar. He can put more or less weight on the bar, but his personal sweet spot is at 220 pounds.

Why? Many factors contribute to the ability of muscle fibers to activate and generate power. Some factors we know, and some we don't yet fully understand. Where the muscle physically attaches to the bone relative to the joint has a profound effect on leverage. The neural pathways between the brain and muscles have varying efficiencies in individuals. The body's ability to supply and process ATP (adenosine triphosphate) to the muscles varies between individuals, as does the mix of slow-twitch and fast-twitch fibers in each muscle. The complex cocktail of blood, oxygen, amino acids, and hormones that supplies the entire process of muscle building has nearly infinite possibilities of variation. But here is the good news. All you have to concentrate on is developing your highest possible Power Factor for each exercise, because it gives a clear indication of what is and is not delivering the most overload to your muscles.

You can't take blood samples and tissue biopsies after each exercise that you perform in order to analyze which technique is generating the greatest metabolic changes. You can't place your body in an MRI machine during each exercise to see what area of a muscle is activated by a particular exercise. You can't perform a CAT scan on your brain to determine what neural pathways are being activated by today's workout. But you don't need to! If your Power Factor is 6,500 pounds per minute this workout, and last workout it was 5,600 pounds per minute, then you are absolutely, positively generating more output from your muscles. And who cares if it's because of hormone secretion, neural pathways, or both? All these systems work together anyway, so isolating one or the other through complex testing does not really provide any practical benefit to the athlete who just wants results. Train by the numbers and everything else will take care of itself.

SIMPLE ARITHMETIC

As you perform your workout, all you need to do is keep track of how many minutes it takes to do each exercise (bench press, deadlifts, shrugs, etc.), how much weight you're using, and how many reps and sets you do with each weight. Record this information as follows on the Workout Record forms included in this book (see Appendixes A and B).

1. Enter the time of day that you begin your workout. This will be used to calculate your overall performance. In all cases, you should be sure to fully warm up before starting the clock on your workout. Take as long as you like to warm up; then start timing your Power Factor Training. Your warm-up should never be counted as part of your Power Factor; doing so will lead to an incentive to use heavy weights too quickly, ultimately causing injury.
2. Enter the time of day that you finish your workout.
3. Subtract your start time from your finish time to get the total time of your workout. Always express this in minutes only (e.g., 95 minutes, not 1 hour and 35 minutes). On the Workout Record, enter this time at the top of the page and on the last line. The total time should include all the time used from the beginning of your workout (but not the warm-up) to the end. It includes rests between sets, rests between exercises, the time you took changing weights, and the time you took to get a drink of water. It is not just the sum of your individual exercise times.
4. Calculate the total weight lifted per set by simple arithmetic. For example, if you perform 20 repetitions with 105 pounds, you multiply the two numbers to get 2,100 pounds. If you do 2 sets at that weight, you multiply by 2 to get 4,200 pounds. Put another way, you've lifted 105 pounds 40 times for a total weight lifted of 4,200 pounds. Again, do not include weight lifted during your warm-up. The warm-up itself should not degenerate into a workout.
5. Calculate the total weight per exercise by adding the row of subtotals.
6. Measure the exercise time from the time you start each individual exercise to the time you finish. It should always include the time you rest in between sets. It should not include warm-up time. You will find a stopwatch very helpful for measuring this time.
7. Calculate the Power Factor by dividing the total weight by the time it took to lift it. So, if you lift 16,730 pounds in 7.5 minutes, your Power Factor is 2,231 pounds per

minute (16,730 ÷ 7.5 = 2,231). This is the power output of your muscles. On average, every minute you lifted 2,231 pounds. If you can increase that number on your next workout, you will know that you have increased the overload and gained strength.

8. To calculate the Power Index, multiply the total weight by the Power Factor, and then divide the product by 1,000,000.

9. Calculate the total weight for the workout by adding the total weight from each exercise (in this example: 16,730 + 13,040 + 8,940 + 72,785 + 72,680 = 184,175 pounds). This number represents the total amount of weight you lifted during your workout.

10. To find the Power Factor for your overall workout, divide the total weight by the total time (in this case: 184,175 ÷ 46 = 4,004).

11. To calculate the Power Index for your workout, multiply the total weight by the Power Factor; then divide the product by 1,000,000 (in this example: 184,175 × 4,004 ÷ 1,000,000 = 737).

Filling in this form will give you all of the data that you need to measure the effectiveness of this workout, engineer the next workout, and keep your progress steady and consistent while avoiding overtraining.

The Power Factor measures the amount of weight lifted (in pounds) in the amount of time (in minutes) that it takes to do the lifting. The Power Factor is expressed in pounds per minute (lbs./min.). It is elegantly simple, yet profound in its result; it measures the muscular output of every exercise you perform! Once a means of quantifying muscular output is achieved, it gives the strength athlete the ability to clearly compare the effectiveness of altering factors such as number of reps per set, number of sets per exercise, slower or faster timing, lighter weights vs. heavier weights, number of days off between workouts, steak and egg breakfast vs. oatmeal breakfast, and so on.

Figure 1.7

WORKOUT RECORD	Date: 7 / 16 / 00

① Start Time: __8 : 05 A.M.__ **②** Finish Time: __8 : 51 A.M.__ **③** Total Time: __46 MINS.__

■ **Exercise: DEADLIFT**

Weight Reps Sets	Weight Reps Sets	Weight Reps Sets	Weight Reps Sets	Weight Reps Sets	Weight Reps Sets
105 × 20 × 2	135 × 20 × 2	155 × 20 × 1	155 × 26 × 1	× ×	× ×
Subtotal = 4,200 lbs.	Subtotal = 5,400 lbs.	Subtotal = 3,100 lbs.	Subtotal = 4,030 lbs.	Subtotal = lbs.	Subtotal = lbs.

Exercise 1:   Total Weight __16,730__ lbs. **⑤**   Time __7½__ mins. **⑥**   Power Factor __2,231__ lbs./min. **⑦**   Power Index __37.3__ **⑧**

■ **Exercise: BENCH PRESS**

Weight Reps Sets	Weight Reps Sets	Weight Reps Sets	Weight Reps Sets	Weight Reps Sets	Weight Reps Sets
120 × 15 × 2	140 × 15 × 2	160 × 13 × 1	160 × 11 × 1	175 × 8 × 1	× ×
Subtotal = 3,600 lbs.	Subtotal = 4,200 lbs.	Subtotal = 2,080 lbs.	Subtotal = 1,760 lbs.	Subtotal = 1,400 lbs.	Subtotal = lbs.

Exercise 2:   Total Weight __13,040__ lbs.   Time __8¼__ mins.   Power Factor __1,581__ lbs./min.   Power Index __20.6__

■ **Exercise: LAT PULLDOWN**

Weight Reps Sets	Weight Reps Sets	Weight Reps Sets	Weight Reps Sets	Weight Reps Sets	Weight Reps Sets
60 × 18 × 2	70 × 18 × 2	80 × 19 × 1	90 × 16 × 1	100 × 13 × 1	× ×
Subtotal = 2,160 lbs.	Subtotal = 2,520 lbs.	Subtotal = 1,520 lbs.	Subtotal = 1,440 lbs.	Subtotal = 1,300 lbs.	Subtotal = lbs.

Exercise 3:   Total Weight __8,940__ lbs.   Time __6¾__ mins.   Power Factor __1,324__ lbs./min.   Power Index __11.8__

■ **Exercise: LEG PRESS**

Weight Reps Sets	Weight Reps Sets	Weight Reps Sets	Weight Reps Sets	Weight Reps Sets	Weight Reps Sets
300 × 20 × 1	400 × 20 × 2	450 × 20 × 2	500 × 23 × 1	525 × 21 × 1	540 × 19 × 1
Subtotal = 6,000 lbs.	Subtotal = 16,000 lbs.	Subtotal = 18,000 lbs.	Subtotal = 11,500 lbs.	Subtotal = 11,025 lbs.	Subtotal = 10,260 lbs.

Exercise 4:   Total Weight __72,785__ lbs.   Time __7½__ mins.   Power Factor __9,705__ lbs./min.   Power Index __706__

■ **Exercise: TOE PRESS**

Weight Reps Sets	Weight Reps Sets	Weight Reps Sets	Weight Reps Sets	Weight Reps Sets	Weight Reps Sets
350 × 20 × 1	400 × 20 × 2	450 × 20 × 2	500 × 24 × 1	525 × 20 × 1	540 × 17 × 1
Subtotal = 7,000 lbs.	Subtotal = 16,000 lbs.	Subtotal = 18,000 lbs.	Subtotal = 12,000 lbs.	Subtotal = 10,500 lbs.	Subtotal = 9,180 lbs.

Exercise 5:   Total Weight __72,680__ lbs.   Time __7__ mins.   Power Factor __10,383__ lbs./min.   Power Index __755__

OVERALL WORKOUT: Total Weight __184,175__ lbs. **⑨**   Time __46__ mins. **③**   Power Factor __4,004__ lbs./min. **⑩**   Power Index __737__ **⑪**

Exercise Subtotal = Weight × Reps × Sets   ■ Power Factor = lbs./min.   ■ Power Index = Total Weight × Power Factor ÷ 1,000,000

2

The Power Index

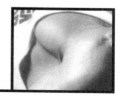

ALPHA STRENGTH AND BETA STRENGTH

The human body is a wonder of engineering. It has a remarkable variety of automatic survival and protection mechanisms that we are only beginning to understand. Breathe in some bacteria, and one mechanism goes to work. Cut your hand, and a different mechanism kicks in. Jump into cold water or get under the hot sun, and your body immediately goes to work compensating for the stress and sending survival signals to your brain. One of those safety systems prevents you from working out too strenuously. Call it fatigue, muscular failure, or running out of gas, it's what protects you from exercising to the point of putting too much stress on your body's recuperative abilities.

Like a machine, the body's strength or power can be measured in two ways. One measure is the rate of lifting that it can achieve, such as 2,000 pounds per minute. The other measure is the amount of time, such as 1 hour, that it can sustain that rate of work. Your protection mechanisms try to prevent you from operating at their extreme limits. That's why you can perform a set to failure but after only a few seconds of rest perform more reps with the same weight. Some people, after only 60 to 90 seconds of rest, can exactly duplicate the first set to failure. That means that they have much more strength capacity but do not tap into all of it in only 1 set.

This phenomenon of hitting an initial wall of fatigue that can be overcome with brief rest is just one more protection mechanism of your body. It keeps extra muscular energy in reserve just in case it's required in the near future. If you never use that reserve amount of strength, it will never grow to a higher level because it doesn't have to.

We call these two forms of human power alpha strength and beta strength. Alpha strength is akin to a snapshot in that it gives a measurement of your rate of lifting for a moment in time, perhaps a minute or two. Beta strength is more like a motion picture that measures how long you can sustain your alpha strength. There is a subtle but extremely important difference between alpha and beta strength.

To illustrate the point, consider that the 1995 edition of the *Guinness Book of Records* lists John "Jack" Atherton as setting a record by bench-pressing 1,134,828 total pounds in 12 hours. That's a rate of lifting of 1,576 pounds per minute, a rate most bodybuilders could duplicate, but he sustained that rate for 12 hours! I can already hear some of you saying, "Twelve hours? That's aerobic exercise!" However, while there is no question that sustaining activity for that long is aerobic in nature, the fact is that it was his muscles that lifted that million-plus pounds, not his well developed heart and lungs.

On the other hand, the Bill Kazmaiers and Anthony Clarks of the world can generate the highest alpha strength. A 700-pound-plus bench press or a 900-pound-plus squat are astronomically high rates of instantaneous muscular output that the human body will sustain for only a very short period of time.

Here is the most important fact for bodybuilders in all of this analysis: both alpha and beta forms of strength build muscle mass. Mass is the ingredient that every bodybuilder is after, but how many realize that if they are not making progress with one method of strength building they can try another? Most bodybuilders don't really care about strength per se; they just want to increase it as a means to gaining more mass. But understanding how strength manifests in the human body can help you measure and guarantee your progress.

If strength can be increased in two ways, then we need to measure it in two ways. We measure alpha strength with the formula W/t or total weight (W) divided by total time (t). The formula for beta strength is $W^2/t \times 10^{-6}$ or total weight (W) squared divided by total time (t) divided by 1,000,000. These two measurements are the Power Factor and Power Index, respectively. The Power Factor measures the intensity of your lifting (e.g., a bench press rate of 2,500 pounds per minute), whereas the Power Index is a relative measurement of how long you can sustain a given rate of lifting. If you sustain 2,500 pounds per minute for 3.5 minutes, for example, your Power Index is 21.9. If you sustain it for 11 minutes, your Power Index is 68.8. Notice that in both cases your Power Factor is the same 2,500 pounds per minute; there is no difference in alpha strength.

In a strict sense, any discussion of how strong or powerful a person is depends on the period of time over which we are measuring. Over a 10-second period, Anthony Clark is king. Over 12 hours, it's the aforementioned Jack Atherton. We wonder which of the two would be stronger over a 2-hour period.

We frequently talk to frustrated bodybuilders who are making no progress because they have fallen into the trap of performing only 1 set, 3 sets, 30 reps, or whatever. What they don't realize is that they are always measuring their progress on a fixed, usually short, time scale. In effect, they measure progress by alpha strength only and never really tax that reserve sustained strength, their beta strength. All of them could make new progress by measuring their beta strength and making sure that it progressively increases from workout to workout.

WHY YOU NEED THE POWER INDEX

There are two ways that you can get stronger. If you lifted 1,700 pounds per minute in your last workout and 2,000 pounds per minute today, then you are stronger. However, if you lifted 1,700 pounds per minute for 5 minutes last workout and 1,700 pounds per minute for 7 minutes today, you are also stronger, even though your Power Factor did not change. Why? Physics, again. If an engine (your muscles) can continue lifting at a certain rate but for a longer period of time, it has to be stronger. You can't get something for nothing; more work done requires more strength.

As your Power Factor Training progresses, you will become familiar with the two ways to achieve higher Power Factors. Basically, you can either lift more total weight, or you can lift the same weight in a shorter period of time. While both achievements represent an increase in muscular output, the tactic of constantly trying to work out in less time has obvious limitations. For one thing, the quicker your workout pace, the greater the likelihood of producing an injury. Also, constantly reducing the time of your workout will ignore beta strength training. Remember, being able to lift at the same rate but for a longer period of time also is an indication of increased strength.

You can achieve an extremely high Power Factor rating by performing certain exercises over a very short period of time. For example, suppose that you perform 6 calf raises with 500 pounds in 6 seconds. Your Power Factor, based on a pounds per minute average, would be a staggering 30,000 pounds per minute! Of course, you really didn't lift 30,000 pounds, nor did you work out for 1 minute, but your rate of lifting for 1/10th of a minute would be 30,000 pounds per minute! This is the limitation of looking at Power Factor numbers in isolation. Theoretically, you could increase your Power Factor every workout by using this tactic, but you'd be cheating yourself. This is where the Power Index measurement comes into play.

The Power Index is a mathematical function of the total weight lifted and the Power Factor. It simultaneously reflects both the total weight you lift and the rate of your lifting. Since the Power Index is calculated by multiplying the total weight (W) by the Power Factor (W/t), the weight component of your workout is actually squared. This produces a very large number, which is then divided by 1,000,000 in order to make it more manageable. Using the above example of 6 calf raises with 500 pounds in 6 seconds (30,000 Power Factor), the Power Index would be just 90 (3,000 lbs. × 30,000 lbs./min. ÷ 1,000,000). By way of contrast, during the development of this system we were routinely achieving Power Indexes in calf raises of well over 4,500!

Because calculating the Power Index involves squaring the total weight lifted, the Power Factor is graphed on a logarithmic scale. Consequently, a modest increase in strength can yield a large increase in the Power Index. These increases can be disproportionate both in raw numbers and in percentages (in fact, you shouldn't use percentages). The only important element is that the trend be in an upward direction. That is an indication of improvement and enough to help you progress.

You can't cheat the Power Index. The only way to make big gains in your Power Index is to work toward lifting at a high Power Factor and to keep it up for as long as you can. In short, you must maintain a high muscular output (pounds per minute) for as long as possible. The Power Index gives you a clear indication of whether your strength is increasing by measuring your capacity to continue lifting at the same rate but for a longer time. The Power Factor gives you a clear indication of whether or not your strength is increasing by measuring your capacity to lift at a higher rate.

Those are the only two ways your muscles (or any engine) can get stronger. By monitoring these two numbers, you will have instant feedback as to which exercises and techniques yield results and which do not. You can also instantly spot overtraining or a plateau. The efficiency of this system is what makes it revolutionary. As you will see, the gains you stand to make will be spectacular.

SISCO'S LAWS OF BODYBUILDING

Momentary Intensity ($I_m = {}^W\!/t$)
1. In the realm of human exertion, there are actually two forms of strength, which we refer to as alpha strength and beta strength. The measure of alpha strength is what we call the Power Factor (*PF*). Momentary intensity is expressed mathematically as $I_m = {}^W\!/t$, where W is the total weight lifted in pounds and t is the total time in minutes. A high intensity of muscular overload is one of

the indispensable conditions of triggering muscle growth. It therefore is important, in the interest of greater precision, to have a means of quantifying that intensity.

When we quantify momentary intensity with the Power Factor (*PF*) measurement, we can identify and increase alpha strength. For example, if a trainee performs 20 reps with 200 pounds in 2 minutes, he has lifted a total weight of 4,000 pounds for a Power Factor of 2,000 pounds per minute (20 × 200 lbs. ÷ 2 mins. = 2,000 lbs./min.) If that same trainee, next time in the gym, performs 20 reps with 200 pounds in only 1.5 minutes, his Power Factor increases to 2,667 pounds per minute (20 × 200 lbs. ÷ 1.5 mins. = 2,667 lbs./min.). This increase in Power Factor accurately reflects the trainee's ability to perform the exercise at a higher intensity. Without this measurement, on both workout days the trainee would simply enter "20 reps at 200 pounds" or "2 sets of 10 reps at 200 pounds" in his logbook and promptly get discouraged that he made no progress when, in fact, he made great progress.

2. *The momentary intensity (I_m) of any exercise is inversely proportionate to the duration (D) over which it can be sustained.* In plain English, the longer the duration of an exercise or workout, the lower the momentary intensity must be. This law is self-evident. You can perform more reps before reaching fatigue with 10 pounds than with 100 pounds, but it takes longer.

Volumetric Intensity ($I_v = {}^{W^2}\!/t \times 10^{-6}$)

3. We measure beta strength in terms of the Power Index through volumetric intensity (I_v). Mathematically, it is expressed as $I_v = {}^{W^2}\!/t \times 10^{-6}$, where W is the total weight lifted in pounds and t is the total time in minutes.

When we measure intensity with the Power Index, we can identify an increase in beta strength. For example, suppose a trainee performs an exercise with a Power Factor of 1,500 pounds per minute (his momentary inten-

sity) and is able to sustain that rate of lifting for 3 minutes before he is at failure. Next time in the gym, he still
has a Power Factor of 1,500 pounds per minute but is able
to sustain it for 4.5 minutes before he reaches failure. If
we look only at his Power Factor (momentary intensity),
he has made no progress. However, it is obvious that he is
stronger, since he can sustain the same high level of muscular output for a longer period of time. This ability is his
beta strength, and it is measured with the Power Index.
His initial Power Index is 6.8, and his second Power
Index is 10.1. This increase in Power Index accurately
reflects the trainee's ability to sustain the intensity for a
longer period of time.

Frequency of Training Is Inversely Proportional to Volumetric Intensity

4. The body needs time to recover, so your Power Index will
be lower when you train more frequently (other things
being equal). In scientific terms, the volumetric intensity
of a workout is inversely proportional to the frequency of
training, due to the trainee's finite recovery capacity.
Stated mathematically, $F = R/I_v$, where F is the frequency
of training, R is the trainee's recovery capacity, and I_v is
the volumetric intensity of the workout.

   Human physiology is such that while a person can
increase his or her muscular strength by a factor of at
least 300 percent, his or her other supporting organs will
not increase their functional capacity at the same time or
to the same degree. For example, there is a limit on how
much cellular waste your kidneys can process in, say, a 24-
hour period. If you double your strength through weight
lifting, your kidneys will not also double their efficiency
or size so they can process more in 24 hours. Since organs
like the kidneys, liver, and pancreas have relatively fixed
rates of performing their functions and will not grow
larger and more efficient with more use, it is necessary to

give them more time to complete their jobs as you get stronger. The fact is, humans have the ability to perform muscular work at a higher rate than their supporting organs can replenish themselves.

At this time, we have no unit of measurement for recovery capacity (R), and it certainly must vary enormously among individuals, as well as in the same person from time to time. For example, when ill or when getting over an illness you would have a greatly diminished recovery capacity. What is important to remember is the principle that, because of a relatively fixed and finite recovery capacity, your frequency of training (F) must decrease as your volumetric intensity (I_v) increases.

This law prevents consistent progress when using a fixed training schedule. In other words, if you always train 3 days per week, you will reach a point where your volumetric intensity (or Power Index) cannot be progressively increased. Without progressive overload, there can be no new growth stimulation. You must decrease training frequency if you want to increase intensity. Like gravity, it's the law.

THE MILLION-POUND CLUB

If you would like an idea of how dramatic a trainee's results can be when Sisco's laws are properly obeyed and applied, consider this example. When we first began the development of Power Factor Training in 1992, our performances were nothing spectacular. A typical workout of shoulders and arms, consisting of three different exercises, yielded an overall workout performance of a 343 Power Factor and a 5.3 Power Index. Similarly, a chest, back, and legs workout, consisting of three different exercises, yielded an 848 Power Factor and a 36 Power Index.

At this point, the twofold benefit of (1) exercising in the strongest range of motion combined with (2) exact monitoring of muscular power output (to avoid both wasted effort and overtraining) led to an explosion of improvement. We were able to add more exercises to our workouts and more weight to each exercise. After 52 days on the program (comprised of only 16 workouts), our shoulder and arm workouts yielded a Power Factor of 3,948 with a Power Index of 1,387. Our chest, back, and leg workouts now yielded a Power Factor of 6,423 and a Power Index of 3,713. Workouts that had begun with bench presses, shrugs, and leg presses of 175 pounds, 135 pounds, and 450 pounds, respectively, were now up to an astounding 500 pounds, 540 pounds, and 1,325 pounds, respectively! And these were not single-repetition weights. These were "sweet spot" workout weights that we used to perform many sets of multiple repetitions.

On day 40 of the program, we arranged a special test of the system. We took a couple of days of extra rest and were careful to carb up with the proper foods. We designed a special workout that combined upper and lower body parts and performed, in effect, a whole-body workout. We used the bench press, deadlift, barbell shrug, leg press, and toe press and, in 131 minutes, we each lifted 1,000,375 pounds. This yielded a Power Factor of 7,636 pounds per minute and a Power Index of 7,639. By way of comparison, that Power Factor is equivalent to lifting two Lincoln Continentals every minute! Further, we kept up that pace for 2 hours and 11 minutes! This clearly and convincingly demonstrates the fantastic muscle-and strength-building capacity and efficiency of this training system.

3

Monitoring for Optimum Results

Never perform a blind workout wherein you just lift weight without regard to the reps, sets, and exact time taken for each exercise. It's a wasted workout. Even if the intensity is sufficient to stimulate some new muscle growth, you'll have no way of knowing what intensity you need next time you're in the gym. It's sloppy, and there is no excuse for it. The most significant ramification of the innovation of the Power Factor and the Power Index is the ability, for the first time in the history of strength training, to provide a simple and mathematically precise indication of muscular output. Once this ability is established, it provides the most effective and efficient way to objectively measure your progress. Theories, myths, folklore, and science can all be put to the ultimate laboratory tests: How much overload does it deliver to the muscles? Does it develop greater strength? How much? How fast?

And this is just the tip of the proverbial iceberg. Henceforth, every factor that contributes to or detracts from your progress now also can be measured. You will be able to accurately measure the effect of more or fewer reps, more or fewer sets, heavier or lighter weight, longer or shorter workouts, extra days off in between workouts, using different supplements, varying other aspects of your diet, and so on. In the domain of body-building, powerlifting, or any other form of strength training, such instant and precise assessment is nothing short of revolutionary. No longer is it necessary for the strength athlete to measure his or her progress by feel or instinct. And all the equipment you need to unleash this powerful new technology is this logbook and a stopwatch—common items in virtually every other sport and yet so crucial in determining and plotting progress.

Could you imagine, for example, an Olympic miler trying to monitor his or her progress by feel while experimenting with running techniques like wind sprints, intervals, running hills, and so on, never measuring progress by using a stopwatch, never having any tangible, objective measure of the effects of his or her training techniques nor of improvement from one month to the next? Yet this is exactly the type of low-tech methodology that strength athletes have always used.

WRITE IT DOWN

During your Power Factor Training workouts, you will record on the Workout Record form the time, sets, reps, and weights that you lifted. After you perform a workout, record your results for each individual exercise and your overall workout performance on the Exercise/Workout Performance Record forms included in this book (see Appendix C). The only calculation you need to carry out on the Exercise/Workout Performance Record forms is the percentage of change from workout to workout. To find the percentage of change, use this simple method:

1. New Number − Old Number = Difference
2. Difference ÷ Old Number × 100% = % Change

For example; suppose your Power Factor goes from 1,675 to 1,890. Find the percentage of change.

$$1,890 - 1,675 = 215$$
$$215 \div 1,675 = .128 \times 100\% = 12.8\%$$

Figure 3.1

DEADLIFT PERFORMANCE RECORD						
Date	Total Weight	% Change	Power Factor	% Change	Power Index	+ or − Change
6/7/00	22,000	—	2,200	—	48	—
6/14/00	31,000	41	2,900	32	90	+42
6/21/00	37,400	20	4,300	48	161	+71
6/28/00	39,800	6	4,500	5	179	+18
7/15/00	48,000	21	4,400	−2	211	+32
7/30/00	61,500	28	6,900	57	424	+213
8/30/00	71,000	15	7,100	3	504	+80

PLAN AHEAD

One of the most powerful aspects of Power Factor Training is its ability to permit you to plan a workout ahead of time in order to achieve a target goal. The calculations necessary to do this are fairly simple, and we encourage you to familiarize yourself with the technique, as it is the key to guaranteeing that every workout is effective, efficient, and progressive. As you do so, keep in mind that the two keys to maximum overload are total weight and time. Those are the only two factors that you will adjust in your workouts.

For example, using the bench press numbers from Figure 3.2, we see that the total weight lifted was 13,040 pounds, and the Power Factor was 1,581 pounds per minute. You can find the time it took you to perform this exercise by looking at the Workout Record or by dividing the total weight by the Power Factor (13,040 ÷ 1,581 = 8.25). Now suppose you set a goal of achieving a 20 percent increase in your total weight and a 10 percent increase in your Power Factor the next time you perform the bench press. Simply follow these steps:

1. Add 20 percent to 13,040 pounds (13,040 × 1.20 = 15,650).
2. Add 10 percent to 1,581 pounds per minute (1,581 × 1.10 = 1,739).
3. Divide the goal total weight by the goal Power Factor. Your result is the time (in minutes) allowed to perform the lifting (15,650 ÷ 1,739 = 9.0).

As a result of having made these simple calculations, you now know exactly what you have to do in your next workout to ensure that your muscular output (overload) is higher: you have to lift 15,650 pounds in 9 minutes (see Figure 3.2). You can achieve your goal total weight simply by increasing your bench press Power Factor (pounds per minute) by adding an extra set or more reps to each set or by using a heavier weight so that the total will be 15,650 pounds. As you work out, keep an eye on your stopwatch to ensure

Figure 3.2

COMPONENTS OF A POWER FACTOR TRAINING GOAL			
	Total Weight (lbs.)	Power Factor (lbs./min.)	Time (mins.)
Current Performance	13,040	1,581	8.25
Goal	15,650	1,739	9.00

that you don't go over the 9 minutes you've set as your target time, and you will be certain that your Power Factor and Power Index have increased.

Here is one of the most important things to keep in mind. Ideally, no two workouts should ever be the same, because each time you return to the gym, you are a different person. If your last workout was properly engineered, it stimulated muscle growth, and if you allowed yourself the required time for recovery and growth, you are stronger when you return to the gym. Therefore, performing the same workout as last time is useless. Since your muscles are now capable of more output, the old workout will not trigger any growth response. Get it? That's what "progressive" overload is all about. Do the same workout every time, and you get nowhere; engineer an ever-increasing overload, and you get steadily stronger. The "engineering" is done with the Power Factor and Power Index numbers.

Goals can be set for one or all exercises you perform and for your total workout as well. It is difficult to overstate the tremendous value of this ability to plan every workout to ensure that it is productive. This is the element of Power Factor Training that creates its efficiency and is the reason that such a high percentage of its trainees can work out once a week or less and still see consistent improvement all the way to the optimum-level muscularity that they desire. Every workout is a positive step toward the trainee's ultimate goal. Compare this to the old system of everyone following a prescribed chart of exercises for 6 weeks, and then switching to another chart for 6 more weeks, and so on, with every trainee using the same daily schedule and repetition schemes regardless of the fact that there is a huge amount of variation among individuals (remember the sweet spot). Power Factor Training gives you the ability to engineer every workout that you perform to be maximally productive for your particular physiology.

GRAPH YOUR RESULTS

This technique of scientifically planning your goals ahead of time and monitoring your results permits the highest possible muscular overload each workout and the greatest possible gains in size and strength. You will readily see your progress by plotting your Power Factor and Power Index numbers on the graph paper located in this logbook. The graph shown in Figure 3.3 reflects one trainee's

Figure 3.3

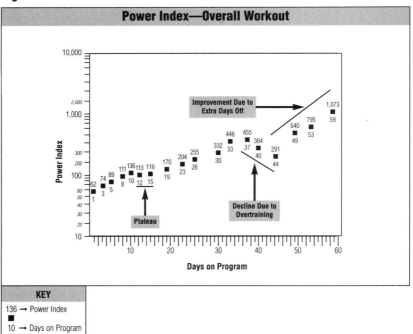

change in overall workout Power Index during a period of 18 workouts over 60 days. The trend that you should see on your graph is a consistent increase in your Power Factor and Power Index numbers, both on individual exercises and on your overall workout.

As in the example, a workout may not always yield an increase, and you may even see a decrease in your numbers. This, as you will discover, can be caused by a variety of circumstances. You may have worked out after eating too few carbohydrates, after having had too little sleep, or when unable to concentrate due to stress. However, the number-one cause of a prolonged inability to improve is overtraining. It is critical to remember that muscular growth takes place only after you have recovered from your last workout. The recovery and growth processes each require time to complete themselves. If you do not allow for this fact, your muscles cannot grow.

Figure 3.3 shows steady progress on a Monday, Wednesday, and Friday schedule, but by day 12 a decline in the Power Index occurs. By switching to a schedule of two days per week, the trainee's metabolism has the required time not only to recover, but to increase muscle mass. On a twice-a-week schedule, tremendous gains are made up to day 33. At this point, rather than just hitting a plateau, muscular output decreases sharply. Once again, this is corrected by adding more time off between workouts, and the trainee's Power Index again shows a tremendous improvement.

You will note that the change in Power Index from day 1 to day 59 is enormous. This reflects a great increase in both the total amount of weight lifted and the rate of lifting (pounds/minute). Such numerical gains can be achieved only through a great increase in muscular strength and therefore create a corresponding increase in muscular size.

Importantly, even subtle changes in the athlete's performance can be quickly and graphically identified and corrected through proper alterations in the workout and/or training schedule. Power Factor Training identifies and prevents the chronic plateaus and overtraining that plague strength athletes who rely on the crude gauge of feel and instinct to measure their performance.

APPENDIX A: Workout Records for Power Factor Workouts A and B

These forms are used each time you perform Power Factor Workout A or B from our book, *Power Factor Training: A Scientific Approach to Building Lean Muscle Mass.* These workouts involve performing five different exercises. (Forms for the specialized routines in our Power Factor Specialization series begin on page 73.)

Simply fill in the amount of weight, number of reps, and number of sets for each exercise. Pages 8 to 10 show the step-by-step calculations that yield your all-important Power Factor and Power Index numbers for each exercise and for each workout. These two numbers measure the intensity of your muscular output and are used to guarantee that each successive workout is progressive and productive.

The Power Factor and Power Index numbers from these pages will also be recorded in Appendix C, to create charts of individual exercise progress, and in Appendix D, to create graphs of individual exercise progress.

WORKOUT A RECORD   Date: ____ / ____ / ____

Start Time: _____   **Finish Time:** _____   **Total Time:** _____

■ **Exercise: STANDING BARBELL PRESS**

Weight Reps Sets	Weight Reps Sets	Weight Reps Sets	Weight Reps Sets	Weight Reps Sets	Weight Reps Sets
× ×	× ×	× ×	× ×	× ×	× ×
Subtotal = lbs.	Subtotal = lbs.	Subtotal = lbs.	Subtotal = lbs.	Subtotal = lbs.	Subtotal = lbs.

Exercise 1:   *Total Weight* _____ *lbs.   Time* _____ *mins.   Power Factor* _____ *lbs./min.   Power Index* _____

■ **Exercise: BARBELL SHRUG**

Weight Reps Sets	Weight Reps Sets	Weight Reps Sets	Weight Reps Sets	Weight Reps Sets	Weight Reps Sets
× ×	× ×	× ×	× ×	× ×	× ×
Subtotal = lbs.	Subtotal = lbs.	Subtotal = lbs.	Subtotal = lbs.	Subtotal = lbs.	Subtotal = lbs.

Exercise 2:   *Total Weight* _____ *lbs.   Time* _____ *mins.   Power Factor* _____ *lbs./min.   Power Index* _____

■ **Exercise: CLOSE-GRIP BENCH PRESS**

Weight Reps Sets	Weight Reps Sets	Weight Reps Sets	Weight Reps Sets	Weight Reps Sets	Weight Reps Sets
× ×	× ×	× ×	× ×	× ×	× ×
Subtotal = lbs.	Subtotal = lbs.	Subtotal = lbs.	Subtotal = lbs.	Subtotal = lbs.	Subtotal = lbs.

Exercise 3:   *Total Weight* _____ *lbs.   Time* _____ *mins.   Power Factor* _____ *lbs./min.   Power Index* _____

■ **Exercise: PREACHER CURL**

Weight Reps Sets	Weight Reps Sets	Weight Reps Sets	Weight Reps Sets	Weight Reps Sets	Weight Reps Sets
× ×	× ×	× ×	× ×	× ×	× ×
Subtotal = lbs.	Subtotal = lbs.	Subtotal = lbs.	Subtotal = lbs.	Subtotal = lbs.	Subtotal = lbs.

Exercise 4:   *Total Weight* _____ *lbs.   Time* _____ *mins.   Power Factor* _____ *lbs./min.   Power Index* _____

■ **Exercise: WEIGHTED CRUNCH**

Weight Reps Sets	Weight Reps Sets	Weight Reps Sets	Weight Reps Sets	Weight Reps Sets	Weight Reps Sets
× ×	× ×	× ×	× ×	× ×	× ×
Subtotal = lbs.	Subtotal = lbs.	Subtotal = lbs.	Subtotal = lbs.	Subtotal = lbs.	Subtotal = lbs.

Exercise 5:   *Total Weight* _____ *lbs.   Time* _____ *mins.   Power Factor* _____ *lbs./min.   Power Index* _____

OVERALL WORKOUT: *Total Weight* _____ *lbs.   Time* _____ *mins.   Power Factor* _____ *lbs./min.   Power Index* _____

Exercise Subtotal = Weight × Reps × Sets   ■ Power Factor = lbs./min.   ■ Power Index = Total Weight × Power Factor ÷ 1,000,000

WORKOUT A RECORD

Date: ____ / ____ / ____

Start Time: _____   Finish Time: _____   Total Time: _____

▪ Exercise: STANDING BARBELL PRESS

Weight Reps Sets	Weight Reps Sets	Weight Reps Sets	Weight Reps Sets	Weight Reps Sets	Weight Reps Sets
✕ ✕	✕ ✕	✕ ✕	✕ ✕	✕ ✕	✕ ✕
Subtotal = lbs.	Subtotal = lbs.	Subtotal = lbs.	Subtotal = lbs.	Subtotal = lbs.	Subtotal = lbs.

Exercise 1:   Total Weight _____ lbs.   Time _____ mins.   Power Factor _____ lbs./min.   Power Index _____

▪ Exercise: BARBELL SHRUG

Weight Reps Sets	Weight Reps Sets	Weight Reps Sets	Weight Reps Sets	Weight Reps Sets	Weight Reps Sets
✕ ✕	✕ ✕	✕ ✕	✕ ✕	✕ ✕	✕ ✕
Subtotal = lbs.	Subtotal = lbs.	Subtotal = lbs.	Subtotal = lbs.	Subtotal = lbs.	Subtotal = lbs.

Exercise 2:   Total Weight _____ lbs.   Time _____ mins.   Power Factor _____ lbs./min.   Power Index _____

▪ Exercise: CLOSE-GRIP BENCH PRESS

Weight Reps Sets	Weight Reps Sets	Weight Reps Sets	Weight Reps Sets	Weight Reps Sets	Weight Reps Sets
✕ ✕	✕ ✕	✕ ✕	✕ ✕	✕ ✕	✕ ✕
Subtotal = lbs.	Subtotal = lbs.	Subtotal = lbs.	Subtotal = lbs.	Subtotal = lbs.	Subtotal = lbs.

Exercise 3:   Total Weight _____ lbs.   Time _____ mins.   Power Factor _____ lbs./min.   Power Index _____

▪ Exercise: PREACHER CURL

Weight Reps Sets	Weight Reps Sets	Weight Reps Sets	Weight Reps Sets	Weight Reps Sets	Weight Reps Sets
✕ ✕	✕ ✕	✕ ✕	✕ ✕	✕ ✕	✕ ✕
Subtotal = lbs.	Subtotal = lbs.	Subtotal = lbs.	Subtotal = lbs.	Subtotal = lbs.	Subtotal = lbs.

Exercise 4:   Total Weight _____ lbs.   Time _____ mins.   Power Factor _____ lbs./min.   Power Index _____

▪ Exercise: WEIGHTED CRUNCH

Weight Reps Sets	Weight Reps Sets	Weight Reps Sets	Weight Reps Sets	Weight Reps Sets	Weight Reps Sets
✕ ✕	✕ ✕	✕ ✕	✕ ✕	✕ ✕	✕ ✕
Subtotal = lbs.	Subtotal = lbs.	Subtotal = lbs.	Subtotal = lbs.	Subtotal = lbs.	Subtotal = lbs.

Exercise 5:   Total Weight _____ lbs.   Time _____ mins.   Power Factor _____ lbs./min.   Power Index _____

OVERALL WORKOUT: Total Weight _____ lbs.   Time _____ mins.   Power Factor _____ lbs./min.   Power Index _____

Exercise Subtotal = Weight ✕ Reps ✕ Sets   ▪ *Power Factor = lbs./min.*   ▪ *Power Index = Total Weight ✕ Power Factor ÷ 1,000,000*

WORKOUT A RECORD

Date: ____ / ____ / ____

Start Time: _____   Finish Time: _____   Total Time: _____

▪ Exercise: STANDING BARBELL PRESS

Weight Reps Sets	Weight Reps Sets	Weight Reps Sets	Weight Reps Sets	Weight Reps Sets	Weight Reps Sets
× ×	× ×	× ×	× ×	× ×	× ×
Subtotal = lbs.	Subtotal = lbs.	Subtotal = lbs.	Subtotal = lbs.	Subtotal = lbs.	Subtotal = lbs.

Exercise 1:   *Total Weight* _____ *lbs.*   *Time* _____ *mins.*   *Power Factor* _____ *lbs./min.*   *Power Index* _____

▪ Exercise: BARBELL SHRUG

Weight Reps Sets	Weight Reps Sets	Weight Reps Sets	Weight Reps Sets	Weight Reps Sets	Weight Reps Sets
× ×	× ×	× ×	× ×	× ×	× ×
Subtotal = lbs.	Subtotal = lbs.	Subtotal = lbs.	Subtotal = lbs.	Subtotal = lbs.	Subtotal = lbs.

Exercise 2:   *Total Weight* _____ *lbs.*   *Time* _____ *mins.*   *Power Factor* _____ *lbs./min.*   *Power Index* _____

▪ Exercise: CLOSE-GRIP BENCH PRESS

Weight Reps Sets	Weight Reps Sets	Weight Reps Sets	Weight Reps Sets	Weight Reps Sets	Weight Reps Sets
× ×	× ×	× ×	× ×	× ×	× ×
Subtotal = lbs.	Subtotal = lbs.	Subtotal = lbs.	Subtotal = lbs.	Subtotal = lbs.	Subtotal = lbs.

Exercise 3:   *Total Weight* _____ *lbs.*   *Time* _____ *mins.*   *Power Factor* _____ *lbs./min.*   *Power Index* _____

▪ Exercise: PREACHER CURL

Weight Reps Sets	Weight Reps Sets	Weight Reps Sets	Weight Reps Sets	Weight Reps Sets	Weight Reps Sets
× ×	× ×	× ×	× ×	× ×	× ×
Subtotal = lbs.	Subtotal = lbs.	Subtotal = lbs.	Subtotal = lbs.	Subtotal = lbs.	Subtotal = lbs.

Exercise 4:   *Total Weight* _____ *lbs.*   *Time* _____ *mins.*   *Power Factor* _____ *lbs./min.*   *Power Index* _____

▪ Exercise: WEIGHTED CRUNCH

Weight Reps Sets	Weight Reps Sets	Weight Reps Sets	Weight Reps Sets	Weight Reps Sets	Weight Reps Sets
× ×	× ×	× ×	× ×	× ×	× ×
Subtotal = lbs.	Subtotal = lbs.	Subtotal = lbs.	Subtotal = lbs.	Subtotal = lbs.	Subtotal = lbs.

Exercise 5:   *Total Weight* _____ *lbs.*   *Time* _____ *mins.*   *Power Factor* _____ *lbs./min.*   *Power Index* _____

OVERALL WORKOUT: *Total Weight* _____ *lbs.*   *Time* _____ *mins.*   *Power Factor* _____ *lbs./min.*   *Power Index* _____

Exercise Subtotal = Weight × Reps × Sets   ▪ *Power Factor = lbs./min.*   ▪ *Power Index = Total Weight × Power Factor ÷ 1,000,000*

WORKOUT A RECORD

Date: ____ / ____ / ____

Start Time: _____ **Finish Time:** _____ **Total Time:** _____

▪ Exercise: STANDING BARBELL PRESS

Weight Reps Sets	Weight Reps Sets	Weight Reps Sets	Weight Reps Sets	Weight Reps Sets	Weight Reps Sets
× ×	× ×	× ×	× ×	× ×	× ×
Subtotal = lbs.	Subtotal = lbs.	Subtotal = lbs.	Subtotal = lbs.	Subtotal = lbs.	Subtotal = lbs.

Exercise 1: *Total Weight* _____ *lbs.* *Time* _____ *mins.* *Power Factor* _____ *lbs./min.* *Power Index* _____

▪ Exercise: BARBELL SHRUG

Weight Reps Sets	Weight Reps Sets	Weight Reps Sets	Weight Reps Sets	Weight Reps Sets	Weight Reps Sets
× ×	× ×	× ×	× ×	× ×	× ×
Subtotal = lbs.	Subtotal = lbs.	Subtotal = lbs.	Subtotal = lbs.	Subtotal = lbs.	Subtotal = lbs.

Exercise 2: *Total Weight* _____ *lbs.* *Time* _____ *mins.* *Power Factor* _____ *lbs./min.* *Power Index* _____

▪ Exercise: CLOSE-GRIP BENCH PRESS

Weight Reps Sets	Weight Reps Sets	Weight Reps Sets	Weight Reps Sets	Weight Reps Sets	Weight Reps Sets
× ×	× ×	× ×	× ×	× ×	× ×
Subtotal = lbs.	Subtotal = lbs.	Subtotal = lbs.	Subtotal = lbs.	Subtotal = lbs.	Subtotal = lbs.

Exercise 3: *Total Weight* _____ *lbs.* *Time* _____ *mins.* *Power Factor* _____ *lbs./min.* *Power Index* _____

▪ Exercise: PREACHER CURL

Weight Reps Sets	Weight Reps Sets	Weight Reps Sets	Weight Reps Sets	Weight Reps Sets	Weight Reps Sets
× ×	× ×	× ×	× ×	× ×	× ×
Subtotal = lbs.	Subtotal = lbs.	Subtotal = lbs.	Subtotal = lbs.	Subtotal = lbs.	Subtotal = lbs.

Exercise 4: *Total Weight* _____ *lbs.* *Time* _____ *mins.* *Power Factor* _____ *lbs./min.* *Power Index* _____

▪ Exercise: WEIGHTED CRUNCH

Weight Reps Sets	Weight Reps Sets	Weight Reps Sets	Weight Reps Sets	Weight Reps Sets	Weight Reps Sets
× ×	× ×	× ×	× ×	× ×	× ×
Subtotal = lbs.	Subtotal = lbs.	Subtotal = lbs.	Subtotal = lbs.	Subtotal = lbs.	Subtotal = lbs.

Exercise 5: *Total Weight* _____ *lbs.* *Time* _____ *mins.* *Power Factor* _____ *lbs./min.* *Power Index* _____

OVERALL WORKOUT: *Total Weight* _____ *lbs.* *Time* _____ *mins.* *Power Factor* _____ *lbs./min.* *Power Index* _____

Exercise Subtotal = Weight × Reps × Sets ▪ *Power Factor = lbs./min.* ▪ *Power Index = Total Weight × Power Factor ÷ 1,000,000*

WORKOUT A RECORD

Date: ____ / ____ / ____

Start Time: _____ Finish Time: _____ Total Time: _____

■ Exercise: STANDING BARBELL PRESS

Weight Reps Sets	Weight Reps Sets	Weight Reps Sets	Weight Reps Sets	Weight Reps Sets	Weight Reps Sets
× ×	× ×	× ×	× ×	× ×	× ×
Subtotal = lbs.	Subtotal = lbs.	Subtotal = lbs.	Subtotal = lbs.	Subtotal = lbs.	Subtotal = lbs.

Exercise 1:   *Total Weight _____ lbs.*   *Time _____ mins.*   *Power Factor _____ lbs./min.*   *Power Index _____*

■ Exercise: BARBELL SHRUG

Weight Reps Sets	Weight Reps Sets	Weight Reps Sets	Weight Reps Sets	Weight Reps Sets	Weight Reps Sets
× ×	× ×	× ×	× ×	× ×	× ×
Subtotal = lbs.	Subtotal = lbs.	Subtotal = lbs.	Subtotal = lbs.	Subtotal = lbs.	Subtotal = lbs.

Exercise 2:   *Total Weight _____ lbs.*   *Time _____ mins.*   *Power Factor _____ lbs./min.*   *Power Index _____*

■ Exercise: CLOSE-GRIP BENCH PRESS

Weight Reps Sets	Weight Reps Sets	Weight Reps Sets	Weight Reps Sets	Weight Reps Sets	Weight Reps Sets
× ×	× ×	× ×	× ×	× ×	× ×
Subtotal = lbs.	Subtotal = lbs.	Subtotal = lbs.	Subtotal = lbs.	Subtotal = lbs.	Subtotal = lbs.

Exercise 3:   *Total Weight _____ lbs.*   *Time _____ mins.*   *Power Factor _____ lbs./min.*   *Power Index _____*

■ Exercise: PREACHER CURL

Weight Reps Sets	Weight Reps Sets	Weight Reps Sets	Weight Reps Sets	Weight Reps Sets	Weight Reps Sets
× ×	× ×	× ×	× ×	× ×	× ×
Subtotal = lbs.	Subtotal = lbs.	Subtotal = lbs.	Subtotal = lbs.	Subtotal = lbs.	Subtotal = lbs.

Exercise 4:   *Total Weight _____ lbs.*   *Time _____ mins.*   *Power Factor _____ lbs./min.*   *Power Index _____*

■ Exercise: WEIGHTED CRUNCH

Weight Reps Sets	Weight Reps Sets	Weight Reps Sets	Weight Reps Sets	Weight Reps Sets	Weight Reps Sets
× ×	× ×	× ×	× ×	× ×	× ×
Subtotal = lbs.	Subtotal = lbs.	Subtotal = lbs.	Subtotal = lbs.	Subtotal = lbs.	Subtotal = lbs.

Exercise 5:   *Total Weight _____ lbs.*   *Time _____ mins.*   *Power Factor _____ lbs./min.*   *Power Index _____*

OVERALL WORKOUT: *Total Weight _____ lbs.*   *Time _____ mins.*   *Power Factor _____ lbs./min.*   *Power Index _____*

Exercise Subtotal = Weight × Reps × Sets   ■ *Power Factor = lbs./min.*   ■ *Power Index = Total Weight × Power Factor ÷ 1,000,000*

WORKOUT A RECORD

Date: ___ / ___ / ___

Start Time: _____   Finish Time: _____   Total Time: _____

▪ Exercise: STANDING BARBELL PRESS

Weight Reps Sets	Weight Reps Sets	Weight Reps Sets	Weight Reps Sets	Weight Reps Sets	Weight Reps Sets
× ×	× ×	× ×	× ×	× ×	× ×
Subtotal = lbs.	Subtotal = lbs.	Subtotal = lbs.	Subtotal = lbs.	Subtotal = lbs.	Subtotal = lbs.

Exercise 1:   *Total Weight _____ lbs.   Time _____ mins.   Power Factor _____ lbs./min.   Power Index _____*

▪ Exercise: BARBELL SHRUG

Weight Reps Sets	Weight Reps Sets	Weight Reps Sets	Weight Reps Sets	Weight Reps Sets	Weight Reps Sets
× ×	× ×	× ×	× ×	× ×	× ×
Subtotal = lbs.	Subtotal = lbs.	Subtotal = lbs.	Subtotal = lbs.	Subtotal = lbs.	Subtotal = lbs.

Exercise 2:   *Total Weight _____ lbs.   Time _____ mins.   Power Factor _____ lbs./min.   Power Index _____*

▪ Exercise: CLOSE-GRIP BENCH PRESS

Weight Reps Sets	Weight Reps Sets	Weight Reps Sets	Weight Reps Sets	Weight Reps Sets	Weight Reps Sets
× ×	× ×	× ×	× ×	× ×	× ×
Subtotal = lbs.	Subtotal = lbs.	Subtotal = lbs.	Subtotal = lbs.	Subtotal = lbs.	Subtotal = lbs.

Exercise 3:   *Total Weight _____ lbs.   Time _____ mins.   Power Factor _____ lbs./min.   Power Index _____*

▪ Exercise: PREACHER CURL

Weight Reps Sets	Weight Reps Sets	Weight Reps Sets	Weight Reps Sets	Weight Reps Sets	Weight Reps Sets
× ×	× ×	× ×	× ×	× ×	× ×
Subtotal = lbs.	Subtotal = lbs.	Subtotal = lbs.	Subtotal = lbs.	Subtotal = lbs.	Subtotal = lbs.

Exercise 4:   *Total Weight _____ lbs.   Time _____ mins.   Power Factor _____ lbs./min.   Power Index _____*

▪ Exercise: WEIGHTED CRUNCH

Weight Reps Sets	Weight Reps Sets	Weight Reps Sets	Weight Reps Sets	Weight Reps Sets	Weight Reps Sets
× ×	× ×	× ×	× ×	× ×	× ×
Subtotal = lbs.	Subtotal = lbs.	Subtotal = lbs.	Subtotal = lbs.	Subtotal = lbs.	Subtotal = lbs.

Exercise 5:   *Total Weight _____ lbs.   Time _____ mins.   Power Factor _____ lbs./min.   Power Index _____*

OVERALL WORKOUT: *Total Weight _____ lbs.   Time _____ mins.   Power Factor _____ lbs./min.   Power Index _____*

Exercise Subtotal = Weight × Reps × Sets   ▪ Power Factor = lbs./min.   ▪ Power Index = Total Weight × Power Factor ÷ 1,000,000

WORKOUT A RECORD

Date: ____ / ____ / ____

Start Time: _____   Finish Time: _____   Total Time: _____

▪ Exercise: STANDING BARBELL PRESS

Weight Reps Sets	Weight Reps Sets	Weight Reps Sets	Weight Reps Sets	Weight Reps Sets	Weight Reps Sets
× ×	× ×	× ×	× ×	× ×	× ×
Subtotal = lbs.	Subtotal = lbs.	Subtotal = lbs.	Subtotal = lbs.	Subtotal = lbs.	Subtotal = lbs.

Exercise 1:   *Total Weight* _____ *lbs.*   *Time* _____ *mins.*   *Power Factor* _____ *lbs./min.*   *Power Index* _____

▪ Exercise: BARBELL SHRUG

Weight Reps Sets	Weight Reps Sets	Weight Reps Sets	Weight Reps Sets	Weight Reps Sets	Weight Reps Sets
× ×	× ×	× ×	× ×	× ×	× ×
Subtotal = lbs.	Subtotal = lbs.	Subtotal = lbs.	Subtotal = lbs.	Subtotal = lbs.	Subtotal = lbs.

Exercise 2:   *Total Weight* _____ *lbs.*   *Time* _____ *mins.*   *Power Factor* _____ *lbs./min.*   *Power Index* _____

▪ Exercise: CLOSE-GRIP BENCH PRESS

Weight Reps Sets	Weight Reps Sets	Weight Reps Sets	Weight Reps Sets	Weight Reps Sets	Weight Reps Sets
× ×	× ×	× ×	× ×	× ×	× ×
Subtotal = lbs.	Subtotal = lbs.	Subtotal = lbs.	Subtotal = lbs.	Subtotal = lbs.	Subtotal = lbs.

Exercise 3:   *Total Weight* _____ *lbs.*   *Time* _____ *mins.*   *Power Factor* _____ *lbs./min.*   *Power Index* _____

▪ Exercise: PREACHER CURL

Weight Reps Sets	Weight Reps Sets	Weight Reps Sets	Weight Reps Sets	Weight Reps Sets	Weight Reps Sets
× ×	× ×	× ×	× ×	× ×	× ×
Subtotal = lbs.	Subtotal = lbs.	Subtotal = lbs.	Subtotal = lbs.	Subtotal = lbs.	Subtotal = lbs.

Exercise 4:   *Total Weight* _____ *lbs.*   *Time* _____ *mins.*   *Power Factor* _____ *lbs./min.*   *Power Index* _____

▪ Exercise: WEIGHTED CRUNCH

Weight Reps Sets	Weight Reps Sets	Weight Reps Sets	Weight Reps Sets	Weight Reps Sets	Weight Reps Sets
× ×	× ×	× ×	× ×	× ×	× ×
Subtotal = lbs.	Subtotal = lbs.	Subtotal = lbs.	Subtotal = lbs.	Subtotal = lbs.	Subtotal = lbs.

Exercise 5:   *Total Weight* _____ *lbs.*   *Time* _____ *mins.*   *Power Factor* _____ *lbs./min.*   *Power Index* _____

OVERALL WORKOUT: *Total Weight* _____ *lbs.*   *Time* _____ *mins.*   *Power Factor* _____ *lbs./min.*   *Power Index* _____

Exercise Subtotal = Weight × Reps × Sets   ▪ *Power Factor = lbs./min.*   ▪ *Power Index = Total Weight × Power Factor ÷ 1,000,000*

WORKOUT A RECORD

Date: ____ / ____ / ____

Start Time: _____ Finish Time: _____ Total Time: _____

■ Exercise: STANDING BARBELL PRESS

Weight Reps Sets	Weight Reps Sets	Weight Reps Sets	Weight Reps Sets	Weight Reps Sets	Weight Reps Sets
× ×	× ×	× ×	× ×	× ×	× ×
Subtotal = lbs.	Subtotal = lbs.	Subtotal = lbs.	Subtotal = lbs.	Subtotal = lbs.	Subtotal = lbs.

Exercise 1:   *Total Weight* _____ *lbs.*   *Time* _____ *mins.*   *Power Factor* _____ *lbs./min.*   *Power Index* _____

■ Exercise: BARBELL SHRUG

Weight Reps Sets	Weight Reps Sets	Weight Reps Sets	Weight Reps Sets	Weight Reps Sets	Weight Reps Sets
× ×	× ×	× ×	× ×	× ×	× ×
Subtotal = lbs.	Subtotal = lbs.	Subtotal = lbs.	Subtotal = lbs.	Subtotal = lbs.	Subtotal = lbs.

Exercise 2:   *Total Weight* _____ *lbs.*   *Time* _____ *mins.*   *Power Factor* _____ *lbs./min.*   *Power Index* _____

■ Exercise: CLOSE-GRIP BENCH PRESS

Weight Reps Sets	Weight Reps Sets	Weight Reps Sets	Weight Reps Sets	Weight Reps Sets	Weight Reps Sets
× ×	× ×	× ×	× ×	× ×	× ×
Subtotal = lbs.	Subtotal = lbs.	Subtotal = lbs.	Subtotal = lbs.	Subtotal = lbs.	Subtotal = lbs.

Exercise 3:   *Total Weight* _____ *lbs.*   *Time* _____ *mins.*   *Power Factor* _____ *lbs./min.*   *Power Index* _____

■ Exercise: PREACHER CURL

Weight Reps Sets	Weight Reps Sets	Weight Reps Sets	Weight Reps Sets	Weight Reps Sets	Weight Reps Sets
× ×	× ×	× ×	× ×	× ×	× ×
Subtotal = lbs.	Subtotal = lbs.	Subtotal = lbs.	Subtotal = lbs.	Subtotal = lbs.	Subtotal = lbs.

Exercise 4:   *Total Weight* _____ *lbs.*   *Time* _____ *mins.*   *Power Factor* _____ *lbs./min.*   *Power Index* _____

■ Exercise: WEIGHTED CRUNCH

Weight Reps Sets	Weight Reps Sets	Weight Reps Sets	Weight Reps Sets	Weight Reps Sets	Weight Reps Sets
× ×	× ×	× ×	× ×	× ×	× ×
Subtotal = lbs.	Subtotal = lbs.	Subtotal = lbs.	Subtotal = lbs.	Subtotal = lbs.	Subtotal = lbs.

Exercise 5:   *Total Weight* _____ *lbs.*   *Time* _____ *mins.*   *Power Factor* _____ *lbs./min.*   *Power Index* _____

OVERALL WORKOUT: *Total Weight* _____ *lbs.*   *Time* _____ *mins.*   *Power Factor* _____ *lbs./min.*   *Power Index* _____

Exercise Subtotal = Weight × Reps × Sets   ■ *Power Factor = lbs./min.*   ■ *Power Index = Total Weight × Power Factor ÷ 1,000,000*

WORKOUT A RECORD   Date: ___ / ___ / ___

Start Time: _____   Finish Time: _____   Total Time: _____

■ Exercise: STANDING BARBELL PRESS

Weight	Reps	Sets	Weight	Reps	Sets	Weight	Reps	Sets	Weight	Reps	Sets	Weight	Reps	Sets	Weight	Reps	Sets
×	×		×	×		×	×		×	×		×	×		×	×	
Subtotal =		lbs.	Subtotal =		lbs.	Subtotal =		lbs.	Subtotal =		lbs.	Subtotal =		lbs.	Subtotal =		lbs.

Exercise 1:   *Total Weight* _____ *lbs.*   *Time* _____ *mins.*   *Power Factor* _____ *lbs./min.*   *Power Index* _____

■ Exercise: BARBELL SHRUG

Weight	Reps	Sets	Weight	Reps	Sets	Weight	Reps	Sets	Weight	Reps	Sets	Weight	Reps	Sets	Weight	Reps	Sets
×	×		×	×		×	×		×	×		×	×		×	×	
Subtotal =		lbs.	Subtotal =		lbs.	Subtotal =		lbs.	Subtotal =		lbs.	Subtotal =		lbs.	Subtotal =		lbs.

Exercise 2:   *Total Weight* _____ *lbs.*   *Time* _____ *mins.*   *Power Factor* _____ *lbs./min.*   *Power Index* _____

■ Exercise: CLOSE-GRIP BENCH PRESS

Weight	Reps	Sets	Weight	Reps	Sets	Weight	Reps	Sets	Weight	Reps	Sets	Weight	Reps	Sets	Weight	Reps	Sets
×	×		×	×		×	×		×	×		×	×		×	×	
Subtotal =		lbs.	Subtotal =		lbs.	Subtotal =		lbs.	Subtotal =		lbs.	Subtotal =		lbs.	Subtotal =		lbs.

Exercise 3:   *Total Weight* _____ *lbs.*   *Time* _____ *mins.*   *Power Factor* _____ *lbs./min.*   *Power Index* _____

■ Exercise: PREACHER CURL

Weight	Reps	Sets	Weight	Reps	Sets	Weight	Reps	Sets	Weight	Reps	Sets	Weight	Reps	Sets	Weight	Reps	Sets
×	×		×	×		×	×		×	×		×	×		×	×	
Subtotal =		lbs.	Subtotal =		lbs.	Subtotal =		lbs.	Subtotal =		lbs.	Subtotal =		lbs.	Subtotal =		lbs.

Exercise 4:   *Total Weight* _____ *lbs.*   *Time* _____ *mins.*   *Power Factor* _____ *lbs./min.*   *Power Index* _____

■ Exercise: WEIGHTED CRUNCH

Weight	Reps	Sets	Weight	Reps	Sets	Weight	Reps	Sets	Weight	Reps	Sets	Weight	Reps	Sets	Weight	Reps	Sets
×	×		×	×		×	×		×	×		×	×		×	×	
Subtotal =		lbs.	Subtotal =		lbs.	Subtotal =		lbs.	Subtotal =		lbs.	Subtotal =		lbs.	Subtotal =		lbs.

Exercise 5:   *Total Weight* _____ *lbs.*   *Time* _____ *mins.*   *Power Factor* _____ *lbs./min.*   *Power Index* _____

OVERALL WORKOUT: *Total Weight* _____ *lbs.*   *Time* _____ *mins.*   *Power Factor* _____ *lbs./min.*   *Power Index* _____

Exercise Subtotal = Weight × Reps × Sets   ■ *Power Factor = lbs./min.*   ■ *Power Index = Total Weight × Power Factor ÷ 1,000,000*

WORKOUT A RECORD

Date: ____ / ____ / ____

Start Time: _____   Finish Time: _____   Total Time: _____

▪ Exercise: STANDING BARBELL PRESS

Weight Reps Sets	Weight Reps Sets	Weight Reps Sets	Weight Reps Sets	Weight Reps Sets	Weight Reps Sets
$\times$ $\times$	$\times$ $\times$	$\times$ $\times$	$\times$ $\times$	$\times$ $\times$	$\times$ $\times$
Subtotal = lbs.	Subtotal = lbs.	Subtotal = lbs.	Subtotal = lbs.	Subtotal = lbs.	Subtotal = lbs.

Exercise 1:   *Total Weight* _____ *lbs.*   *Time* _____ *mins.*   *Power Factor* _____ *lbs./min.*   *Power Index* _____

▪ Exercise: BARBELL SHRUG

Weight Reps Sets	Weight Reps Sets	Weight Reps Sets	Weight Reps Sets	Weight Reps Sets	Weight Reps Sets
$\times$ $\times$	$\times$ $\times$	$\times$ $\times$	$\times$ $\times$	$\times$ $\times$	$\times$ $\times$
Subtotal = lbs.	Subtotal = lbs.	Subtotal = lbs.	Subtotal = lbs.	Subtotal = lbs.	Subtotal = lbs.

Exercise 2:   *Total Weight* _____ *lbs.*   *Time* _____ *mins.*   *Power Factor* _____ *lbs./min.*   *Power Index* _____

▪ Exercise: CLOSE-GRIP BENCH PRESS

Weight Reps Sets	Weight Reps Sets	Weight Reps Sets	Weight Reps Sets	Weight Reps Sets	Weight Reps Sets
$\times$ $\times$	$\times$ $\times$	$\times$ $\times$	$\times$ $\times$	$\times$ $\times$	$\times$ $\times$
Subtotal = lbs.	Subtotal = lbs.	Subtotal = lbs.	Subtotal = lbs.	Subtotal = lbs.	Subtotal = lbs.

Exercise 3:   *Total Weight* _____ *lbs.*   *Time* _____ *mins.*   *Power Factor* _____ *lbs./min.*   *Power Index* _____

▪ Exercise: PREACHER CURL

Weight Reps Sets	Weight Reps Sets	Weight Reps Sets	Weight Reps Sets	Weight Reps Sets	Weight Reps Sets
$\times$ $\times$	$\times$ $\times$	$\times$ $\times$	$\times$ $\times$	$\times$ $\times$	$\times$ $\times$
Subtotal = lbs.	Subtotal = lbs.	Subtotal = lbs.	Subtotal = lbs.	Subtotal = lbs.	Subtotal = lbs.

Exercise 4:   *Total Weight* _____ *lbs.*   *Time* _____ *mins.*   *Power Factor* _____ *lbs./min.*   *Power Index* _____

▪ Exercise: WEIGHTED CRUNCH

Weight Reps Sets	Weight Reps Sets	Weight Reps Sets	Weight Reps Sets	Weight Reps Sets	Weight Reps Sets
$\times$ $\times$	$\times$ $\times$	$\times$ $\times$	$\times$ $\times$	$\times$ $\times$	$\times$ $\times$
Subtotal = lbs.	Subtotal = lbs.	Subtotal = lbs.	Subtotal = lbs.	Subtotal = lbs.	Subtotal = lbs.

Exercise 5:   *Total Weight* _____ *lbs.*   *Time* _____ *mins.*   *Power Factor* _____ *lbs./min.*   *Power Index* _____

OVERALL WORKOUT: *Total Weight* _____ *lbs.*   *Time* _____ *mins.*   *Power Factor* _____ *lbs./min.*   *Power Index* _____

Exercise Subtotal = Weight $\times$ Reps $\times$ Sets   ▪ *Power Factor = lbs./min.*   ▪ *Power Index = Total Weight $\times$ Power Factor $\div$ 1,000,000*

WORKOUT A RECORD

Date: ____ / ____ / ____

Start Time: _____   Finish Time: _____   Total Time: _____

■ **Exercise: STANDING BARBELL PRESS**

Weight Reps Sets	Weight Reps Sets	Weight Reps Sets	Weight Reps Sets	Weight Reps Sets	Weight Reps Sets
× ×	× ×	× ×	× ×	× ×	× ×
Subtotal = lbs.	Subtotal = lbs.	Subtotal = lbs.	Subtotal = lbs.	Subtotal = lbs.	Subtotal = lbs.

Exercise 1:   *Total Weight* _____ *lbs.*   *Time* _____ *mins.*   *Power Factor* _____ *lbs./min.*   *Power Index* _____

■ **Exercise: BARBELL SHRUG**

Weight Reps Sets	Weight Reps Sets	Weight Reps Sets	Weight Reps Sets	Weight Reps Sets	Weight Reps Sets
× ×	× ×	× ×	× ×	× ×	× ×
Subtotal = lbs.	Subtotal = lbs.	Subtotal = lbs.	Subtotal = lbs.	Subtotal = lbs.	Subtotal = lbs.

Exercise 2:   *Total Weight* _____ *lbs.*   *Time* _____ *mins.*   *Power Factor* _____ *lbs./min.*   *Power Index* _____

■ **Exercise: CLOSE-GRIP BENCH PRESS**

Weight Reps Sets	Weight Reps Sets	Weight Reps Sets	Weight Reps Sets	Weight Reps Sets	Weight Reps Sets
× ×	× ×	× ×	× ×	× ×	× ×
Subtotal = lbs.	Subtotal = lbs.	Subtotal = lbs.	Subtotal = lbs.	Subtotal = lbs.	Subtotal = lbs.

Exercise 3:   *Total Weight* _____ *lbs.*   *Time* _____ *mins.*   *Power Factor* _____ *lbs./min.*   *Power Index* _____

■ **Exercise: PREACHER CURL**

Weight Reps Sets	Weight Reps Sets	Weight Reps Sets	Weight Reps Sets	Weight Reps Sets	Weight Reps Sets
× ×	× ×	× ×	× ×	× ×	× ×
Subtotal = lbs.	Subtotal = lbs.	Subtotal = lbs.	Subtotal = lbs.	Subtotal = lbs.	Subtotal = lbs.

Exercise 4:   *Total Weight* _____ *lbs.*   *Time* _____ *mins.*   *Power Factor* _____ *lbs./min.*   *Power Index* _____

■ **Exercise: WEIGHTED CRUNCH**

Weight Reps Sets	Weight Reps Sets	Weight Reps Sets	Weight Reps Sets	Weight Reps Sets	Weight Reps Sets
× ×	× ×	× ×	× ×	× ×	× ×
Subtotal = lbs.	Subtotal = lbs.	Subtotal = lbs.	Subtotal = lbs.	Subtotal = lbs.	Subtotal = lbs.

Exercise 5:   *Total Weight* _____ *lbs.*   *Time* _____ *mins.*   *Power Factor* _____ *lbs./min.*   *Power Index* _____

OVERALL WORKOUT: *Total Weight* _____ *lbs.*   *Time* _____ *mins.*   *Power Factor* _____ *lbs./min.*   *Power Index* _____

Exercise Subtotal = Weight × Reps × Sets   ■ *Power Factor = lbs./min.*   ■ *Power Index = Total Weight × Power Factor ÷ 1,000,000*

WORKOUT A RECORD

Date: ____ / ____ / ____

Start Time: _____   Finish Time: _____   Total Time: _____

■ Exercise: STANDING BARBELL PRESS

Weight Reps Sets	Weight Reps Sets	Weight Reps Sets	Weight Reps Sets	Weight Reps Sets	Weight Reps Sets
× ×	× ×	× ×	× ×	× ×	× ×
Subtotal = lbs.	Subtotal = lbs.	Subtotal = lbs.	Subtotal = lbs.	Subtotal = lbs.	Subtotal = lbs.

Exercise 1:   *Total Weight* _____ *lbs.*   *Time* _____ *mins.*   *Power Factor* _____ *lbs./min.*   *Power Index* _____

■ Exercise: BARBELL SHRUG

Weight Reps Sets	Weight Reps Sets	Weight Reps Sets	Weight Reps Sets	Weight Reps Sets	Weight Reps Sets
× ×	× ×	× ×	× ×	× ×	× ×
Subtotal = lbs.	Subtotal = lbs.	Subtotal = lbs.	Subtotal = lbs.	Subtotal = lbs.	Subtotal = lbs.

Exercise 2:   *Total Weight* _____ *lbs.*   *Time* _____ *mins.*   *Power Factor* _____ *lbs./min.*   *Power Index* _____

■ Exercise: CLOSE-GRIP BENCH PRESS

Weight Reps Sets	Weight Reps Sets	Weight Reps Sets	Weight Reps Sets	Weight Reps Sets	Weight Reps Sets
× ×	× ×	× ×	× ×	× ×	× ×
Subtotal = lbs.	Subtotal = lbs.	Subtotal = lbs.	Subtotal = lbs.	Subtotal = lbs.	Subtotal = lbs.

Exercise 3:   *Total Weight* _____ *lbs.*   *Time* _____ *mins.*   *Power Factor* _____ *lbs./min.*   *Power Index* _____

■ Exercise: PREACHER CURL

Weight Reps Sets	Weight Reps Sets	Weight Reps Sets	Weight Reps Sets	Weight Reps Sets	Weight Reps Sets
× ×	× ×	× ×	× ×	× ×	× ×
Subtotal = lbs.	Subtotal = lbs.	Subtotal = lbs.	Subtotal = lbs.	Subtotal = lbs.	Subtotal = lbs.

Exercise 4:   *Total Weight* _____ *lbs.*   *Time* _____ *mins.*   *Power Factor* _____ *lbs./min.*   *Power Index* _____

■ Exercise: WEIGHTED CRUNCH

Weight Reps Sets	Weight Reps Sets	Weight Reps Sets	Weight Reps Sets	Weight Reps Sets	Weight Reps Sets
× ×	× ×	× ×	× ×	× ×	× ×
Subtotal = lbs.	Subtotal = lbs.	Subtotal = lbs.	Subtotal = lbs.	Subtotal = lbs.	Subtotal = lbs.

Exercise 5:   *Total Weight* _____ *lbs.*   *Time* _____ *mins.*   *Power Factor* _____ *lbs./min.*   *Power Index* _____

OVERALL WORKOUT: *Total Weight* _____ *lbs.*   *Time* _____ *mins.*   *Power Factor* _____ *lbs./min.*   *Power Index* _____

Exercise Subtotal = Weight × Reps × Sets   ■ *Power Factor = lbs./min.*   ■ *Power Index = Total Weight × Power Factor ÷ 1,000,000*

WORKOUT A RECORD   Date: ___ / ___ / ___

Start Time: _____   Finish Time: _____   Total Time: _____

■ **Exercise: STANDING BARBELL PRESS**

Weight Reps Sets	Weight Reps Sets	Weight Reps Sets	Weight Reps Sets	Weight Reps Sets	Weight Reps Sets
× ×	× ×	× ×	× ×	× ×	× ×
Subtotal = lbs.	Subtotal = lbs.	Subtotal = lbs.	Subtotal = lbs.	Subtotal = lbs.	Subtotal = lbs.

Exercise 1:   Total Weight _____ lbs.   Time _____ mins.   Power Factor _____ lbs./min.   Power Index _____

■ **Exercise: BARBELL SHRUG**

Weight Reps Sets	Weight Reps Sets	Weight Reps Sets	Weight Reps Sets	Weight Reps Sets	Weight Reps Sets
× ×	× ×	× ×	× ×	× ×	× ×
Subtotal = lbs.	Subtotal = lbs.	Subtotal = lbs.	Subtotal = lbs.	Subtotal = lbs.	Subtotal = lbs.

Exercise 2:   Total Weight _____ lbs.   Time _____ mins.   Power Factor _____ lbs./min.   Power Index _____

■ **Exercise: CLOSE-GRIP BENCH PRESS**

Weight Reps Sets	Weight Reps Sets	Weight Reps Sets	Weight Reps Sets	Weight Reps Sets	Weight Reps Sets
× ×	× ×	× ×	× ×	× ×	× ×
Subtotal = lbs.	Subtotal = lbs.	Subtotal = lbs.	Subtotal = lbs.	Subtotal = lbs.	Subtotal = lbs.

Exercise 3:   Total Weight _____ lbs.   Time _____ mins.   Power Factor _____ lbs./min.   Power Index _____

■ **Exercise: PREACHER CURL**

Weight Reps Sets	Weight Reps Sets	Weight Reps Sets	Weight Reps Sets	Weight Reps Sets	Weight Reps Sets
× ×	× ×	× ×	× ×	× ×	× ×
Subtotal = lbs.	Subtotal = lbs.	Subtotal = lbs.	Subtotal = lbs.	Subtotal = lbs.	Subtotal = lbs.

Exercise 4:   Total Weight _____ lbs.   Time _____ mins.   Power Factor _____ lbs./min.   Power Index _____

■ **Exercise: WEIGHTED CRUNCH**

Weight Reps Sets	Weight Reps Sets	Weight Reps Sets	Weight Reps Sets	Weight Reps Sets	Weight Reps Sets
× ×	× ×	× ×	× ×	× ×	× ×
Subtotal = lbs.	Subtotal = lbs.	Subtotal = lbs.	Subtotal = lbs.	Subtotal = lbs.	Subtotal = lbs.

Exercise 5:   Total Weight _____ lbs.   Time _____ mins.   Power Factor _____ lbs./min.   Power Index _____

OVERALL WORKOUT: Total Weight _____ lbs.   Time _____ mins.   Power Factor _____ lbs./min.   Power Index _____

Exercise Subtotal = Weight × Reps × Sets   ■ *Power Factor = lbs./min.*   ■ *Power Index = Total Weight × Power Factor ÷ 1,000,000*

WORKOUT A RECORD

Date: ____ / ____ / ____

Start Time: _____   Finish Time: _____   Total Time: _____

▪ Exercise: STANDING BARBELL PRESS

Weight Reps Sets	Weight Reps Sets	Weight Reps Sets	Weight Reps Sets	Weight Reps Sets	Weight Reps Sets
× ×	× ×	× ×	× ×	× ×	× ×
Subtotal = lbs.	Subtotal = lbs.	Subtotal = lbs.	Subtotal = lbs.	Subtotal = lbs.	Subtotal = lbs.

Exercise 1: Total Weight _____ lbs. Time _____ mins. Power Factor _____ lbs./min. Power Index _____

▪ Exercise: BARBELL SHRUG

Weight Reps Sets	Weight Reps Sets	Weight Reps Sets	Weight Reps Sets	Weight Reps Sets	Weight Reps Sets
× ×	× ×	× ×	× ×	× ×	× ×
Subtotal = lbs.	Subtotal = lbs.	Subtotal = lbs.	Subtotal = lbs.	Subtotal = lbs.	Subtotal = lbs.

Exercise 2: Total Weight _____ lbs. Time _____ mins. Power Factor _____ lbs./min. Power Index _____

▪ Exercise: CLOSE-GRIP BENCH PRESS

Weight Reps Sets	Weight Reps Sets	Weight Reps Sets	Weight Reps Sets	Weight Reps Sets	Weight Reps Sets
× ×	× ×	× ×	× ×	× ×	× ×
Subtotal = lbs.	Subtotal = lbs.	Subtotal = lbs.	Subtotal = lbs.	Subtotal = lbs.	Subtotal = lbs.

Exercise 3: Total Weight _____ lbs. Time _____ mins. Power Factor _____ lbs./min. Power Index _____

▪ Exercise: PREACHER CURL

Weight Reps Sets	Weight Reps Sets	Weight Reps Sets	Weight Reps Sets	Weight Reps Sets	Weight Reps Sets
× ×	× ×	× ×	× ×	× ×	× ×
Subtotal = lbs.	Subtotal = lbs.	Subtotal = lbs.	Subtotal = lbs.	Subtotal = lbs.	Subtotal = lbs.

Exercise 4: Total Weight _____ lbs. Time _____ mins. Power Factor _____ lbs./min. Power Index _____

▪ Exercise: WEIGHTED CRUNCH

Weight Reps Sets	Weight Reps Sets	Weight Reps Sets	Weight Reps Sets	Weight Reps Sets	Weight Reps Sets
× ×	× ×	× ×	× ×	× ×	× ×
Subtotal = lbs.	Subtotal = lbs.	Subtotal = lbs.	Subtotal = lbs.	Subtotal = lbs.	Subtotal = lbs.

Exercise 5: Total Weight _____ lbs. Time _____ mins. Power Factor _____ lbs./min. Power Index _____

OVERALL WORKOUT: Total Weight _____ lbs. Time _____ mins. Power Factor _____ lbs./min. Power Index _____

Exercise Subtotal = Weight × Reps × Sets ▪ *Power Factor = lbs./min.* ▪ *Power Index = Total Weight × Power Factor ÷ 1,000,000*

WORKOUT A RECORD

Date: ____ / ____ / ____

Start Time: _____   Finish Time: _____   Total Time: _____

■ **Exercise: STANDING BARBELL PRESS**

Weight Reps Sets	Weight Reps Sets	Weight Reps Sets	Weight Reps Sets	Weight Reps Sets	Weight Reps Sets
× ×	× ×	× ×	× ×	× ×	× ×
Subtotal = lbs.	Subtotal = lbs.	Subtotal = lbs.	Subtotal = lbs.	Subtotal = lbs.	Subtotal = lbs.

Exercise 1:   *Total Weight* _____ *lbs.*   *Time* _____ *mins.*   *Power Factor* _____ *lbs./min.*   *Power Index* _____

■ **Exercise: BARBELL SHRUG**

Weight Reps Sets	Weight Reps Sets	Weight Reps Sets	Weight Reps Sets	Weight Reps Sets	Weight Reps Sets
× ×	× ×	× ×	× ×	× ×	× ×
Subtotal = lbs.	Subtotal = lbs.	Subtotal = lbs.	Subtotal = lbs.	Subtotal = lbs.	Subtotal = lbs.

Exercise 2:   *Total Weight* _____ *lbs.*   *Time* _____ *mins.*   *Power Factor* _____ *lbs./min.*   *Power Index* _____

■ **Exercise: CLOSE-GRIP BENCH PRESS**

Weight Reps Sets	Weight Reps Sets	Weight Reps Sets	Weight Reps Sets	Weight Reps Sets	Weight Reps Sets
× ×	× ×	× ×	× ×	× ×	× ×
Subtotal = lbs.	Subtotal = lbs.	Subtotal = lbs.	Subtotal = lbs.	Subtotal = lbs.	Subtotal = lbs.

Exercise 3:   *Total Weight* _____ *lbs.*   *Time* _____ *mins.*   *Power Factor* _____ *lbs./min.*   *Power Index* _____

■ **Exercise: PREACHER CURL**

Weight Reps Sets	Weight Reps Sets	Weight Reps Sets	Weight Reps Sets	Weight Reps Sets	Weight Reps Sets
× ×	× ×	× ×	× ×	× ×	× ×
Subtotal = lbs.	Subtotal = lbs.	Subtotal = lbs.	Subtotal = lbs.	Subtotal = lbs.	Subtotal = lbs.

Exercise 4:   *Total Weight* _____ *lbs.*   *Time* _____ *mins.*   *Power Factor* _____ *lbs./min.*   *Power Index* _____

■ **Exercise: WEIGHTED CRUNCH**

Weight Reps Sets	Weight Reps Sets	Weight Reps Sets	Weight Reps Sets	Weight Reps Sets	Weight Reps Sets
× ×	× ×	× ×	× ×	× ×	× ×
Subtotal = lbs.	Subtotal = lbs.	Subtotal = lbs.	Subtotal = lbs.	Subtotal = lbs.	Subtotal = lbs.

Exercise 5:   *Total Weight* _____ *lbs.*   *Time* _____ *mins.*   *Power Factor* _____ *lbs./min.*   *Power Index* _____

OVERALL WORKOUT: *Total Weight* _____ *lbs.*   *Time* _____ *mins.*   *Power Factor* _____ *lbs./min.*   *Power Index* _____

Exercise Subtotal = Weight × Reps × Sets   ■   *Power Factor = lbs./min.*   ■   *Power Index = Total Weight × Power Factor ÷ 1,000,000*

WORKOUT A RECORD

Date: ____ / ____ / ____

Start Time: _____   Finish Time: _____   Total Time: _____

■ **Exercise: STANDING BARBELL PRESS**

Weight Reps Sets	Weight Reps Sets	Weight Reps Sets	Weight Reps Sets	Weight Reps Sets	Weight Reps Sets
× ×	× ×	× ×	× ×	× ×	× ×
Subtotal = lbs.	Subtotal = lbs.	Subtotal = lbs.	Subtotal = lbs.	Subtotal = lbs.	Subtotal = lbs.

Exercise 1:   *Total Weight* _____ *lbs.*   *Time* _____ *mins.*   *Power Factor* _____ *lbs./min.*   *Power Index* _____

■ **Exercise: BARBELL SHRUG**

Weight Reps Sets	Weight Reps Sets	Weight Reps Sets	Weight Reps Sets	Weight Reps Sets	Weight Reps Sets
× ×	× ×	× ×	× ×	× ×	× ×
Subtotal = lbs.	Subtotal = lbs.	Subtotal = lbs.	Subtotal = lbs.	Subtotal = lbs.	Subtotal = lbs.

Exercise 2:   *Total Weight* _____ *lbs.*   *Time* _____ *mins.*   *Power Factor* _____ *lbs./min.*   *Power Index* _____

■ **Exercise: CLOSE-GRIP BENCH PRESS**

Weight Reps Sets	Weight Reps Sets	Weight Reps Sets	Weight Reps Sets	Weight Reps Sets	Weight Reps Sets
× ×	× ×	× ×	× ×	× ×	× ×
Subtotal = lbs.	Subtotal = lbs.	Subtotal = lbs.	Subtotal = lbs.	Subtotal = lbs.	Subtotal = lbs.

Exercise 3:   *Total Weight* _____ *lbs.*   *Time* _____ *mins.*   *Power Factor* _____ *lbs./min.*   *Power Index* _____

■ **Exercise: PREACHER CURL**

Weight Reps Sets	Weight Reps Sets	Weight Reps Sets	Weight Reps Sets	Weight Reps Sets	Weight Reps Sets
× ×	× ×	× ×	× ×	× ×	× ×
Subtotal = lbs.	Subtotal = lbs.	Subtotal = lbs.	Subtotal = lbs.	Subtotal = lbs.	Subtotal = lbs.

Exercise 4:   *Total Weight* _____ *lbs.*   *Time* _____ *mins.*   *Power Factor* _____ *lbs./min.*   *Power Index* _____

■ **Exercise: WEIGHTED CRUNCH**

Weight Reps Sets	Weight Reps Sets	Weight Reps Sets	Weight Reps Sets	Weight Reps Sets	Weight Reps Sets
× ×	× ×	× ×	× ×	× ×	× ×
Subtotal = lbs.	Subtotal = lbs.	Subtotal = lbs.	Subtotal = lbs.	Subtotal = lbs.	Subtotal = lbs.

Exercise 5:   *Total Weight* _____ *lbs.*   *Time* _____ *mins.*   *Power Factor* _____ *lbs./min.*   *Power Index* _____

OVERALL WORKOUT: *Total Weight* _____ *lbs.*   *Time* _____ *mins.*   *Power Factor* _____ *lbs./min.*   *Power Index* _____

Exercise Subtotal = Weight × Reps × Sets   ■ *Power Factor = lbs./min.*   ■ *Power Index = Total Weight × Power Factor ÷ 1,000,000*

WORKOUT A RECORD   Date: ___ / ___ / ___

Start Time: _____   **Finish Time:** _____   **Total Time:** _____

▪ Exercise: STANDING BARBELL PRESS

Weight Reps Sets	Weight Reps Sets	Weight Reps Sets	Weight Reps Sets	Weight Reps Sets	Weight Reps Sets
× ×	× ×	× ×	× ×	× ×	× ×
Subtotal = lbs.	Subtotal = lbs.	Subtotal = lbs.	Subtotal = lbs.	Subtotal = lbs.	Subtotal = lbs.

Exercise 1:   *Total Weight _____ lbs.   Time _____ mins.   Power Factor _____ lbs./min.   Power Index _____*

▪ Exercise: BARBELL SHRUG

Weight Reps Sets	Weight Reps Sets	Weight Reps Sets	Weight Reps Sets	Weight Reps Sets	Weight Reps Sets
× ×	× ×	× ×	× ×	× ×	× ×
Subtotal = lbs.	Subtotal = lbs.	Subtotal = lbs.	Subtotal = lbs.	Subtotal = lbs.	Subtotal = lbs.

Exercise 2:   *Total Weight _____ lbs.   Time _____ mins.   Power Factor _____ lbs./min.   Power Index _____*

▪ Exercise: CLOSE-GRIP BENCH PRESS

Weight Reps Sets	Weight Reps Sets	Weight Reps Sets	Weight Reps Sets	Weight Reps Sets	Weight Reps Sets
× ×	× ×	× ×	× ×	× ×	× ×
Subtotal = lbs.	Subtotal = lbs.	Subtotal = lbs.	Subtotal = lbs.	Subtotal = lbs.	Subtotal = lbs.

Exercise 3:   *Total Weight _____ lbs.   Time _____ mins.   Power Factor _____ lbs./min.   Power Index _____*

▪ Exercise: PREACHER CURL

Weight Reps Sets	Weight Reps Sets	Weight Reps Sets	Weight Reps Sets	Weight Reps Sets	Weight Reps Sets
× ×	× ×	× ×	× ×	× ×	× ×
Subtotal = lbs.	Subtotal = lbs.	Subtotal = lbs.	Subtotal = lbs.	Subtotal = lbs.	Subtotal = lbs.

Exercise 4:   *Total Weight _____ lbs.   Time _____ mins.   Power Factor _____ lbs./min.   Power Index _____*

▪ Exercise: WEIGHTED CRUNCH

Weight Reps Sets	Weight Reps Sets	Weight Reps Sets	Weight Reps Sets	Weight Reps Sets	Weight Reps Sets
× ×	× ×	× ×	× ×	× ×	× ×
Subtotal = lbs.	Subtotal = lbs.	Subtotal = lbs.	Subtotal = lbs.	Subtotal = lbs.	Subtotal = lbs.

Exercise 5:   *Total Weight _____ lbs.   Time _____ mins.   Power Factor _____ lbs./min.   Power Index _____*

OVERALL WORKOUT: *Total Weight _____ lbs.   Time _____ mins.   Power Factor _____ lbs./min.   Power Index _____*

Exercise Subtotal = Weight × Reps × Sets   ▪ Power Factor = lbs./min.   ▪ Power Index = Total Weight × Power Factor ÷ 1,000,000

WORKOUT A RECORD   Date: ____ / ____ / ____

Start Time: _____   Finish Time: _____   Total Time: _____

■ Exercise: STANDING BARBELL PRESS

Weight Reps Sets	Weight Reps Sets	Weight Reps Sets	Weight Reps Sets	Weight Reps Sets	Weight Reps Sets
× ×	× ×	× ×	× ×	× ×	× ×
Subtotal = lbs.	Subtotal = lbs.	Subtotal = lbs.	Subtotal = lbs.	Subtotal = lbs.	Subtotal = lbs.

Exercise 1:   *Total Weight* _____ *lbs.*   *Time* _____ *mins.*   *Power Factor* _____ *lbs./min.*   *Power Index* _____

■ Exercise: BARBELL SHRUG

Weight Reps Sets	Weight Reps Sets	Weight Reps Sets	Weight Reps Sets	Weight Reps Sets	Weight Reps Sets
× ×	× ×	× ×	× ×	× ×	× ×
Subtotal = lbs.	Subtotal = lbs.	Subtotal = lbs.	Subtotal = lbs.	Subtotal = lbs.	Subtotal = lbs.

Exercise 2:   *Total Weight* _____ *lbs.*   *Time* _____ *mins.*   *Power Factor* _____ *lbs./min.*   *Power Index* _____

■ Exercise: CLOSE-GRIP BENCH PRESS

Weight Reps Sets	Weight Reps Sets	Weight Reps Sets	Weight Reps Sets	Weight Reps Sets	Weight Reps Sets
× ×	× ×	× ×	× ×	× ×	× ×
Subtotal = lbs.	Subtotal = lbs.	Subtotal = lbs.	Subtotal = lbs.	Subtotal = lbs.	Subtotal = lbs.

Exercise 3:   *Total Weight* _____ *lbs.*   *Time* _____ *mins.*   *Power Factor* _____ *lbs./min.*   *Power Index* _____

■ Exercise: PREACHER CURL

Weight Reps Sets	Weight Reps Sets	Weight Reps Sets	Weight Reps Sets	Weight Reps Sets	Weight Reps Sets
× ×	× ×	× ×	× ×	× ×	× ×
Subtotal = lbs.	Subtotal = lbs.	Subtotal = lbs.	Subtotal = lbs.	Subtotal = lbs.	Subtotal = lbs.

Exercise 4:   *Total Weight* _____ *lbs.*   *Time* _____ *mins.*   *Power Factor* _____ *lbs./min.*   *Power Index* _____

■ Exercise: WEIGHTED CRUNCH

Weight Reps Sets	Weight Reps Sets	Weight Reps Sets	Weight Reps Sets	Weight Reps Sets	Weight Reps Sets
× ×	× ×	× ×	× ×	× ×	× ×
Subtotal = lbs.	Subtotal = lbs.	Subtotal = lbs.	Subtotal = lbs.	Subtotal = lbs.	Subtotal = lbs.

Exercise 5:   *Total Weight* _____ *lbs.*   *Time* _____ *mins.*   *Power Factor* _____ *lbs./min.*   *Power Index* _____

OVERALL WORKOUT: *Total Weight* _____ *lbs.*   *Time* _____ *mins.*   *Power Factor* _____ *lbs./min.*   *Power Index* _____

Exercise Subtotal = Weight × Reps × Sets   ■ *Power Factor = lbs./min.*   ■ *Power Index = Total Weight × Power Factor ÷ 1,000,000*

WORKOUT A RECORD   Date: ___ / ___ / ___

Start Time: _____   **Finish Time:** _____   **Total Time:** _____

■ **Exercise: STANDING BARBELL PRESS**

Weight Reps Sets	Weight Reps Sets	Weight Reps Sets	Weight Reps Sets	Weight Reps Sets	Weight Reps Sets
× ×	× ×	× ×	× ×	× ×	× ×
Subtotal = lbs.	Subtotal = lbs.	Subtotal = lbs.	Subtotal = lbs.	Subtotal = lbs.	Subtotal = lbs.

Exercise 1:   *Total Weight* _____ *lbs.*   *Time* _____ *mins.*   *Power Factor* _____ *lbs./min.*   *Power Index* _____

■ **Exercise: BARBELL SHRUG**

Weight Reps Sets	Weight Reps Sets	Weight Reps Sets	Weight Reps Sets	Weight Reps Sets	Weight Reps Sets
× ×	× ×	× ×	× ×	× ×	× ×
Subtotal = lbs.	Subtotal = lbs.	Subtotal = lbs.	Subtotal = lbs.	Subtotal = lbs.	Subtotal = lbs.

Exercise 2:   *Total Weight* _____ *lbs.*   *Time* _____ *mins.*   *Power Factor* _____ *lbs./min.*   *Power Index* _____

■ **Exercise: CLOSE-GRIP BENCH PRESS**

Weight Reps Sets	Weight Reps Sets	Weight Reps Sets	Weight Reps Sets	Weight Reps Sets	Weight Reps Sets
× ×	× ×	× ×	× ×	× ×	× ×
Subtotal = lbs.	Subtotal = lbs.	Subtotal = lbs.	Subtotal = lbs.	Subtotal = lbs.	Subtotal = lbs.

Exercise 3:   *Total Weight* _____ *lbs.*   *Time* _____ *mins.*   *Power Factor* _____ *lbs./min.*   *Power Index* _____

■ **Exercise: PREACHER CURL**

Weight Reps Sets	Weight Reps Sets	Weight Reps Sets	Weight Reps Sets	Weight Reps Sets	Weight Reps Sets
× ×	× ×	× ×	× ×	× ×	× ×
Subtotal = lbs.	Subtotal = lbs.	Subtotal = lbs.	Subtotal = lbs.	Subtotal = lbs.	Subtotal = lbs.

Exercise 4:   *Total Weight* _____ *lbs.*   *Time* _____ *mins.*   *Power Factor* _____ *lbs./min.*   *Power Index* _____

■ **Exercise: WEIGHTED CRUNCH**

Weight Reps Sets	Weight Reps Sets	Weight Reps Sets	Weight Reps Sets	Weight Reps Sets	Weight Reps Sets
× ×	× ×	× ×	× ×	× ×	× ×
Subtotal = lbs.	Subtotal = lbs.	Subtotal = lbs.	Subtotal = lbs.	Subtotal = lbs.	Subtotal = lbs.

Exercise 5:   *Total Weight* _____ *lbs.*   *Time* _____ *mins.*   *Power Factor* _____ *lbs./min.*   *Power Index* _____

OVERALL WORKOUT: *Total Weight* _____ *lbs.*   *Time* _____ *mins.*   *Power Factor* _____ *lbs./min.*   *Power Index* _____

Exercise Subtotal = Weight × Reps × Sets   ■ *Power Factor = lbs./min.*   ■ *Power Index = Total Weight × Power Factor ÷ 1,000,000*

WORKOUT A RECORD

Date: ____ / ____ / ____

Start Time: _____   Finish Time: _____   Total Time: _____

■ **Exercise: STANDING BARBELL PRESS**

Weight Reps Sets	Weight Reps Sets	Weight Reps Sets	Weight Reps Sets	Weight Reps Sets	Weight Reps Sets
✕ ✕	✕ ✕	✕ ✕	✕ ✕	✕ ✕	✕ ✕
Subtotal = ____ lbs.	Subtotal = ____ lbs.	Subtotal = ____ lbs.	Subtotal = ____ lbs.	Subtotal = ____ lbs.	Subtotal = ____ lbs.

Exercise 1:   *Total Weight* _____ *lbs.*   *Time* _____ *mins.*   *Power Factor* _____ *lbs./min.*   *Power Index* _____

■ **Exercise: BARBELL SHRUG**

Weight Reps Sets	Weight Reps Sets	Weight Reps Sets	Weight Reps Sets	Weight Reps Sets	Weight Reps Sets
✕ ✕	✕ ✕	✕ ✕	✕ ✕	✕ ✕	✕ ✕
Subtotal = ____ lbs.	Subtotal = ____ lbs.	Subtotal = ____ lbs.	Subtotal = ____ lbs.	Subtotal = ____ lbs.	Subtotal = ____ lbs.

Exercise 2:   *Total Weight* _____ *lbs.*   *Time* _____ *mins.*   *Power Factor* _____ *lbs./min.*   *Power Index* _____

■ **Exercise: CLOSE-GRIP BENCH PRESS**

Weight Reps Sets	Weight Reps Sets	Weight Reps Sets	Weight Reps Sets	Weight Reps Sets	Weight Reps Sets
✕ ✕	✕ ✕	✕ ✕	✕ ✕	✕ ✕	✕ ✕
Subtotal = ____ lbs.	Subtotal = ____ lbs.	Subtotal = ____ lbs.	Subtotal = ____ lbs.	Subtotal = ____ lbs.	Subtotal = ____ lbs.

Exercise 3:   *Total Weight* _____ *lbs.*   *Time* _____ *mins.*   *Power Factor* _____ *lbs./min.*   *Power Index* _____

■ **Exercise: PREACHER CURL**

Weight Reps Sets	Weight Reps Sets	Weight Reps Sets	Weight Reps Sets	Weight Reps Sets	Weight Reps Sets
✕ ✕	✕ ✕	✕ ✕	✕ ✕	✕ ✕	✕ ✕
Subtotal = ____ lbs.	Subtotal = ____ lbs.	Subtotal = ____ lbs.	Subtotal = ____ lbs.	Subtotal = ____ lbs.	Subtotal = ____ lbs.

Exercise 4:   *Total Weight* _____ *lbs.*   *Time* _____ *mins.*   *Power Factor* _____ *lbs./min.*   *Power Index* _____

■ **Exercise: WEIGHTED CRUNCH**

Weight Reps Sets	Weight Reps Sets	Weight Reps Sets	Weight Reps Sets	Weight Reps Sets	Weight Reps Sets
✕ ✕	✕ ✕	✕ ✕	✕ ✕	✕ ✕	✕ ✕
Subtotal = ____ lbs.	Subtotal = ____ lbs.	Subtotal = ____ lbs.	Subtotal = ____ lbs.	Subtotal = ____ lbs.	Subtotal = ____ lbs.

Exercise 5:   *Total Weight* _____ *lbs.*   *Time* _____ *mins.*   *Power Factor* _____ *lbs./min.*   *Power Index* _____

OVERALL WORKOUT: *Total Weight* _____ *lbs.*   *Time* _____ *mins.*   *Power Factor* _____ *lbs./min.*   *Power Index* _____

Exercise Subtotal = Weight ✕ Reps ✕ Sets   ■ *Power Factor = lbs./min.*   ■ *Power Index = Total Weight ✕ Power Factor ÷ 1,000,000*

WORKOUT B RECORD   Date: ___ / ___ / ___

Start Time: _____   Finish Time: _____   Total Time: _____

■ Exercise: DEADLIFT

Weight	Reps	Sets	Weight	Reps	Sets	Weight	Reps	Sets	Weight	Reps	Sets	Weight	Reps	Sets	Weight	Reps	Sets
×	×		×	×		×	×		×	×		×	×		×	×	
Subtotal =		lbs.	Subtotal =		lbs.	Subtotal =		lbs.	Subtotal =		lbs.	Subtotal =		lbs.	Subtotal =		lbs.

Exercise 1:   *Total Weight _____ lbs.   Time _____ mins.   Power Factor _____ lbs./min.   Power Index _____*

■ Exercise: BENCH PRESS

Weight	Reps	Sets	Weight	Reps	Sets	Weight	Reps	Sets	Weight	Reps	Sets	Weight	Reps	Sets	Weight	Reps	Sets
×	×		×	×		×	×		×	×		×	×		×	×	
Subtotal =		lbs.	Subtotal =		lbs.	Subtotal =		lbs.	Subtotal =		lbs.	Subtotal =		lbs.	Subtotal =		lbs.

Exercise 2:   *Total Weight _____ lbs.   Time _____ mins.   Power Factor _____ lbs./min.   Power Index _____*

■ Exercise: LAT PULLDOWN

Weight	Reps	Sets	Weight	Reps	Sets	Weight	Reps	Sets	Weight	Reps	Sets	Weight	Reps	Sets	Weight	Reps	Sets
×	×		×	×		×	×		×	×		×	×		×	×	
Subtotal =		lbs.	Subtotal =		lbs.	Subtotal =		lbs.	Subtotal =		lbs.	Subtotal =		lbs.	Subtotal =		lbs.

Exercise 3:   *Total Weight _____ lbs.   Time _____ mins.   Power Factor _____ lbs./min.   Power Index _____*

■ Exercise: LEG PRESS

Weight	Reps	Sets	Weight	Reps	Sets	Weight	Reps	Sets	Weight	Reps	Sets	Weight	Reps	Sets	Weight	Reps	Sets
×	×		×	×		×	×		×	×		×	×		×	×	
Subtotal =		lbs.	Subtotal =		lbs.	Subtotal =		lbs.	Subtotal =		lbs.	Subtotal =		lbs.	Subtotal =		lbs.

Exercise 4:   *Total Weight _____ lbs.   Time _____ mins.   Power Factor _____ lbs./min.   Power Index _____*

■ Exercise: TOE PRESS

Weight	Reps	Sets	Weight	Reps	Sets	Weight	Reps	Sets	Weight	Reps	Sets	Weight	Reps	Sets	Weight	Reps	Sets
×	×		×	×		×	×		×	×		×	×		×	×	
Subtotal =		lbs.	Subtotal =		lbs.	Subtotal =		lbs.	Subtotal =		lbs.	Subtotal =		lbs.	Subtotal =		lbs.

Exercise 5:   *Total Weight _____ lbs.   Time _____ mins.   Power Factor _____ lbs./min.   Power Index _____*

OVERALL WORKOUT: *Total Weight _____ lbs.   Time _____ mins.   Power Factor _____ lbs./min.   Power Index _____*

Exercise Subtotal = Weight × Reps × Sets   ■ Power Factor = lbs./min.   ■ Power Index = Total Weight × Power Factor ÷ 1,000,000

WORKOUT B RECORD   Date: ____ / ____ / ____

Start Time: _____   **Finish Time:** _____   **Total Time:** _____

■ Exercise: DEADLIFT

Weight	Reps	Sets	Weight	Reps	Sets	Weight	Reps	Sets	Weight	Reps	Sets	Weight	Reps	Sets	Weight	Reps	Sets
×	×		×	×		×	×		×	×		×	×		×	×	
Subtotal =		lbs.	Subtotal =		lbs.	Subtotal =		lbs.	Subtotal =		lbs.	Subtotal =		lbs.	Subtotal =		lbs.

Exercise 1:   *Total Weight* _____ *lbs.   Time* _____ *mins.   Power Factor* _____ *lbs./min.   Power Index* _____

■ Exercise: BENCH PRESS

Weight	Reps	Sets	Weight	Reps	Sets	Weight	Reps	Sets	Weight	Reps	Sets	Weight	Reps	Sets	Weight	Reps	Sets
×	×		×	×		×	×		×	×		×	×		×	×	
Subtotal =		lbs.	Subtotal =		lbs.	Subtotal =		lbs.	Subtotal =		lbs.	Subtotal =		lbs.	Subtotal =		lbs.

Exercise 2:   *Total Weight* _____ *lbs.   Time* _____ *mins.   Power Factor* _____ *lbs./min.   Power Index* _____

■ Exercise: LAT PULLDOWN

Weight	Reps	Sets	Weight	Reps	Sets	Weight	Reps	Sets	Weight	Reps	Sets	Weight	Reps	Sets	Weight	Reps	Sets
×	×		×	×		×	×		×	×		×	×		×	×	
Subtotal =		lbs.	Subtotal =		lbs.	Subtotal =		lbs.	Subtotal =		lbs.	Subtotal =		lbs.	Subtotal =		lbs.

Exercise 3:   *Total Weight* _____ *lbs.   Time* _____ *mins.   Power Factor* _____ *lbs./min.   Power Index* _____

■ Exercise: LEG PRESS

Weight	Reps	Sets	Weight	Reps	Sets	Weight	Reps	Sets	Weight	Reps	Sets	Weight	Reps	Sets	Weight	Reps	Sets
×	×		×	×		×	×		×	×		×	×		×	×	
Subtotal =		lbs.	Subtotal =		lbs.	Subtotal =		lbs.	Subtotal =		lbs.	Subtotal =		lbs.	Subtotal =		lbs.

Exercise 4:   *Total Weight* _____ *lbs.   Time* _____ *mins.   Power Factor* _____ *lbs./min.   Power Index* _____

■ Exercise: TOE PRESS

Weight	Reps	Sets	Weight	Reps	Sets	Weight	Reps	Sets	Weight	Reps	Sets	Weight	Reps	Sets	Weight	Reps	Sets
×	×		×	×		×	×		×	×		×	×		×	×	
Subtotal =		lbs.	Subtotal =		lbs.	Subtotal =		lbs.	Subtotal =		lbs.	Subtotal =		lbs.	Subtotal =		lbs.

Exercise 5:   *Total Weight* _____ *lbs.   Time* _____ *mins.   Power Factor* _____ *lbs./min.   Power Index* _____

OVERALL WORKOUT: *Total Weight* _____ *lbs.   Time* _____ *mins.   Power Factor* _____ *lbs./min.   Power Index* _____

Exercise Subtotal = Weight × Reps × Sets   ■ *Power Factor = lbs./min.*   ■ *Power Index = Total Weight × Power Factor ÷ 1,000,000*

WORKOUT B RECORD

Date: ____ / ____ / ____

Start Time: _____   Finish Time: _____   Total Time: _____

■ Exercise: DEADLIFT

Weight	Reps	Sets	Weight	Reps	Sets	Weight	Reps	Sets	Weight	Reps	Sets	Weight	Reps	Sets	Weight	Reps	Sets
×	×		×	×		×	×		×	×		×	×		×	×	
Subtotal =		lbs.	Subtotal =		lbs.	Subtotal =		lbs.	Subtotal =		lbs.	Subtotal =		lbs.	Subtotal =		lbs.

Exercise 1: _____   *Total Weight* _____ *lbs.*   *Time* _____ *mins.*   *Power Factor* _____ *lbs./min.*   *Power Index* _____

■ Exercise: BENCH PRESS

Weight	Reps	Sets	Weight	Reps	Sets	Weight	Reps	Sets	Weight	Reps	Sets	Weight	Reps	Sets	Weight	Reps	Sets
×	×		×	×		×	×		×	×		×	×		×	×	
Subtotal =		lbs.	Subtotal =		lbs.	Subtotal =		lbs.	Subtotal =		lbs.	Subtotal =		lbs.	Subtotal =		lbs.

Exercise 2: _____   *Total Weight* _____ *lbs.*   *Time* _____ *mins.*   *Power Factor* _____ *lbs./min.*   *Power Index* _____

■ Exercise: LAT PULLDOWN

Weight	Reps	Sets	Weight	Reps	Sets	Weight	Reps	Sets	Weight	Reps	Sets	Weight	Reps	Sets	Weight	Reps	Sets
×	×		×	×		×	×		×	×		×	×		×	×	
Subtotal =		lbs.	Subtotal =		lbs.	Subtotal =		lbs.	Subtotal =		lbs.	Subtotal =		lbs.	Subtotal =		lbs.

Exercise 3: _____   *Total Weight* _____ *lbs.*   *Time* _____ *mins.*   *Power Factor* _____ *lbs./min.*   *Power Index* _____

■ Exercise: LEG PRESS

Weight	Reps	Sets	Weight	Reps	Sets	Weight	Reps	Sets	Weight	Reps	Sets	Weight	Reps	Sets	Weight	Reps	Sets
×	×		×	×		×	×		×	×		×	×		×	×	
Subtotal =		lbs.	Subtotal =		lbs.	Subtotal =		lbs.	Subtotal =		lbs.	Subtotal =		lbs.	Subtotal =		lbs.

Exercise 4: _____   *Total Weight* _____ *lbs.*   *Time* _____ *mins.*   *Power Factor* _____ *lbs./min.*   *Power Index* _____

■ Exercise: TOE PRESS

Weight	Reps	Sets	Weight	Reps	Sets	Weight	Reps	Sets	Weight	Reps	Sets	Weight	Reps	Sets	Weight	Reps	Sets
×	×		×	×		×	×		×	×		×	×		×	×	
Subtotal =		lbs.	Subtotal =		lbs.	Subtotal =		lbs.	Subtotal =		lbs.	Subtotal =		lbs.	Subtotal =		lbs.

Exercise 5: _____   *Total Weight* _____ *lbs.*   *Time* _____ *mins.*   *Power Factor* _____ *lbs./min.*   *Power Index* _____

OVERALL WORKOUT: *Total Weight* _____ *lbs.*   *Time* _____ *mins.*   *Power Factor* _____ *lbs./min.*   *Power Index* _____

Exercise Subtotal = Weight × Reps × Sets   ■ *Power Factor = lbs./min.*   ■ *Power Index = Total Weight × Power Factor ÷ 1,000,000*

WORKOUT B RECORD   Date: ____ / ____ / ____

Start Time: _____   Finish Time: _____   Total Time: _____

- **Exercise: DEADLIFT**

Weight Reps Sets	Weight Reps Sets	Weight Reps Sets	Weight Reps Sets	Weight Reps Sets	Weight Reps Sets
× ×	× ×	× ×	× ×	× ×	× ×
Subtotal = lbs.	Subtotal = lbs.	Subtotal = lbs.	Subtotal = lbs.	Subtotal = lbs.	Subtotal = lbs.

Exercise 1:   *Total Weight _____ lbs.   Time _____ mins.   Power Factor _____ lbs./min.   Power Index _____*

- **Exercise: BENCH PRESS**

Weight Reps Sets	Weight Reps Sets	Weight Reps Sets	Weight Reps Sets	Weight Reps Sets	Weight Reps Sets
× ×	× ×	× ×	× ×	× ×	× ×
Subtotal = lbs.	Subtotal = lbs.	Subtotal = lbs.	Subtotal = lbs.	Subtotal = lbs.	Subtotal = lbs.

Exercise 2:   *Total Weight _____ lbs.   Time _____ mins.   Power Factor _____ lbs./min.   Power Index _____*

- **Exercise: LAT PULLDOWN**

Weight Reps Sets	Weight Reps Sets	Weight Reps Sets	Weight Reps Sets	Weight Reps Sets	Weight Reps Sets
× ×	× ×	× ×	× ×	× ×	× ×
Subtotal = lbs.	Subtotal = lbs.	Subtotal = lbs.	Subtotal = lbs.	Subtotal = lbs.	Subtotal = lbs.

Exercise 3:   *Total Weight _____ lbs.   Time _____ mins.   Power Factor _____ lbs./min.   Power Index _____*

- **Exercise: LEG PRESS**

Weight Reps Sets	Weight Reps Sets	Weight Reps Sets	Weight Reps Sets	Weight Reps Sets	Weight Reps Sets
× ×	× ×	× ×	× ×	× ×	× ×
Subtotal = lbs.	Subtotal = lbs.	Subtotal = lbs.	Subtotal = lbs.	Subtotal = lbs.	Subtotal = lbs.

Exercise 4:   *Total Weight _____ lbs.   Time _____ mins.   Power Factor _____ lbs./min.   Power Index _____*

- **Exercise: TOE PRESS**

Weight Reps Sets	Weight Reps Sets	Weight Reps Sets	Weight Reps Sets	Weight Reps Sets	Weight Reps Sets
× ×	× ×	× ×	× ×	× ×	× ×
Subtotal = lbs.	Subtotal = lbs.	Subtotal = lbs.	Subtotal = lbs.	Subtotal = lbs.	Subtotal = lbs.

Exercise 5:   *Total Weight _____ lbs.   Time _____ mins.   Power Factor _____ lbs./min.   Power Index _____*

OVERALL WORKOUT: *Total Weight _____ lbs.   Time _____ mins.   Power Factor _____ lbs./min.   Power Index _____*

Exercise Subtotal = Weight × Reps × Sets   ■ Power Factor = lbs./min.   ■ Power Index = Total Weight × Power Factor ÷ 1,000,000

WORKOUT B RECORD   Date: ___ / ___ / ___

Start Time: _____   **Finish Time:** _____   **Total Time:** _____

▪ Exercise: DEADLIFT

Weight Reps Sets	Weight Reps Sets	Weight Reps Sets	Weight Reps Sets	Weight Reps Sets	Weight Reps Sets
× ×	× ×	× ×	× ×	× ×	× ×
Subtotal = lbs.	Subtotal = lbs.	Subtotal = lbs.	Subtotal = lbs.	Subtotal = lbs.	Subtotal = lbs.

Exercise 1:   *Total Weight* _____ *lbs.*   *Time* _____ *mins.*   *Power Factor* _____ *lbs./min.*   *Power Index* _____

▪ Exercise: BENCH PRESS

Weight Reps Sets	Weight Reps Sets	Weight Reps Sets	Weight Reps Sets	Weight Reps Sets	Weight Reps Sets
× ×	× ×	× ×	× ×	× ×	× ×
Subtotal = lbs.	Subtotal = lbs.	Subtotal = lbs.	Subtotal = lbs.	Subtotal = lbs.	Subtotal = lbs.

Exercise 2:   *Total Weight* _____ *lbs.*   *Time* _____ *mins.*   *Power Factor* _____ *lbs./min.*   *Power Index* _____

▪ Exercise: LAT PULLDOWN

Weight Reps Sets	Weight Reps Sets	Weight Reps Sets	Weight Reps Sets	Weight Reps Sets	Weight Reps Sets
× ×	× ×	× ×	× ×	× ×	× ×
Subtotal = lbs.	Subtotal = lbs.	Subtotal = lbs.	Subtotal = lbs.	Subtotal = lbs.	Subtotal = lbs.

Exercise 3:   *Total Weight* _____ *lbs.*   *Time* _____ *mins.*   *Power Factor* _____ *lbs./min.*   *Power Index* _____

▪ Exercise: LEG PRESS

Weight Reps Sets	Weight Reps Sets	Weight Reps Sets	Weight Reps Sets	Weight Reps Sets	Weight Reps Sets
× ×	× ×	× ×	× ×	× ×	× ×
Subtotal = lbs.	Subtotal = lbs.	Subtotal = lbs.	Subtotal = lbs.	Subtotal = lbs.	Subtotal = lbs.

Exercise 4:   *Total Weight* _____ *lbs.*   *Time* _____ *mins.*   *Power Factor* _____ *lbs./min.*   *Power Index* _____

▪ Exercise: TOE PRESS

Weight Reps Sets	Weight Reps Sets	Weight Reps Sets	Weight Reps Sets	Weight Reps Sets	Weight Reps Sets
× ×	× ×	× ×	× ×	× ×	× ×
Subtotal = lbs.	Subtotal = lbs.	Subtotal = lbs.	Subtotal = lbs.	Subtotal = lbs.	Subtotal = lbs.

Exercise 5:   *Total Weight* _____ *lbs.*   *Time* _____ *mins.*   *Power Factor* _____ *lbs./min.*   *Power Index* _____

OVERALL WORKOUT: *Total Weight* _____ *lbs.*   *Time* _____ *mins.*   *Power Factor* _____ *lbs./min.*   *Power Index* _____

Exercise Subtotal = Weight × Reps × Sets   ▪ *Power Factor = lbs./min.*   ▪ *Power Index = Total Weight × Power Factor ÷ 1,000,000*

WORKOUT B RECORD   Date: ___ / ___ / ___

Start Time: _____   **Finish Time:** _____   **Total Time:** _____

▪ Exercise: DEADLIFT

Weight Reps Sets	Weight Reps Sets	Weight Reps Sets	Weight Reps Sets	Weight Reps Sets	Weight Reps Sets
× ×	× ×	× ×	× ×	× ×	× ×
Subtotal = lbs.	Subtotal = lbs.	Subtotal = lbs.	Subtotal = lbs.	Subtotal = lbs.	Subtotal = lbs.

Exercise 1:   *Total Weight* _____ *lbs.*   *Time* _____ *mins.*   *Power Factor* _____ *lbs./min.*   *Power Index* _____

▪ Exercise: BENCH PRESS

Weight Reps Sets	Weight Reps Sets	Weight Reps Sets	Weight Reps Sets	Weight Reps Sets	Weight Reps Sets
× ×	× ×	× ×	× ×	× ×	× ×
Subtotal = lbs.	Subtotal = lbs.	Subtotal = lbs.	Subtotal = lbs.	Subtotal = lbs.	Subtotal = lbs.

Exercise 2:   *Total Weight* _____ *lbs.*   *Time* _____ *mins.*   *Power Factor* _____ *lbs./min.*   *Power Index* _____

▪ Exercise: LAT PULLDOWN

Weight Reps Sets	Weight Reps Sets	Weight Reps Sets	Weight Reps Sets	Weight Reps Sets	Weight Reps Sets
× ×	× ×	× ×	× ×	× ×	× ×
Subtotal = lbs.	Subtotal = lbs.	Subtotal = lbs.	Subtotal = lbs.	Subtotal = lbs.	Subtotal = lbs.

Exercise 3:   *Total Weight* _____ *lbs.*   *Time* _____ *mins.*   *Power Factor* _____ *lbs./min.*   *Power Index* _____

▪ Exercise: LEG PRESS

Weight Reps Sets	Weight Reps Sets	Weight Reps Sets	Weight Reps Sets	Weight Reps Sets	Weight Reps Sets
× ×	× ×	× ×	× ×	× ×	× ×
Subtotal = lbs.	Subtotal = lbs.	Subtotal = lbs.	Subtotal = lbs.	Subtotal = lbs.	Subtotal = lbs.

Exercise 4:   *Total Weight* _____ *lbs.*   *Time* _____ *mins.*   *Power Factor* _____ *lbs./min.*   *Power Index* _____

▪ Exercise: TOE PRESS

Weight Reps Sets	Weight Reps Sets	Weight Reps Sets	Weight Reps Sets	Weight Reps Sets	Weight Reps Sets
× ×	× ×	× ×	× ×	× ×	× ×
Subtotal = lbs.	Subtotal = lbs.	Subtotal = lbs.	Subtotal = lbs.	Subtotal = lbs.	Subtotal = lbs.

Exercise 5:   *Total Weight* _____ *lbs.*   *Time* _____ *mins.*   *Power Factor* _____ *lbs./min.*   *Power Index* _____

OVERALL WORKOUT: *Total Weight* _____ *lbs.*   *Time* _____ *mins.*   *Power Factor* _____ *lbs./min.*   *Power Index* _____

Exercise Subtotal = Weight × Reps × Sets   ▪ *Power Factor = lbs./min.*   ▪ *Power Index = Total Weight × Power Factor ÷ 1,000,000*

WORKOUT B RECORD

Date: ___ / ___ / ___

Start Time: _____   Finish Time: _____   Total Time: _____

▪ Exercise: DEADLIFT

Weight Reps Sets	Weight Reps Sets	Weight Reps Sets	Weight Reps Sets	Weight Reps Sets	Weight Reps Sets
× ×	× ×	× ×	× ×	× ×	× ×
Subtotal = lbs.	Subtotal = lbs.	Subtotal = lbs.	Subtotal = lbs.	Subtotal = lbs.	Subtotal = lbs.

Exercise 1:   Total Weight _____ lbs.   Time _____ mins.   Power Factor _____ lbs./min.   Power Index _____

▪ Exercise: BENCH PRESS

Weight Reps Sets	Weight Reps Sets	Weight Reps Sets	Weight Reps Sets	Weight Reps Sets	Weight Reps Sets
× ×	× ×	× ×	× ×	× ×	× ×
Subtotal = lbs.	Subtotal = lbs.	Subtotal = lbs.	Subtotal = lbs.	Subtotal = lbs.	Subtotal = lbs.

Exercise 2:   Total Weight _____ lbs.   Time _____ mins.   Power Factor _____ lbs./min.   Power Index _____

▪ Exercise: LAT PULLDOWN

Weight Reps Sets	Weight Reps Sets	Weight Reps Sets	Weight Reps Sets	Weight Reps Sets	Weight Reps Sets
× ×	× ×	× ×	× ×	× ×	× ×
Subtotal = lbs.	Subtotal = lbs.	Subtotal = lbs.	Subtotal = lbs.	Subtotal = lbs.	Subtotal = lbs.

Exercise 3:   Total Weight _____ lbs.   Time _____ mins.   Power Factor _____ lbs./min.   Power Index _____

▪ Exercise: LEG PRESS

Weight Reps Sets	Weight Reps Sets	Weight Reps Sets	Weight Reps Sets	Weight Reps Sets	Weight Reps Sets
× ×	× ×	× ×	× ×	× ×	× ×
Subtotal = lbs.	Subtotal = lbs.	Subtotal = lbs.	Subtotal = lbs.	Subtotal = lbs.	Subtotal = lbs.

Exercise 4:   Total Weight _____ lbs.   Time _____ mins.   Power Factor _____ lbs./min.   Power Index _____

▪ Exercise: TOE PRESS

Weight Reps Sets	Weight Reps Sets	Weight Reps Sets	Weight Reps Sets	Weight Reps Sets	Weight Reps Sets
× ×	× ×	× ×	× ×	× ×	× ×
Subtotal = lbs.	Subtotal = lbs.	Subtotal = lbs.	Subtotal = lbs.	Subtotal = lbs.	Subtotal = lbs.

Exercise 5:   Total Weight _____ lbs.   Time _____ mins.   Power Factor _____ lbs./min.   Power Index _____

OVERALL WORKOUT: *Total Weight _____ lbs.   Time _____ mins.   Power Factor _____ lbs./min.   Power Index _____*

Exercise Subtotal = Weight × Reps × Sets   ▪ Power Factor = lbs./min.   ▪ Power Index = Total Weight × Power Factor ÷ 1,000,000

WORKOUT B RECORD

Date: ____ / ____ / ____

Start Time: _____ Finish Time: _____ Total Time: _____

■ **Exercise: DEADLIFT**

Weight	Reps	Sets	Weight	Reps	Sets	Weight	Reps	Sets	Weight	Reps	Sets	Weight	Reps	Sets	Weight	Reps	Sets
×	×		×	×		×	×		×	×		×	×		×	×	
Subtotal =	lbs.		Subtotal =	lbs.		Subtotal =	lbs.		Subtotal =	lbs.		Subtotal =	lbs.		Subtotal =	lbs.	

Exercise 1:   *Total Weight* _____ *lbs.*   *Time* _____ *mins.*   *Power Factor* _____ *lbs./min.*   *Power Index* _____

■ **Exercise: BENCH PRESS**

Weight	Reps	Sets	Weight	Reps	Sets	Weight	Reps	Sets	Weight	Reps	Sets	Weight	Reps	Sets	Weight	Reps	Sets
×	×		×	×		×	×		×	×		×	×		×	×	
Subtotal =	lbs.		Subtotal =	lbs.		Subtotal =	lbs.		Subtotal =	lbs.		Subtotal =	lbs.		Subtotal =	lbs.	

Exercise 2:   *Total Weight* _____ *lbs.*   *Time* _____ *mins.*   *Power Factor* _____ *lbs./min.*   *Power Index* _____

■ **Exercise: LAT PULLDOWN**

Weight	Reps	Sets	Weight	Reps	Sets	Weight	Reps	Sets	Weight	Reps	Sets	Weight	Reps	Sets	Weight	Reps	Sets
×	×		×	×		×	×		×	×		×	×		×	×	
Subtotal =	lbs.		Subtotal =	lbs.		Subtotal =	lbs.		Subtotal =	lbs.		Subtotal =	lbs.		Subtotal =	lbs.	

Exercise 3:   *Total Weight* _____ *lbs.*   *Time* _____ *mins.*   *Power Factor* _____ *lbs./min.*   *Power Index* _____

■ **Exercise: LEG PRESS**

Weight	Reps	Sets	Weight	Reps	Sets	Weight	Reps	Sets	Weight	Reps	Sets	Weight	Reps	Sets	Weight	Reps	Sets
×	×		×	×		×	×		×	×		×	×		×	×	
Subtotal =	lbs.		Subtotal =	lbs.		Subtotal =	lbs.		Subtotal =	lbs.		Subtotal =	lbs.		Subtotal =	lbs.	

Exercise 4:   *Total Weight* _____ *lbs.*   *Time* _____ *mins.*   *Power Factor* _____ *lbs./min.*   *Power Index* _____

■ **Exercise: TOE PRESS**

Weight	Reps	Sets	Weight	Reps	Sets	Weight	Reps	Sets	Weight	Reps	Sets	Weight	Reps	Sets	Weight	Reps	Sets
×	×		×	×		×	×		×	×		×	×		×	×	
Subtotal =	lbs.		Subtotal =	lbs.		Subtotal =	lbs.		Subtotal =	lbs.		Subtotal =	lbs.		Subtotal =	lbs.	

Exercise 5:   *Total Weight* _____ *lbs.*   *Time* _____ *mins.*   *Power Factor* _____ *lbs./min.*   *Power Index* _____

OVERALL WORKOUT: *Total Weight* _____ *lbs.*   *Time* _____ *mins.*   *Power Factor* _____ *lbs./min.*   *Power Index* _____

Exercise Subtotal = Weight × Reps × Sets ■ *Power Factor = lbs./min.* ■ *Power Index = Total Weight × Power Factor ÷ 1,000,000*

WORKOUT B RECORD   Date: ____ / ____ / ____

Start Time: _____   Finish Time: _____   Total Time: _____

■ Exercise: DEADLIFT

Weight Reps Sets	Weight Reps Sets	Weight Reps Sets	Weight Reps Sets	Weight Reps Sets	Weight Reps Sets
× ×	× ×	× ×	× ×	× ×	× ×
Subtotal = lbs.	Subtotal = lbs.	Subtotal = lbs.	Subtotal = lbs.	Subtotal = lbs.	Subtotal = lbs.

Exercise 1:   Total Weight _____ lbs.   Time _____ mins.   Power Factor _____ lbs./min.   Power Index _____

■ Exercise: BENCH PRESS

Weight Reps Sets	Weight Reps Sets	Weight Reps Sets	Weight Reps Sets	Weight Reps Sets	Weight Reps Sets
× ×	× ×	× ×	× ×	× ×	× ×
Subtotal = lbs.	Subtotal = lbs.	Subtotal = lbs.	Subtotal = lbs.	Subtotal = lbs.	Subtotal = lbs.

Exercise 2:   Total Weight _____ lbs.   Time _____ mins.   Power Factor _____ lbs./min.   Power Index _____

■ Exercise: LAT PULLDOWN

Weight Reps Sets	Weight Reps Sets	Weight Reps Sets	Weight Reps Sets	Weight Reps Sets	Weight Reps Sets
× ×	× ×	× ×	× ×	× ×	× ×
Subtotal = lbs.	Subtotal = lbs.	Subtotal = lbs.	Subtotal = lbs.	Subtotal = lbs.	Subtotal = lbs.

Exercise 3:   Total Weight _____ lbs.   Time _____ mins.   Power Factor _____ lbs./min.   Power Index _____

■ Exercise: LEG PRESS

Weight Reps Sets	Weight Reps Sets	Weight Reps Sets	Weight Reps Sets	Weight Reps Sets	Weight Reps Sets
× ×	× ×	× ×	× ×	× ×	× ×
Subtotal = lbs.	Subtotal = lbs.	Subtotal = lbs.	Subtotal = lbs.	Subtotal = lbs.	Subtotal = lbs.

Exercise 4:   Total Weight _____ lbs.   Time _____ mins.   Power Factor _____ lbs./min.   Power Index _____

■ Exercise: TOE PRESS

Weight Reps Sets	Weight Reps Sets	Weight Reps Sets	Weight Reps Sets	Weight Reps Sets	Weight Reps Sets
× ×	× ×	× ×	× ×	× ×	× ×
Subtotal = lbs.	Subtotal = lbs.	Subtotal = lbs.	Subtotal = lbs.	Subtotal = lbs.	Subtotal = lbs.

Exercise 5:   Total Weight _____ lbs.   Time _____ mins.   Power Factor _____ lbs./min.   Power Index _____

OVERALL WORKOUT: *Total Weight* _____ lbs.   *Time* _____ mins.   *Power Factor* _____ lbs./min.   *Power Index* _____

Exercise Subtotal = Weight × Reps × Sets   ■ *Power Factor = lbs./min.*   ■ *Power Index = Total Weight × Power Factor ÷ 1,000,000*

WORKOUT B RECORD

Date: ____ / ____ / ____

Start Time: _____   Finish Time: _____   Total Time: _____

▪ Exercise: DEADLIFT

Weight Reps Sets	Weight Reps Sets	Weight Reps Sets	Weight Reps Sets	Weight Reps Sets	Weight Reps Sets
× ×	× ×	× ×	× ×	× ×	× ×
Subtotal = lbs.	Subtotal = lbs.	Subtotal = lbs.	Subtotal = lbs.	Subtotal = lbs.	Subtotal = lbs.

Exercise 1:   *Total Weight* _____ *lbs.*   *Time* _____ *mins.*   *Power Factor* _____ *lbs./min.*   *Power Index* _____

▪ Exercise: BENCH PRESS

Weight Reps Sets	Weight Reps Sets	Weight Reps Sets	Weight Reps Sets	Weight Reps Sets	Weight Reps Sets
× ×	× ×	× ×	× ×	× ×	× ×
Subtotal = lbs.	Subtotal = lbs.	Subtotal = lbs.	Subtotal = lbs.	Subtotal = lbs.	Subtotal = lbs.

Exercise 2:   *Total Weight* _____ *lbs.*   *Time* _____ *mins.*   *Power Factor* _____ *lbs./min.*   *Power Index* _____

▪ Exercise: LAT PULLDOWN

Weight Reps Sets	Weight Reps Sets	Weight Reps Sets	Weight Reps Sets	Weight Reps Sets	Weight Reps Sets
× ×	× ×	× ×	× ×	× ×	× ×
Subtotal = lbs.	Subtotal = lbs.	Subtotal = lbs.	Subtotal = lbs.	Subtotal = lbs.	Subtotal = lbs.

Exercise 3:   *Total Weight* _____ *lbs.*   *Time* _____ *mins.*   *Power Factor* _____ *lbs./min.*   *Power Index* _____

▪ Exercise: LEG PRESS

Weight Reps Sets	Weight Reps Sets	Weight Reps Sets	Weight Reps Sets	Weight Reps Sets	Weight Reps Sets
× ×	× ×	× ×	× ×	× ×	× ×
Subtotal = lbs.	Subtotal = lbs.	Subtotal = lbs.	Subtotal = lbs.	Subtotal = lbs.	Subtotal = lbs.

Exercise 4:   *Total Weight* _____ *lbs.*   *Time* _____ *mins.*   *Power Factor* _____ *lbs./min.*   *Power Index* _____

▪ Exercise: TOE PRESS

Weight Reps Sets	Weight Reps Sets	Weight Reps Sets	Weight Reps Sets	Weight Reps Sets	Weight Reps Sets
× ×	× ×	× ×	× ×	× ×	× ×
Subtotal = lbs.	Subtotal = lbs.	Subtotal = lbs.	Subtotal = lbs.	Subtotal = lbs.	Subtotal = lbs.

Exercise 5:   *Total Weight* _____ *lbs.*   *Time* _____ *mins.*   *Power Factor* _____ *lbs./min.*   *Power Index* _____

OVERALL WORKOUT: *Total Weight* _____ *lbs.*   *Time* _____ *mins.*   *Power Factor* _____ *lbs./min.*   *Power Index* _____

Exercise Subtotal = Weight × Reps × Sets   ▪ *Power Factor = lbs./min.*   ▪ *Power Index = Total Weight × Power Factor ÷ 1,000,000*

WORKOUT B RECORD

Date: ____ / ____ / ____

Start Time: _____   Finish Time: _____   Total Time: _____

■ **Exercise: DEADLIFT**

Weight Reps Sets	Weight Reps Sets	Weight Reps Sets	Weight Reps Sets	Weight Reps Sets	Weight Reps Sets
× ×	× ×	× ×	× ×	× ×	× ×
Subtotal = lbs.	Subtotal = lbs.	Subtotal = lbs.	Subtotal = lbs.	Subtotal = lbs.	Subtotal = lbs.

Exercise 1:   Total Weight _____ lbs.   Time _____ mins.   Power Factor _____ lbs./min.   Power Index _____

■ **Exercise: BENCH PRESS**

Weight Reps Sets	Weight Reps Sets	Weight Reps Sets	Weight Reps Sets	Weight Reps Sets	Weight Reps Sets
× ×	× ×	× ×	× ×	× ×	× ×
Subtotal = lbs.	Subtotal = lbs.	Subtotal = lbs.	Subtotal = lbs.	Subtotal = lbs.	Subtotal = lbs.

Exercise 2:   Total Weight _____ lbs.   Time _____ mins.   Power Factor _____ lbs./min.   Power Index _____

■ **Exercise: LAT PULLDOWN**

Weight Reps Sets	Weight Reps Sets	Weight Reps Sets	Weight Reps Sets	Weight Reps Sets	Weight Reps Sets
× ×	× ×	× ×	× ×	× ×	× ×
Subtotal = lbs.	Subtotal = lbs.	Subtotal = lbs.	Subtotal = lbs.	Subtotal = lbs.	Subtotal = lbs.

Exercise 3:   Total Weight _____ lbs.   Time _____ mins.   Power Factor _____ lbs./min.   Power Index _____

■ **Exercise: LEG PRESS**

Weight Reps Sets	Weight Reps Sets	Weight Reps Sets	Weight Reps Sets	Weight Reps Sets	Weight Reps Sets
× ×	× ×	× ×	× ×	× ×	× ×
Subtotal = lbs.	Subtotal = lbs.	Subtotal = lbs.	Subtotal = lbs.	Subtotal = lbs.	Subtotal = lbs.

Exercise 4:   Total Weight _____ lbs.   Time _____ mins.   Power Factor _____ lbs./min.   Power Index _____

■ **Exercise: TOE PRESS**

Weight Reps Sets	Weight Reps Sets	Weight Reps Sets	Weight Reps Sets	Weight Reps Sets	Weight Reps Sets
× ×	× ×	× ×	× ×	× ×	× ×
Subtotal = lbs.	Subtotal = lbs.	Subtotal = lbs.	Subtotal = lbs.	Subtotal = lbs.	Subtotal = lbs.

Exercise 5:   Total Weight _____ lbs.   Time _____ mins.   Power Factor _____ lbs./min.   Power Index _____

OVERALL WORKOUT: Total Weight _____ lbs.   Time _____ mins.   Power Factor _____ lbs./min.   Power Index _____

Exercise Subtotal = Weight × Reps × Sets   ■   *Power Factor = lbs./min.*   ■   *Power Index = Total Weight × Power Factor ÷ 1,000,000*

WORKOUT B RECORD

Date: ____ / ____ / ____

Start Time: _____   Finish Time: _____   Total Time: _____

■ Exercise: DEADLIFT

Weight Reps Sets	Weight Reps Sets	Weight Reps Sets	Weight Reps Sets	Weight Reps Sets	Weight Reps Sets
× ×	× ×	× ×	× ×	× ×	× ×
Subtotal = lbs.	Subtotal = lbs.	Subtotal = lbs.	Subtotal = lbs.	Subtotal = lbs.	Subtotal = lbs.

Exercise 1:   *Total Weight* _____ *lbs.*   *Time* _____ *mins.*   *Power Factor* _____ *lbs./min.*   *Power Index* _____

■ Exercise: BENCH PRESS

Weight Reps Sets	Weight Reps Sets	Weight Reps Sets	Weight Reps Sets	Weight Reps Sets	Weight Reps Sets
× ×	× ×	× ×	× ×	× ×	× ×
Subtotal = lbs.	Subtotal = lbs.	Subtotal = lbs.	Subtotal = lbs.	Subtotal = lbs.	Subtotal = lbs.

Exercise 2:   *Total Weight* _____ *lbs.*   *Time* _____ *mins.*   *Power Factor* _____ *lbs./min.*   *Power Index* _____

■ Exercise: LAT PULLDOWN

Weight Reps Sets	Weight Reps Sets	Weight Reps Sets	Weight Reps Sets	Weight Reps Sets	Weight Reps Sets
× ×	× ×	× ×	× ×	× ×	× ×
Subtotal = lbs.	Subtotal = lbs.	Subtotal = lbs.	Subtotal = lbs.	Subtotal = lbs.	Subtotal = lbs.

Exercise 3:   *Total Weight* _____ *lbs.*   *Time* _____ *mins.*   *Power Factor* _____ *lbs./min.*   *Power Index* _____

■ Exercise: LEG PRESS

Weight Reps Sets	Weight Reps Sets	Weight Reps Sets	Weight Reps Sets	Weight Reps Sets	Weight Reps Sets
× ×	× ×	× ×	× ×	× ×	× ×
Subtotal = lbs.	Subtotal = lbs.	Subtotal = lbs.	Subtotal = lbs.	Subtotal = lbs.	Subtotal = lbs.

Exercise 4:   *Total Weight* _____ *lbs.*   *Time* _____ *mins.*   *Power Factor* _____ *lbs./min.*   *Power Index* _____

■ Exercise: TOE PRESS

Weight Reps Sets	Weight Reps Sets	Weight Reps Sets	Weight Reps Sets	Weight Reps Sets	Weight Reps Sets
× ×	× ×	× ×	× ×	× ×	× ×
Subtotal = lbs.	Subtotal = lbs.	Subtotal = lbs.	Subtotal = lbs.	Subtotal = lbs.	Subtotal = lbs.

Exercise 5:   *Total Weight* _____ *lbs.*   *Time* _____ *mins.*   *Power Factor* _____ *lbs./min.*   *Power Index* _____

OVERALL WORKOUT: *Total Weight* _____ *lbs.*   *Time* _____ *mins.*   *Power Factor* _____ *lbs./min.*   *Power Index* _____

Exercise Subtotal = Weight × Reps × Sets   ■ *Power Factor = lbs./min.*   ■ *Power Index = Total Weight × Power Factor ÷ 1,000,000*

WORKOUT B RECORD

Date: ____ / ____ / ____

Start Time: _____ Finish Time: _____ Total Time: _____

■ Exercise: DEADLIFT

Weight Reps Sets	Weight Reps Sets	Weight Reps Sets	Weight Reps Sets	Weight Reps Sets	Weight Reps Sets
× ×	× ×	× ×	× ×	× ×	× ×
Subtotal = lbs.	Subtotal = lbs.	Subtotal = lbs.	Subtotal = lbs.	Subtotal = lbs.	Subtotal = lbs.

Exercise 1:   *Total Weight* _____ *lbs.*   *Time* _____ *mins.*   *Power Factor* _____ *lbs./min.*   *Power Index* _____

■ Exercise: BENCH PRESS

Weight Reps Sets	Weight Reps Sets	Weight Reps Sets	Weight Reps Sets	Weight Reps Sets	Weight Reps Sets
× ×	× ×	× ×	× ×	× ×	× ×
Subtotal = lbs.	Subtotal = lbs.	Subtotal = lbs.	Subtotal = lbs.	Subtotal = lbs.	Subtotal = lbs.

Exercise 2:   *Total Weight* _____ *lbs.*   *Time* _____ *mins.*   *Power Factor* _____ *lbs./min.*   *Power Index* _____

■ Exercise: LAT PULLDOWN

Weight Reps Sets	Weight Reps Sets	Weight Reps Sets	Weight Reps Sets	Weight Reps Sets	Weight Reps Sets
× ×	× ×	× ×	× ×	× ×	× ×
Subtotal = lbs.	Subtotal = lbs.	Subtotal = lbs.	Subtotal = lbs.	Subtotal = lbs.	Subtotal = lbs.

Exercise 3:   *Total Weight* _____ *lbs.*   *Time* _____ *mins.*   *Power Factor* _____ *lbs./min.*   *Power Index* _____

■ Exercise: LEG PRESS

Weight Reps Sets	Weight Reps Sets	Weight Reps Sets	Weight Reps Sets	Weight Reps Sets	Weight Reps Sets
× ×	× ×	× ×	× ×	× ×	× ×
Subtotal = lbs.	Subtotal = lbs.	Subtotal = lbs.	Subtotal = lbs.	Subtotal = lbs.	Subtotal = lbs.

Exercise 4:   *Total Weight* _____ *lbs.*   *Time* _____ *mins.*   *Power Factor* _____ *lbs./min.*   *Power Index* _____

■ Exercise: TOE PRESS

Weight Reps Sets	Weight Reps Sets	Weight Reps Sets	Weight Reps Sets	Weight Reps Sets	Weight Reps Sets
× ×	× ×	× ×	× ×	× ×	× ×
Subtotal = lbs.	Subtotal = lbs.	Subtotal = lbs.	Subtotal = lbs.	Subtotal = lbs.	Subtotal = lbs.

Exercise 5:   *Total Weight* _____ *lbs.*   *Time* _____ *mins.*   *Power Factor* _____ *lbs./min.*   *Power Index* _____

OVERALL WORKOUT: *Total Weight* _____ *lbs.*   *Time* _____ *mins.*   *Power Factor* _____ *lbs./min.*   *Power Index* _____

Exercise Subtotal = Weight × Reps × Sets   ■ *Power Factor = lbs./min.*   ■ *Power Index = Total Weight × Power Factor ÷ 1,000,000*

WORKOUT B RECORD

Date: ____ / ____ / ____

Start Time: _____   **Finish Time:** _____   **Total Time:** _____

▪ Exercise: DEADLIFT

Weight Reps Sets	Weight Reps Sets	Weight Reps Sets	Weight Reps Sets	Weight Reps Sets	Weight Reps Sets
× ×	× ×	× ×	× ×	× ×	× ×
Subtotal = lbs.	Subtotal = lbs.	Subtotal = lbs.	Subtotal = lbs.	Subtotal = lbs.	Subtotal = lbs.

Exercise 1:   Total Weight _____ lbs.   Time _____ mins.   Power Factor _____ lbs./min.   Power Index _____

▪ Exercise: BENCH PRESS

Weight Reps Sets	Weight Reps Sets	Weight Reps Sets	Weight Reps Sets	Weight Reps Sets	Weight Reps Sets
× ×	× ×	× ×	× ×	× ×	× ×
Subtotal = lbs.	Subtotal = lbs.	Subtotal = lbs.	Subtotal = lbs.	Subtotal = lbs.	Subtotal = lbs.

Exercise 2:   Total Weight _____ lbs.   Time _____ mins.   Power Factor _____ lbs./min.   Power Index _____

▪ Exercise: LAT PULLDOWN

Weight Reps Sets	Weight Reps Sets	Weight Reps Sets	Weight Reps Sets	Weight Reps Sets	Weight Reps Sets
× ×	× ×	× ×	× ×	× ×	× ×
Subtotal = lbs.	Subtotal = lbs.	Subtotal = lbs.	Subtotal = lbs.	Subtotal = lbs.	Subtotal = lbs.

Exercise 3:   Total Weight _____ lbs.   Time _____ mins.   Power Factor _____ lbs./min.   Power Index _____

▪ Exercise: LEG PRESS

Weight Reps Sets	Weight Reps Sets	Weight Reps Sets	Weight Reps Sets	Weight Reps Sets	Weight Reps Sets
× ×	× ×	× ×	× ×	× ×	× ×
Subtotal = lbs.	Subtotal = lbs.	Subtotal = lbs.	Subtotal = lbs.	Subtotal = lbs.	Subtotal = lbs.

Exercise 4:   Total Weight _____ lbs.   Time _____ mins.   Power Factor _____ lbs./min.   Power Index _____

▪ Exercise: TOE PRESS

Weight Reps Sets	Weight Reps Sets	Weight Reps Sets	Weight Reps Sets	Weight Reps Sets	Weight Reps Sets
× ×	× ×	× ×	× ×	× ×	× ×
Subtotal = lbs.	Subtotal = lbs.	Subtotal = lbs.	Subtotal = lbs.	Subtotal = lbs.	Subtotal = lbs.

Exercise 5:   Total Weight _____ lbs.   Time _____ mins.   Power Factor _____ lbs./min.   Power Index _____

OVERALL WORKOUT: Total Weight _____ lbs.   Time _____ mins.   Power Factor _____ lbs./min.   Power Index _____

Exercise Subtotal = Weight × Reps × Sets ▪ *Power Factor = lbs./min.* ▪ *Power Index = Total Weight × Power Factor ÷ 1,000,000*

WORKOUT B RECORD

Date: ___ / ___ / ___

Start Time: _____   Finish Time: _____   Total Time: _____

■ **Exercise: DEADLIFT**

Weight Reps Sets	Weight Reps Sets	Weight Reps Sets	Weight Reps Sets	Weight Reps Sets	Weight Reps Sets
× ×	× ×	× ×	× ×	× ×	× ×
Subtotal = lbs.	Subtotal = lbs.	Subtotal = lbs.	Subtotal = lbs.	Subtotal = lbs.	Subtotal = lbs.

Exercise 1:   *Total Weight* _____ *lbs.*   *Time* _____ *mins.*   *Power Factor* _____ *lbs./min.*   *Power Index* _____

■ **Exercise: BENCH PRESS**

Weight Reps Sets	Weight Reps Sets	Weight Reps Sets	Weight Reps Sets	Weight Reps Sets	Weight Reps Sets
× ×	× ×	× ×	× ×	× ×	× ×
Subtotal = lbs.	Subtotal = lbs.	Subtotal = lbs.	Subtotal = lbs.	Subtotal = lbs.	Subtotal = lbs.

Exercise 2:   *Total Weight* _____ *lbs.*   *Time* _____ *mins.*   *Power Factor* _____ *lbs./min.*   *Power Index* _____

■ **Exercise: LAT PULLDOWN**

Weight Reps Sets	Weight Reps Sets	Weight Reps Sets	Weight Reps Sets	Weight Reps Sets	Weight Reps Sets
× ×	× ×	× ×	× ×	× ×	× ×
Subtotal = lbs.	Subtotal = lbs.	Subtotal = lbs.	Subtotal = lbs.	Subtotal = lbs.	Subtotal = lbs.

Exercise 3:   *Total Weight* _____ *lbs.*   *Time* _____ *mins.*   *Power Factor* _____ *lbs./min.*   *Power Index* _____

■ **Exercise: LEG PRESS**

Weight Reps Sets	Weight Reps Sets	Weight Reps Sets	Weight Reps Sets	Weight Reps Sets	Weight Reps Sets
× ×	× ×	× ×	× ×	× ×	× ×
Subtotal = lbs.	Subtotal = lbs.	Subtotal = lbs.	Subtotal = lbs.	Subtotal = lbs.	Subtotal = lbs.

Exercise 4:   *Total Weight* _____ *lbs.*   *Time* _____ *mins.*   *Power Factor* _____ *lbs./min.*   *Power Index* _____

■ **Exercise: TOE PRESS**

Weight Reps Sets	Weight Reps Sets	Weight Reps Sets	Weight Reps Sets	Weight Reps Sets	Weight Reps Sets
× ×	× ×	× ×	× ×	× ×	× ×
Subtotal = lbs.	Subtotal = lbs.	Subtotal = lbs.	Subtotal = lbs.	Subtotal = lbs.	Subtotal = lbs.

Exercise 5:   *Total Weight* _____ *lbs.*   *Time* _____ *mins.*   *Power Factor* _____ *lbs./min.*   *Power Index* _____

OVERALL WORKOUT: *Total Weight* _____ *lbs.*   *Time* _____ *mins.*   *Power Factor* _____ *lbs./min.*   *Power Index* _____

Exercise Subtotal = Weight × Reps × Sets   ■ *Power Factor = lbs./min.*   ■ *Power Index = Total Weight × Power Factor ÷ 1,000,000*

WORKOUT B RECORD   Date: ___ / ___ / ___

Start Time: _____   **Finish Time:** _____   **Total Time:** _____

■ Exercise: DEADLIFT

Weight Reps Sets	Weight Reps Sets	Weight Reps Sets	Weight Reps Sets	Weight Reps Sets	Weight Reps Sets
× ×	× ×	× ×	× ×	× ×	× ×
Subtotal = lbs.	Subtotal = lbs.	Subtotal = lbs.	Subtotal = lbs.	Subtotal = lbs.	Subtotal = lbs.

Exercise 1:   Total Weight _____ lbs.   Time _____ mins.   Power Factor _____ lbs./min.   Power Index _____

■ Exercise: BENCH PRESS

Weight Reps Sets	Weight Reps Sets	Weight Reps Sets	Weight Reps Sets	Weight Reps Sets	Weight Reps Sets
× ×	× ×	× ×	× ×	× ×	× ×
Subtotal = lbs.	Subtotal = lbs.	Subtotal = lbs.	Subtotal = lbs.	Subtotal = lbs.	Subtotal = lbs.

Exercise 2:   Total Weight _____ lbs.   Time _____ mins.   Power Factor _____ lbs./min.   Power Index _____

■ Exercise: LAT PULLDOWN

Weight Reps Sets	Weight Reps Sets	Weight Reps Sets	Weight Reps Sets	Weight Reps Sets	Weight Reps Sets
× ×	× ×	× ×	× ×	× ×	× ×
Subtotal = lbs.	Subtotal = lbs.	Subtotal = lbs.	Subtotal = lbs.	Subtotal = lbs.	Subtotal = lbs.

Exercise 3:   Total Weight _____ lbs.   Time _____ mins.   Power Factor _____ lbs./min.   Power Index _____

■ Exercise: LEG PRESS

Weight Reps Sets	Weight Reps Sets	Weight Reps Sets	Weight Reps Sets	Weight Reps Sets	Weight Reps Sets
× ×	× ×	× ×	× ×	× ×	× ×
Subtotal = lbs.	Subtotal = lbs.	Subtotal = lbs.	Subtotal = lbs.	Subtotal = lbs.	Subtotal = lbs.

Exercise 4:   Total Weight _____ lbs.   Time _____ mins.   Power Factor _____ lbs./min.   Power Index _____

■ Exercise: TOE PRESS

Weight Reps Sets	Weight Reps Sets	Weight Reps Sets	Weight Reps Sets	Weight Reps Sets	Weight Reps Sets
× ×	× ×	× ×	× ×	× ×	× ×
Subtotal = lbs.	Subtotal = lbs.	Subtotal = lbs.	Subtotal = lbs.	Subtotal = lbs.	Subtotal = lbs.

Exercise 5:   Total Weight _____ lbs.   Time _____ mins.   Power Factor _____ lbs./min.   Power Index _____

OVERALL WORKOUT: Total Weight _____ lbs.   Time _____ mins.   Power Factor _____ lbs./min.   Power Index _____

Exercise Subtotal = Weight × Reps × Sets   ■ *Power Factor = lbs./min.*   ■ *Power Index = Total Weight × Power Factor ÷ 1,000,000*

WORKOUT B RECORD   Date: ___ / ___ / ___

Start Time: _____   Finish Time: _____   Total Time: _____

■ Exercise: DEADLIFT

Weight Reps Sets	Weight Reps Sets	Weight Reps Sets	Weight Reps Sets	Weight Reps Sets	Weight Reps Sets
× ×	× ×	× ×	× ×	× ×	× ×
Subtotal = lbs.	Subtotal = lbs.	Subtotal = lbs.	Subtotal = lbs.	Subtotal = lbs.	Subtotal = lbs.

Exercise 1:   *Total Weight _____ lbs.   Time _____ mins.   Power Factor _____ lbs./min.   Power Index _____*

■ Exercise: BENCH PRESS

Weight Reps Sets	Weight Reps Sets	Weight Reps Sets	Weight Reps Sets	Weight Reps Sets	Weight Reps Sets
× ×	× ×	× ×	× ×	× ×	× ×
Subtotal = lbs.	Subtotal = lbs.	Subtotal = lbs.	Subtotal = lbs.	Subtotal = lbs.	Subtotal = lbs.

Exercise 2:   *Total Weight _____ lbs.   Time _____ mins.   Power Factor _____ lbs./min.   Power Index _____*

■ Exercise: LAT PULLDOWN

Weight Reps Sets	Weight Reps Sets	Weight Reps Sets	Weight Reps Sets	Weight Reps Sets	Weight Reps Sets
× ×	× ×	× ×	× ×	× ×	× ×
Subtotal = lbs.	Subtotal = lbs.	Subtotal = lbs.	Subtotal = lbs.	Subtotal = lbs.	Subtotal = lbs.

Exercise 3:   *Total Weight _____ lbs.   Time _____ mins.   Power Factor _____ lbs./min.   Power Index _____*

■ Exercise: LEG PRESS

Weight Reps Sets	Weight Reps Sets	Weight Reps Sets	Weight Reps Sets	Weight Reps Sets	Weight Reps Sets
× ×	× ×	× ×	× ×	× ×	× ×
Subtotal = lbs.	Subtotal = lbs.	Subtotal = lbs.	Subtotal = lbs.	Subtotal = lbs.	Subtotal = lbs.

Exercise 4:   *Total Weight _____ lbs.   Time _____ mins.   Power Factor _____ lbs./min.   Power Index _____*

■ Exercise: TOE PRESS

Weight Reps Sets	Weight Reps Sets	Weight Reps Sets	Weight Reps Sets	Weight Reps Sets	Weight Reps Sets
× ×	× ×	× ×	× ×	× ×	× ×
Subtotal = lbs.	Subtotal = lbs.	Subtotal = lbs.	Subtotal = lbs.	Subtotal = lbs.	Subtotal = lbs.

Exercise 5:   *Total Weight _____ lbs.   Time _____ mins.   Power Factor _____ lbs./min.   Power Index _____*

OVERALL WORKOUT: *Total Weight _____ lbs.   Time _____ mins.   Power Factor _____ lbs./min.   Power Index _____*

Exercise Subtotal = Weight × Reps × Sets   ■ Power Factor = lbs./min.   ■ Power Index = Total Weight × Power Factor ÷ 1,000,000

WORKOUT B RECORD

Date: ____ / ____ / ____

Start Time: _____ Finish Time: _____ Total Time: _____

■ Exercise: DEADLIFT

Weight	Reps	Sets	Weight	Reps	Sets	Weight	Reps	Sets	Weight	Reps	Sets	Weight	Reps	Sets	Weight	Reps	Sets
×	×		×	×		×	×		×	×		×	×		×	×	
Subtotal =		lbs.	Subtotal =		lbs.	Subtotal =		lbs.	Subtotal =		lbs.	Subtotal =		lbs.	Subtotal =		lbs.

Exercise 1:   Total Weight _____ lbs.   Time _____ mins.   Power Factor _____ lbs./min.   Power Index _____

■ Exercise: BENCH PRESS

Weight	Reps	Sets	Weight	Reps	Sets	Weight	Reps	Sets	Weight	Reps	Sets	Weight	Reps	Sets	Weight	Reps	Sets
×	×		×	×		×	×		×	×		×	×		×	×	
Subtotal =		lbs.	Subtotal =		lbs.	Subtotal =		lbs.	Subtotal =		lbs.	Subtotal =		lbs.	Subtotal =		lbs.

Exercise 2:   Total Weight _____ lbs.   Time _____ mins.   Power Factor _____ lbs./min.   Power Index _____

■ Exercise: LAT PULLDOWN

Weight	Reps	Sets	Weight	Reps	Sets	Weight	Reps	Sets	Weight	Reps	Sets	Weight	Reps	Sets	Weight	Reps	Sets
×	×		×	×		×	×		×	×		×	×		×	×	
Subtotal =		lbs.	Subtotal =		lbs.	Subtotal =		lbs.	Subtotal =		lbs.	Subtotal =		lbs.	Subtotal =		lbs.

Exercise 3:   Total Weight _____ lbs.   Time _____ mins.   Power Factor _____ lbs./min.   Power Index _____

■ Exercise: LEG PRESS

Weight	Reps	Sets	Weight	Reps	Sets	Weight	Reps	Sets	Weight	Reps	Sets	Weight	Reps	Sets	Weight	Reps	Sets
×	×		×	×		×	×		×	×		×	×		×	×	
Subtotal =		lbs.	Subtotal =		lbs.	Subtotal =		lbs.	Subtotal =		lbs.	Subtotal =		lbs.	Subtotal =		lbs.

Exercise 4:   Total Weight _____ lbs.   Time _____ mins.   Power Factor _____ lbs./min.   Power Index _____

■ Exercise: TOE PRESS

Weight	Reps	Sets	Weight	Reps	Sets	Weight	Reps	Sets	Weight	Reps	Sets	Weight	Reps	Sets	Weight	Reps	Sets
×	×		×	×		×	×		×	×		×	×		×	×	
Subtotal =		lbs.	Subtotal =		lbs.	Subtotal =		lbs.	Subtotal =		lbs.	Subtotal =		lbs.	Subtotal =		lbs.

Exercise 5:   Total Weight _____ lbs.   Time _____ mins.   Power Factor _____ lbs./min.   Power Index _____

OVERALL WORKOUT: Total Weight _____ lbs.   Time _____ mins.   Power Factor _____ lbs./min.   Power Index _____

Exercise Subtotal = Weight × Reps × Sets   ■ *Power Factor = lbs./min.*   ■ *Power Index = Total Weight × Power Factor ÷ 1,000,000*

WORKOUT B RECORD

Date: ___ / ___ / ___

Start Time: _____   **Finish Time:** _____   **Total Time:** _____

■ Exercise: DEADLIFT

Weight Reps Sets	Weight Reps Sets	Weight Reps Sets	Weight Reps Sets	Weight Reps Sets	Weight Reps Sets
× ×	× ×	× ×	× ×	× ×	× ×
Subtotal = lbs.	Subtotal = lbs.	Subtotal = lbs.	Subtotal = lbs.	Subtotal = lbs.	Subtotal = lbs.

Exercise 1:   *Total Weight* _____ *lbs.*   *Time* _____ *mins.*   *Power Factor* _____ *lbs./min.*   *Power Index* _____

■ Exercise: BENCH PRESS

Weight Reps Sets	Weight Reps Sets	Weight Reps Sets	Weight Reps Sets	Weight Reps Sets	Weight Reps Sets
× ×	× ×	× ×	× ×	× ×	× ×
Subtotal = lbs.	Subtotal = lbs.	Subtotal = lbs.	Subtotal = lbs.	Subtotal = lbs.	Subtotal = lbs.

Exercise 2:   *Total Weight* _____ *lbs.*   *Time* _____ *mins.*   *Power Factor* _____ *lbs./min.*   *Power Index* _____

■ Exercise: LAT PULLDOWN

Weight Reps Sets	Weight Reps Sets	Weight Reps Sets	Weight Reps Sets	Weight Reps Sets	Weight Reps Sets
× ×	× ×	× ×	× ×	× ×	× ×
Subtotal = lbs.	Subtotal = lbs.	Subtotal = lbs.	Subtotal = lbs.	Subtotal = lbs.	Subtotal = lbs.

Exercise 3:   *Total Weight* _____ *lbs.*   *Time* _____ *mins.*   *Power Factor* _____ *lbs./min.*   *Power Index* _____

■ Exercise: LEG PRESS

Weight Reps Sets	Weight Reps Sets	Weight Reps Sets	Weight Reps Sets	Weight Reps Sets	Weight Reps Sets
× ×	× ×	× ×	× ×	× ×	× ×
Subtotal = lbs.	Subtotal = lbs.	Subtotal = lbs.	Subtotal = lbs.	Subtotal = lbs.	Subtotal = lbs.

Exercise 4:   *Total Weight* _____ *lbs.*   *Time* _____ *mins.*   *Power Factor* _____ *lbs./min.*   *Power Index* _____

■ Exercise: TOE PRESS

Weight Reps Sets	Weight Reps Sets	Weight Reps Sets	Weight Reps Sets	Weight Reps Sets	Weight Reps Sets
× ×	× ×	× ×	× ×	× ×	× ×
Subtotal = lbs.	Subtotal = lbs.	Subtotal = lbs.	Subtotal = lbs.	Subtotal = lbs.	Subtotal = lbs.

Exercise 5:   *Total Weight* _____ *lbs.*   *Time* _____ *mins.*   *Power Factor* _____ *lbs./min.*   *Power Index* _____

OVERALL WORKOUT: *Total Weight* _____ *lbs.*   *Time* _____ *mins.*   *Power Factor* _____ *lbs./min.*   *Power Index* _____

Exercise Subtotal = Weight × Reps × Sets   ■ *Power Factor = lbs./min.*   ■ *Power Index = Total Weight × Power Factor ÷ 1,000,000*

WORKOUT B RECORD   Date: ____ / ____ / ____

Start Time: _____   Finish Time: _____   Total Time: _____

▪ Exercise: DEADLIFT

Weight Reps Sets	Weight Reps Sets	Weight Reps Sets	Weight Reps Sets	Weight Reps Sets	Weight Reps Sets
× ×	× ×	× ×	× ×	× ×	× ×
Subtotal = lbs.	Subtotal = lbs.	Subtotal = lbs.	Subtotal = lbs.	Subtotal = lbs.	Subtotal = lbs.

Exercise 1:   *Total Weight _____ lbs.   Time _____ mins.   Power Factor _____ lbs./min.   Power Index _____*

▪ Exercise: BENCH PRESS

Weight Reps Sets	Weight Reps Sets	Weight Reps Sets	Weight Reps Sets	Weight Reps Sets	Weight Reps Sets
× ×	× ×	× ×	× ×	× ×	× ×
Subtotal = lbs.	Subtotal = lbs.	Subtotal = lbs.	Subtotal = lbs.	Subtotal = lbs.	Subtotal = lbs.

Exercise 2:   *Total Weight _____ lbs.   Time _____ mins.   Power Factor _____ lbs./min.   Power Index _____*

▪ Exercise: LAT PULLDOWN

Weight Reps Sets	Weight Reps Sets	Weight Reps Sets	Weight Reps Sets	Weight Reps Sets	Weight Reps Sets
× ×	× ×	× ×	× ×	× ×	× ×
Subtotal = lbs.	Subtotal = lbs.	Subtotal = lbs.	Subtotal = lbs.	Subtotal = lbs.	Subtotal = lbs.

Exercise 3:   *Total Weight _____ lbs.   Time _____ mins.   Power Factor _____ lbs./min.   Power Index _____*

▪ Exercise: LEG PRESS

Weight Reps Sets	Weight Reps Sets	Weight Reps Sets	Weight Reps Sets	Weight Reps Sets	Weight Reps Sets
× ×	× ×	× ×	× ×	× ×	× ×
Subtotal = lbs.	Subtotal = lbs.	Subtotal = lbs.	Subtotal = lbs.	Subtotal = lbs.	Subtotal = lbs.

Exercise 4:   *Total Weight _____ lbs.   Time _____ mins.   Power Factor _____ lbs./min.   Power Index _____*

▪ Exercise: TOE PRESS

Weight Reps Sets	Weight Reps Sets	Weight Reps Sets	Weight Reps Sets	Weight Reps Sets	Weight Reps Sets
× ×	× ×	× ×	× ×	× ×	× ×
Subtotal = lbs.	Subtotal = lbs.	Subtotal = lbs.	Subtotal = lbs.	Subtotal = lbs.	Subtotal = lbs.

Exercise 5:   *Total Weight _____ lbs.   Time _____ mins.   Power Factor _____ lbs./min.   Power Index _____*

OVERALL WORKOUT: *Total Weight _____ lbs.   Time _____ mins.   Power Factor _____ lbs./min.   Power Index _____*

Exercise Subtotal = Weight × Reps × Sets   ▪ *Power Factor = lbs./min.*   ▪ *Power Index = Total Weight × Power Factor ÷ 1,000,000*

APPENDIX B: Workout Records for Power Factor Specialization Routines

These forms are used each time you perform a specialization routine from our Power Factor Specialization series (*Power Factor Specialization: Chest & Arms, Power Factor Specialization: Shoulders & Back,* and *Power Factor Specialization: Abs & Legs*).

Simply fill in the amount of weight, number of reps, and number of sets for each exercise. Pages 8 to 10 show the step-by-step calculations that yield your all-important Power Factor and Power Index numbers for each exercise and for each workout. These two numbers measure the intensity of your muscular output and are used to guarantee that each successive workout is progressive and productive.

Please note that additional space is provided on each form to include the exercises that may be available to you and that yield the best results. See our *Power Factor Specialization* books for the ratings of the most common specialization exercises.

The Power Factor and Power Index numbers from these pages will also be recorded in Appendix C, to create charts of individual exercise progress, and in Appendix D, to create graphs of individual exercise progress.

CHEST SPECIALIZATION WORKOUT RECORD   Date: ___ / ___ / ___

Start Time: _____   **Finish Time:** _____   **Total Time:** _____

■ Exercise: BENCH PRESS

Weight Reps Sets	Weight Reps Sets	Weight Reps Sets	Weight Reps Sets	Weight Reps Sets	Weight Reps Sets
× ×	× ×	× ×	× ×	× ×	× ×
Subtotal = lbs.	Subtotal = lbs.	Subtotal = lbs.	Subtotal = lbs.	Subtotal = lbs.	Subtotal = lbs.

Exercise 1:   Total Weight _____ lbs.   Time _____ mins.   Power Factor _____ lbs./min.   Power Index _____

■ Exercise: BARBELL DECLINE BENCH PRESS

Weight Reps Sets	Weight Reps Sets	Weight Reps Sets	Weight Reps Sets	Weight Reps Sets	Weight Reps Sets
× ×	× ×	× ×	× ×	× ×	× ×
Subtotal = lbs.	Subtotal = lbs.	Subtotal = lbs.	Subtotal = lbs.	Subtotal = lbs.	Subtotal = lbs.

Exercise 2:   Total Weight _____ lbs.   Time _____ mins.   Power Factor _____ lbs./min.   Power Index _____

■ Exercise: HIGH-PULLEY CABLE CROSSOVER

Weight Reps Sets	Weight Reps Sets	Weight Reps Sets	Weight Reps Sets	Weight Reps Sets	Weight Reps Sets
× ×	× ×	× ×	× ×	× ×	× ×
Subtotal = lbs.	Subtotal = lbs.	Subtotal = lbs.	Subtotal = lbs.	Subtotal = lbs.	Subtotal = lbs.

Exercise 3:   Total Weight _____ lbs.   Time _____ mins.   Power Factor _____ lbs./min.   Power Index _____

■ Exercise:

Weight Reps Sets	Weight Reps Sets	Weight Reps Sets	Weight Reps Sets	Weight Reps Sets	Weight Reps Sets
× ×	× ×	× ×	× ×	× ×	× ×
Subtotal = lbs.	Subtotal = lbs.	Subtotal = lbs.	Subtotal = lbs.	Subtotal = lbs.	Subtotal = lbs.

Exercise 4:   Total Weight _____ lbs.   Time _____ mins.   Power Factor _____ lbs./min.   Power Index _____

■ Exercise:

Weight Reps Sets	Weight Reps Sets	Weight Reps Sets	Weight Reps Sets	Weight Reps Sets	Weight Reps Sets
× ×	× ×	× ×	× ×	× ×	× ×
Subtotal = lbs.	Subtotal = lbs.	Subtotal = lbs.	Subtotal = lbs.	Subtotal = lbs.	Subtotal = lbs.

Exercise 5:   Total Weight _____ lbs.   Time _____ mins.   Power Factor _____ lbs./min.   Power Index _____

OVERALL WORKOUT: Total Weight _____ lbs.   Time _____ mins.   Power Factor _____ lbs./min.   Power Index _____

Exercise Subtotal = Weight × Reps × Sets   ■ *Power Factor = lbs./min.*   ■ *Power Index = Total Weight × Power Factor ÷ 1,000,000*

CHEST SPECIALIZATION WORKOUT RECORD   Date: ___ / ___ / ___

Start Time: _____   Finish Time: _____   Total Time: _____

▪ Exercise: BENCH PRESS

Weight	Reps	Sets	Weight	Reps	Sets	Weight	Reps	Sets	Weight	Reps	Sets	Weight	Reps	Sets	Weight	Reps	Sets
×	×		×	×		×	×		×	×		×	×		×	×	
Subtotal =		lbs.	Subtotal =		lbs.	Subtotal =		lbs.	Subtotal =		lbs.	Subtotal =		lbs.	Subtotal =		lbs.

Exercise 1:   *Total Weight _____ lbs.*   *Time _____ mins.*   *Power Factor _____ lbs./min.*   *Power Index _____*

▪ Exercise: BARBELL DECLINE BENCH PRESS

Weight	Reps	Sets	Weight	Reps	Sets	Weight	Reps	Sets	Weight	Reps	Sets	Weight	Reps	Sets	Weight	Reps	Sets
×	×		×	×		×	×		×	×		×	×		×	×	
Subtotal =		lbs.	Subtotal =		lbs.	Subtotal =		lbs.	Subtotal =		lbs.	Subtotal =		lbs.	Subtotal =		lbs.

Exercise 2:   *Total Weight _____ lbs.*   *Time _____ mins.*   *Power Factor _____ lbs./min.*   *Power Index _____*

▪ Exercise: HIGH-PULLEY CABLE CROSSOVER

Weight	Reps	Sets	Weight	Reps	Sets	Weight	Reps	Sets	Weight	Reps	Sets	Weight	Reps	Sets	Weight	Reps	Sets
×	×		×	×		×	×		×	×		×	×		×	×	
Subtotal =		lbs.	Subtotal =		lbs.	Subtotal =		lbs.	Subtotal =		lbs.	Subtotal =		lbs.	Subtotal =		lbs.

Exercise 3:   *Total Weight _____ lbs.*   *Time _____ mins.*   *Power Factor _____ lbs./min.*   *Power Index _____*

▪ Exercise:

Weight	Reps	Sets	Weight	Reps	Sets	Weight	Reps	Sets	Weight	Reps	Sets	Weight	Reps	Sets	Weight	Reps	Sets
×	×		×	×		×	×		×	×		×	×		×	×	
Subtotal =		lbs.	Subtotal =		lbs.	Subtotal =		lbs.	Subtotal =		lbs.	Subtotal =		lbs.	Subtotal =		lbs.

Exercise 4:   *Total Weight _____ lbs.*   *Time _____ mins.*   *Power Factor _____ lbs./min.*   *Power Index _____*

▪ Exercise:

Weight	Reps	Sets	Weight	Reps	Sets	Weight	Reps	Sets	Weight	Reps	Sets	Weight	Reps	Sets	Weight	Reps	Sets
×	×		×	×		×	×		×	×		×	×		×	×	
Subtotal =		lbs.	Subtotal =		lbs.	Subtotal =		lbs.	Subtotal =		lbs.	Subtotal =		lbs.	Subtotal =		lbs.

Exercise 5:   *Total Weight _____ lbs.*   *Time _____ mins.*   *Power Factor _____ lbs./min.*   *Power Index _____*

OVERALL WORKOUT: *Total Weight _____ lbs.*   *Time _____ mins.*   *Power Factor _____ lbs./min.*   *Power Index _____*

Exercise Subtotal = Weight × Reps × Sets   ▪ *Power Factor = lbs./min.*   ▪ *Power Index = Total Weight × Power Factor ÷ 1,000,000*

CHEST SPECIALIZATION WORKOUT RECORD   Date: ___ / ___ / ___

Start Time: _____   Finish Time: _____   Total Time: _____

■ **Exercise: BENCH PRESS**

Weight Reps Sets	Weight Reps Sets	Weight Reps Sets	Weight Reps Sets	Weight Reps Sets	Weight Reps Sets
× ×	× ×	× ×	× ×	× ×	× ×
Subtotal = lbs.	Subtotal = lbs.	Subtotal = lbs.	Subtotal = lbs.	Subtotal = lbs.	Subtotal = lbs.

Exercise 1:   *Total Weight* _____ *lbs.*   *Time* _____ *mins.*   *Power Factor* _____ *lbs./min.*   *Power Index* _____

■ **Exercise: BARBELL DECLINE BENCH PRESS**

Weight Reps Sets	Weight Reps Sets	Weight Reps Sets	Weight Reps Sets	Weight Reps Sets	Weight Reps Sets
× ×	× ×	× ×	× ×	× ×	× ×
Subtotal = lbs.	Subtotal = lbs.	Subtotal = lbs.	Subtotal = lbs.	Subtotal = lbs.	Subtotal = lbs.

Exercise 2:   *Total Weight* _____ *lbs.*   *Time* _____ *mins.*   *Power Factor* _____ *lbs./min.*   *Power Index* _____

■ **Exercise: HIGH-PULLEY CABLE CROSSOVER**

Weight Reps Sets	Weight Reps Sets	Weight Reps Sets	Weight Reps Sets	Weight Reps Sets	Weight Reps Sets
× ×	× ×	× ×	× ×	× ×	× ×
Subtotal = lbs.	Subtotal = lbs.	Subtotal = lbs.	Subtotal = lbs.	Subtotal = lbs.	Subtotal = lbs.

Exercise 3:   *Total Weight* _____ *lbs.*   *Time* _____ *mins.*   *Power Factor* _____ *lbs./min.*   *Power Index* _____

■ **Exercise:**

Weight Reps Sets	Weight Reps Sets	Weight Reps Sets	Weight Reps Sets	Weight Reps Sets	Weight Reps Sets
× ×	× ×	× ×	× ×	× ×	× ×
Subtotal = lbs.	Subtotal = lbs.	Subtotal = lbs.	Subtotal = lbs.	Subtotal = lbs.	Subtotal = lbs.

Exercise 4:   *Total Weight* _____ *lbs.*   *Time* _____ *mins.*   *Power Factor* _____ *lbs./min.*   *Power Index* _____

■ **Exercise:**

Weight Reps Sets	Weight Reps Sets	Weight Reps Sets	Weight Reps Sets	Weight Reps Sets	Weight Reps Sets
× ×	× ×	× ×	× ×	× ×	× ×
Subtotal = lbs.	Subtotal = lbs.	Subtotal = lbs.	Subtotal = lbs.	Subtotal = lbs.	Subtotal = lbs.

Exercise 5:   *Total Weight* _____ *lbs.*   *Time* _____ *mins.*   *Power Factor* _____ *lbs./min.*   *Power Index* _____

OVERALL WORKOUT: *Total Weight* _____ *lbs.*   *Time* _____ *mins.*   *Power Factor* _____ *lbs./min.*   *Power Index* _____

Exercise Subtotal = Weight × Reps × Sets   ■ *Power Factor = lbs./min.*   ■ *Power Index = Total Weight × Power Factor ÷ 1,000,000*

CHEST SPECIALIZATION WORKOUT RECORD   Date: ____ / ____ / ____

Start Time: _____   **Finish Time:** _____   **Total Time:** _____

▪ Exercise: BENCH PRESS

Weight Reps Sets	Weight Reps Sets	Weight Reps Sets	Weight Reps Sets	Weight Reps Sets	Weight Reps Sets
× ×	× ×	× ×	× ×	× ×	× ×
Subtotal = lbs.	Subtotal = lbs.	Subtotal = lbs.	Subtotal = lbs.	Subtotal = lbs.	Subtotal = lbs.

Exercise 1:   *Total Weight* _____ *lbs.*   *Time* _____ *mins.*   *Power Factor* _____ *lbs./min.*   *Power Index* _____

▪ Exercise: BARBELL DECLINE BENCH PRESS

Weight Reps Sets	Weight Reps Sets	Weight Reps Sets	Weight Reps Sets	Weight Reps Sets	Weight Reps Sets
× ×	× ×	× ×	× ×	× ×	× ×
Subtotal = lbs.	Subtotal = lbs.	Subtotal = lbs.	Subtotal = lbs.	Subtotal = lbs.	Subtotal = lbs.

Exercise 2:   *Total Weight* _____ *lbs.*   *Time* _____ *mins.*   *Power Factor* _____ *lbs./min.*   *Power Index* _____

▪ Exercise: HIGH-PULLEY CABLE CROSSOVER

Weight Reps Sets	Weight Reps Sets	Weight Reps Sets	Weight Reps Sets	Weight Reps Sets	Weight Reps Sets
× ×	× ×	× ×	× ×	× ×	× ×
Subtotal = lbs.	Subtotal = lbs.	Subtotal = lbs.	Subtotal = lbs.	Subtotal = lbs.	Subtotal = lbs.

Exercise 3:   *Total Weight* _____ *lbs.*   *Time* _____ *mins.*   *Power Factor* _____ *lbs./min.*   *Power Index* _____

▪ Exercise:

Weight Reps Sets	Weight Reps Sets	Weight Reps Sets	Weight Reps Sets	Weight Reps Sets	Weight Reps Sets
× ×	× ×	× ×	× ×	× ×	× ×
Subtotal = lbs.	Subtotal = lbs.	Subtotal = lbs.	Subtotal = lbs.	Subtotal = lbs.	Subtotal = lbs.

Exercise 4:   *Total Weight* _____ *lbs.*   *Time* _____ *mins.*   *Power Factor* _____ *lbs./min.*   *Power Index* _____

▪ Exercise:

Weight Reps Sets	Weight Reps Sets	Weight Reps Sets	Weight Reps Sets	Weight Reps Sets	Weight Reps Sets
× ×	× ×	× ×	× ×	× ×	× ×
Subtotal = lbs.	Subtotal = lbs.	Subtotal = lbs.	Subtotal = lbs.	Subtotal = lbs.	Subtotal = lbs.

Exercise 5:   *Total Weight* _____ *lbs.*   *Time* _____ *mins.*   *Power Factor* _____ *lbs./min.*   *Power Index* _____

OVERALL WORKOUT: *Total Weight* _____ *lbs.*   *Time* _____ *mins.*   *Power Factor* _____ *lbs./min.*   *Power Index* _____

Exercise Subtotal = Weight × Reps × Sets   ▪ *Power Factor = lbs./min.*   ▪ *Power Index = Total Weight × Power Factor ÷ 1,000,000*

CHEST SPECIALIZATION WORKOUT RECORD   Date: ___ / ___ / ___

Start Time: _____   Finish Time: _____   Total Time: _____

■ **Exercise: BENCH PRESS**

Weight Reps Sets	Weight Reps Sets	Weight Reps Sets	Weight Reps Sets	Weight Reps Sets	Weight Reps Sets
× ×	× ×	× ×	× ×	× ×	× ×
Subtotal = lbs.	Subtotal = lbs.	Subtotal = lbs.	Subtotal = lbs.	Subtotal = lbs.	Subtotal = lbs.

Exercise 1:   *Total Weight* _____ *lbs.*   *Time* _____ *mins.*   *Power Factor* _____ *lbs./min.*   *Power Index* _____

■ **Exercise: BARBELL DECLINE BENCH PRESS**

Weight Reps Sets	Weight Reps Sets	Weight Reps Sets	Weight Reps Sets	Weight Reps Sets	Weight Reps Sets
× ×	× ×	× ×	× ×	× ×	× ×
Subtotal = lbs.	Subtotal = lbs.	Subtotal = lbs.	Subtotal = lbs.	Subtotal = lbs.	Subtotal = lbs.

Exercise 2:   *Total Weight* _____ *lbs.*   *Time* _____ *mins.*   *Power Factor* _____ *lbs./min.*   *Power Index* _____

■ **Exercise: HIGH-PULLEY CABLE CROSSOVER**

Weight Reps Sets	Weight Reps Sets	Weight Reps Sets	Weight Reps Sets	Weight Reps Sets	Weight Reps Sets
× ×	× ×	× ×	× ×	× ×	× ×
Subtotal = lbs.	Subtotal = lbs.	Subtotal = lbs.	Subtotal = lbs.	Subtotal = lbs.	Subtotal = lbs.

Exercise 3:   *Total Weight* _____ *lbs.*   *Time* _____ *mins.*   *Power Factor* _____ *lbs./min.*   *Power Index* _____

■ **Exercise:**

Weight Reps Sets	Weight Reps Sets	Weight Reps Sets	Weight Reps Sets	Weight Reps Sets	Weight Reps Sets
× ×	× ×	× ×	× ×	× ×	× ×
Subtotal = lbs.	Subtotal = lbs.	Subtotal = lbs.	Subtotal = lbs.	Subtotal = lbs.	Subtotal = lbs.

Exercise 4:   *Total Weight* _____ *lbs.*   *Time* _____ *mins.*   *Power Factor* _____ *lbs./min.*   *Power Index* _____

■ **Exercise:**

Weight Reps Sets	Weight Reps Sets	Weight Reps Sets	Weight Reps Sets	Weight Reps Sets	Weight Reps Sets
× ×	× ×	× ×	× ×	× ×	× ×
Subtotal = lbs.	Subtotal = lbs.	Subtotal = lbs.	Subtotal = lbs.	Subtotal = lbs.	Subtotal = lbs.

Exercise 5:   *Total Weight* _____ *lbs.*   *Time* _____ *mins.*   *Power Factor* _____ *lbs./min.*   *Power Index* _____

OVERALL WORKOUT: *Total Weight* _____ *lbs.*   *Time* _____ *mins.*   *Power Factor* _____ *lbs./min.*   *Power Index* _____

Exercise Subtotal = Weight × Reps × Sets   ■ *Power Factor = lbs./min.*   ■ *Power Index = Total Weight × Power Factor ÷ 1,000,000*

CHEST SPECIALIZATION WORKOUT RECORD   Date: ____ / ____ / ____

Start Time: _____   **Finish Time:** _____   **Total Time:** _____

▪ Exercise: BENCH PRESS

Weight Reps Sets	Weight Reps Sets	Weight Reps Sets	Weight Reps Sets	Weight Reps Sets	Weight Reps Sets
× ×	× ×	× ×	× ×	× ×	× ×
Subtotal = lbs.	Subtotal = lbs.	Subtotal = lbs.	Subtotal = lbs.	Subtotal = lbs.	Subtotal = lbs.

Exercise 1:   *Total Weight* _____ *lbs.   Time* _____ *mins.   Power Factor* _____ *lbs./min.   Power Index* _____

▪ Exercise: BARBELL DECLINE BENCH PRESS

Weight Reps Sets	Weight Reps Sets	Weight Reps Sets	Weight Reps Sets	Weight Reps Sets	Weight Reps Sets
× ×	× ×	× ×	× ×	× ×	× ×
Subtotal = lbs.	Subtotal = lbs.	Subtotal = lbs.	Subtotal = lbs.	Subtotal = lbs.	Subtotal = lbs.

Exercise 2:   *Total Weight* _____ *lbs.   Time* _____ *mins.   Power Factor* _____ *lbs./min.   Power Index* _____

▪ Exercise: HIGH-PULLEY CABLE CROSSOVER

Weight Reps Sets	Weight Reps Sets	Weight Reps Sets	Weight Reps Sets	Weight Reps Sets	Weight Reps Sets
× ×	× ×	× ×	× ×	× ×	× ×
Subtotal = lbs.	Subtotal = lbs.	Subtotal = lbs.	Subtotal = lbs.	Subtotal = lbs.	Subtotal = lbs.

Exercise 3:   *Total Weight* _____ *lbs.   Time* _____ *mins.   Power Factor* _____ *lbs./min.   Power Index* _____

▪ Exercise:

Weight Reps Sets	Weight Reps Sets	Weight Reps Sets	Weight Reps Sets	Weight Reps Sets	Weight Reps Sets
× ×	× ×	× ×	× ×	× ×	× ×
Subtotal = lbs.	Subtotal = lbs.	Subtotal = lbs.	Subtotal = lbs.	Subtotal = lbs.	Subtotal = lbs.

Exercise 4:   *Total Weight* _____ *lbs.   Time* _____ *mins.   Power Factor* _____ *lbs./min.   Power Index* _____

▪ Exercise:

Weight Reps Sets	Weight Reps Sets	Weight Reps Sets	Weight Reps Sets	Weight Reps Sets	Weight Reps Sets
× ×	× ×	× ×	× ×	× ×	× ×
Subtotal = lbs.	Subtotal = lbs.	Subtotal = lbs.	Subtotal = lbs.	Subtotal = lbs.	Subtotal = lbs.

Exercise 5:   *Total Weight* _____ *lbs.   Time* _____ *mins.   Power Factor* _____ *lbs./min.   Power Index* _____

OVERALL WORKOUT: *Total Weight* _____ *lbs.   Time* _____ *mins.   Power Factor* _____ *lbs./min.   Power Index* _____

Exercise Subtotal = Weight × Reps × Sets   ▪ Power Factor = lbs./min.   ▪ Power Index = Total Weight × Power Factor ÷ 1,000,000

CHEST SPECIALIZATION WORKOUT RECORD   Date: ___ / ___ / ___

Start Time: _____   **Finish Time:** _____   **Total Time:** _____

■ **Exercise: BENCH PRESS**

Weight Reps Sets	Weight Reps Sets	Weight Reps Sets	Weight Reps Sets	Weight Reps Sets	Weight Reps Sets
× ×	× ×	× ×	× ×	× ×	× ×
Subtotal = lbs.	Subtotal = lbs.	Subtotal = lbs.	Subtotal = lbs.	Subtotal = lbs.	Subtotal = lbs.

Exercise 1:   *Total Weight* _____ *lbs.*   *Time* _____ *mins.*   *Power Factor* _____ *lbs./min.*   *Power Index* _____

■ **Exercise: BARBELL DECLINE BENCH PRESS**

Weight Reps Sets	Weight Reps Sets	Weight Reps Sets	Weight Reps Sets	Weight Reps Sets	Weight Reps Sets
× ×	× ×	× ×	× ×	× ×	× ×
Subtotal = lbs.	Subtotal = lbs.	Subtotal = lbs.	Subtotal = lbs.	Subtotal = lbs.	Subtotal = lbs.

Exercise 2:   *Total Weight* _____ *lbs.*   *Time* _____ *mins.*   *Power Factor* _____ *lbs./min.*   *Power Index* _____

■ **Exercise: HIGH-PULLEY CABLE CROSSOVER**

Weight Reps Sets	Weight Reps Sets	Weight Reps Sets	Weight Reps Sets	Weight Reps Sets	Weight Reps Sets
× ×	× ×	× ×	× ×	× ×	× ×
Subtotal = lbs.	Subtotal = lbs.	Subtotal = lbs.	Subtotal = lbs.	Subtotal = lbs.	Subtotal = lbs.

Exercise 3:   *Total Weight* _____ *lbs.*   *Time* _____ *mins.*   *Power Factor* _____ *lbs./min.*   *Power Index* _____

■ **Exercise:**

Weight Reps Sets	Weight Reps Sets	Weight Reps Sets	Weight Reps Sets	Weight Reps Sets	Weight Reps Sets
× ×	× ×	× ×	× ×	× ×	× ×
Subtotal = lbs.	Subtotal = lbs.	Subtotal = lbs.	Subtotal = lbs.	Subtotal = lbs.	Subtotal = lbs.

Exercise 4:   *Total Weight* _____ *lbs.*   *Time* _____ *mins.*   *Power Factor* _____ *lbs./min.*   *Power Index* _____

■ **Exercise:**

Weight Reps Sets	Weight Reps Sets	Weight Reps Sets	Weight Reps Sets	Weight Reps Sets	Weight Reps Sets
× ×	× ×	× ×	× ×	× ×	× ×
Subtotal = lbs.	Subtotal = lbs.	Subtotal = lbs.	Subtotal = lbs.	Subtotal = lbs.	Subtotal = lbs.

Exercise 5:   *Total Weight* _____ *lbs.*   *Time* _____ *mins.*   *Power Factor* _____ *lbs./min.*   *Power Index* _____

OVERALL WORKOUT: *Total Weight* _____ *lbs.*   *Time* _____ *mins.*   *Power Factor* _____ *lbs./min.*   *Power Index* _____

Exercise Subtotal = Weight × Reps × Sets   ■ *Power Factor = lbs./min.*   ■ *Power Index = Total Weight × Power Factor ÷ 1,000,000*

CHEST SPECIALIZATION WORKOUT RECORD   Date: ___ / ___ / ___

Start Time: _____   **Finish Time:** _____   **Total Time:** _____

■ **Exercise: BENCH PRESS**

Weight Reps Sets	Weight Reps Sets	Weight Reps Sets	Weight Reps Sets	Weight Reps Sets	Weight Reps Sets
× ×	× ×	× ×	× ×	× ×	× ×
Subtotal = lbs.	Subtotal = lbs.	Subtotal = lbs.	Subtotal = lbs.	Subtotal = lbs.	Subtotal = lbs.

Exercise 1:   *Total Weight _____ lbs.   Time _____ mins.   Power Factor _____ lbs./min.   Power Index _____*

■ **Exercise: BARBELL DECLINE BENCH PRESS**

Weight Reps Sets	Weight Reps Sets	Weight Reps Sets	Weight Reps Sets	Weight Reps Sets	Weight Reps Sets
× ×	× ×	× ×	× ×	× ×	× ×
Subtotal = lbs.	Subtotal = lbs.	Subtotal = lbs.	Subtotal = lbs.	Subtotal = lbs.	Subtotal = lbs.

Exercise 2:   *Total Weight _____ lbs.   Time _____ mins.   Power Factor _____ lbs./min.   Power Index _____*

■ **Exercise: HIGH-PULLEY CABLE CROSSOVER**

Weight Reps Sets	Weight Reps Sets	Weight Reps Sets	Weight Reps Sets	Weight Reps Sets	Weight Reps Sets
× ×	× ×	× ×	× ×	× ×	× ×
Subtotal = lbs.	Subtotal = lbs.	Subtotal = lbs.	Subtotal = lbs.	Subtotal = lbs.	Subtotal = lbs.

Exercise 3:   *Total Weight _____ lbs.   Time _____ mins.   Power Factor _____ lbs./min.   Power Index _____*

■ **Exercise:**

Weight Reps Sets	Weight Reps Sets	Weight Reps Sets	Weight Reps Sets	Weight Reps Sets	Weight Reps Sets
× ×	× ×	× ×	× ×	× ×	× ×
Subtotal = lbs.	Subtotal = lbs.	Subtotal = lbs.	Subtotal = lbs.	Subtotal = lbs.	Subtotal = lbs.

Exercise 4:   *Total Weight _____ lbs.   Time _____ mins.   Power Factor _____ lbs./min.   Power Index _____*

■ **Exercise:**

Weight Reps Sets	Weight Reps Sets	Weight Reps Sets	Weight Reps Sets	Weight Reps Sets	Weight Reps Sets
× ×	× ×	× ×	× ×	× ×	× ×
Subtotal = lbs.	Subtotal = lbs.	Subtotal = lbs.	Subtotal = lbs.	Subtotal = lbs.	Subtotal = lbs.

Exercise 5:   *Total Weight _____ lbs.   Time _____ mins.   Power Factor _____ lbs./min.   Power Index _____*

OVERALL WORKOUT: *Total Weight _____ lbs.   Time _____ mins.   Power Factor _____ lbs./min.   Power Index _____*

Exercise Subtotal = Weight × Reps × Sets   ■ *Power Factor = lbs./min.*   ■ *Power Index = Total Weight × Power Factor ÷ 1,000,000*

CHEST SPECIALIZATION WORKOUT RECORD   Date: ___ / ___ / ___

Start Time: _____   Finish Time: _____   Total Time: _____

- **Exercise: BENCH PRESS**

Weight Reps Sets	Weight Reps Sets	Weight Reps Sets	Weight Reps Sets	Weight Reps Sets	Weight Reps Sets
× ×	× ×	× ×	× ×	× ×	× ×
Subtotal = lbs.	Subtotal = lbs.	Subtotal = lbs.	Subtotal = lbs.	Subtotal = lbs.	Subtotal = lbs.

Exercise 1:   *Total Weight _____ lbs.   Time _____ mins.   Power Factor _____ lbs./min.   Power Index _____*

- **Exercise: BARBELL DECLINE BENCH PRESS**

Weight Reps Sets	Weight Reps Sets	Weight Reps Sets	Weight Reps Sets	Weight Reps Sets	Weight Reps Sets
× ×	× ×	× ×	× ×	× ×	× ×
Subtotal = lbs.	Subtotal = lbs.	Subtotal = lbs.	Subtotal = lbs.	Subtotal = lbs.	Subtotal = lbs.

Exercise 2:   *Total Weight _____ lbs.   Time _____ mins.   Power Factor _____ lbs./min.   Power Index _____*

- **Exercise: HIGH-PULLEY CABLE CROSSOVER**

Weight Reps Sets	Weight Reps Sets	Weight Reps Sets	Weight Reps Sets	Weight Reps Sets	Weight Reps Sets
× ×	× ×	× ×	× ×	× ×	× ×
Subtotal = lbs.	Subtotal = lbs.	Subtotal = lbs.	Subtotal = lbs.	Subtotal = lbs.	Subtotal = lbs.

Exercise 3:   *Total Weight _____ lbs.   Time _____ mins.   Power Factor _____ lbs./min.   Power Index _____*

- **Exercise:**

Weight Reps Sets	Weight Reps Sets	Weight Reps Sets	Weight Reps Sets	Weight Reps Sets	Weight Reps Sets
× ×	× ×	× ×	× ×	× ×	× ×
Subtotal = lbs.	Subtotal = lbs.	Subtotal = lbs.	Subtotal = lbs.	Subtotal = lbs.	Subtotal = lbs.

Exercise 4:   *Total Weight _____ lbs.   Time _____ mins.   Power Factor _____ lbs./min.   Power Index _____*

- **Exercise:**

Weight Reps Sets	Weight Reps Sets	Weight Reps Sets	Weight Reps Sets	Weight Reps Sets	Weight Reps Sets
× ×	× ×	× ×	× ×	× ×	× ×
Subtotal = lbs.	Subtotal = lbs.	Subtotal = lbs.	Subtotal = lbs.	Subtotal = lbs.	Subtotal = lbs.

Exercise 5:   *Total Weight _____ lbs.   Time _____ mins.   Power Factor _____ lbs./min.   Power Index _____*

OVERALL WORKOUT: *Total Weight _____ lbs.   Time _____ mins.   Power Factor _____ lbs./min.   Power Index _____*

Exercise Subtotal = Weight × Reps × Sets   ■ *Power Factor = lbs./min.*   ■ *Power Index = Total Weight × Power Factor ÷ 1,000,000*

CHEST SPECIALIZATION WORKOUT RECORD Date: ___ / ___ / ___

Start Time: _____ Finish Time: _____ Total Time: _____

▪ Exercise: BENCH PRESS

Weight Reps Sets	Weight Reps Sets	Weight Reps Sets	Weight Reps Sets	Weight Reps Sets	Weight Reps Sets
× ×	× ×	× ×	× ×	× ×	× ×
Subtotal = lbs.	Subtotal = lbs.	Subtotal = lbs.	Subtotal = lbs.	Subtotal = lbs.	Subtotal = lbs.

Exercise 1:   *Total Weight* _____ *lbs.*   *Time* _____ *mins.*   *Power Factor* _____ *lbs./min.*   *Power Index* _____

▪ Exercise: BARBELL DECLINE BENCH PRESS

Weight Reps Sets	Weight Reps Sets	Weight Reps Sets	Weight Reps Sets	Weight Reps Sets	Weight Reps Sets
× ×	× ×	× ×	× ×	× ×	× ×
Subtotal = lbs.	Subtotal = lbs.	Subtotal = lbs.	Subtotal = lbs.	Subtotal = lbs.	Subtotal = lbs.

Exercise 2:   *Total Weight* _____ *lbs.*   *Time* _____ *mins.*   *Power Factor* _____ *lbs./min.*   *Power Index* _____

▪ Exercise: HIGH-PULLEY CABLE CROSSOVER

Weight Reps Sets	Weight Reps Sets	Weight Reps Sets	Weight Reps Sets	Weight Reps Sets	Weight Reps Sets
× ×	× ×	× ×	× ×	× ×	× ×
Subtotal = lbs.	Subtotal = lbs.	Subtotal = lbs.	Subtotal = lbs.	Subtotal = lbs.	Subtotal = lbs.

Exercise 3:   *Total Weight* _____ *lbs.*   *Time* _____ *mins.*   *Power Factor* _____ *lbs./min.*   *Power Index* _____

▪ Exercise:

Weight Reps Sets	Weight Reps Sets	Weight Reps Sets	Weight Reps Sets	Weight Reps Sets	Weight Reps Sets
× ×	× ×	× ×	× ×	× ×	× ×
Subtotal = lbs.	Subtotal = lbs.	Subtotal = lbs.	Subtotal = lbs.	Subtotal = lbs.	Subtotal = lbs.

Exercise 4:   *Total Weight* _____ *lbs.*   *Time* _____ *mins.*   *Power Factor* _____ *lbs./min.*   *Power Index* _____

▪ Exercise:

Weight Reps Sets	Weight Reps Sets	Weight Reps Sets	Weight Reps Sets	Weight Reps Sets	Weight Reps Sets
× ×	× ×	× ×	× ×	× ×	× ×
Subtotal = lbs.	Subtotal = lbs.	Subtotal = lbs.	Subtotal = lbs.	Subtotal = lbs.	Subtotal = lbs.

Exercise 5:   *Total Weight* _____ *lbs.*   *Time* _____ *mins.*   *Power Factor* _____ *lbs./min.*   *Power Index* _____

OVERALL WORKOUT: *Total Weight* _____ *lbs.*   *Time* _____ *mins.*   *Power Factor* _____ *lbs./min.*   *Power Index* _____

Exercise Subtotal = Weight × Reps × Sets   ▪ *Power Factor = lbs./min.*   ▪ *Power Index = Total Weight × Power Factor ÷ 1,000,000*

CHEST SPECIALIZATION WORKOUT RECORD   Date: ___ / ___ / ___

Start Time: _____   Finish Time: _____   Total Time: _____

■ Exercise: BENCH PRESS

Weight	Reps	Sets	Weight	Reps	Sets	Weight	Reps	Sets	Weight	Reps	Sets	Weight	Reps	Sets	Weight	Reps	Sets
	×	×		×	×		×	×		×	×		×	×		×	×
Subtotal =		lbs.	Subtotal =		lbs.	Subtotal =		lbs.	Subtotal =		lbs.	Subtotal =		lbs.	Subtotal =		lbs.

Exercise 1:   *Total Weight* _____ *lbs.*   *Time* _____ *mins.*   *Power Factor* _____ *lbs./min.*   *Power Index* _____

■ Exercise: BARBELL DECLINE BENCH PRESS

Weight	Reps	Sets	Weight	Reps	Sets	Weight	Reps	Sets	Weight	Reps	Sets	Weight	Reps	Sets	Weight	Reps	Sets
	×	×		×	×		×	×		×	×		×	×		×	×
Subtotal =		lbs.	Subtotal =		lbs.	Subtotal =		lbs.	Subtotal =		lbs.	Subtotal =		lbs.	Subtotal =		lbs.

Exercise 2:   *Total Weight* _____ *lbs.*   *Time* _____ *mins.*   *Power Factor* _____ *lbs./min.*   *Power Index* _____

■ Exercise: HIGH-PULLEY CABLE CROSSOVER

Weight	Reps	Sets	Weight	Reps	Sets	Weight	Reps	Sets	Weight	Reps	Sets	Weight	Reps	Sets	Weight	Reps	Sets
	×	×		×	×		×	×		×	×		×	×		×	×
Subtotal =		lbs.	Subtotal =		lbs.	Subtotal =		lbs.	Subtotal =		lbs.	Subtotal =		lbs.	Subtotal =		lbs.

Exercise 3:   *Total Weight* _____ *lbs.*   *Time* _____ *mins.*   *Power Factor* _____ *lbs./min.*   *Power Index* _____

■ Exercise:

Weight	Reps	Sets	Weight	Reps	Sets	Weight	Reps	Sets	Weight	Reps	Sets	Weight	Reps	Sets	Weight	Reps	Sets
	×	×		×	×		×	×		×	×		×	×		×	×
Subtotal =		lbs.	Subtotal =		lbs.	Subtotal =		lbs.	Subtotal =		lbs.	Subtotal =		lbs.	Subtotal =		lbs.

Exercise 4:   *Total Weight* _____ *lbs.*   *Time* _____ *mins.*   *Power Factor* _____ *lbs./min.*   *Power Index* _____

■ Exercise:

Weight	Reps	Sets	Weight	Reps	Sets	Weight	Reps	Sets	Weight	Reps	Sets	Weight	Reps	Sets	Weight	Reps	Sets
	×	×		×	×		×	×		×	×		×	×		×	×
Subtotal =		lbs.	Subtotal =		lbs.	Subtotal =		lbs.	Subtotal =		lbs.	Subtotal =		lbs.	Subtotal =		lbs.

Exercise 5:   *Total Weight* _____ *lbs.*   *Time* _____ *mins.*   *Power Factor* _____ *lbs./min.*   *Power Index* _____

OVERALL WORKOUT: *Total Weight* _____ *lbs.*   *Time* _____ *mins.*   *Power Factor* _____ *lbs./min.*   *Power Index* _____

Exercise Subtotal = Weight × Reps × Sets   ■ *Power Factor = lbs./min.*   ■ *Power Index = Total Weight × Power Factor ÷ 1,000,000*

CHEST SPECIALIZATION WORKOUT RECORD Date: ___ / ___ / ___

Start Time: _____ **Finish Time:** _____ **Total Time:** _____

▪ Exercise: BENCH PRESS

Weight Reps Sets	Weight Reps Sets	Weight Reps Sets	Weight Reps Sets	Weight Reps Sets	Weight Reps Sets
× ×	× ×	× ×	× ×	× ×	× ×
Subtotal = lbs.	Subtotal = lbs.	Subtotal = lbs.	Subtotal = lbs.	Subtotal = lbs.	Subtotal = lbs.

Exercise 1: *Total Weight* _____ *lbs.* *Time* _____ *mins.* *Power Factor* _____ *lbs./min.* *Power Index* _____

▪ Exercise: BARBELL DECLINE BENCH PRESS

Weight Reps Sets	Weight Reps Sets	Weight Reps Sets	Weight Reps Sets	Weight Reps Sets	Weight Reps Sets
× ×	× ×	× ×	× ×	× ×	× ×
Subtotal = lbs.	Subtotal = lbs.	Subtotal = lbs.	Subtotal = lbs.	Subtotal = lbs.	Subtotal = lbs.

Exercise 2: *Total Weight* _____ *lbs.* *Time* _____ *mins.* *Power Factor* _____ *lbs./min.* *Power Index* _____

▪ Exercise: HIGH-PULLEY CABLE CROSSOVER

Weight Reps Sets	Weight Reps Sets	Weight Reps Sets	Weight Reps Sets	Weight Reps Sets	Weight Reps Sets
× ×	× ×	× ×	× ×	× ×	× ×
Subtotal = lbs.	Subtotal = lbs.	Subtotal = lbs.	Subtotal = lbs.	Subtotal = lbs.	Subtotal = lbs.

Exercise 3: *Total Weight* _____ *lbs.* *Time* _____ *mins.* *Power Factor* _____ *lbs./min.* *Power Index* _____

▪ Exercise:

Weight Reps Sets	Weight Reps Sets	Weight Reps Sets	Weight Reps Sets	Weight Reps Sets	Weight Reps Sets
× ×	× ×	× ×	× ×	× ×	× ×
Subtotal = lbs.	Subtotal = lbs.	Subtotal = lbs.	Subtotal = lbs.	Subtotal = lbs.	Subtotal = lbs.

Exercise 4: *Total Weight* _____ *lbs.* *Time* _____ *mins.* *Power Factor* _____ *lbs./min.* *Power Index* _____

▪ Exercise:

Weight Reps Sets	Weight Reps Sets	Weight Reps Sets	Weight Reps Sets	Weight Reps Sets	Weight Reps Sets
× ×	× ×	× ×	× ×	× ×	× ×
Subtotal = lbs.	Subtotal = lbs.	Subtotal = lbs.	Subtotal = lbs.	Subtotal = lbs.	Subtotal = lbs.

Exercise 5: *Total Weight* _____ *lbs.* *Time* _____ *mins.* *Power Factor* _____ *lbs./min.* *Power Index* _____

OVERALL WORKOUT: *Total Weight* _____ *lbs.* *Time* _____ *mins.* *Power Factor* _____ *lbs./min.* *Power Index* _____

Exercise Subtotal = Weight × Reps × Sets ▪ *Power Factor = lbs./min.* ▪ *Power Index = Total Weight × Power Factor ÷ 1,000,000*

CHEST SPECIALIZATION WORKOUT RECORD   Date: ____ / ____ / ____

Start Time: _____   **Finish Time:** _____   **Total Time:** _____

■ Exercise: BENCH PRESS

Weight Reps Sets	Weight Reps Sets	Weight Reps Sets	Weight Reps Sets	Weight Reps Sets	Weight Reps Sets
× ×	× ×	× ×	× ×	× ×	× ×
Subtotal = lbs.	Subtotal = lbs.	Subtotal = lbs.	Subtotal = lbs.	Subtotal = lbs.	Subtotal = lbs.

Exercise 1:   *Total Weight* _____ *lbs.*   *Time* _____ *mins.*   *Power Factor* _____ *lbs./min.*   *Power Index* _____

■ Exercise: BARBELL DECLINE BENCH PRESS

Weight Reps Sets	Weight Reps Sets	Weight Reps Sets	Weight Reps Sets	Weight Reps Sets	Weight Reps Sets
× ×	× ×	× ×	× ×	× ×	× ×
Subtotal = lbs.	Subtotal = lbs.	Subtotal = lbs.	Subtotal = lbs.	Subtotal = lbs.	Subtotal = lbs.

Exercise 2:   *Total Weight* _____ *lbs.*   *Time* _____ *mins.*   *Power Factor* _____ *lbs./min.*   *Power Index* _____

■ Exercise: HIGH-PULLEY CABLE CROSSOVER

Weight Reps Sets	Weight Reps Sets	Weight Reps Sets	Weight Reps Sets	Weight Reps Sets	Weight Reps Sets
× ×	× ×	× ×	× ×	× ×	× ×
Subtotal = lbs.	Subtotal = lbs.	Subtotal = lbs.	Subtotal = lbs.	Subtotal = lbs.	Subtotal = lbs.

Exercise 3:   *Total Weight* _____ *lbs.*   *Time* _____ *mins.*   *Power Factor* _____ *lbs./min.*   *Power Index* _____

■ Exercise:

Weight Reps Sets	Weight Reps Sets	Weight Reps Sets	Weight Reps Sets	Weight Reps Sets	Weight Reps Sets
× ×	× ×	× ×	× ×	× ×	× ×
Subtotal = lbs.	Subtotal = lbs.	Subtotal = lbs.	Subtotal = lbs.	Subtotal = lbs.	Subtotal = lbs.

Exercise 4:   *Total Weight* _____ *lbs.*   *Time* _____ *mins.*   *Power Factor* _____ *lbs./min.*   *Power Index* _____

■ Exercise:

Weight Reps Sets	Weight Reps Sets	Weight Reps Sets	Weight Reps Sets	Weight Reps Sets	Weight Reps Sets
× ×	× ×	× ×	× ×	× ×	× ×
Subtotal = lbs.	Subtotal = lbs.	Subtotal = lbs.	Subtotal = lbs.	Subtotal = lbs.	Subtotal = lbs.

Exercise 5:   *Total Weight* _____ *lbs.*   *Time* _____ *mins.*   *Power Factor* _____ *lbs./min.*   *Power Index* _____

OVERALL WORKOUT: *Total Weight* _____ *lbs.*   *Time* _____ *mins.*   *Power Factor* _____ *lbs./min.*   *Power Index* _____

Exercise Subtotal = Weight × Reps × Sets   ■ *Power Factor = lbs./min.*   ■ *Power Index = Total Weight × Power Factor ÷ 1,000,000*

CHEST SPECIALIZATION WORKOUT RECORD   Date: ___ / ___ / ___

Start Time: _____   Finish Time: _____   Total Time: _____

▪ Exercise: BENCH PRESS

Weight Reps Sets	Weight Reps Sets	Weight Reps Sets	Weight Reps Sets	Weight Reps Sets	Weight Reps Sets
× ×	× ×	× ×	× ×	× ×	× ×
Subtotal = lbs.	Subtotal = lbs.	Subtotal = lbs.	Subtotal = lbs.	Subtotal = lbs.	Subtotal = lbs.

Exercise 1:   *Total Weight _____ lbs.   Time _____ mins.   Power Factor _____ lbs./min.   Power Index _____*

▪ Exercise: BARBELL DECLINE BENCH PRESS

Weight Reps Sets	Weight Reps Sets	Weight Reps Sets	Weight Reps Sets	Weight Reps Sets	Weight Reps Sets
× ×	× ×	× ×	× ×	× ×	× ×
Subtotal = lbs.	Subtotal = lbs.	Subtotal = lbs.	Subtotal = lbs.	Subtotal = lbs.	Subtotal = lbs.

Exercise 2:   *Total Weight _____ lbs.   Time _____ mins.   Power Factor _____ lbs./min.   Power Index _____*

▪ Exercise: HIGH-PULLEY CABLE CROSSOVER

Weight Reps Sets	Weight Reps Sets	Weight Reps Sets	Weight Reps Sets	Weight Reps Sets	Weight Reps Sets
× ×	× ×	× ×	× ×	× ×	× ×
Subtotal = lbs.	Subtotal = lbs.	Subtotal = lbs.	Subtotal = lbs.	Subtotal = lbs.	Subtotal = lbs.

Exercise 3:   *Total Weight _____ lbs.   Time _____ mins.   Power Factor _____ lbs./min.   Power Index _____*

▪ Exercise:

Weight Reps Sets	Weight Reps Sets	Weight Reps Sets	Weight Reps Sets	Weight Reps Sets	Weight Reps Sets
× ×	× ×	× ×	× ×	× ×	× ×
Subtotal = lbs.	Subtotal = lbs.	Subtotal = lbs.	Subtotal = lbs.	Subtotal = lbs.	Subtotal = lbs.

Exercise 4:   *Total Weight _____ lbs.   Time _____ mins.   Power Factor _____ lbs./min.   Power Index _____*

▪ Exercise:

Weight Reps Sets	Weight Reps Sets	Weight Reps Sets	Weight Reps Sets	Weight Reps Sets	Weight Reps Sets
× ×	× ×	× ×	× ×	× ×	× ×
Subtotal = lbs.	Subtotal = lbs.	Subtotal = lbs.	Subtotal = lbs.	Subtotal = lbs.	Subtotal = lbs.

Exercise 5:   *Total Weight _____ lbs.   Time _____ mins.   Power Factor _____ lbs./min.   Power Index _____*

OVERALL WORKOUT: *Total Weight _____ lbs.   Time _____ mins.   Power Factor _____ lbs./min.   Power Index _____*

Exercise Subtotal = Weight × Reps × Sets   ▪ *Power Factor = lbs./min.*   ▪ *Power Index = Total Weight × Power Factor ÷ 1,000,000*

CHEST SPECIALIZATION WORKOUT RECORD   Date: ____ / ____ / ____

Start Time: _____   **Finish Time:** _____   **Total Time:** _____

■ **Exercise: BENCH PRESS**

Weight Reps Sets	Weight Reps Sets	Weight Reps Sets	Weight Reps Sets	Weight Reps Sets	Weight Reps Sets
× ×	× ×	× ×	× ×	× ×	× ×
Subtotal = lbs.	Subtotal = lbs.	Subtotal = lbs.	Subtotal = lbs.	Subtotal = lbs.	Subtotal = lbs.

Exercise 1:   *Total Weight* _____ *lbs.*   *Time* _____ *mins.*   *Power Factor* _____ *lbs./min.*   *Power Index* _____

■ **Exercise: BARBELL DECLINE BENCH PRESS**

Weight Reps Sets	Weight Reps Sets	Weight Reps Sets	Weight Reps Sets	Weight Reps Sets	Weight Reps Sets
× ×	× ×	× ×	× ×	× ×	× ×
Subtotal = lbs.	Subtotal = lbs.	Subtotal = lbs.	Subtotal = lbs.	Subtotal = lbs.	Subtotal = lbs.

Exercise 2:   *Total Weight* _____ *lbs.*   *Time* _____ *mins.*   *Power Factor* _____ *lbs./min.*   *Power Index* _____

■ **Exercise: HIGH-PULLEY CABLE CROSSOVER**

Weight Reps Sets	Weight Reps Sets	Weight Reps Sets	Weight Reps Sets	Weight Reps Sets	Weight Reps Sets
× ×	× ×	× ×	× ×	× ×	× ×
Subtotal = lbs.	Subtotal = lbs.	Subtotal = lbs.	Subtotal = lbs.	Subtotal = lbs.	Subtotal = lbs.

Exercise 3:   *Total Weight* _____ *lbs.*   *Time* _____ *mins.*   *Power Factor* _____ *lbs./min.*   *Power Index* _____

■ **Exercise:**

Weight Reps Sets	Weight Reps Sets	Weight Reps Sets	Weight Reps Sets	Weight Reps Sets	Weight Reps Sets
× ×	× ×	× ×	× ×	× ×	× ×
Subtotal = lbs.	Subtotal = lbs.	Subtotal = lbs.	Subtotal = lbs.	Subtotal = lbs.	Subtotal = lbs.

Exercise 4:   *Total Weight* _____ *lbs.*   *Time* _____ *mins.*   *Power Factor* _____ *lbs./min.*   *Power Index* _____

■ **Exercise:**

Weight Reps Sets	Weight Reps Sets	Weight Reps Sets	Weight Reps Sets	Weight Reps Sets	Weight Reps Sets
× ×	× ×	× ×	× ×	× ×	× ×
Subtotal = lbs.	Subtotal = lbs.	Subtotal = lbs.	Subtotal = lbs.	Subtotal = lbs.	Subtotal = lbs.

Exercise 5:   *Total Weight* _____ *lbs.*   *Time* _____ *mins.*   *Power Factor* _____ *lbs./min.*   *Power Index* _____

OVERALL WORKOUT: *Total Weight* _____ *lbs.*   *Time* _____ *mins.*   *Power Factor* _____ *lbs./min.*   *Power Index* _____

Exercise Subtotal = Weight × Reps × Sets   ■   *Power Factor = lbs./min.*   ■   *Power Index = Total Weight × Power Factor ÷ 1,000,000*

CHEST SPECIALIZATION WORKOUT RECORD   Date: ___ / ___ / ___

Start Time: _____   Finish Time: _____   Total Time: _____

■ Exercise: BENCH PRESS

Weight	Reps	Sets	Weight	Reps	Sets	Weight	Reps	Sets	Weight	Reps	Sets	Weight	Reps	Sets	Weight	Reps	Sets
×		×		×		×		×		×		×		×		×	
Subtotal =		lbs.	Subtotal =		lbs.	Subtotal =		lbs.	Subtotal =		lbs.	Subtotal =		lbs.	Subtotal =		lbs.

Exercise 1:   Total Weight _____ lbs.   Time _____ mins.   Power Factor _____ lbs./min.   Power Index _____

■ Exercise: BARBELL DECLINE BENCH PRESS

Weight	Reps	Sets	Weight	Reps	Sets	Weight	Reps	Sets	Weight	Reps	Sets	Weight	Reps	Sets	Weight	Reps	Sets
×		×		×		×		×		×		×		×		×	
Subtotal =		lbs.	Subtotal =		lbs.	Subtotal =		lbs.	Subtotal =		lbs.	Subtotal =		lbs.	Subtotal =		lbs.

Exercise 2:   Total Weight _____ lbs.   Time _____ mins.   Power Factor _____ lbs./min.   Power Index _____

■ Exercise: HIGH-PULLEY CABLE CROSSOVER

Weight	Reps	Sets	Weight	Reps	Sets	Weight	Reps	Sets	Weight	Reps	Sets	Weight	Reps	Sets	Weight	Reps	Sets
×		×		×		×		×		×		×		×		×	
Subtotal =		lbs.	Subtotal =		lbs.	Subtotal =		lbs.	Subtotal =		lbs.	Subtotal =		lbs.	Subtotal =		lbs.

Exercise 3:   Total Weight _____ lbs.   Time _____ mins.   Power Factor _____ lbs./min.   Power Index _____

■ Exercise:

Weight	Reps	Sets	Weight	Reps	Sets	Weight	Reps	Sets	Weight	Reps	Sets	Weight	Reps	Sets	Weight	Reps	Sets
×		×		×		×		×		×		×		×		×	
Subtotal =		lbs.	Subtotal =		lbs.	Subtotal =		lbs.	Subtotal =		lbs.	Subtotal =		lbs.	Subtotal =		lbs.

Exercise 4:   Total Weight _____ lbs.   Time _____ mins.   Power Factor _____ lbs./min.   Power Index _____

■ Exercise:

Weight	Reps	Sets	Weight	Reps	Sets	Weight	Reps	Sets	Weight	Reps	Sets	Weight	Reps	Sets	Weight	Reps	Sets
×		×		×		×		×		×		×		×		×	
Subtotal =		lbs.	Subtotal =		lbs.	Subtotal =		lbs.	Subtotal =		lbs.	Subtotal =		lbs.	Subtotal =		lbs.

Exercise 5:   Total Weight _____ lbs.   Time _____ mins.   Power Factor _____ lbs./min.   Power Index _____

OVERALL WORKOUT: *Total Weight _____ lbs.   Time _____ mins.   Power Factor _____ lbs./min.   Power Index _____*

Exercise Subtotal = Weight × Reps × Sets   ■ *Power Factor = lbs./min.*   ■ *Power Index = Total Weight × Power Factor ÷ 1,000,000*

CHEST SPECIALIZATION WORKOUT RECORD Date: ___ / ___ / ___

Start Time: _____   **Finish Time:** _____   **Total Time:** _____

■ Exercise: BENCH PRESS

Weight	Reps	Sets	Weight	Reps	Sets	Weight	Reps	Sets	Weight	Reps	Sets	Weight	Reps	Sets	Weight	Reps	Sets
×	×		×	×		×	×		×	×		×	×		×	×	
Subtotal =	lbs.		Subtotal =	lbs.		Subtotal =	lbs.		Subtotal =	lbs.		Subtotal =	lbs.		Subtotal =	lbs.	

Exercise 1:   *Total Weight* _____ *lbs.*   *Time* _____ *mins.*   *Power Factor* _____ *lbs./min.*   *Power Index* _____

■ Exercise: BARBELL DECLINE BENCH PRESS

Weight	Reps	Sets	Weight	Reps	Sets	Weight	Reps	Sets	Weight	Reps	Sets	Weight	Reps	Sets	Weight	Reps	Sets
×	×		×	×		×	×		×	×		×	×		×	×	
Subtotal =	lbs.		Subtotal =	lbs.		Subtotal =	lbs.		Subtotal =	lbs.		Subtotal =	lbs.		Subtotal =	lbs.	

Exercise 2:   *Total Weight* _____ *lbs.*   *Time* _____ *mins.*   *Power Factor* _____ *lbs./min.*   *Power Index* _____

■ Exercise: HIGH-PULLEY CABLE CROSSOVER

Weight	Reps	Sets	Weight	Reps	Sets	Weight	Reps	Sets	Weight	Reps	Sets	Weight	Reps	Sets	Weight	Reps	Sets
×	×		×	×		×	×		×	×		×	×		×	×	
Subtotal =	lbs.		Subtotal =	lbs.		Subtotal =	lbs.		Subtotal =	lbs.		Subtotal =	lbs.		Subtotal =	lbs.	

Exercise 3:   *Total Weight* _____ *lbs.*   *Time* _____ *mins.*   *Power Factor* _____ *lbs./min.*   *Power Index* _____

■ Exercise:

Weight	Reps	Sets	Weight	Reps	Sets	Weight	Reps	Sets	Weight	Reps	Sets	Weight	Reps	Sets	Weight	Reps	Sets
×	×		×	×		×	×		×	×		×	×		×	×	
Subtotal =	lbs.		Subtotal =	lbs.		Subtotal =	lbs.		Subtotal =	lbs.		Subtotal =	lbs.		Subtotal =	lbs.	

Exercise 4:   *Total Weight* _____ *lbs.*   *Time* _____ *mins.*   *Power Factor* _____ *lbs./min.*   *Power Index* _____

■ Exercise:

Weight	Reps	Sets	Weight	Reps	Sets	Weight	Reps	Sets	Weight	Reps	Sets	Weight	Reps	Sets	Weight	Reps	Sets
×	×		×	×		×	×		×	×		×	×		×	×	
Subtotal =	lbs.		Subtotal =	lbs.		Subtotal =	lbs.		Subtotal =	lbs.		Subtotal =	lbs.		Subtotal =	lbs.	

Exercise 5:   *Total Weight* _____ *lbs.*   *Time* _____ *mins.*   *Power Factor* _____ *lbs./min.*   *Power Index* _____

OVERALL WORKOUT: *Total Weight* _____ *lbs.*   *Time* _____ *mins.*   *Power Factor* _____ *lbs./min.*   *Power Index* _____

Exercise Subtotal = Weight × Reps × Sets ■ *Power Factor = lbs./min.* ■ *Power Index = Total Weight × Power Factor ÷ 1,000,000*

CHEST SPECIALIZATION WORKOUT RECORD Date: ___ / ___ / ___

Start Time: _____ Finish Time: _____ Total Time: _____

■ Exercise: BENCH PRESS

Weight Reps Sets	Weight Reps Sets	Weight Reps Sets	Weight Reps Sets	Weight Reps Sets	Weight Reps Sets
× ×	× ×	× ×	× ×	× ×	× ×
Subtotal = lbs.	Subtotal = lbs.	Subtotal = lbs.	Subtotal = lbs.	Subtotal = lbs.	Subtotal = lbs.

Exercise 1: Total Weight _____ lbs. Time _____ mins. Power Factor _____ lbs./min. Power Index _____

■ Exercise: BARBELL DECLINE BENCH PRESS

Weight Reps Sets	Weight Reps Sets	Weight Reps Sets	Weight Reps Sets	Weight Reps Sets	Weight Reps Sets
× ×	× ×	× ×	× ×	× ×	× ×
Subtotal = lbs.	Subtotal = lbs.	Subtotal = lbs.	Subtotal = lbs.	Subtotal = lbs.	Subtotal = lbs.

Exercise 2: Total Weight _____ lbs. Time _____ mins. Power Factor _____ lbs./min. Power Index _____

■ Exercise: HIGH-PULLEY CABLE CROSSOVER

Weight Reps Sets	Weight Reps Sets	Weight Reps Sets	Weight Reps Sets	Weight Reps Sets	Weight Reps Sets
× ×	× ×	× ×	× ×	× ×	× ×
Subtotal = lbs.	Subtotal = lbs.	Subtotal = lbs.	Subtotal = lbs.	Subtotal = lbs.	Subtotal = lbs.

Exercise 3: Total Weight _____ lbs. Time _____ mins. Power Factor _____ lbs./min. Power Index _____

■ Exercise:

Weight Reps Sets	Weight Reps Sets	Weight Reps Sets	Weight Reps Sets	Weight Reps Sets	Weight Reps Sets
× ×	× ×	× ×	× ×	× ×	× ×
Subtotal = lbs.	Subtotal = lbs.	Subtotal = lbs.	Subtotal = lbs.	Subtotal = lbs.	Subtotal = lbs.

Exercise 4: Total Weight _____ lbs. Time _____ mins. Power Factor _____ lbs./min. Power Index _____

■ Exercise:

Weight Reps Sets	Weight Reps Sets	Weight Reps Sets	Weight Reps Sets	Weight Reps Sets	Weight Reps Sets
× ×	× ×	× ×	× ×	× ×	× ×
Subtotal = lbs.	Subtotal = lbs.	Subtotal = lbs.	Subtotal = lbs.	Subtotal = lbs.	Subtotal = lbs.

Exercise 5: Total Weight _____ lbs. Time _____ mins. Power Factor _____ lbs./min. Power Index _____

OVERALL WORKOUT: *Total Weight _____ lbs. Time _____ mins. Power Factor _____ lbs./min. Power Index _____*

Exercise Subtotal = Weight × Reps × Sets ■ *Power Factor = lbs./min.* ■ *Power Index = Total Weight × Power Factor ÷ 1,000,000*

CHEST SPECIALIZATION WORKOUT RECORD   Date: ___ / ___ / ___

Start Time: _____   Finish Time: _____   Total Time: _____

■ Exercise: BENCH PRESS

Weight	Reps	Sets	Weight	Reps	Sets	Weight	Reps	Sets	Weight	Reps	Sets	Weight	Reps	Sets	Weight	Reps	Sets
×	×		×	×		×	×		×	×		×	×		×	×	
Subtotal =		lbs.	Subtotal =		lbs.	Subtotal =		lbs.	Subtotal =		lbs.	Subtotal =		lbs.	Subtotal =		lbs.

Exercise 1:   *Total Weight _____ lbs.   Time _____ mins.   Power Factor _____ lbs./min.   Power Index _____*

■ Exercise: BARBELL DECLINE BENCH PRESS

Weight	Reps	Sets	Weight	Reps	Sets	Weight	Reps	Sets	Weight	Reps	Sets	Weight	Reps	Sets	Weight	Reps	Sets
×	×		×	×		×	×		×	×		×	×		×	×	
Subtotal =		lbs.	Subtotal =		lbs.	Subtotal =		lbs.	Subtotal =		lbs.	Subtotal =		lbs.	Subtotal =		lbs.

Exercise 2:   *Total Weight _____ lbs.   Time _____ mins.   Power Factor _____ lbs./min.   Power Index _____*

■ Exercise: HIGH-PULLEY CABLE CROSSOVER

Weight	Reps	Sets	Weight	Reps	Sets	Weight	Reps	Sets	Weight	Reps	Sets	Weight	Reps	Sets	Weight	Reps	Sets
×	×		×	×		×	×		×	×		×	×		×	×	
Subtotal =		lbs.	Subtotal =		lbs.	Subtotal =		lbs.	Subtotal =		lbs.	Subtotal =		lbs.	Subtotal =		lbs.

Exercise 3:   *Total Weight _____ lbs.   Time _____ mins.   Power Factor _____ lbs./min.   Power Index _____*

■ Exercise:

Weight	Reps	Sets	Weight	Reps	Sets	Weight	Reps	Sets	Weight	Reps	Sets	Weight	Reps	Sets	Weight	Reps	Sets
×	×		×	×		×	×		×	×		×	×		×	×	
Subtotal =		lbs.	Subtotal =		lbs.	Subtotal =		lbs.	Subtotal =		lbs.	Subtotal =		lbs.	Subtotal =		lbs.

Exercise 4:   *Total Weight _____ lbs.   Time _____ mins.   Power Factor _____ lbs./min.   Power Index _____*

■ Exercise:

Weight	Reps	Sets	Weight	Reps	Sets	Weight	Reps	Sets	Weight	Reps	Sets	Weight	Reps	Sets	Weight	Reps	Sets
×	×		×	×		×	×		×	×		×	×		×	×	
Subtotal =		lbs.	Subtotal =		lbs.	Subtotal =		lbs.	Subtotal =		lbs.	Subtotal =		lbs.	Subtotal =		lbs.

Exercise 5:   *Total Weight _____ lbs.   Time _____ mins.   Power Factor _____ lbs./min.   Power Index _____*

OVERALL WORKOUT: *Total Weight _____ lbs.   Time _____ mins.   Power Factor _____ lbs./min.   Power Index _____*

Exercise Subtotal = Weight × Reps × Sets   ■ Power Factor = lbs./min.   ■ Power Index = Total Weight × Power Factor ÷ 1,000,000

CHEST SPECIALIZATION WORKOUT RECORD   Date: ___ / ___ / ___

Start Time: _____   **Finish Time:** _____   **Total Time:** _____

▪ Exercise: BENCH PRESS

Weight Reps Sets	Weight Reps Sets	Weight Reps Sets	Weight Reps Sets	Weight Reps Sets	Weight Reps Sets
× ×	× ×	× ×	× ×	× ×	× ×
Subtotal = lbs.	Subtotal = lbs.	Subtotal = lbs.	Subtotal = lbs.	Subtotal = lbs.	Subtotal = lbs.

Exercise 1:   *Total Weight* _____ *lbs.*   *Time* _____ *mins.*   *Power Factor* _____ *lbs./min.*   *Power Index* _____

▪ Exercise: BARBELL DECLINE BENCH PRESS

Weight Reps Sets	Weight Reps Sets	Weight Reps Sets	Weight Reps Sets	Weight Reps Sets	Weight Reps Sets
× ×	× ×	× ×	× ×	× ×	× ×
Subtotal = lbs.	Subtotal = lbs.	Subtotal = lbs.	Subtotal = lbs.	Subtotal = lbs.	Subtotal = lbs.

Exercise 2:   *Total Weight* _____ *lbs.*   *Time* _____ *mins.*   *Power Factor* _____ *lbs./min.*   *Power Index* _____

▪ Exercise: HIGH-PULLEY CABLE CROSSOVER

Weight Reps Sets	Weight Reps Sets	Weight Reps Sets	Weight Reps Sets	Weight Reps Sets	Weight Reps Sets
× ×	× ×	× ×	× ×	× ×	× ×
Subtotal = lbs.	Subtotal = lbs.	Subtotal = lbs.	Subtotal = lbs.	Subtotal = lbs.	Subtotal = lbs.

Exercise 3:   *Total Weight* _____ *lbs.*   *Time* _____ *mins.*   *Power Factor* _____ *lbs./min.*   *Power Index* _____

▪ Exercise:

Weight Reps Sets	Weight Reps Sets	Weight Reps Sets	Weight Reps Sets	Weight Reps Sets	Weight Reps Sets
× ×	× ×	× ×	× ×	× ×	× ×
Subtotal = lbs.	Subtotal = lbs.	Subtotal = lbs.	Subtotal = lbs.	Subtotal = lbs.	Subtotal = lbs.

Exercise 4:   *Total Weight* _____ *lbs.*   *Time* _____ *mins.*   *Power Factor* _____ *lbs./min.*   *Power Index* _____

▪ Exercise:

Weight Reps Sets	Weight Reps Sets	Weight Reps Sets	Weight Reps Sets	Weight Reps Sets	Weight Reps Sets
× ×	× ×	× ×	× ×	× ×	× ×
Subtotal = lbs.	Subtotal = lbs.	Subtotal = lbs.	Subtotal = lbs.	Subtotal = lbs.	Subtotal = lbs.

Exercise 5:   *Total Weight* _____ *lbs.*   *Time* _____ *mins.*   *Power Factor* _____ *lbs./min.*   *Power Index* _____

OVERALL WORKOUT: *Total Weight* _____ *lbs.*   *Time* _____ *mins.*   *Power Factor* _____ *lbs./min.*   *Power Index* _____

Exercise Subtotal = Weight × Reps × Sets   ▪ *Power Factor = lbs./min.*   ▪ *Power Index = Total Weight × Power Factor ÷ 1,000,000*

TRICEPS SPECIALIZATION WORKOUT RECORD Date: ___ / ___ / ___

Start Time: _____   Finish Time: _____   Total Time: _____

▪ Exercise: DIP (OR CLOSE-GRIP BENCH PRESS)

Weight Reps Sets	Weight Reps Sets	Weight Reps Sets	Weight Reps Sets	Weight Reps Sets	Weight Reps Sets
× ×	× ×	× ×	× ×	× ×	× ×
Subtotal = lbs.	Subtotal = lbs.	Subtotal = lbs.	Subtotal = lbs.	Subtotal = lbs.	Subtotal = lbs.

Exercise 1:   *Total Weight* _____ *lbs.*   *Time* _____ *mins.*   *Power Factor* _____ *lbs./min.*   *Power Index* _____

▪ Exercise: SEATED BARBELL TRICEPS EXTENSION

Weight Reps Sets	Weight Reps Sets	Weight Reps Sets	Weight Reps Sets	Weight Reps Sets	Weight Reps Sets
× ×	× ×	× ×	× ×	× ×	× ×
Subtotal = lbs.	Subtotal = lbs.	Subtotal = lbs.	Subtotal = lbs.	Subtotal = lbs.	Subtotal = lbs.

Exercise 2:   *Total Weight* _____ *lbs.*   *Time* _____ *mins.*   *Power Factor* _____ *lbs./min.*   *Power Index* _____

▪ Exercise:

Weight Reps Sets	Weight Reps Sets	Weight Reps Sets	Weight Reps Sets	Weight Reps Sets	Weight Reps Sets
× ×	× ×	× ×	× ×	× ×	× ×
Subtotal = lbs.	Subtotal = lbs.	Subtotal = lbs.	Subtotal = lbs.	Subtotal = lbs.	Subtotal = lbs.

Exercise 3:   *Total Weight* _____ *lbs.*   *Time* _____ *mins.*   *Power Factor* _____ *lbs./min.*   *Power Index* _____

▪ Exercise:

Weight Reps Sets	Weight Reps Sets	Weight Reps Sets	Weight Reps Sets	Weight Reps Sets	Weight Reps Sets
× ×	× ×	× ×	× ×	× ×	× ×
Subtotal = lbs.	Subtotal = lbs.	Subtotal = lbs.	Subtotal = lbs.	Subtotal = lbs.	Subtotal = lbs.

Exercise 4:   *Total Weight* _____ *lbs.*   *Time* _____ *mins.*   *Power Factor* _____ *lbs./min.*   *Power Index* _____

▪ Exercise:

Weight Reps Sets	Weight Reps Sets	Weight Reps Sets	Weight Reps Sets	Weight Reps Sets	Weight Reps Sets
× ×	× ×	× ×	× ×	× ×	× ×
Subtotal = lbs.	Subtotal = lbs.	Subtotal = lbs.	Subtotal = lbs.	Subtotal = lbs.	Subtotal = lbs.

Exercise 5:   *Total Weight* _____ *lbs.*   *Time* _____ *mins.*   *Power Factor* _____ *lbs./min.*   *Power Index* _____

OVERALL WORKOUT: *Total Weight* _____ *lbs.*   *Time* _____ *mins.*   *Power Factor* _____ *lbs./min.*   *Power Index* _____

Exercise Subtotal = Weight × Reps × Sets   ▪ *Power Factor = lbs./min.*   ▪ *Power Index = Total Weight × Power Factor ÷ 1,000,000*

TRICEPS SPECIALIZATION WORKOUT RECORD Date: ___ / ___ / ___

Start Time: _____   **Finish Time:** _____   **Total Time:** _____

■ Exercise: DIP (OR CLOSE-GRIP BENCH PRESS)

Weight Reps Sets	Weight Reps Sets	Weight Reps Sets	Weight Reps Sets	Weight Reps Sets	Weight Reps Sets
× ×	× ×	× ×	× ×	× ×	× ×
Subtotal = lbs.	Subtotal = lbs.	Subtotal = lbs.	Subtotal = lbs.	Subtotal = lbs.	Subtotal = lbs.

Exercise 1:   *Total Weight _____ lbs.   Time _____ mins.   Power Factor _____ lbs./min.   Power Index _____*

■ Exercise: SEATED BARBELL TRICEPS EXTENSION

Weight Reps Sets	Weight Reps Sets	Weight Reps Sets	Weight Reps Sets	Weight Reps Sets	Weight Reps Sets
× ×	× ×	× ×	× ×	× ×	× ×
Subtotal = lbs.	Subtotal = lbs.	Subtotal = lbs.	Subtotal = lbs.	Subtotal = lbs.	Subtotal = lbs.

Exercise 2:   *Total Weight _____ lbs.   Time _____ mins.   Power Factor _____ lbs./min.   Power Index _____*

■ Exercise:

Weight Reps Sets	Weight Reps Sets	Weight Reps Sets	Weight Reps Sets	Weight Reps Sets	Weight Reps Sets
× ×	× ×	× ×	× ×	× ×	× ×
Subtotal = lbs.	Subtotal = lbs.	Subtotal = lbs.	Subtotal = lbs.	Subtotal = lbs.	Subtotal = lbs.

Exercise 3:   *Total Weight _____ lbs.   Time _____ mins.   Power Factor _____ lbs./min.   Power Index _____*

■ Exercise:

Weight Reps Sets	Weight Reps Sets	Weight Reps Sets	Weight Reps Sets	Weight Reps Sets	Weight Reps Sets
× ×	× ×	× ×	× ×	× ×	× ×
Subtotal = lbs.	Subtotal = lbs.	Subtotal = lbs.	Subtotal = lbs.	Subtotal = lbs.	Subtotal = lbs.

Exercise 4:   *Total Weight _____ lbs.   Time _____ mins.   Power Factor _____ lbs./min.   Power Index _____*

■ Exercise:

Weight Reps Sets	Weight Reps Sets	Weight Reps Sets	Weight Reps Sets	Weight Reps Sets	Weight Reps Sets
× ×	× ×	× ×	× ×	× ×	× ×
Subtotal = lbs.	Subtotal = lbs.	Subtotal = lbs.	Subtotal = lbs.	Subtotal = lbs.	Subtotal = lbs.

Exercise 5:   *Total Weight _____ lbs.   Time _____ mins.   Power Factor _____ lbs./min.   Power Index _____*

OVERALL WORKOUT: *Total Weight _____ lbs.   Time _____ mins.   Power Factor _____ lbs./min.   Power Index _____*

Exercise Subtotal = Weight × Reps × Sets   ■ *Power Factor = lbs./min.*   ■ *Power Index = Total Weight × Power Factor ÷ 1,000,000*

TRICEPS SPECIALIZATION WORKOUT RECORD Date: ___ / ___ / ___

Start Time: _____ **Finish Time:** _____ **Total Time:** _____

■ Exercise: DIP (OR CLOSE-GRIP BENCH PRESS)

Weight Reps Sets	Weight Reps Sets	Weight Reps Sets	Weight Reps Sets	Weight Reps Sets	Weight Reps Sets
× ×	× ×	× ×	× ×	× ×	× ×
Subtotal = lbs.	Subtotal = lbs.	Subtotal = lbs.	Subtotal = lbs.	Subtotal = lbs.	Subtotal = lbs.

Exercise 1:   *Total Weight* _____ *lbs.*   *Time* _____ *mins.*   *Power Factor* _____ *lbs./min.*   *Power Index* _____

■ Exercise: SEATED BARBELL TRICEPS EXTENSION

Weight Reps Sets	Weight Reps Sets	Weight Reps Sets	Weight Reps Sets	Weight Reps Sets	Weight Reps Sets
× ×	× ×	× ×	× ×	× ×	× ×
Subtotal = lbs.	Subtotal = lbs.	Subtotal = lbs.	Subtotal = lbs.	Subtotal = lbs.	Subtotal = lbs.

Exercise 2:   *Total Weight* _____ *lbs.*   *Time* _____ *mins.*   *Power Factor* _____ *lbs./min.*   *Power Index* _____

■ Exercise:

Weight Reps Sets	Weight Reps Sets	Weight Reps Sets	Weight Reps Sets	Weight Reps Sets	Weight Reps Sets
× ×	× ×	× ×	× ×	× ×	× ×
Subtotal = lbs.	Subtotal = lbs.	Subtotal = lbs.	Subtotal = lbs.	Subtotal = lbs.	Subtotal = lbs.

Exercise 3:   *Total Weight* _____ *lbs.*   *Time* _____ *mins.*   *Power Factor* _____ *lbs./min.*   *Power Index* _____

■ Exercise:

Weight Reps Sets	Weight Reps Sets	Weight Reps Sets	Weight Reps Sets	Weight Reps Sets	Weight Reps Sets
× ×	× ×	× ×	× ×	× ×	× ×
Subtotal = lbs.	Subtotal = lbs.	Subtotal = lbs.	Subtotal = lbs.	Subtotal = lbs.	Subtotal = lbs.

Exercise 4:   *Total Weight* _____ *lbs.*   *Time* _____ *mins.*   *Power Factor* _____ *lbs./min.*   *Power Index* _____

■ Exercise:

Weight Reps Sets	Weight Reps Sets	Weight Reps Sets	Weight Reps Sets	Weight Reps Sets	Weight Reps Sets
× ×	× ×	× ×	× ×	× ×	× ×
Subtotal = lbs.	Subtotal = lbs.	Subtotal = lbs.	Subtotal = lbs.	Subtotal = lbs.	Subtotal = lbs.

Exercise 5:   *Total Weight* _____ *lbs.*   *Time* _____ *mins.*   *Power Factor* _____ *lbs./min.*   *Power Index* _____

OVERALL WORKOUT: *Total Weight* _____ *lbs.*   *Time* _____ *mins.*   *Power Factor* _____ *lbs./min.*   *Power Index* _____

Exercise Subtotal = Weight × Reps × Sets   ■ *Power Factor = lbs./min.*   ■ *Power Index = Total Weight × Power Factor ÷ 1,000,000*

TRICEPS SPECIALIZATION WORKOUT RECORD　Date: ___ / ___ / ___

Start Time: _____　Finish Time: _____　Total Time: _____

■ Exercise:　DIP (OR CLOSE-GRIP BENCH PRESS)

Weight Reps Sets	Weight Reps Sets	Weight Reps Sets	Weight Reps Sets	Weight Reps Sets	Weight Reps Sets
× ×	× ×	× ×	× ×	× ×	× ×
Subtotal = lbs.	Subtotal = lbs.	Subtotal = lbs.	Subtotal = lbs.	Subtotal = lbs.	Subtotal = lbs.

Exercise 1:　　*Total Weight _____ lbs.　Time _____ mins.　Power Factor _____ lbs./min.　Power Index _____*

■ Exercise:　SEATED BARBELL TRICEPS EXTENSION

Weight Reps Sets	Weight Reps Sets	Weight Reps Sets	Weight Reps Sets	Weight Reps Sets	Weight Reps Sets
× ×	× ×	× ×	× ×	× ×	× ×
Subtotal = lbs.	Subtotal = lbs.	Subtotal = lbs.	Subtotal = lbs.	Subtotal = lbs.	Subtotal = lbs.

Exercise 2:　　*Total Weight _____ lbs.　Time _____ mins.　Power Factor _____ lbs./min.　Power Index _____*

■ Exercise:

Weight Reps Sets	Weight Reps Sets	Weight Reps Sets	Weight Reps Sets	Weight Reps Sets	Weight Reps Sets
× ×	× ×	× ×	× ×	× ×	× ×
Subtotal = lbs.	Subtotal = lbs.	Subtotal = lbs.	Subtotal = lbs.	Subtotal = lbs.	Subtotal = lbs.

Exercise 3:　　*Total Weight _____ lbs.　Time _____ mins.　Power Factor _____ lbs./min.　Power Index _____*

■ Exercise:

Weight Reps Sets	Weight Reps Sets	Weight Reps Sets	Weight Reps Sets	Weight Reps Sets	Weight Reps Sets
× ×	× ×	× ×	× ×	× ×	× ×
Subtotal = lbs.	Subtotal = lbs.	Subtotal = lbs.	Subtotal = lbs.	Subtotal = lbs.	Subtotal = lbs.

Exercise 4:　　*Total Weight _____ lbs.　Time _____ mins.　Power Factor _____ lbs./min.　Power Index _____*

■ Exercise:

Weight Reps Sets	Weight Reps Sets	Weight Reps Sets	Weight Reps Sets	Weight Reps Sets	Weight Reps Sets
× ×	× ×	× ×	× ×	× ×	× ×
Subtotal = lbs.	Subtotal = lbs.	Subtotal = lbs.	Subtotal = lbs.	Subtotal = lbs.	Subtotal = lbs.

Exercise 5:　　*Total Weight _____ lbs.　Time _____ mins.　Power Factor _____ lbs./min.　Power Index _____*

OVERALL WORKOUT:　*Total Weight _____ lbs.　Time _____ mins.　Power Factor _____ lbs./min.　Power Index _____*

Exercise Subtotal = Weight × Reps × Sets　■ *Power Factor = lbs./min.*　■ *Power Index = Total Weight × Power Factor ÷ 1,000,000*

TRICEPS SPECIALIZATION WORKOUT RECORD Date: ___ / ___ / ___

Start Time: _____   Finish Time: _____   Total Time: _____

■ Exercise: DIP (OR CLOSE-GRIP BENCH PRESS)

Weight Reps Sets	Weight Reps Sets	Weight Reps Sets	Weight Reps Sets	Weight Reps Sets	Weight Reps Sets
× ×	× ×	× ×	× ×	× ×	× ×
Subtotal = lbs.	Subtotal = lbs.	Subtotal = lbs.	Subtotal = lbs.	Subtotal = lbs.	Subtotal = lbs.

Exercise 1:   *Total Weight* _____ *lbs.*   *Time* _____ *mins.*   *Power Factor* _____ *lbs./min.*   *Power Index* _____

■ Exercise: SEATED BARBELL TRICEPS EXTENSION

Weight Reps Sets	Weight Reps Sets	Weight Reps Sets	Weight Reps Sets	Weight Reps Sets	Weight Reps Sets
× ×	× ×	× ×	× ×	× ×	× ×
Subtotal = lbs.	Subtotal = lbs.	Subtotal = lbs.	Subtotal = lbs.	Subtotal = lbs.	Subtotal = lbs.

Exercise 2:   *Total Weight* _____ *lbs.*   *Time* _____ *mins.*   *Power Factor* _____ *lbs./min.*   *Power Index* _____

■ Exercise:

Weight Reps Sets	Weight Reps Sets	Weight Reps Sets	Weight Reps Sets	Weight Reps Sets	Weight Reps Sets
× ×	× ×	× ×	× ×	× ×	× ×
Subtotal = lbs.	Subtotal = lbs.	Subtotal = lbs.	Subtotal = lbs.	Subtotal = lbs.	Subtotal = lbs.

Exercise 3:   *Total Weight* _____ *lbs.*   *Time* _____ *mins.*   *Power Factor* _____ *lbs./min.*   *Power Index* _____

■ Exercise:

Weight Reps Sets	Weight Reps Sets	Weight Reps Sets	Weight Reps Sets	Weight Reps Sets	Weight Reps Sets
× ×	× ×	× ×	× ×	× ×	× ×
Subtotal = lbs.	Subtotal = lbs.	Subtotal = lbs.	Subtotal = lbs.	Subtotal = lbs.	Subtotal = lbs.

Exercise 4:   *Total Weight* _____ *lbs.*   *Time* _____ *mins.*   *Power Factor* _____ *lbs./min.*   *Power Index* _____

■ Exercise:

Weight Reps Sets	Weight Reps Sets	Weight Reps Sets	Weight Reps Sets	Weight Reps Sets	Weight Reps Sets
× ×	× ×	× ×	× ×	× ×	× ×
Subtotal = lbs.	Subtotal = lbs.	Subtotal = lbs.	Subtotal = lbs.	Subtotal = lbs.	Subtotal = lbs.

Exercise 5:   *Total Weight* _____ *lbs.*   *Time* _____ *mins.*   *Power Factor* _____ *lbs./min.*   *Power Index* _____

OVERALL WORKOUT: *Total Weight* _____ *lbs.*   *Time* _____ *mins.*   *Power Factor* _____ *lbs./min.*   *Power Index* _____

Exercise Subtotal = Weight × Reps × Sets ■ *Power Factor = lbs./min.* ■ *Power Index = Total Weight × Power Factor ÷ 1,000,000*

TRICEPS SPECIALIZATION WORKOUT RECORD Date: ___ / ___ / ___

Start Time: _____   Finish Time: _____   Total Time: _____

■ Exercise: DIP (OR CLOSE-GRIP BENCH PRESS)

Weight Reps Sets	Weight Reps Sets	Weight Reps Sets	Weight Reps Sets	Weight Reps Sets	Weight Reps Sets
× ×	× ×	× ×	× ×	× ×	× ×
Subtotal = lbs.	Subtotal = lbs.	Subtotal = lbs.	Subtotal = lbs.	Subtotal = lbs.	Subtotal = lbs.

Exercise 1:   *Total Weight* _____ *lbs.*   *Time* _____ *mins.*   *Power Factor* _____ *lbs./min.*   *Power Index* _____

■ Exercise: SEATED BARBELL TRICEPS EXTENSION

Weight Reps Sets	Weight Reps Sets	Weight Reps Sets	Weight Reps Sets	Weight Reps Sets	Weight Reps Sets
× ×	× ×	× ×	× ×	× ×	× ×
Subtotal = lbs.	Subtotal = lbs.	Subtotal = lbs.	Subtotal = lbs.	Subtotal = lbs.	Subtotal = lbs.

Exercise 2:   *Total Weight* _____ *lbs.*   *Time* _____ *mins.*   *Power Factor* _____ *lbs./min.*   *Power Index* _____

■ Exercise:

Weight Reps Sets	Weight Reps Sets	Weight Reps Sets	Weight Reps Sets	Weight Reps Sets	Weight Reps Sets
× ×	× ×	× ×	× ×	× ×	× ×
Subtotal = lbs.	Subtotal = lbs.	Subtotal = lbs.	Subtotal = lbs.	Subtotal = lbs.	Subtotal = lbs.

Exercise 3:   *Total Weight* _____ *lbs.*   *Time* _____ *mins.*   *Power Factor* _____ *lbs./min.*   *Power Index* _____

■ Exercise:

Weight Reps Sets	Weight Reps Sets	Weight Reps Sets	Weight Reps Sets	Weight Reps Sets	Weight Reps Sets
× ×	× ×	× ×	× ×	× ×	× ×
Subtotal = lbs.	Subtotal = lbs.	Subtotal = lbs.	Subtotal = lbs.	Subtotal = lbs.	Subtotal = lbs.

Exercise 4:   *Total Weight* _____ *lbs.*   *Time* _____ *mins.*   *Power Factor* _____ *lbs./min.*   *Power Index* _____

■ Exercise:

Weight Reps Sets	Weight Reps Sets	Weight Reps Sets	Weight Reps Sets	Weight Reps Sets	Weight Reps Sets
× ×	× ×	× ×	× ×	× ×	× ×
Subtotal = lbs.	Subtotal = lbs.	Subtotal = lbs.	Subtotal = lbs.	Subtotal = lbs.	Subtotal = lbs.

Exercise 5:   *Total Weight* _____ *lbs.*   *Time* _____ *mins.*   *Power Factor* _____ *lbs./min.*   *Power Index* _____

OVERALL WORKOUT: *Total Weight* _____ *lbs.*   *Time* _____ *mins.*   *Power Factor* _____ *lbs./min.*   *Power Index* _____

Exercise Subtotal = Weight × Reps × Sets   ■ *Power Factor = lbs./min.*   ■ *Power Index = Total Weight × Power Factor ÷ 1,000,000*

TRICEPS SPECIALIZATION WORKOUT RECORD Date: ___ / ___ / ___

Start Time: _____   **Finish Time:** _____   **Total Time:** _____

■ **Exercise: DIP (OR CLOSE-GRIP BENCH PRESS)**

Weight Reps Sets	Weight Reps Sets	Weight Reps Sets	Weight Reps Sets	Weight Reps Sets	Weight Reps Sets
× ×	× ×	× ×	× ×	× ×	× ×
Subtotal = lbs.	Subtotal = lbs.	Subtotal = lbs.	Subtotal = lbs.	Subtotal = lbs.	Subtotal = lbs.

Exercise 1: _____ *Total Weight* _____ *lbs.* *Time* _____ *mins.* *Power Factor* _____ *lbs./min.* *Power Index* _____

■ **Exercise: SEATED BARBELL TRICEPS EXTENSION**

Weight Reps Sets	Weight Reps Sets	Weight Reps Sets	Weight Reps Sets	Weight Reps Sets	Weight Reps Sets
× ×	× ×	× ×	× ×	× ×	× ×
Subtotal = lbs.	Subtotal = lbs.	Subtotal = lbs.	Subtotal = lbs.	Subtotal = lbs.	Subtotal = lbs.

Exercise 2: _____ *Total Weight* _____ *lbs.* *Time* _____ *mins.* *Power Factor* _____ *lbs./min.* *Power Index* _____

■ **Exercise:**

Weight Reps Sets	Weight Reps Sets	Weight Reps Sets	Weight Reps Sets	Weight Reps Sets	Weight Reps Sets
× ×	× ×	× ×	× ×	× ×	× ×
Subtotal = lbs.	Subtotal = lbs.	Subtotal = lbs.	Subtotal = lbs.	Subtotal = lbs.	Subtotal = lbs.

Exercise 3: _____ *Total Weight* _____ *lbs.* *Time* _____ *mins.* *Power Factor* _____ *lbs./min.* *Power Index* _____

■ **Exercise:**

Weight Reps Sets	Weight Reps Sets	Weight Reps Sets	Weight Reps Sets	Weight Reps Sets	Weight Reps Sets
× ×	× ×	× ×	× ×	× ×	× ×
Subtotal = lbs.	Subtotal = lbs.	Subtotal = lbs.	Subtotal = lbs.	Subtotal = lbs.	Subtotal = lbs.

Exercise 4: _____ *Total Weight* _____ *lbs.* *Time* _____ *mins.* *Power Factor* _____ *lbs./min.* *Power Index* _____

■ **Exercise:**

Weight Reps Sets	Weight Reps Sets	Weight Reps Sets	Weight Reps Sets	Weight Reps Sets	Weight Reps Sets
× ×	× ×	× ×	× ×	× ×	× ×
Subtotal = lbs.	Subtotal = lbs.	Subtotal = lbs.	Subtotal = lbs.	Subtotal = lbs.	Subtotal = lbs.

Exercise 5: _____ *Total Weight* _____ *lbs.* *Time* _____ *mins.* *Power Factor* _____ *lbs./min.* *Power Index* _____

OVERALL WORKOUT: *Total Weight* _____ *lbs.* *Time* _____ *mins.* *Power Factor* _____ *lbs./min.* *Power Index* _____

Exercise Subtotal = Weight × Reps × Sets ■ *Power Factor = lbs./min.* ■ *Power Index = Total Weight × Power Factor ÷ 1,000,000*

TRICEPS SPECIALIZATION WORKOUT RECORD Date: ___ / ___ / ___

Start Time: _____ **Finish Time:** _____ **Total Time:** _____

▪ Exercise: DIP (OR CLOSE-GRIP BENCH PRESS)

Weight Reps Sets	Weight Reps Sets	Weight Reps Sets	Weight Reps Sets	Weight Reps Sets	Weight Reps Sets
× ×	× ×	× ×	× ×	× ×	× ×
Subtotal = lbs.	Subtotal = lbs.	Subtotal = lbs.	Subtotal = lbs.	Subtotal = lbs.	Subtotal = lbs.

Exercise 1:   *Total Weight* _____ *lbs.*   *Time* _____ *mins.*   *Power Factor* _____ *lbs./min.*   *Power Index* _____

▪ Exercise: SEATED BARBELL TRICEPS EXTENSION

Weight Reps Sets	Weight Reps Sets	Weight Reps Sets	Weight Reps Sets	Weight Reps Sets	Weight Reps Sets
× ×	× ×	× ×	× ×	× ×	× ×
Subtotal = lbs.	Subtotal = lbs.	Subtotal = lbs.	Subtotal = lbs.	Subtotal = lbs.	Subtotal = lbs.

Exercise 2:   *Total Weight* _____ *lbs.*   *Time* _____ *mins.*   *Power Factor* _____ *lbs./min.*   *Power Index* _____

▪ Exercise:

Weight Reps Sets	Weight Reps Sets	Weight Reps Sets	Weight Reps Sets	Weight Reps Sets	Weight Reps Sets
× ×	× ×	× ×	× ×	× ×	× ×
Subtotal = lbs.	Subtotal = lbs.	Subtotal = lbs.	Subtotal = lbs.	Subtotal = lbs.	Subtotal = lbs.

Exercise 3:   *Total Weight* _____ *lbs.*   *Time* _____ *mins.*   *Power Factor* _____ *lbs./min.*   *Power Index* _____

▪ Exercise:

Weight Reps Sets	Weight Reps Sets	Weight Reps Sets	Weight Reps Sets	Weight Reps Sets	Weight Reps Sets
× ×	× ×	× ×	× ×	× ×	× ×
Subtotal = lbs.	Subtotal = lbs.	Subtotal = lbs.	Subtotal = lbs.	Subtotal = lbs.	Subtotal = lbs.

Exercise 4:   *Total Weight* _____ *lbs.*   *Time* _____ *mins.*   *Power Factor* _____ *lbs./min.*   *Power Index* _____

▪ Exercise:

Weight Reps Sets	Weight Reps Sets	Weight Reps Sets	Weight Reps Sets	Weight Reps Sets	Weight Reps Sets
× ×	× ×	× ×	× ×	× ×	× ×
Subtotal = lbs.	Subtotal = lbs.	Subtotal = lbs.	Subtotal = lbs.	Subtotal = lbs.	Subtotal = lbs.

Exercise 5:   *Total Weight* _____ *lbs.*   *Time* _____ *mins.*   *Power Factor* _____ *lbs./min.*   *Power Index* _____

OVERALL WORKOUT: *Total Weight* _____ *lbs.*   *Time* _____ *mins.*   *Power Factor* _____ *lbs./min.*   *Power Index* _____

Exercise Subtotal = Weight × Reps × Sets   ▪ *Power Factor = lbs./min.*   ▪ *Power Index = Total Weight × Power Factor ÷ 1,000,000*

TRICEPS SPECIALIZATION WORKOUT RECORD Date: ____ / ____ / ____

Start Time: _____   **Finish Time:** _____   **Total Time:** _____

■ **Exercise: DIP (OR CLOSE-GRIP BENCH PRESS)**

Weight	Reps	Sets	Weight	Reps	Sets	Weight	Reps	Sets	Weight	Reps	Sets	Weight	Reps	Sets	Weight	Reps	Sets
	×	×		×	×		×	×		×	×		×	×		×	×
Subtotal =		lbs.	Subtotal =		lbs.	Subtotal =		lbs.	Subtotal =		lbs.	Subtotal =		lbs.	Subtotal =		lbs.

Exercise 1:   *Total Weight* _____ *lbs.   Time* _____ *mins.   Power Factor* _____ *lbs./min.   Power Index* _____

■ **Exercise: SEATED BARBELL TRICEPS EXTENSION**

Weight	Reps	Sets	Weight	Reps	Sets	Weight	Reps	Sets	Weight	Reps	Sets	Weight	Reps	Sets	Weight	Reps	Sets
	×	×		×	×		×	×		×	×		×	×		×	×
Subtotal =		lbs.	Subtotal =		lbs.	Subtotal =		lbs.	Subtotal =		lbs.	Subtotal =		lbs.	Subtotal =		lbs.

Exercise 2:   *Total Weight* _____ *lbs.   Time* _____ *mins.   Power Factor* _____ *lbs./min.   Power Index* _____

■ **Exercise:**

Weight	Reps	Sets	Weight	Reps	Sets	Weight	Reps	Sets	Weight	Reps	Sets	Weight	Reps	Sets	Weight	Reps	Sets
	×	×		×	×		×	×		×	×		×	×		×	×
Subtotal =		lbs.	Subtotal =		lbs.	Subtotal =		lbs.	Subtotal =		lbs.	Subtotal =		lbs.	Subtotal =		lbs.

Exercise 3:   *Total Weight* _____ *lbs.   Time* _____ *mins.   Power Factor* _____ *lbs./min.   Power Index* _____

■ **Exercise:**

Weight	Reps	Sets	Weight	Reps	Sets	Weight	Reps	Sets	Weight	Reps	Sets	Weight	Reps	Sets	Weight	Reps	Sets
	×	×		×	×		×	×		×	×		×	×		×	×
Subtotal =		lbs.	Subtotal =		lbs.	Subtotal =		lbs.	Subtotal =		lbs.	Subtotal =		lbs.	Subtotal =		lbs.

Exercise 4:   *Total Weight* _____ *lbs.   Time* _____ *mins.   Power Factor* _____ *lbs./min.   Power Index* _____

■ **Exercise:**

Weight	Reps	Sets	Weight	Reps	Sets	Weight	Reps	Sets	Weight	Reps	Sets	Weight	Reps	Sets	Weight	Reps	Sets
	×	×		×	×		×	×		×	×		×	×		×	×
Subtotal =		lbs.	Subtotal =		lbs.	Subtotal =		lbs.	Subtotal =		lbs.	Subtotal =		lbs.	Subtotal =		lbs.

Exercise 5:   *Total Weight* _____ *lbs.   Time* _____ *mins.   Power Factor* _____ *lbs./min.   Power Index* _____

OVERALL WORKOUT: *Total Weight* _____ *lbs.   Time* _____ *mins.   Power Factor* _____ *lbs./min.   Power Index* _____

Exercise Subtotal = Weight × Reps × Sets   ■ *Power Factor = lbs./min.*   ■ *Power Index = Total Weight × Power Factor ÷ 1,000,000*

TRICEPS SPECIALIZATION WORKOUT RECORD   Date: ___ / ___ / ___

Start Time: _____   **Finish Time:** _____   **Total Time:** _____

■ Exercise: DIP (OR CLOSE-GRIP BENCH PRESS)

Weight Reps Sets	Weight Reps Sets	Weight Reps Sets	Weight Reps Sets	Weight Reps Sets	Weight Reps Sets
× ×	× ×	× ×	× ×	× ×	× ×
Subtotal = lbs.	Subtotal = lbs.	Subtotal = lbs.	Subtotal = lbs.	Subtotal = lbs.	Subtotal = lbs.

Exercise 1:   *Total Weight* _____ *lbs.*   *Time* _____ *mins.*   *Power Factor* _____ *lbs./min.*   *Power Index* _____

■ Exercise: SEATED BARBELL TRICEPS EXTENSION

Weight Reps Sets	Weight Reps Sets	Weight Reps Sets	Weight Reps Sets	Weight Reps Sets	Weight Reps Sets
× ×	× ×	× ×	× ×	× ×	× ×
Subtotal = lbs.	Subtotal = lbs.	Subtotal = lbs.	Subtotal = lbs.	Subtotal = lbs.	Subtotal = lbs.

Exercise 2:   *Total Weight* _____ *lbs.*   *Time* _____ *mins.*   *Power Factor* _____ *lbs./min.*   *Power Index* _____

■ Exercise:

Weight Reps Sets	Weight Reps Sets	Weight Reps Sets	Weight Reps Sets	Weight Reps Sets	Weight Reps Sets
× ×	× ×	× ×	× ×	× ×	× ×
Subtotal = lbs.	Subtotal = lbs.	Subtotal = lbs.	Subtotal = lbs.	Subtotal = lbs.	Subtotal = lbs.

Exercise 3:   *Total Weight* _____ *lbs.*   *Time* _____ *mins.*   *Power Factor* _____ *lbs./min.*   *Power Index* _____

■ Exercise:

Weight Reps Sets	Weight Reps Sets	Weight Reps Sets	Weight Reps Sets	Weight Reps Sets	Weight Reps Sets
× ×	× ×	× ×	× ×	× ×	× ×
Subtotal = lbs.	Subtotal = lbs.	Subtotal = lbs.	Subtotal = lbs.	Subtotal = lbs.	Subtotal = lbs.

Exercise 4:   *Total Weight* _____ *lbs.*   *Time* _____ *mins.*   *Power Factor* _____ *lbs./min.*   *Power Index* _____

■ Exercise:

Weight Reps Sets	Weight Reps Sets	Weight Reps Sets	Weight Reps Sets	Weight Reps Sets	Weight Reps Sets
× ×	× ×	× ×	× ×	× ×	× ×
Subtotal = lbs.	Subtotal = lbs.	Subtotal = lbs.	Subtotal = lbs.	Subtotal = lbs.	Subtotal = lbs.

Exercise 5:   *Total Weight* _____ *lbs.*   *Time* _____ *mins.*   *Power Factor* _____ *lbs./min.*   *Power Index* _____

OVERALL WORKOUT: *Total Weight* _____ *lbs.*   *Time* _____ *mins.*   *Power Factor* _____ *lbs./min.*   *Power Index* _____

Exercise Subtotal = Weight × Reps × Sets   ■ *Power Factor = lbs./min.*   ■ *Power Index = Total Weight × Power Factor ÷ 1,000,000*

TRICEPS SPECIALIZATION WORKOUT RECORD Date: ___ / ___ / ___

Start Time: _____   Finish Time: _____   Total Time: _____

■ Exercise: DIP (OR CLOSE-GRIP BENCH PRESS)

Weight Reps Sets	Weight Reps Sets	Weight Reps Sets	Weight Reps Sets	Weight Reps Sets	Weight Reps Sets
× ×	× ×	× ×	× ×	× ×	× ×
Subtotal = lbs.	Subtotal = lbs.	Subtotal = lbs.	Subtotal = lbs.	Subtotal = lbs.	Subtotal = lbs.

Exercise 1: *Total Weight _____ lbs. Time _____ mins. Power Factor _____ lbs./min. Power Index _____*

■ Exercise: SEATED BARBELL TRICEPS EXTENSION

Weight Reps Sets	Weight Reps Sets	Weight Reps Sets	Weight Reps Sets	Weight Reps Sets	Weight Reps Sets
× ×	× ×	× ×	× ×	× ×	× ×
Subtotal = lbs.	Subtotal = lbs.	Subtotal = lbs.	Subtotal = lbs.	Subtotal = lbs.	Subtotal = lbs.

Exercise 2: *Total Weight _____ lbs. Time _____ mins. Power Factor _____ lbs./min. Power Index _____*

■ Exercise:

Weight Reps Sets	Weight Reps Sets	Weight Reps Sets	Weight Reps Sets	Weight Reps Sets	Weight Reps Sets
× ×	× ×	× ×	× ×	× ×	× ×
Subtotal = lbs.	Subtotal = lbs.	Subtotal = lbs.	Subtotal = lbs.	Subtotal = lbs.	Subtotal = lbs.

Exercise 3: *Total Weight _____ lbs. Time _____ mins. Power Factor _____ lbs./min. Power Index _____*

■ Exercise:

Weight Reps Sets	Weight Reps Sets	Weight Reps Sets	Weight Reps Sets	Weight Reps Sets	Weight Reps Sets
× ×	× ×	× ×	× ×	× ×	× ×
Subtotal = lbs.	Subtotal = lbs.	Subtotal = lbs.	Subtotal = lbs.	Subtotal = lbs.	Subtotal = lbs.

Exercise 4: *Total Weight _____ lbs. Time _____ mins. Power Factor _____ lbs./min. Power Index _____*

■ Exercise:

Weight Reps Sets	Weight Reps Sets	Weight Reps Sets	Weight Reps Sets	Weight Reps Sets	Weight Reps Sets
× ×	× ×	× ×	× ×	× ×	× ×
Subtotal = lbs.	Subtotal = lbs.	Subtotal = lbs.	Subtotal = lbs.	Subtotal = lbs.	Subtotal = lbs.

Exercise 5: *Total Weight _____ lbs. Time _____ mins. Power Factor _____ lbs./min. Power Index _____*

OVERALL WORKOUT: *Total Weight _____ lbs. Time _____ mins. Power Factor _____ lbs./min. Power Index _____*

Exercise Subtotal = Weight × Reps × Sets   ■ Power Factor = lbs./min.   ■ Power Index = Total Weight × Power Factor ÷ 1,000,000

TRICEPS SPECIALIZATION WORKOUT RECORD Date: ___ / ___ / ___

Start Time: _____ **Finish Time:** _____ **Total Time:** _____

▪ Exercise: DIP (OR CLOSE-GRIP BENCH PRESS)

Weight Reps Sets	Weight Reps Sets	Weight Reps Sets	Weight Reps Sets	Weight Reps Sets	Weight Reps Sets
× ×	× ×	× ×	× ×	× ×	× ×
Subtotal = lbs.	Subtotal = lbs.	Subtotal = lbs.	Subtotal = lbs.	Subtotal = lbs.	Subtotal = lbs.

Exercise 1: *Total Weight* _____ *lbs.* *Time* _____ *mins.* *Power Factor* _____ *lbs./min.* *Power Index* _____

▪ Exercise: SEATED BARBELL TRICEPS EXTENSION

Weight Reps Sets	Weight Reps Sets	Weight Reps Sets	Weight Reps Sets	Weight Reps Sets	Weight Reps Sets
× ×	× ×	× ×	× ×	× ×	× ×
Subtotal = lbs.	Subtotal = lbs.	Subtotal = lbs.	Subtotal = lbs.	Subtotal = lbs.	Subtotal = lbs.

Exercise 2: *Total Weight* _____ *lbs.* *Time* _____ *mins.* *Power Factor* _____ *lbs./min.* *Power Index* _____

▪ Exercise:

Weight Reps Sets	Weight Reps Sets	Weight Reps Sets	Weight Reps Sets	Weight Reps Sets	Weight Reps Sets
× ×	× ×	× ×	× ×	× ×	× ×
Subtotal = lbs.	Subtotal = lbs.	Subtotal = lbs.	Subtotal = lbs.	Subtotal = lbs.	Subtotal = lbs.

Exercise 3: *Total Weight* _____ *lbs.* *Time* _____ *mins.* *Power Factor* _____ *lbs./min.* *Power Index* _____

▪ Exercise:

Weight Reps Sets	Weight Reps Sets	Weight Reps Sets	Weight Reps Sets	Weight Reps Sets	Weight Reps Sets
× ×	× ×	× ×	× ×	× ×	× ×
Subtotal = lbs.	Subtotal = lbs.	Subtotal = lbs.	Subtotal = lbs.	Subtotal = lbs.	Subtotal = lbs.

Exercise 4: *Total Weight* _____ *lbs.* *Time* _____ *mins.* *Power Factor* _____ *lbs./min.* *Power Index* _____

▪ Exercise:

Weight Reps Sets	Weight Reps Sets	Weight Reps Sets	Weight Reps Sets	Weight Reps Sets	Weight Reps Sets
× ×	× ×	× ×	× ×	× ×	× ×
Subtotal = lbs.	Subtotal = lbs.	Subtotal = lbs.	Subtotal = lbs.	Subtotal = lbs.	Subtotal = lbs.

Exercise 5: *Total Weight* _____ *lbs.* *Time* _____ *mins.* *Power Factor* _____ *lbs./min.* *Power Index* _____

OVERALL WORKOUT: *Total Weight* _____ *lbs.* *Time* _____ *mins.* *Power Factor* _____ *lbs./min.* *Power Index* _____

Exercise Subtotal = Weight × Reps × Sets ▪ *Power Factor = lbs./min.* ▪ *Power Index = Total Weight × Power Factor ÷ 1,000,000*

TRICEPS SPECIALIZATION WORKOUT RECORD   Date: ___ / ___ / ___

Start Time: _____   Finish Time: _____   Total Time: _____

■ Exercise: DIP (OR CLOSE-GRIP BENCH PRESS)

Weight Reps Sets	Weight Reps Sets	Weight Reps Sets	Weight Reps Sets	Weight Reps Sets	Weight Reps Sets
× ×	× ×	× ×	× ×	× ×	× ×
Subtotal = lbs.	Subtotal = lbs.	Subtotal = lbs.	Subtotal = lbs.	Subtotal = lbs.	Subtotal = lbs.

Exercise 1:   *Total Weight* _____ *lbs.*   *Time* _____ *mins.*   *Power Factor* _____ *lbs./min.*   *Power Index* _____

■ Exercise: SEATED BARBELL TRICEPS EXTENSION

Weight Reps Sets	Weight Reps Sets	Weight Reps Sets	Weight Reps Sets	Weight Reps Sets	Weight Reps Sets
× ×	× ×	× ×	× ×	× ×	× ×
Subtotal = lbs.	Subtotal = lbs.	Subtotal = lbs.	Subtotal = lbs.	Subtotal = lbs.	Subtotal = lbs.

Exercise 2:   *Total Weight* _____ *lbs.*   *Time* _____ *mins.*   *Power Factor* _____ *lbs./min.*   *Power Index* _____

■ Exercise:

Weight Reps Sets	Weight Reps Sets	Weight Reps Sets	Weight Reps Sets	Weight Reps Sets	Weight Reps Sets
× ×	× ×	× ×	× ×	× ×	× ×
Subtotal = lbs.	Subtotal = lbs.	Subtotal = lbs.	Subtotal = lbs.	Subtotal = lbs.	Subtotal = lbs.

Exercise 3:   *Total Weight* _____ *lbs.*   *Time* _____ *mins.*   *Power Factor* _____ *lbs./min.*   *Power Index* _____

■ Exercise:

Weight Reps Sets	Weight Reps Sets	Weight Reps Sets	Weight Reps Sets	Weight Reps Sets	Weight Reps Sets
× ×	× ×	× ×	× ×	× ×	× ×
Subtotal = lbs.	Subtotal = lbs.	Subtotal = lbs.	Subtotal = lbs.	Subtotal = lbs.	Subtotal = lbs.

Exercise 4:   *Total Weight* _____ *lbs.*   *Time* _____ *mins.*   *Power Factor* _____ *lbs./min.*   *Power Index* _____

■ Exercise:

Weight Reps Sets	Weight Reps Sets	Weight Reps Sets	Weight Reps Sets	Weight Reps Sets	Weight Reps Sets
× ×	× ×	× ×	× ×	× ×	× ×
Subtotal = lbs.	Subtotal = lbs.	Subtotal = lbs.	Subtotal = lbs.	Subtotal = lbs.	Subtotal = lbs.

Exercise 5:   *Total Weight* _____ *lbs.*   *Time* _____ *mins.*   *Power Factor* _____ *lbs./min.*   *Power Index* _____

OVERALL WORKOUT: *Total Weight* _____ *lbs.*   *Time* _____ *mins.*   *Power Factor* _____ *lbs./min.*   *Power Index* _____

Exercise Subtotal = Weight × Reps × Sets   ■ *Power Factor = lbs./min.*   ■ *Power Index = Total Weight × Power Factor ÷ 1,000,000*

TRICEPS SPECIALIZATION WORKOUT RECORD Date: ___ / ___ / ___

Start Time: _____   Finish Time: _____   Total Time: _____

■ **Exercise: DIP (OR CLOSE-GRIP BENCH PRESS)**

Weight Reps Sets	Weight Reps Sets	Weight Reps Sets	Weight Reps Sets	Weight Reps Sets	Weight Reps Sets
× ×	× ×	× ×	× ×	× ×	× ×
Subtotal = lbs.	Subtotal = lbs.	Subtotal = lbs.	Subtotal = lbs.	Subtotal = lbs.	Subtotal = lbs.

Exercise 1:   *Total Weight* _____ *lbs.*   *Time* _____ *mins.*   *Power Factor* _____ *lbs./min.*   *Power Index* _____

■ **Exercise: SEATED BARBELL TRICEPS EXTENSION**

Weight Reps Sets	Weight Reps Sets	Weight Reps Sets	Weight Reps Sets	Weight Reps Sets	Weight Reps Sets
× ×	× ×	× ×	× ×	× ×	× ×
Subtotal = lbs.	Subtotal = lbs.	Subtotal = lbs.	Subtotal = lbs.	Subtotal = lbs.	Subtotal = lbs.

Exercise 2:   *Total Weight* _____ *lbs.*   *Time* _____ *mins.*   *Power Factor* _____ *lbs./min.*   *Power Index* _____

■ **Exercise:**

Weight Reps Sets	Weight Reps Sets	Weight Reps Sets	Weight Reps Sets	Weight Reps Sets	Weight Reps Sets
× ×	× ×	× ×	× ×	× ×	× ×
Subtotal = lbs.	Subtotal = lbs.	Subtotal = lbs.	Subtotal = lbs.	Subtotal = lbs.	Subtotal = lbs.

Exercise 3:   *Total Weight* _____ *lbs.*   *Time* _____ *mins.*   *Power Factor* _____ *lbs./min.*   *Power Index* _____

■ **Exercise:**

Weight Reps Sets	Weight Reps Sets	Weight Reps Sets	Weight Reps Sets	Weight Reps Sets	Weight Reps Sets
× ×	× ×	× ×	× ×	× ×	× ×
Subtotal = lbs.	Subtotal = lbs.	Subtotal = lbs.	Subtotal = lbs.	Subtotal = lbs.	Subtotal = lbs.

Exercise 4:   *Total Weight* _____ *lbs.*   *Time* _____ *mins.*   *Power Factor* _____ *lbs./min.*   *Power Index* _____

■ **Exercise:**

Weight Reps Sets	Weight Reps Sets	Weight Reps Sets	Weight Reps Sets	Weight Reps Sets	Weight Reps Sets
× ×	× ×	× ×	× ×	× ×	× ×
Subtotal = lbs.	Subtotal = lbs.	Subtotal = lbs.	Subtotal = lbs.	Subtotal = lbs.	Subtotal = lbs.

Exercise 5:   *Total Weight* _____ *lbs.*   *Time* _____ *mins.*   *Power Factor* _____ *lbs./min.*   *Power Index* _____

OVERALL WORKOUT: *Total Weight* _____ *lbs.*   *Time* _____ *mins.*   *Power Factor* _____ *lbs./min.*   *Power Index* _____

Exercise Subtotal = Weight × Reps × Sets   ■ *Power Factor = lbs./min.*   ■ *Power Index = Total Weight × Power Factor ÷ 1,000,000*

TRICEPS SPECIALIZATION WORKOUT RECORD   Date: ___ / ___ / ___

Start Time: _____   Finish Time: _____   Total Time: _____

■ **Exercise: DIP (OR CLOSE-GRIP BENCH PRESS)**

Weight Reps Sets	Weight Reps Sets	Weight Reps Sets	Weight Reps Sets	Weight Reps Sets	Weight Reps Sets
× ×	× ×	× ×	× ×	× ×	× ×
Subtotal = lbs.	Subtotal = lbs.	Subtotal = lbs.	Subtotal = lbs.	Subtotal = lbs.	Subtotal = lbs.

Exercise 1:   *Total Weight* _____ *lbs.*   *Time* _____ *mins.*   *Power Factor* _____ *lbs./min.*   *Power Index* _____

■ **Exercise: SEATED BARBELL TRICEPS EXTENSION**

Weight Reps Sets	Weight Reps Sets	Weight Reps Sets	Weight Reps Sets	Weight Reps Sets	Weight Reps Sets
× ×	× ×	× ×	× ×	× ×	× ×
Subtotal = lbs.	Subtotal = lbs.	Subtotal = lbs.	Subtotal = lbs.	Subtotal = lbs.	Subtotal = lbs.

Exercise 2:   *Total Weight* _____ *lbs.*   *Time* _____ *mins.*   *Power Factor* _____ *lbs./min.*   *Power Index* _____

■ **Exercise:**

Weight Reps Sets	Weight Reps Sets	Weight Reps Sets	Weight Reps Sets	Weight Reps Sets	Weight Reps Sets
× ×	× ×	× ×	× ×	× ×	× ×
Subtotal = lbs.	Subtotal = lbs.	Subtotal = lbs.	Subtotal = lbs.	Subtotal = lbs.	Subtotal = lbs.

Exercise 3:   *Total Weight* _____ *lbs.*   *Time* _____ *mins.*   *Power Factor* _____ *lbs./min.*   *Power Index* _____

■ **Exercise:**

Weight Reps Sets	Weight Reps Sets	Weight Reps Sets	Weight Reps Sets	Weight Reps Sets	Weight Reps Sets
× ×	× ×	× ×	× ×	× ×	× ×
Subtotal = lbs.	Subtotal = lbs.	Subtotal = lbs.	Subtotal = lbs.	Subtotal = lbs.	Subtotal = lbs.

Exercise 4:   *Total Weight* _____ *lbs.*   *Time* _____ *mins.*   *Power Factor* _____ *lbs./min.*   *Power Index* _____

■ **Exercise:**

Weight Reps Sets	Weight Reps Sets	Weight Reps Sets	Weight Reps Sets	Weight Reps Sets	Weight Reps Sets
× ×	× ×	× ×	× ×	× ×	× ×
Subtotal = lbs.	Subtotal = lbs.	Subtotal = lbs.	Subtotal = lbs.	Subtotal = lbs.	Subtotal = lbs.

Exercise 5:   *Total Weight* _____ *lbs.*   *Time* _____ *mins.*   *Power Factor* _____ *lbs./min.*   *Power Index* _____

OVERALL WORKOUT: *Total Weight* _____ *lbs.*   *Time* _____ *mins.*   *Power Factor* _____ *lbs./min.*   *Power Index* _____

Exercise Subtotal = Weight × Reps × Sets   ■ *Power Factor = lbs./min.*   ■ *Power Index = Total Weight × Power Factor ÷ 1,000,000*

TRICEPS SPECIALIZATION WORKOUT RECORD Date: ___ / ___ / ___

Start Time: _____   Finish Time: _____   Total Time: _____

▪ Exercise: DIP (OR CLOSE-GRIP BENCH PRESS)

Weight Reps Sets	Weight Reps Sets	Weight Reps Sets	Weight Reps Sets	Weight Reps Sets	Weight Reps Sets
× ×	× ×	× ×	× ×	× ×	× ×
Subtotal = lbs.	Subtotal = lbs.	Subtotal = lbs.	Subtotal = lbs.	Subtotal = lbs.	Subtotal = lbs.

Exercise 1: Total Weight _____ lbs. Time _____ mins. Power Factor _____ lbs./min. Power Index _____

▪ Exercise: SEATED BARBELL TRICEPS EXTENSION

Weight Reps Sets	Weight Reps Sets	Weight Reps Sets	Weight Reps Sets	Weight Reps Sets	Weight Reps Sets
× ×	× ×	× ×	× ×	× ×	× ×
Subtotal = lbs.	Subtotal = lbs.	Subtotal = lbs.	Subtotal = lbs.	Subtotal = lbs.	Subtotal = lbs.

Exercise 2: Total Weight _____ lbs. Time _____ mins. Power Factor _____ lbs./min. Power Index _____

▪ Exercise:

Weight Reps Sets	Weight Reps Sets	Weight Reps Sets	Weight Reps Sets	Weight Reps Sets	Weight Reps Sets
× ×	× ×	× ×	× ×	× ×	× ×
Subtotal = lbs.	Subtotal = lbs.	Subtotal = lbs.	Subtotal = lbs.	Subtotal = lbs.	Subtotal = lbs.

Exercise 3: Total Weight _____ lbs. Time _____ mins. Power Factor _____ lbs./min. Power Index _____

▪ Exercise:

Weight Reps Sets	Weight Reps Sets	Weight Reps Sets	Weight Reps Sets	Weight Reps Sets	Weight Reps Sets
× ×	× ×	× ×	× ×	× ×	× ×
Subtotal = lbs.	Subtotal = lbs.	Subtotal = lbs.	Subtotal = lbs.	Subtotal = lbs.	Subtotal = lbs.

Exercise 4: Total Weight _____ lbs. Time _____ mins. Power Factor _____ lbs./min. Power Index _____

▪ Exercise:

Weight Reps Sets	Weight Reps Sets	Weight Reps Sets	Weight Reps Sets	Weight Reps Sets	Weight Reps Sets
× ×	× ×	× ×	× ×	× ×	× ×
Subtotal = lbs.	Subtotal = lbs.	Subtotal = lbs.	Subtotal = lbs.	Subtotal = lbs.	Subtotal = lbs.

Exercise 5: Total Weight _____ lbs. Time _____ mins. Power Factor _____ lbs./min. Power Index _____

OVERALL WORKOUT: Total Weight _____ lbs. Time _____ mins. Power Factor _____ lbs./min. Power Index _____

Exercise Subtotal = Weight × Reps × Sets ▪ *Power Factor = lbs./min.* ▪ *Power Index = Total Weight × Power Factor ÷ 1,000,000*

TRICEPS SPECIALIZATION WORKOUT RECORD Date: ___ / ___ / ___

Start Time: _____   Finish Time: _____   Total Time: _____

▪ Exercise: DIP (OR CLOSE-GRIP BENCH PRESS)

Weight Reps Sets	Weight Reps Sets	Weight Reps Sets	Weight Reps Sets	Weight Reps Sets	Weight Reps Sets
× ×	× ×	× ×	× ×	× ×	× ×
Subtotal = ___ lbs.	Subtotal = ___ lbs.	Subtotal = ___ lbs.	Subtotal = ___ lbs.	Subtotal = ___ lbs.	Subtotal = ___ lbs.

Exercise 1:   *Total Weight* ___ *lbs.*   *Time* ___ *mins.*   *Power Factor* ___ *lbs./min.*   *Power Index* ___

▪ Exercise: SEATED BARBELL TRICEPS EXTENSION

Weight Reps Sets	Weight Reps Sets	Weight Reps Sets	Weight Reps Sets	Weight Reps Sets	Weight Reps Sets
× ×	× ×	× ×	× ×	× ×	× ×
Subtotal = ___ lbs.	Subtotal = ___ lbs.	Subtotal = ___ lbs.	Subtotal = ___ lbs.	Subtotal = ___ lbs.	Subtotal = ___ lbs.

Exercise 2:   *Total Weight* ___ *lbs.*   *Time* ___ *mins.*   *Power Factor* ___ *lbs./min.*   *Power Index* ___

▪ Exercise:

Weight Reps Sets	Weight Reps Sets	Weight Reps Sets	Weight Reps Sets	Weight Reps Sets	Weight Reps Sets
× ×	× ×	× ×	× ×	× ×	× ×
Subtotal = ___ lbs.	Subtotal = ___ lbs.	Subtotal = ___ lbs.	Subtotal = ___ lbs.	Subtotal = ___ lbs.	Subtotal = ___ lbs.

Exercise 3:   *Total Weight* ___ *lbs.*   *Time* ___ *mins.*   *Power Factor* ___ *lbs./min.*   *Power Index* ___

▪ Exercise:

Weight Reps Sets	Weight Reps Sets	Weight Reps Sets	Weight Reps Sets	Weight Reps Sets	Weight Reps Sets
× ×	× ×	× ×	× ×	× ×	× ×
Subtotal = ___ lbs.	Subtotal = ___ lbs.	Subtotal = ___ lbs.	Subtotal = ___ lbs.	Subtotal = ___ lbs.	Subtotal = ___ lbs.

Exercise 4:   *Total Weight* ___ *lbs.*   *Time* ___ *mins.*   *Power Factor* ___ *lbs./min.*   *Power Index* ___

▪ Exercise:

Weight Reps Sets	Weight Reps Sets	Weight Reps Sets	Weight Reps Sets	Weight Reps Sets	Weight Reps Sets
× ×	× ×	× ×	× ×	× ×	× ×
Subtotal = ___ lbs.	Subtotal = ___ lbs.	Subtotal = ___ lbs.	Subtotal = ___ lbs.	Subtotal = ___ lbs.	Subtotal = ___ lbs.

Exercise 5:   *Total Weight* ___ *lbs.*   *Time* ___ *mins.*   *Power Factor* ___ *lbs./min.*   *Power Index* ___

OVERALL WORKOUT: *Total Weight* ___ *lbs.*   *Time* ___ *mins.*   *Power Factor* ___ *lbs./min.*   *Power Index* ___

Exercise Subtotal = Weight × Reps × Sets   ▪ Power Factor = lbs./min.   ▪ Power Index = Total Weight × Power Factor ÷ 1,000,000

TRICEPS SPECIALIZATION WORKOUT RECORD Date: ___ / ___ / ___

Start Time: _____ Finish Time: _____ Total Time: _____

■ Exercise: DIP (OR CLOSE-GRIP BENCH PRESS)

Weight Reps Sets	Weight Reps Sets	Weight Reps Sets	Weight Reps Sets	Weight Reps Sets	Weight Reps Sets
× ×	× ×	× ×	× ×	× ×	× ×
Subtotal = lbs.	Subtotal = lbs.	Subtotal = lbs.	Subtotal = lbs.	Subtotal = lbs.	Subtotal = lbs.

Exercise 1:   *Total Weight _____ lbs.   Time _____ mins.   Power Factor _____ lbs./min.   Power Index _____*

■ Exercise: SEATED BARBELL TRICEPS EXTENSION

Weight Reps Sets	Weight Reps Sets	Weight Reps Sets	Weight Reps Sets	Weight Reps Sets	Weight Reps Sets
× ×	× ×	× ×	× ×	× ×	× ×
Subtotal = lbs.	Subtotal = lbs.	Subtotal = lbs.	Subtotal = lbs.	Subtotal = lbs.	Subtotal = lbs.

Exercise 2:   *Total Weight _____ lbs.   Time _____ mins.   Power Factor _____ lbs./min.   Power Index _____*

■ Exercise:

Weight Reps Sets	Weight Reps Sets	Weight Reps Sets	Weight Reps Sets	Weight Reps Sets	Weight Reps Sets
× ×	× ×	× ×	× ×	× ×	× ×
Subtotal = lbs.	Subtotal = lbs.	Subtotal = lbs.	Subtotal = lbs.	Subtotal = lbs.	Subtotal = lbs.

Exercise 3:   *Total Weight _____ lbs.   Time _____ mins.   Power Factor _____ lbs./min.   Power Index _____*

■ Exercise:

Weight Reps Sets	Weight Reps Sets	Weight Reps Sets	Weight Reps Sets	Weight Reps Sets	Weight Reps Sets
× ×	× ×	× ×	× ×	× ×	× ×
Subtotal = lbs.	Subtotal = lbs.	Subtotal = lbs.	Subtotal = lbs.	Subtotal = lbs.	Subtotal = lbs.

Exercise 4:   *Total Weight _____ lbs.   Time _____ mins.   Power Factor _____ lbs./min.   Power Index _____*

■ Exercise:

Weight Reps Sets	Weight Reps Sets	Weight Reps Sets	Weight Reps Sets	Weight Reps Sets	Weight Reps Sets
× ×	× ×	× ×	× ×	× ×	× ×
Subtotal = lbs.	Subtotal = lbs.	Subtotal = lbs.	Subtotal = lbs.	Subtotal = lbs.	Subtotal = lbs.

Exercise 5:   *Total Weight _____ lbs.   Time _____ mins.   Power Factor _____ lbs./min.   Power Index _____*

OVERALL WORKOUT: *Total Weight _____ lbs.   Time _____ mins.   Power Factor _____ lbs./min.   Power Index _____*

Exercise Subtotal = Weight × Reps × Sets   ■ *Power Factor = lbs./min.*   ■ *Power Index = Total Weight × Power Factor ÷ 1,000,000*

TRICEPS SPECIALIZATION WORKOUT RECORD Date: ___ / ___ / ___

Start Time: _____   Finish Time: _____   Total Time: _____

■ Exercise: DIP (OR CLOSE-GRIP BENCH PRESS)

Weight Reps Sets	Weight Reps Sets	Weight Reps Sets	Weight Reps Sets	Weight Reps Sets	Weight Reps Sets
× ×	× ×	× ×	× ×	× ×	× ×
Subtotal = lbs.	Subtotal = lbs.	Subtotal = lbs.	Subtotal = lbs.	Subtotal = lbs.	Subtotal = lbs.

Exercise 1:   Total Weight _____ lbs.   Time _____ mins.   Power Factor _____ lbs./min.   Power Index _____

■ Exercise: SEATED BARBELL TRICEPS EXTENSION

Weight Reps Sets	Weight Reps Sets	Weight Reps Sets	Weight Reps Sets	Weight Reps Sets	Weight Reps Sets
× ×	× ×	× ×	× ×	× ×	× ×
Subtotal = lbs.	Subtotal = lbs.	Subtotal = lbs.	Subtotal = lbs.	Subtotal = lbs.	Subtotal = lbs.

Exercise 2:   Total Weight _____ lbs.   Time _____ mins.   Power Factor _____ lbs./min.   Power Index _____

■ Exercise:

Weight Reps Sets	Weight Reps Sets	Weight Reps Sets	Weight Reps Sets	Weight Reps Sets	Weight Reps Sets
× ×	× ×	× ×	× ×	× ×	× ×
Subtotal = lbs.	Subtotal = lbs.	Subtotal = lbs.	Subtotal = lbs.	Subtotal = lbs.	Subtotal = lbs.

Exercise 3:   Total Weight _____ lbs.   Time _____ mins.   Power Factor _____ lbs./min.   Power Index _____

■ Exercise:

Weight Reps Sets	Weight Reps Sets	Weight Reps Sets	Weight Reps Sets	Weight Reps Sets	Weight Reps Sets
× ×	× ×	× ×	× ×	× ×	× ×
Subtotal = lbs.	Subtotal = lbs.	Subtotal = lbs.	Subtotal = lbs.	Subtotal = lbs.	Subtotal = lbs.

Exercise 4:   Total Weight _____ lbs.   Time _____ mins.   Power Factor _____ lbs./min.   Power Index _____

■ Exercise:

Weight Reps Sets	Weight Reps Sets	Weight Reps Sets	Weight Reps Sets	Weight Reps Sets	Weight Reps Sets
× ×	× ×	× ×	× ×	× ×	× ×
Subtotal = lbs.	Subtotal = lbs.	Subtotal = lbs.	Subtotal = lbs.	Subtotal = lbs.	Subtotal = lbs.

Exercise 5:   Total Weight _____ lbs.   Time _____ mins.   Power Factor _____ lbs./min.   Power Index _____

OVERALL WORKOUT: Total Weight _____ lbs.   Time _____ mins.   Power Factor _____ lbs./min.   Power Index _____

Exercise Subtotal = Weight × Reps × Sets   ■ *Power Factor = lbs./min.*   ■ *Power Index = Total Weight × Power Factor ÷ 1,000,000*

TRICEPS SPECIALIZATION WORKOUT RECORD Date: ___ / ___ / ___

Start Time: _____   **Finish Time:** _____   **Total Time:** _____

▪ Exercise: DIP (OR CLOSE-GRIP BENCH PRESS)

Weight Reps Sets	Weight Reps Sets	Weight Reps Sets	Weight Reps Sets	Weight Reps Sets	Weight Reps Sets
× ×	× ×	× ×	× ×	× ×	× ×
Subtotal = lbs.	Subtotal = lbs.	Subtotal = lbs.	Subtotal = lbs.	Subtotal = lbs.	Subtotal = lbs.

Exercise 1:   *Total Weight* _____ *lbs.*   *Time* _____ *mins.*   *Power Factor* _____ *lbs./min.*   *Power Index* _____

▪ Exercise: SEATED BARBELL TRICEPS EXTENSION

Weight Reps Sets	Weight Reps Sets	Weight Reps Sets	Weight Reps Sets	Weight Reps Sets	Weight Reps Sets
× ×	× ×	× ×	× ×	× ×	× ×
Subtotal = lbs.	Subtotal = lbs.	Subtotal = lbs.	Subtotal = lbs.	Subtotal = lbs.	Subtotal = lbs.

Exercise 2:   *Total Weight* _____ *lbs.*   *Time* _____ *mins.*   *Power Factor* _____ *lbs./min.*   *Power Index* _____

▪ Exercise:

Weight Reps Sets	Weight Reps Sets	Weight Reps Sets	Weight Reps Sets	Weight Reps Sets	Weight Reps Sets
× ×	× ×	× ×	× ×	× ×	× ×
Subtotal = lbs.	Subtotal = lbs.	Subtotal = lbs.	Subtotal = lbs.	Subtotal = lbs.	Subtotal = lbs.

Exercise 3:   *Total Weight* _____ *lbs.*   *Time* _____ *mins.*   *Power Factor* _____ *lbs./min.*   *Power Index* _____

▪ Exercise:

Weight Reps Sets	Weight Reps Sets	Weight Reps Sets	Weight Reps Sets	Weight Reps Sets	Weight Reps Sets
× ×	× ×	× ×	× ×	× ×	× ×
Subtotal = lbs.	Subtotal = lbs.	Subtotal = lbs.	Subtotal = lbs.	Subtotal = lbs.	Subtotal = lbs.

Exercise 4:   *Total Weight* _____ *lbs.*   *Time* _____ *mins.*   *Power Factor* _____ *lbs./min.*   *Power Index* _____

▪ Exercise:

Weight Reps Sets	Weight Reps Sets	Weight Reps Sets	Weight Reps Sets	Weight Reps Sets	Weight Reps Sets
× ×	× ×	× ×	× ×	× ×	× ×
Subtotal = lbs.	Subtotal = lbs.	Subtotal = lbs.	Subtotal = lbs.	Subtotal = lbs.	Subtotal = lbs.

Exercise 5:   *Total Weight* _____ *lbs.*   *Time* _____ *mins.*   *Power Factor* _____ *lbs./min.*   *Power Index* _____

OVERALL WORKOUT: *Total Weight* _____ *lbs.*   *Time* _____ *mins.*   *Power Factor* _____ *lbs./min.*   *Power Index* _____

Exercise Subtotal = Weight × Reps × Sets   ▪ *Power Factor = lbs./min.*   ▪ *Power Index = Total Weight × Power Factor ÷ 1,000,000*

BICEPS SPECIALIZATION WORKOUT RECORD   Date: ___ / ___ / ___

Start Time: _____   Finish Time: _____   Total Time: _____

▪ Exercise: SEATED BARBELL CURL

Weight Reps Sets	Weight Reps Sets	Weight Reps Sets	Weight Reps Sets	Weight Reps Sets	Weight Reps Sets
× ×	× ×	× ×	× ×	× ×	× ×
Subtotal = lbs.	Subtotal = lbs.	Subtotal = lbs.	Subtotal = lbs.	Subtotal = lbs.	Subtotal = lbs.

Exercise 1:   *Total Weight* _____ *lbs.*   *Time* _____ *mins.*   *Power Factor* _____ *lbs./min.*   *Power Index* _____

▪ Exercise: STANDING BARBELL CURL

Weight Reps Sets	Weight Reps Sets	Weight Reps Sets	Weight Reps Sets	Weight Reps Sets	Weight Reps Sets
× ×	× ×	× ×	× ×	× ×	× ×
Subtotal = lbs.	Subtotal = lbs.	Subtotal = lbs.	Subtotal = lbs.	Subtotal = lbs.	Subtotal = lbs.

Exercise 2:   *Total Weight* _____ *lbs.*   *Time* _____ *mins.*   *Power Factor* _____ *lbs./min.*   *Power Index* _____

▪ Exercise:

Weight Reps Sets	Weight Reps Sets	Weight Reps Sets	Weight Reps Sets	Weight Reps Sets	Weight Reps Sets
× ×	× ×	× ×	× ×	× ×	× ×
Subtotal = lbs.	Subtotal = lbs.	Subtotal = lbs.	Subtotal = lbs.	Subtotal = lbs.	Subtotal = lbs.

Exercise 3:   *Total Weight* _____ *lbs.*   *Time* _____ *mins.*   *Power Factor* _____ *lbs./min.*   *Power Index* _____

▪ Exercise:

Weight Reps Sets	Weight Reps Sets	Weight Reps Sets	Weight Reps Sets	Weight Reps Sets	Weight Reps Sets
× ×	× ×	× ×	× ×	× ×	× ×
Subtotal = lbs.	Subtotal = lbs.	Subtotal = lbs.	Subtotal = lbs.	Subtotal = lbs.	Subtotal = lbs.

Exercise 4:   *Total Weight* _____ *lbs.*   *Time* _____ *mins.*   *Power Factor* _____ *lbs./min.*   *Power Index* _____

▪ Exercise:

Weight Reps Sets	Weight Reps Sets	Weight Reps Sets	Weight Reps Sets	Weight Reps Sets	Weight Reps Sets
× ×	× ×	× ×	× ×	× ×	× ×
Subtotal = lbs.	Subtotal = lbs.	Subtotal = lbs.	Subtotal = lbs.	Subtotal = lbs.	Subtotal = lbs.

Exercise 5:   *Total Weight* _____ *lbs.*   *Time* _____ *mins.*   *Power Factor* _____ *lbs./min.*   *Power Index* _____

OVERALL WORKOUT: *Total Weight* _____ *lbs.*   *Time* _____ *mins.*   *Power Factor* _____ *lbs./min.*   *Power Index* _____

Exercise Subtotal = Weight × Reps × Sets   ▪ *Power Factor = lbs./min.*   ▪ *Power Index = Total Weight × Power Factor ÷ 1,000,000*

BICEPS SPECIALIZATION WORKOUT RECORD Date: ___ / ___ / ___

Start Time: _____   Finish Time: _____   Total Time: _____

■ Exercise: SEATED BARBELL CURL

Weight Reps Sets	Weight Reps Sets	Weight Reps Sets	Weight Reps Sets	Weight Reps Sets	Weight Reps Sets
× ×	× ×	× ×	× ×	× ×	× ×
Subtotal = lbs.	Subtotal = lbs.	Subtotal = lbs.	Subtotal = lbs.	Subtotal = lbs.	Subtotal = lbs.

Exercise 1:   *Total Weight* _____ *lbs.*   *Time* _____ *mins.*   *Power Factor* _____ *lbs./min.*   *Power Index* _____

■ Exercise: STANDING BARBELL CURL

Weight Reps Sets	Weight Reps Sets	Weight Reps Sets	Weight Reps Sets	Weight Reps Sets	Weight Reps Sets
× ×	× ×	× ×	× ×	× ×	× ×
Subtotal = lbs.	Subtotal = lbs.	Subtotal = lbs.	Subtotal = lbs.	Subtotal = lbs.	Subtotal = lbs.

Exercise 2:   *Total Weight* _____ *lbs.*   *Time* _____ *mins.*   *Power Factor* _____ *lbs./min.*   *Power Index* _____

■ Exercise:

Weight Reps Sets	Weight Reps Sets	Weight Reps Sets	Weight Reps Sets	Weight Reps Sets	Weight Reps Sets
× ×	× ×	× ×	× ×	× ×	× ×
Subtotal = lbs.	Subtotal = lbs.	Subtotal = lbs.	Subtotal = lbs.	Subtotal = lbs.	Subtotal = lbs.

Exercise 3:   *Total Weight* _____ *lbs.*   *Time* _____ *mins.*   *Power Factor* _____ *lbs./min.*   *Power Index* _____

■ Exercise:

Weight Reps Sets	Weight Reps Sets	Weight Reps Sets	Weight Reps Sets	Weight Reps Sets	Weight Reps Sets
× ×	× ×	× ×	× ×	× ×	× ×
Subtotal = lbs.	Subtotal = lbs.	Subtotal = lbs.	Subtotal = lbs.	Subtotal = lbs.	Subtotal = lbs.

Exercise 4:   *Total Weight* _____ *lbs.*   *Time* _____ *mins.*   *Power Factor* _____ *lbs./min.*   *Power Index* _____

■ Exercise:

Weight Reps Sets	Weight Reps Sets	Weight Reps Sets	Weight Reps Sets	Weight Reps Sets	Weight Reps Sets
× ×	× ×	× ×	× ×	× ×	× ×
Subtotal = lbs.	Subtotal = lbs.	Subtotal = lbs.	Subtotal = lbs.	Subtotal = lbs.	Subtotal = lbs.

Exercise 5:   *Total Weight* _____ *lbs.*   *Time* _____ *mins.*   *Power Factor* _____ *lbs./min.*   *Power Index* _____

OVERALL WORKOUT: *Total Weight* _____ *lbs.*   *Time* _____ *mins.*   *Power Factor* _____ *lbs./min.*   *Power Index* _____

Exercise Subtotal = Weight × Reps × Sets   ■ *Power Factor = lbs./min.*   ■ *Power Index = Total Weight × Power Factor ÷ 1,000,000*

BICEPS SPECIALIZATION WORKOUT RECORD   Date: ___ / ___ / ___

Start Time: _____   **Finish Time:** _____   **Total Time:** _____

■ Exercise: SEATED BARBELL CURL

Weight Reps Sets	Weight Reps Sets	Weight Reps Sets	Weight Reps Sets	Weight Reps Sets	Weight Reps Sets
× ×	× ×	× ×	× ×	× ×	× ×
Subtotal = lbs.	Subtotal = lbs.	Subtotal = lbs.	Subtotal = lbs.	Subtotal = lbs.	Subtotal = lbs.

Exercise 1:   *Total Weight* _____ *lbs.*   *Time* _____ *mins.*   *Power Factor* _____ *lbs./min.*   *Power Index* _____

■ Exercise: STANDING BARBELL CURL

Weight Reps Sets	Weight Reps Sets	Weight Reps Sets	Weight Reps Sets	Weight Reps Sets	Weight Reps Sets
× ×	× ×	× ×	× ×	× ×	× ×
Subtotal = lbs.	Subtotal = lbs.	Subtotal = lbs.	Subtotal = lbs.	Subtotal = lbs.	Subtotal = lbs.

Exercise 2:   *Total Weight* _____ *lbs.*   *Time* _____ *mins.*   *Power Factor* _____ *lbs./min.*   *Power Index* _____

■ Exercise:

Weight Reps Sets	Weight Reps Sets	Weight Reps Sets	Weight Reps Sets	Weight Reps Sets	Weight Reps Sets
× ×	× ×	× ×	× ×	× ×	× ×
Subtotal = lbs.	Subtotal = lbs.	Subtotal = lbs.	Subtotal = lbs.	Subtotal = lbs.	Subtotal = lbs.

Exercise 3:   *Total Weight* _____ *lbs.*   *Time* _____ *mins.*   *Power Factor* _____ *lbs./min.*   *Power Index* _____

■ Exercise:

Weight Reps Sets	Weight Reps Sets	Weight Reps Sets	Weight Reps Sets	Weight Reps Sets	Weight Reps Sets
× ×	× ×	× ×	× ×	× ×	× ×
Subtotal = lbs.	Subtotal = lbs.	Subtotal = lbs.	Subtotal = lbs.	Subtotal = lbs.	Subtotal = lbs.

Exercise 4:   *Total Weight* _____ *lbs.*   *Time* _____ *mins.*   *Power Factor* _____ *lbs./min.*   *Power Index* _____

■ Exercise:

Weight Reps Sets	Weight Reps Sets	Weight Reps Sets	Weight Reps Sets	Weight Reps Sets	Weight Reps Sets
× ×	× ×	× ×	× ×	× ×	× ×
Subtotal = lbs.	Subtotal = lbs.	Subtotal = lbs.	Subtotal = lbs.	Subtotal = lbs.	Subtotal = lbs.

Exercise 5:   *Total Weight* _____ *lbs.*   *Time* _____ *mins.*   *Power Factor* _____ *lbs./min.*   *Power Index* _____

OVERALL WORKOUT: *Total Weight* _____ *lbs.*   *Time* _____ *mins.*   *Power Factor* _____ *lbs./min.*   *Power Index* _____

Exercise Subtotal = Weight × Reps × Sets   ■ *Power Factor = lbs./min.*   ■ *Power Index = Total Weight × Power Factor ÷ 1,000,000*

BICEPS SPECIALIZATION WORKOUT RECORD   Date: ___ / ___ / ___

Start Time: _____   **Finish Time:** _____   **Total Time:** _____

■ Exercise: SEATED BARBELL CURL

Weight Reps Sets	Weight Reps Sets	Weight Reps Sets	Weight Reps Sets	Weight Reps Sets	Weight Reps Sets
× ×	× ×	× ×	× ×	× ×	× ×
Subtotal = lbs.	Subtotal = lbs.	Subtotal = lbs.	Subtotal = lbs.	Subtotal = lbs.	Subtotal = lbs.

Exercise 1:   *Total Weight* _____ *lbs.*   *Time* _____ *mins.*   *Power Factor* _____ *lbs./min.*   *Power Index* _____

■ Exercise: STANDING BARBELL CURL

Weight Reps Sets	Weight Reps Sets	Weight Reps Sets	Weight Reps Sets	Weight Reps Sets	Weight Reps Sets
× ×	× ×	× ×	× ×	× ×	× ×
Subtotal = lbs.	Subtotal = lbs.	Subtotal = lbs.	Subtotal = lbs.	Subtotal = lbs.	Subtotal = lbs.

Exercise 2:   *Total Weight* _____ *lbs.*   *Time* _____ *mins.*   *Power Factor* _____ *lbs./min.*   *Power Index* _____

■ Exercise:

Weight Reps Sets	Weight Reps Sets	Weight Reps Sets	Weight Reps Sets	Weight Reps Sets	Weight Reps Sets
× ×	× ×	× ×	× ×	× ×	× ×
Subtotal = lbs.	Subtotal = lbs.	Subtotal = lbs.	Subtotal = lbs.	Subtotal = lbs.	Subtotal = lbs.

Exercise 3:   *Total Weight* _____ *lbs.*   *Time* _____ *mins.*   *Power Factor* _____ *lbs./min.*   *Power Index* _____

■ Exercise:

Weight Reps Sets	Weight Reps Sets	Weight Reps Sets	Weight Reps Sets	Weight Reps Sets	Weight Reps Sets
× ×	× ×	× ×	× ×	× ×	× ×
Subtotal = lbs.	Subtotal = lbs.	Subtotal = lbs.	Subtotal = lbs.	Subtotal = lbs.	Subtotal = lbs.

Exercise 4:   *Total Weight* _____ *lbs.*   *Time* _____ *mins.*   *Power Factor* _____ *lbs./min.*   *Power Index* _____

■ Exercise:

Weight Reps Sets	Weight Reps Sets	Weight Reps Sets	Weight Reps Sets	Weight Reps Sets	Weight Reps Sets
× ×	× ×	× ×	× ×	× ×	× ×
Subtotal = lbs.	Subtotal = lbs.	Subtotal = lbs.	Subtotal = lbs.	Subtotal = lbs.	Subtotal = lbs.

Exercise 5:   *Total Weight* _____ *lbs.*   *Time* _____ *mins.*   *Power Factor* _____ *lbs./min.*   *Power Index* _____

OVERALL WORKOUT: *Total Weight* _____ *lbs.*   *Time* _____ *mins.*   *Power Factor* _____ *lbs./min.*   *Power Index* _____

Exercise Subtotal = Weight × Reps × Sets   ■ *Power Factor = lbs./min.*   ■ *Power Index = Total Weight × Power Factor ÷ 1,000,000*

BICEPS SPECIALIZATION WORKOUT RECORD Date: ___ / ___ / ___

Start Time: _____   Finish Time: _____   Total Time: _____

■ Exercise: SEATED BARBELL CURL

Weight Reps Sets	Weight Reps Sets	Weight Reps Sets	Weight Reps Sets	Weight Reps Sets	Weight Reps Sets
× ×	× ×	× ×	× ×	× ×	× ×
Subtotal = lbs.	Subtotal = lbs.	Subtotal = lbs.	Subtotal = lbs.	Subtotal = lbs.	Subtotal = lbs.

Exercise 1:   *Total Weight _____ lbs.   Time _____ mins.   Power Factor _____ lbs./min.   Power Index _____*

■ Exercise: STANDING BARBELL CURL

Weight Reps Sets	Weight Reps Sets	Weight Reps Sets	Weight Reps Sets	Weight Reps Sets	Weight Reps Sets
× ×	× ×	× ×	× ×	× ×	× ×
Subtotal = lbs.	Subtotal = lbs.	Subtotal = lbs.	Subtotal = lbs.	Subtotal = lbs.	Subtotal = lbs.

Exercise 2:   *Total Weight _____ lbs.   Time _____ mins.   Power Factor _____ lbs./min.   Power Index _____*

■ Exercise:

Weight Reps Sets	Weight Reps Sets	Weight Reps Sets	Weight Reps Sets	Weight Reps Sets	Weight Reps Sets
× ×	× ×	× ×	× ×	× ×	× ×
Subtotal = lbs.	Subtotal = lbs.	Subtotal = lbs.	Subtotal = lbs.	Subtotal = lbs.	Subtotal = lbs.

Exercise 3:   *Total Weight _____ lbs.   Time _____ mins.   Power Factor _____ lbs./min.   Power Index _____*

■ Exercise:

Weight Reps Sets	Weight Reps Sets	Weight Reps Sets	Weight Reps Sets	Weight Reps Sets	Weight Reps Sets
× ×	× ×	× ×	× ×	× ×	× ×
Subtotal = lbs.	Subtotal = lbs.	Subtotal = lbs.	Subtotal = lbs.	Subtotal = lbs.	Subtotal = lbs.

Exercise 4:   *Total Weight _____ lbs.   Time _____ mins.   Power Factor _____ lbs./min.   Power Index _____*

■ Exercise:

Weight Reps Sets	Weight Reps Sets	Weight Reps Sets	Weight Reps Sets	Weight Reps Sets	Weight Reps Sets
× ×	× ×	× ×	× ×	× ×	× ×
Subtotal = lbs.	Subtotal = lbs.	Subtotal = lbs.	Subtotal = lbs.	Subtotal = lbs.	Subtotal = lbs.

Exercise 5:   *Total Weight _____ lbs.   Time _____ mins.   Power Factor _____ lbs./min.   Power Index _____*

OVERALL WORKOUT: *Total Weight _____ lbs.   Time _____ mins.   Power Factor _____ lbs./min.   Power Index _____*

Exercise Subtotal = Weight × Reps × Sets   ■ *Power Factor = lbs./min.*   ■ *Power Index = Total Weight × Power Factor ÷ 1,000,000*

BICEPS SPECIALIZATION WORKOUT RECORD   Date: ____ / ____ / ____

Start Time: _____   **Finish Time:** _____   **Total Time:** _____

■ **Exercise: SEATED BARBELL CURL**

Weight Reps Sets	Weight Reps Sets	Weight Reps Sets	Weight Reps Sets	Weight Reps Sets	Weight Reps Sets
× ×	× ×	× ×	× ×	× ×	× ×
Subtotal = lbs.	Subtotal = lbs.	Subtotal = lbs.	Subtotal = lbs.	Subtotal = lbs.	Subtotal = lbs.

Exercise 1:   *Total Weight* _____ *lbs.   Time* _____ *mins.   Power Factor* _____ *lbs./min.   Power Index* _____

■ **Exercise: STANDING BARBELL CURL**

Weight Reps Sets	Weight Reps Sets	Weight Reps Sets	Weight Reps Sets	Weight Reps Sets	Weight Reps Sets
× ×	× ×	× ×	× ×	× ×	× ×
Subtotal = lbs.	Subtotal = lbs.	Subtotal = lbs.	Subtotal = lbs.	Subtotal = lbs.	Subtotal = lbs.

Exercise 2:   *Total Weight* _____ *lbs.   Time* _____ *mins.   Power Factor* _____ *lbs./min.   Power Index* _____

■ **Exercise:**

Weight Reps Sets	Weight Reps Sets	Weight Reps Sets	Weight Reps Sets	Weight Reps Sets	Weight Reps Sets
× ×	× ×	× ×	× ×	× ×	× ×
Subtotal = lbs.	Subtotal = lbs.	Subtotal = lbs.	Subtotal = lbs.	Subtotal = lbs.	Subtotal = lbs.

Exercise 3:   *Total Weight* _____ *lbs.   Time* _____ *mins.   Power Factor* _____ *lbs./min.   Power Index* _____

■ **Exercise:**

Weight Reps Sets	Weight Reps Sets	Weight Reps Sets	Weight Reps Sets	Weight Reps Sets	Weight Reps Sets
× ×	× ×	× ×	× ×	× ×	× ×
Subtotal = lbs.	Subtotal = lbs.	Subtotal = lbs.	Subtotal = lbs.	Subtotal = lbs.	Subtotal = lbs.

Exercise 4:   *Total Weight* _____ *lbs.   Time* _____ *mins.   Power Factor* _____ *lbs./min.   Power Index* _____

■ **Exercise:**

Weight Reps Sets	Weight Reps Sets	Weight Reps Sets	Weight Reps Sets	Weight Reps Sets	Weight Reps Sets
× ×	× ×	× ×	× ×	× ×	× ×
Subtotal = lbs.	Subtotal = lbs.	Subtotal = lbs.	Subtotal = lbs.	Subtotal = lbs.	Subtotal = lbs.

Exercise 5:   *Total Weight* _____ *lbs.   Time* _____ *mins.   Power Factor* _____ *lbs./min.   Power Index* _____

OVERALL WORKOUT: *Total Weight* _____ *lbs.   Time* _____ *mins.   Power Factor* _____ *lbs./min.   Power Index* _____

Exercise Subtotal = Weight × Reps × Sets   ■ *Power Factor = lbs./min.*   ■ *Power Index = Total Weight × Power Factor ÷ 1,000,000*

BICEPS SPECIALIZATION WORKOUT RECORD   Date: ___ / ___ / ___

Start Time: _____   Finish Time: _____   Total Time: _____

■ Exercise: SEATED BARBELL CURL

Weight Reps Sets	Weight Reps Sets	Weight Reps Sets	Weight Reps Sets	Weight Reps Sets	Weight Reps Sets
× ×	× ×	× ×	× ×	× ×	× ×
Subtotal = lbs.	Subtotal = lbs.	Subtotal = lbs.	Subtotal = lbs.	Subtotal = lbs.	Subtotal = lbs.

Exercise 1:   *Total Weight _____ lbs.   Time _____ mins.   Power Factor _____ lbs./min.   Power Index _____*

■ Exercise: STANDING BARBELL CURL

Weight Reps Sets	Weight Reps Sets	Weight Reps Sets	Weight Reps Sets	Weight Reps Sets	Weight Reps Sets
× ×	× ×	× ×	× ×	× ×	× ×
Subtotal = lbs.	Subtotal = lbs.	Subtotal = lbs.	Subtotal = lbs.	Subtotal = lbs.	Subtotal = lbs.

Exercise 2:   *Total Weight _____ lbs.   Time _____ mins.   Power Factor _____ lbs./min.   Power Index _____*

■ Exercise:

Weight Reps Sets	Weight Reps Sets	Weight Reps Sets	Weight Reps Sets	Weight Reps Sets	Weight Reps Sets
× ×	× ×	× ×	× ×	× ×	× ×
Subtotal = lbs.	Subtotal = lbs.	Subtotal = lbs.	Subtotal = lbs.	Subtotal = lbs.	Subtotal = lbs.

Exercise 3:   *Total Weight _____ lbs.   Time _____ mins.   Power Factor _____ lbs./min.   Power Index _____*

■ Exercise:

Weight Reps Sets	Weight Reps Sets	Weight Reps Sets	Weight Reps Sets	Weight Reps Sets	Weight Reps Sets
× ×	× ×	× ×	× ×	× ×	× ×
Subtotal = lbs.	Subtotal = lbs.	Subtotal = lbs.	Subtotal = lbs.	Subtotal = lbs.	Subtotal = lbs.

Exercise 4:   *Total Weight _____ lbs.   Time _____ mins.   Power Factor _____ lbs./min.   Power Index _____*

■ Exercise:

Weight Reps Sets	Weight Reps Sets	Weight Reps Sets	Weight Reps Sets	Weight Reps Sets	Weight Reps Sets
× ×	× ×	× ×	× ×	× ×	× ×
Subtotal = lbs.	Subtotal = lbs.	Subtotal = lbs.	Subtotal = lbs.	Subtotal = lbs.	Subtotal = lbs.

Exercise 5:   *Total Weight _____ lbs.   Time _____ mins.   Power Factor _____ lbs./min.   Power Index _____*

OVERALL WORKOUT: *Total Weight _____ lbs.   Time _____ mins.   Power Factor _____ lbs./min.   Power Index _____*

Exercise Subtotal = Weight × Reps × Sets   ■ *Power Factor = lbs./min.*   ■ *Power Index = Total Weight × Power Factor ÷ 1,000,000*

BICEPS SPECIALIZATION WORKOUT RECORD   Date: ___ / ___ / ___

Start Time: _____   Finish Time: _____   Total Time: _____

▪ Exercise: SEATED BARBELL CURL

Weight Reps Sets	Weight Reps Sets	Weight Reps Sets	Weight Reps Sets	Weight Reps Sets	Weight Reps Sets
× ×	× ×	× ×	× ×	× ×	× ×
Subtotal = lbs.	Subtotal = lbs.	Subtotal = lbs.	Subtotal = lbs.	Subtotal = lbs.	Subtotal = lbs.

Exercise 1:   *Total Weight _____ lbs.   Time _____ mins.   Power Factor _____ lbs./min.   Power Index _____*

▪ Exercise: STANDING BARBELL CURL

Weight Reps Sets	Weight Reps Sets	Weight Reps Sets	Weight Reps Sets	Weight Reps Sets	Weight Reps Sets
× ×	× ×	× ×	× ×	× ×	× ×
Subtotal = lbs.	Subtotal = lbs.	Subtotal = lbs.	Subtotal = lbs.	Subtotal = lbs.	Subtotal = lbs.

Exercise 2:   *Total Weight _____ lbs.   Time _____ mins.   Power Factor _____ lbs./min.   Power Index _____*

▪ Exercise:

Weight Reps Sets	Weight Reps Sets	Weight Reps Sets	Weight Reps Sets	Weight Reps Sets	Weight Reps Sets
× ×	× ×	× ×	× ×	× ×	× ×
Subtotal = lbs.	Subtotal = lbs.	Subtotal = lbs.	Subtotal = lbs.	Subtotal = lbs.	Subtotal = lbs.

Exercise 3:   *Total Weight _____ lbs.   Time _____ mins.   Power Factor _____ lbs./min.   Power Index _____*

▪ Exercise:

Weight Reps Sets	Weight Reps Sets	Weight Reps Sets	Weight Reps Sets	Weight Reps Sets	Weight Reps Sets
× ×	× ×	× ×	× ×	× ×	× ×
Subtotal = lbs.	Subtotal = lbs.	Subtotal = lbs.	Subtotal = lbs.	Subtotal = lbs.	Subtotal = lbs.

Exercise 4:   *Total Weight _____ lbs.   Time _____ mins.   Power Factor _____ lbs./min.   Power Index _____*

▪ Exercise:

Weight Reps Sets	Weight Reps Sets	Weight Reps Sets	Weight Reps Sets	Weight Reps Sets	Weight Reps Sets
× ×	× ×	× ×	× ×	× ×	× ×
Subtotal = lbs.	Subtotal = lbs.	Subtotal = lbs.	Subtotal = lbs.	Subtotal = lbs.	Subtotal = lbs.

Exercise 5:   *Total Weight _____ lbs.   Time _____ mins.   Power Factor _____ lbs./min.   Power Index _____*

OVERALL WORKOUT: *Total Weight _____ lbs.   Time _____ mins.   Power Factor _____ lbs./min.   Power Index _____*

Exercise Subtotal = Weight × Reps × Sets   ▪ *Power Factor = lbs./min.*   ▪ *Power Index = Total Weight × Power Factor ÷ 1,000,000*

BICEPS SPECIALIZATION WORKOUT RECORD   Date: ___ / ___ / ___

Start Time: _____   Finish Time: _____   Total Time: _____

▪ Exercise: SEATED BARBELL CURL

Weight Reps Sets	Weight Reps Sets	Weight Reps Sets	Weight Reps Sets	Weight Reps Sets	Weight Reps Sets
× ×	× ×	× ×	× ×	× ×	× ×
Subtotal = lbs.	Subtotal = lbs.	Subtotal = lbs.	Subtotal = lbs.	Subtotal = lbs.	Subtotal = lbs.

Exercise 1:   *Total Weight* _____ *lbs.*   *Time* _____ *mins.*   *Power Factor* _____ *lbs./min.*   *Power Index* _____

▪ Exercise: STANDING BARBELL CURL

Weight Reps Sets	Weight Reps Sets	Weight Reps Sets	Weight Reps Sets	Weight Reps Sets	Weight Reps Sets
× ×	× ×	× ×	× ×	× ×	× ×
Subtotal = lbs.	Subtotal = lbs.	Subtotal = lbs.	Subtotal = lbs.	Subtotal = lbs.	Subtotal = lbs.

Exercise 2:   *Total Weight* _____ *lbs.*   *Time* _____ *mins.*   *Power Factor* _____ *lbs./min.*   *Power Index* _____

▪ Exercise:

Weight Reps Sets	Weight Reps Sets	Weight Reps Sets	Weight Reps Sets	Weight Reps Sets	Weight Reps Sets
× ×	× ×	× ×	× ×	× ×	× ×
Subtotal = lbs.	Subtotal = lbs.	Subtotal = lbs.	Subtotal = lbs.	Subtotal = lbs.	Subtotal = lbs.

Exercise 3:   *Total Weight* _____ *lbs.*   *Time* _____ *mins.*   *Power Factor* _____ *lbs./min.*   *Power Index* _____

▪ Exercise:

Weight Reps Sets	Weight Reps Sets	Weight Reps Sets	Weight Reps Sets	Weight Reps Sets	Weight Reps Sets
× ×	× ×	× ×	× ×	× ×	× ×
Subtotal = lbs.	Subtotal = lbs.	Subtotal = lbs.	Subtotal = lbs.	Subtotal = lbs.	Subtotal = lbs.

Exercise 4:   *Total Weight* _____ *lbs.*   *Time* _____ *mins.*   *Power Factor* _____ *lbs./min.*   *Power Index* _____

▪ Exercise:

Weight Reps Sets	Weight Reps Sets	Weight Reps Sets	Weight Reps Sets	Weight Reps Sets	Weight Reps Sets
× ×	× ×	× ×	× ×	× ×	× ×
Subtotal = lbs.	Subtotal = lbs.	Subtotal = lbs.	Subtotal = lbs.	Subtotal = lbs.	Subtotal = lbs.

Exercise 5:   *Total Weight* _____ *lbs.*   *Time* _____ *mins.*   *Power Factor* _____ *lbs./min.*   *Power Index* _____

OVERALL WORKOUT: *Total Weight* _____ *lbs.*   *Time* _____ *mins.*   *Power Factor* _____ *lbs./min.*   *Power Index* _____

Exercise Subtotal = Weight × Reps × Sets   ▪ *Power Factor = lbs./min.*   ▪ *Power Index = Total Weight × Power Factor ÷ 1,000,000*

BICEPS SPECIALIZATION WORKOUT RECORD Date: ___ / ___ / ___

Start Time: _____   Finish Time: _____   Total Time: _____

■ Exercise: SEATED BARBELL CURL

Weight Reps Sets	Weight Reps Sets	Weight Reps Sets	Weight Reps Sets	Weight Reps Sets	Weight Reps Sets
× ×	× ×	× ×	× ×	× ×	× ×
Subtotal = lbs.	Subtotal = lbs.	Subtotal = lbs.	Subtotal = lbs.	Subtotal = lbs.	Subtotal = lbs.

Exercise 1:   *Total Weight _____ lbs.*   *Time _____ mins.*   *Power Factor _____ lbs./min.*   *Power Index _____*

■ Exercise: STANDING BARBELL CURL

Weight Reps Sets	Weight Reps Sets	Weight Reps Sets	Weight Reps Sets	Weight Reps Sets	Weight Reps Sets
× ×	× ×	× ×	× ×	× ×	× ×
Subtotal = lbs.	Subtotal = lbs.	Subtotal = lbs.	Subtotal = lbs.	Subtotal = lbs.	Subtotal = lbs.

Exercise 2:   *Total Weight _____ lbs.*   *Time _____ mins.*   *Power Factor _____ lbs./min.*   *Power Index _____*

■ Exercise:

Weight Reps Sets	Weight Reps Sets	Weight Reps Sets	Weight Reps Sets	Weight Reps Sets	Weight Reps Sets
× ×	× ×	× ×	× ×	× ×	× ×
Subtotal = lbs.	Subtotal = lbs.	Subtotal = lbs.	Subtotal = lbs.	Subtotal = lbs.	Subtotal = lbs.

Exercise 3:   *Total Weight _____ lbs.*   *Time _____ mins.*   *Power Factor _____ lbs./min.*   *Power Index _____*

■ Exercise:

Weight Reps Sets	Weight Reps Sets	Weight Reps Sets	Weight Reps Sets	Weight Reps Sets	Weight Reps Sets
× ×	× ×	× ×	× ×	× ×	× ×
Subtotal = lbs.	Subtotal = lbs.	Subtotal = lbs.	Subtotal = lbs.	Subtotal = lbs.	Subtotal = lbs.

Exercise 4:   *Total Weight _____ lbs.*   *Time _____ mins.*   *Power Factor _____ lbs./min.*   *Power Index _____*

■ Exercise:

Weight Reps Sets	Weight Reps Sets	Weight Reps Sets	Weight Reps Sets	Weight Reps Sets	Weight Reps Sets
× ×	× ×	× ×	× ×	× ×	× ×
Subtotal = lbs.	Subtotal = lbs.	Subtotal = lbs.	Subtotal = lbs.	Subtotal = lbs.	Subtotal = lbs.

Exercise 5:   *Total Weight _____ lbs.*   *Time _____ mins.*   *Power Factor _____ lbs./min.*   *Power Index _____*

OVERALL WORKOUT: *Total Weight _____ lbs.*   *Time _____ mins.*   *Power Factor _____ lbs./min.*   *Power Index _____*

Exercise Subtotal = Weight × Reps × Sets   ■ *Power Factor = lbs./min.*   ■ *Power Index = Total Weight × Power Factor ÷ 1,000,000*

BICEPS SPECIALIZATION WORKOUT RECORD   Date: ___ / ___ / ___

Start Time: _____   **Finish Time:** _____   **Total Time:** _____

■ Exercise: SEATED BARBELL CURL

Weight Reps Sets	Weight Reps Sets	Weight Reps Sets	Weight Reps Sets	Weight Reps Sets	Weight Reps Sets
× ×	× ×	× ×	× ×	× ×	× ×
Subtotal = lbs.	Subtotal = lbs.	Subtotal = lbs.	Subtotal = lbs.	Subtotal = lbs.	Subtotal = lbs.

Exercise 1:   *Total Weight _____ lbs.   Time _____ mins.   Power Factor _____ lbs./min.   Power Index _____*

■ Exercise: STANDING BARBELL CURL

Weight Reps Sets	Weight Reps Sets	Weight Reps Sets	Weight Reps Sets	Weight Reps Sets	Weight Reps Sets
× ×	× ×	× ×	× ×	× ×	× ×
Subtotal = lbs.	Subtotal = lbs.	Subtotal = lbs.	Subtotal = lbs.	Subtotal = lbs.	Subtotal = lbs.

Exercise 2:   *Total Weight _____ lbs.   Time _____ mins.   Power Factor _____ lbs./min.   Power Index _____*

■ Exercise:

Weight Reps Sets	Weight Reps Sets	Weight Reps Sets	Weight Reps Sets	Weight Reps Sets	Weight Reps Sets
× ×	× ×	× ×	× ×	× ×	× ×
Subtotal = lbs.	Subtotal = lbs.	Subtotal = lbs.	Subtotal = lbs.	Subtotal = lbs.	Subtotal = lbs.

Exercise 3:   *Total Weight _____ lbs.   Time _____ mins.   Power Factor _____ lbs./min.   Power Index _____*

■ Exercise:

Weight Reps Sets	Weight Reps Sets	Weight Reps Sets	Weight Reps Sets	Weight Reps Sets	Weight Reps Sets
× ×	× ×	× ×	× ×	× ×	× ×
Subtotal = lbs.	Subtotal = lbs.	Subtotal = lbs.	Subtotal = lbs.	Subtotal = lbs.	Subtotal = lbs.

Exercise 4:   *Total Weight _____ lbs.   Time _____ mins.   Power Factor _____ lbs./min.   Power Index _____*

■ Exercise:

Weight Reps Sets	Weight Reps Sets	Weight Reps Sets	Weight Reps Sets	Weight Reps Sets	Weight Reps Sets
× ×	× ×	× ×	× ×	× ×	× ×
Subtotal = lbs.	Subtotal = lbs.	Subtotal = lbs.	Subtotal = lbs.	Subtotal = lbs.	Subtotal = lbs.

Exercise 5:   *Total Weight _____ lbs.   Time _____ mins.   Power Factor _____ lbs./min.   Power Index _____*

OVERALL WORKOUT: *Total Weight _____ lbs.   Time _____ mins.   Power Factor _____ lbs./min.   Power Index _____*

Exercise Subtotal = Weight × Reps × Sets   ■ Power Factor = lbs./min.   ■ Power Index = Total Weight × Power Factor ÷ 1,000,000

BICEPS SPECIALIZATION WORKOUT RECORD   Date: ____ / ____ / ____

Start Time: _____   Finish Time: _____   Total Time: _____

■ Exercise: SEATED BARBELL CURL

Weight Reps Sets	Weight Reps Sets	Weight Reps Sets	Weight Reps Sets	Weight Reps Sets	Weight Reps Sets
× ×	× ×	× ×	× ×	× ×	× ×
Subtotal = lbs.	Subtotal = lbs.	Subtotal = lbs.	Subtotal = lbs.	Subtotal = lbs.	Subtotal = lbs.

Exercise 1:   *Total Weight* _____ *lbs.*   *Time* _____ *mins.*   *Power Factor* _____ *lbs./min.*   *Power Index* _____

■ Exercise: STANDING BARBELL CURL

Weight Reps Sets	Weight Reps Sets	Weight Reps Sets	Weight Reps Sets	Weight Reps Sets	Weight Reps Sets
× ×	× ×	× ×	× ×	× ×	× ×
Subtotal = lbs.	Subtotal = lbs.	Subtotal = lbs.	Subtotal = lbs.	Subtotal = lbs.	Subtotal = lbs.

Exercise 2:   *Total Weight* _____ *lbs.*   *Time* _____ *mins.*   *Power Factor* _____ *lbs./min.*   *Power Index* _____

■ Exercise:

Weight Reps Sets	Weight Reps Sets	Weight Reps Sets	Weight Reps Sets	Weight Reps Sets	Weight Reps Sets
× ×	× ×	× ×	× ×	× ×	× ×
Subtotal = lbs.	Subtotal = lbs.	Subtotal = lbs.	Subtotal = lbs.	Subtotal = lbs.	Subtotal = lbs.

Exercise 3:   *Total Weight* _____ *lbs.*   *Time* _____ *mins.*   *Power Factor* _____ *lbs./min.*   *Power Index* _____

■ Exercise:

Weight Reps Sets	Weight Reps Sets	Weight Reps Sets	Weight Reps Sets	Weight Reps Sets	Weight Reps Sets
× ×	× ×	× ×	× ×	× ×	× ×
Subtotal = lbs.	Subtotal = lbs.	Subtotal = lbs.	Subtotal = lbs.	Subtotal = lbs.	Subtotal = lbs.

Exercise 4:   *Total Weight* _____ *lbs.*   *Time* _____ *mins.*   *Power Factor* _____ *lbs./min.*   *Power Index* _____

■ Exercise:

Weight Reps Sets	Weight Reps Sets	Weight Reps Sets	Weight Reps Sets	Weight Reps Sets	Weight Reps Sets
× ×	× ×	× ×	× ×	× ×	× ×
Subtotal = lbs.	Subtotal = lbs.	Subtotal = lbs.	Subtotal = lbs.	Subtotal = lbs.	Subtotal = lbs.

Exercise 5:   *Total Weight* _____ *lbs.*   *Time* _____ *mins.*   *Power Factor* _____ *lbs./min.*   *Power Index* _____

OVERALL WORKOUT: *Total Weight* _____ *lbs.*   *Time* _____ *mins.*   *Power Factor* _____ *lbs./min.*   *Power Index* _____

Exercise Subtotal = Weight × Reps × Sets   ■ *Power Factor = lbs./min.*   ■ *Power Index = Total Weight × Power Factor ÷ 1,000,000*

BICEPS SPECIALIZATION WORKOUT RECORD   Date: ____ / ____ / ____

Start Time: _____   **Finish Time:** _____   **Total Time:** _____

■ **Exercise: SEATED BARBELL CURL**

Weight Reps Sets	Weight Reps Sets	Weight Reps Sets	Weight Reps Sets	Weight Reps Sets	Weight Reps Sets
× ×	× ×	× ×	× ×	× ×	× ×
Subtotal = lbs.	Subtotal = lbs.	Subtotal = lbs.	Subtotal = lbs.	Subtotal = lbs.	Subtotal = lbs.

Exercise 1:   *Total Weight* _____ *lbs.*   *Time* _____ *mins.*   *Power Factor* _____ *lbs./min.*   *Power Index* _____

■ **Exercise: STANDING BARBELL CURL**

Weight Reps Sets	Weight Reps Sets	Weight Reps Sets	Weight Reps Sets	Weight Reps Sets	Weight Reps Sets
× ×	× ×	× ×	× ×	× ×	× ×
Subtotal = lbs.	Subtotal = lbs.	Subtotal = lbs.	Subtotal = lbs.	Subtotal = lbs.	Subtotal = lbs.

Exercise 2:   *Total Weight* _____ *lbs.*   *Time* _____ *mins.*   *Power Factor* _____ *lbs./min.*   *Power Index* _____

■ **Exercise:**

Weight Reps Sets	Weight Reps Sets	Weight Reps Sets	Weight Reps Sets	Weight Reps Sets	Weight Reps Sets
× ×	× ×	× ×	× ×	× ×	× ×
Subtotal = lbs.	Subtotal = lbs.	Subtotal = lbs.	Subtotal = lbs.	Subtotal = lbs.	Subtotal = lbs.

Exercise 3:   *Total Weight* _____ *lbs.*   *Time* _____ *mins.*   *Power Factor* _____ *lbs./min.*   *Power Index* _____

■ **Exercise:**

Weight Reps Sets	Weight Reps Sets	Weight Reps Sets	Weight Reps Sets	Weight Reps Sets	Weight Reps Sets
× ×	× ×	× ×	× ×	× ×	× ×
Subtotal = lbs.	Subtotal = lbs.	Subtotal = lbs.	Subtotal = lbs.	Subtotal = lbs.	Subtotal = lbs.

Exercise 4:   *Total Weight* _____ *lbs.*   *Time* _____ *mins.*   *Power Factor* _____ *lbs./min.*   *Power Index* _____

■ **Exercise:**

Weight Reps Sets	Weight Reps Sets	Weight Reps Sets	Weight Reps Sets	Weight Reps Sets	Weight Reps Sets
× ×	× ×	× ×	× ×	× ×	× ×
Subtotal = lbs.	Subtotal = lbs.	Subtotal = lbs.	Subtotal = lbs.	Subtotal = lbs.	Subtotal = lbs.

Exercise 5:   *Total Weight* _____ *lbs.*   *Time* _____ *mins.*   *Power Factor* _____ *lbs./min.*   *Power Index* _____

OVERALL WORKOUT: *Total Weight* _____ *lbs.*   *Time* _____ *mins.*   *Power Factor* _____ *lbs./min.*   *Power Index* _____

Exercise Subtotal = Weight × Reps × Sets   ■ *Power Factor = lbs./min.*   ■ *Power Index = Total Weight × Power Factor ÷ 1,000,000*

BICEPS SPECIALIZATION WORKOUT RECORD   Date: ___ / ___ / ___

Start Time: _____   **Finish Time:** _____   **Total Time:** _____

■ Exercise: SEATED BARBELL CURL

Weight Reps Sets	Weight Reps Sets	Weight Reps Sets	Weight Reps Sets	Weight Reps Sets	Weight Reps Sets
× ×	× ×	× ×	× ×	× ×	× ×
Subtotal = lbs.	Subtotal = lbs.	Subtotal = lbs.	Subtotal = lbs.	Subtotal = lbs.	Subtotal = lbs.

Exercise 1:   *Total Weight* _____ *lbs.* *Time* _____ *mins.* *Power Factor* _____ *lbs./min.* *Power Index* _____

■ Exercise: STANDING BARBELL CURL

Weight Reps Sets	Weight Reps Sets	Weight Reps Sets	Weight Reps Sets	Weight Reps Sets	Weight Reps Sets
× ×	× ×	× ×	× ×	× ×	× ×
Subtotal = lbs.	Subtotal = lbs.	Subtotal = lbs.	Subtotal = lbs.	Subtotal = lbs.	Subtotal = lbs.

Exercise 2:   *Total Weight* _____ *lbs.* *Time* _____ *mins.* *Power Factor* _____ *lbs./min.* *Power Index* _____

■ Exercise:

Weight Reps Sets	Weight Reps Sets	Weight Reps Sets	Weight Reps Sets	Weight Reps Sets	Weight Reps Sets
× ×	× ×	× ×	× ×	× ×	× ×
Subtotal = lbs.	Subtotal = lbs.	Subtotal = lbs.	Subtotal = lbs.	Subtotal = lbs.	Subtotal = lbs.

Exercise 3:   *Total Weight* _____ *lbs.* *Time* _____ *mins.* *Power Factor* _____ *lbs./min.* *Power Index* _____

■ Exercise:

Weight Reps Sets	Weight Reps Sets	Weight Reps Sets	Weight Reps Sets	Weight Reps Sets	Weight Reps Sets
× ×	× ×	× ×	× ×	× ×	× ×
Subtotal = lbs.	Subtotal = lbs.	Subtotal = lbs.	Subtotal = lbs.	Subtotal = lbs.	Subtotal = lbs.

Exercise 4:   *Total Weight* _____ *lbs.* *Time* _____ *mins.* *Power Factor* _____ *lbs./min.* *Power Index* _____

■ Exercise:

Weight Reps Sets	Weight Reps Sets	Weight Reps Sets	Weight Reps Sets	Weight Reps Sets	Weight Reps Sets
× ×	× ×	× ×	× ×	× ×	× ×
Subtotal = lbs.	Subtotal = lbs.	Subtotal = lbs.	Subtotal = lbs.	Subtotal = lbs.	Subtotal = lbs.

Exercise 5:   *Total Weight* _____ *lbs.* *Time* _____ *mins.* *Power Factor* _____ *lbs./min.* *Power Index* _____

OVERALL WORKOUT: *Total Weight* _____ *lbs.* *Time* _____ *mins.* *Power Factor* _____ *lbs./min.* *Power Index* _____

Exercise Subtotal = Weight × Reps × Sets   ■ *Power Factor = lbs./min.*   ■ *Power Index = Total Weight × Power Factor ÷ 1,000,000*

BICEPS SPECIALIZATION WORKOUT RECORD Date: ___ / ___ / ___

Start Time: _____   Finish Time: _____   Total Time: _____

■ **Exercise: SEATED BARBELL CURL**

Weight Reps Sets	Weight Reps Sets	Weight Reps Sets	Weight Reps Sets	Weight Reps Sets	Weight Reps Sets
× ×	× ×	× ×	× ×	× ×	× ×
Subtotal = lbs.	Subtotal = lbs.	Subtotal = lbs.	Subtotal = lbs.	Subtotal = lbs.	Subtotal = lbs.

Exercise 1:   *Total Weight _____ lbs.   Time _____ mins.   Power Factor _____ lbs./min.   Power Index _____*

■ **Exercise: STANDING BARBELL CURL**

Weight Reps Sets	Weight Reps Sets	Weight Reps Sets	Weight Reps Sets	Weight Reps Sets	Weight Reps Sets
× ×	× ×	× ×	× ×	× ×	× ×
Subtotal = lbs.	Subtotal = lbs.	Subtotal = lbs.	Subtotal = lbs.	Subtotal = lbs.	Subtotal = lbs.

Exercise 2:   *Total Weight _____ lbs.   Time _____ mins.   Power Factor _____ lbs./min.   Power Index _____*

■ **Exercise:**

Weight Reps Sets	Weight Reps Sets	Weight Reps Sets	Weight Reps Sets	Weight Reps Sets	Weight Reps Sets
× ×	× ×	× ×	× ×	× ×	× ×
Subtotal = lbs.	Subtotal = lbs.	Subtotal = lbs.	Subtotal = lbs.	Subtotal = lbs.	Subtotal = lbs.

Exercise 3:   *Total Weight _____ lbs.   Time _____ mins.   Power Factor _____ lbs./min.   Power Index _____*

■ **Exercise:**

Weight Reps Sets	Weight Reps Sets	Weight Reps Sets	Weight Reps Sets	Weight Reps Sets	Weight Reps Sets
× ×	× ×	× ×	× ×	× ×	× ×
Subtotal = lbs.	Subtotal = lbs.	Subtotal = lbs.	Subtotal = lbs.	Subtotal = lbs.	Subtotal = lbs.

Exercise 4:   *Total Weight _____ lbs.   Time _____ mins.   Power Factor _____ lbs./min.   Power Index _____*

■ **Exercise:**

Weight Reps Sets	Weight Reps Sets	Weight Reps Sets	Weight Reps Sets	Weight Reps Sets	Weight Reps Sets
× ×	× ×	× ×	× ×	× ×	× ×
Subtotal = lbs.	Subtotal = lbs.	Subtotal = lbs.	Subtotal = lbs.	Subtotal = lbs.	Subtotal = lbs.

Exercise 5:   *Total Weight _____ lbs.   Time _____ mins.   Power Factor _____ lbs./min.   Power Index _____*

OVERALL WORKOUT: *Total Weight _____ lbs.   Time _____ mins.   Power Factor _____ lbs./min.   Power Index _____*

Exercise Subtotal = Weight × Reps × Sets   ■ Power Factor = lbs./min.   ■ Power Index = Total Weight × Power Factor ÷ 1,000,000

BICEPS SPECIALIZATION WORKOUT RECORD   Date: ___ / ___ / ___

Start Time: _____   Finish Time: _____   Total Time: _____

▪ Exercise: SEATED BARBELL CURL

Weight Reps Sets	Weight Reps Sets	Weight Reps Sets	Weight Reps Sets	Weight Reps Sets	Weight Reps Sets
× ×	× ×	× ×	× ×	× ×	× ×
Subtotal = lbs.	Subtotal = lbs.	Subtotal = lbs.	Subtotal = lbs.	Subtotal = lbs.	Subtotal = lbs.

Exercise 1:   Total Weight _____ lbs.   Time _____ mins.   Power Factor _____ lbs./min.   Power Index _____

▪ Exercise: STANDING BARBELL CURL

Weight Reps Sets	Weight Reps Sets	Weight Reps Sets	Weight Reps Sets	Weight Reps Sets	Weight Reps Sets
× ×	× ×	× ×	× ×	× ×	× ×
Subtotal = lbs.	Subtotal = lbs.	Subtotal = lbs.	Subtotal = lbs.	Subtotal = lbs.	Subtotal = lbs.

Exercise 2:   Total Weight _____ lbs.   Time _____ mins.   Power Factor _____ lbs./min.   Power Index _____

▪ Exercise:

Weight Reps Sets	Weight Reps Sets	Weight Reps Sets	Weight Reps Sets	Weight Reps Sets	Weight Reps Sets
× ×	× ×	× ×	× ×	× ×	× ×
Subtotal = lbs.	Subtotal = lbs.	Subtotal = lbs.	Subtotal = lbs.	Subtotal = lbs.	Subtotal = lbs.

Exercise 3:   Total Weight _____ lbs.   Time _____ mins.   Power Factor _____ lbs./min.   Power Index _____

▪ Exercise:

Weight Reps Sets	Weight Reps Sets	Weight Reps Sets	Weight Reps Sets	Weight Reps Sets	Weight Reps Sets
× ×	× ×	× ×	× ×	× ×	× ×
Subtotal = lbs.	Subtotal = lbs.	Subtotal = lbs.	Subtotal = lbs.	Subtotal = lbs.	Subtotal = lbs.

Exercise 4:   Total Weight _____ lbs.   Time _____ mins.   Power Factor _____ lbs./min.   Power Index _____

▪ Exercise:

Weight Reps Sets	Weight Reps Sets	Weight Reps Sets	Weight Reps Sets	Weight Reps Sets	Weight Reps Sets
× ×	× ×	× ×	× ×	× ×	× ×
Subtotal = lbs.	Subtotal = lbs.	Subtotal = lbs.	Subtotal = lbs.	Subtotal = lbs.	Subtotal = lbs.

Exercise 5:   Total Weight _____ lbs.   Time _____ mins.   Power Factor _____ lbs./min.   Power Index _____

OVERALL WORKOUT: Total Weight _____ lbs.   Time _____ mins.   Power Factor _____ lbs./min.   Power Index _____

Exercise Subtotal = Weight × Reps × Sets ▪ *Power Factor = lbs./min.* ▪ *Power Index = Total Weight × Power Factor ÷ 1,000,000*

BICEPS SPECIALIZATION WORKOUT RECORD Date: ____ / ____ / ____

Start Time: _____   Finish Time: _____   Total Time: _____

■ Exercise: SEATED BARBELL CURL

Weight Reps Sets	Weight Reps Sets	Weight Reps Sets	Weight Reps Sets	Weight Reps Sets	Weight Reps Sets
× ×	× ×	× ×	× ×	× ×	× ×
Subtotal = lbs.	Subtotal = lbs.	Subtotal = lbs.	Subtotal = lbs.	Subtotal = lbs.	Subtotal = lbs.

Exercise 1:   *Total Weight* _____ *lbs.*   *Time* _____ *mins.*   *Power Factor* _____ *lbs./min.*   *Power Index* _____

■ Exercise: STANDING BARBELL CURL

Weight Reps Sets	Weight Reps Sets	Weight Reps Sets	Weight Reps Sets	Weight Reps Sets	Weight Reps Sets
× ×	× ×	× ×	× ×	× ×	× ×
Subtotal = lbs.	Subtotal = lbs.	Subtotal = lbs.	Subtotal = lbs.	Subtotal = lbs.	Subtotal = lbs.

Exercise 2:   *Total Weight* _____ *lbs.*   *Time* _____ *mins.*   *Power Factor* _____ *lbs./min.*   *Power Index* _____

■ Exercise:

Weight Reps Sets	Weight Reps Sets	Weight Reps Sets	Weight Reps Sets	Weight Reps Sets	Weight Reps Sets
× ×	× ×	× ×	× ×	× ×	× ×
Subtotal = lbs.	Subtotal = lbs.	Subtotal = lbs.	Subtotal = lbs.	Subtotal = lbs.	Subtotal = lbs.

Exercise 3:   *Total Weight* _____ *lbs.*   *Time* _____ *mins.*   *Power Factor* _____ *lbs./min.*   *Power Index* _____

■ Exercise:

Weight Reps Sets	Weight Reps Sets	Weight Reps Sets	Weight Reps Sets	Weight Reps Sets	Weight Reps Sets
× ×	× ×	× ×	× ×	× ×	× ×
Subtotal = lbs.	Subtotal = lbs.	Subtotal = lbs.	Subtotal = lbs.	Subtotal = lbs.	Subtotal = lbs.

Exercise 4:   *Total Weight* _____ *lbs.*   *Time* _____ *mins.*   *Power Factor* _____ *lbs./min.*   *Power Index* _____

■ Exercise:

Weight Reps Sets	Weight Reps Sets	Weight Reps Sets	Weight Reps Sets	Weight Reps Sets	Weight Reps Sets
× ×	× ×	× ×	× ×	× ×	× ×
Subtotal = lbs.	Subtotal = lbs.	Subtotal = lbs.	Subtotal = lbs.	Subtotal = lbs.	Subtotal = lbs.

Exercise 5:   *Total Weight* _____ *lbs.*   *Time* _____ *mins.*   *Power Factor* _____ *lbs./min.*   *Power Index* _____

OVERALL WORKOUT: *Total Weight* _____ *lbs.*   *Time* _____ *mins.*   *Power Factor* _____ *lbs./min.*   *Power Index* _____

Exercise Subtotal = Weight × Reps × Sets   ■ *Power Factor = lbs./min.*   ■ *Power Index = Total Weight × Power Factor ÷ 1,000,000*

BICEPS SPECIALIZATION WORKOUT RECORD   Date: ___ / ___ / ___

Start Time: _____   **Finish Time:** _____   **Total Time:** _____

■ Exercise: SEATED BARBELL CURL

Weight Reps Sets	Weight Reps Sets	Weight Reps Sets	Weight Reps Sets	Weight Reps Sets	Weight Reps Sets
✕ ✕	✕ ✕	✕ ✕	✕ ✕	✕ ✕	✕ ✕
Subtotal = lbs.	Subtotal = lbs.	Subtotal = lbs.	Subtotal = lbs.	Subtotal = lbs.	Subtotal = lbs.

Exercise 1:   *Total Weight* _____ *lbs.*   *Time* _____ *mins.*   *Power Factor* _____ *lbs./min.*   *Power Index* _____

■ Exercise: STANDING BARBELL CURL

Weight Reps Sets	Weight Reps Sets	Weight Reps Sets	Weight Reps Sets	Weight Reps Sets	Weight Reps Sets
✕ ✕	✕ ✕	✕ ✕	✕ ✕	✕ ✕	✕ ✕
Subtotal = lbs.	Subtotal = lbs.	Subtotal = lbs.	Subtotal = lbs.	Subtotal = lbs.	Subtotal = lbs.

Exercise 2:   *Total Weight* _____ *lbs.*   *Time* _____ *mins.*   *Power Factor* _____ *lbs./min.*   *Power Index* _____

■ Exercise:

Weight Reps Sets	Weight Reps Sets	Weight Reps Sets	Weight Reps Sets	Weight Reps Sets	Weight Reps Sets
✕ ✕	✕ ✕	✕ ✕	✕ ✕	✕ ✕	✕ ✕
Subtotal = lbs.	Subtotal = lbs.	Subtotal = lbs.	Subtotal = lbs.	Subtotal = lbs.	Subtotal = lbs.

Exercise 3:   *Total Weight* _____ *lbs.*   *Time* _____ *mins.*   *Power Factor* _____ *lbs./min.*   *Power Index* _____

■ Exercise:

Weight Reps Sets	Weight Reps Sets	Weight Reps Sets	Weight Reps Sets	Weight Reps Sets	Weight Reps Sets
✕ ✕	✕ ✕	✕ ✕	✕ ✕	✕ ✕	✕ ✕
Subtotal = lbs.	Subtotal = lbs.	Subtotal = lbs.	Subtotal = lbs.	Subtotal = lbs.	Subtotal = lbs.

Exercise 4:   *Total Weight* _____ *lbs.*   *Time* _____ *mins.*   *Power Factor* _____ *lbs./min.*   *Power Index* _____

■ Exercise:

Weight Reps Sets	Weight Reps Sets	Weight Reps Sets	Weight Reps Sets	Weight Reps Sets	Weight Reps Sets
✕ ✕	✕ ✕	✕ ✕	✕ ✕	✕ ✕	✕ ✕
Subtotal = lbs.	Subtotal = lbs.	Subtotal = lbs.	Subtotal = lbs.	Subtotal = lbs.	Subtotal = lbs.

Exercise 5:   *Total Weight* _____ *lbs.*   *Time* _____ *mins.*   *Power Factor* _____ *lbs./min.*   *Power Index* _____

OVERALL WORKOUT: *Total Weight* _____ *lbs.*   *Time* _____ *mins.*   *Power Factor* _____ *lbs./min.*   *Power Index* _____

Exercise Subtotal = Weight ✕ Reps ✕ Sets   ■ *Power Factor = lbs./min.*   ■ *Power Index = Total Weight ✕ Power Factor ÷ 1,000,000*

BICEPS SPECIALIZATION WORKOUT RECORD Date: ___ / ___ / ___

Start Time: _____　　Finish Time: _____　　Total Time: _____

■ **Exercise: SEATED BARBELL CURL**

Weight Reps Sets	Weight Reps Sets	Weight Reps Sets	Weight Reps Sets	Weight Reps Sets	Weight Reps Sets
× ×	× ×	× ×	× ×	× ×	× ×
Subtotal = lbs.	Subtotal = lbs.	Subtotal = lbs.	Subtotal = lbs.	Subtotal = lbs.	Subtotal = lbs.

Exercise 1: 　　*Total Weight* _____ *lbs.*　*Time* _____ *mins.*　*Power Factor* _____ *lbs./min.*　*Power Index* _____

■ **Exercise: STANDING BARBELL CURL**

Weight Reps Sets	Weight Reps Sets	Weight Reps Sets	Weight Reps Sets	Weight Reps Sets	Weight Reps Sets
× ×	× ×	× ×	× ×	× ×	× ×
Subtotal = lbs.	Subtotal = lbs.	Subtotal = lbs.	Subtotal = lbs.	Subtotal = lbs.	Subtotal = lbs.

Exercise 2: 　　*Total Weight* _____ *lbs.*　*Time* _____ *mins.*　*Power Factor* _____ *lbs./min.*　*Power Index* _____

■ **Exercise:**

Weight Reps Sets	Weight Reps Sets	Weight Reps Sets	Weight Reps Sets	Weight Reps Sets	Weight Reps Sets
× ×	× ×	× ×	× ×	× ×	× ×
Subtotal = lbs.	Subtotal = lbs.	Subtotal = lbs.	Subtotal = lbs.	Subtotal = lbs.	Subtotal = lbs.

Exercise 3: 　　*Total Weight* _____ *lbs.*　*Time* _____ *mins.*　*Power Factor* _____ *lbs./min.*　*Power Index* _____

■ **Exercise:**

Weight Reps Sets	Weight Reps Sets	Weight Reps Sets	Weight Reps Sets	Weight Reps Sets	Weight Reps Sets
× ×	× ×	× ×	× ×	× ×	× ×
Subtotal = lbs.	Subtotal = lbs.	Subtotal = lbs.	Subtotal = lbs.	Subtotal = lbs.	Subtotal = lbs.

Exercise 4: 　　*Total Weight* _____ *lbs.*　*Time* _____ *mins.*　*Power Factor* _____ *lbs./min.*　*Power Index* _____

■ **Exercise:**

Weight Reps Sets	Weight Reps Sets	Weight Reps Sets	Weight Reps Sets	Weight Reps Sets	Weight Reps Sets
× ×	× ×	× ×	× ×	× ×	× ×
Subtotal = lbs.	Subtotal = lbs.	Subtotal = lbs.	Subtotal = lbs.	Subtotal = lbs.	Subtotal = lbs.

Exercise 5: 　　*Total Weight* _____ *lbs.*　*Time* _____ *mins.*　*Power Factor* _____ *lbs./min.*　*Power Index* _____

OVERALL WORKOUT:　*Total Weight* _____ *lbs.*　*Time* _____ *mins.*　*Power Factor* _____ *lbs./min.*　*Power Index* _____

Exercise Subtotal = Weight × Reps × Sets　■ *Power Factor = lbs./min.*　■ *Power Index = Total Weight × Power Factor ÷ 1,000,000*

BICEPS SPECIALIZATION WORKOUT RECORD   Date: ___ / ___ / ___

Start Time: _____   **Finish Time:** _____   **Total Time:** _____

■ Exercise: SEATED BARBELL CURL

Weight Reps Sets	Weight Reps Sets	Weight Reps Sets	Weight Reps Sets	Weight Reps Sets	Weight Reps Sets
× ×	× ×	× ×	× ×	× ×	× ×
Subtotal = lbs.	Subtotal = lbs.	Subtotal = lbs.	Subtotal = lbs.	Subtotal = lbs.	Subtotal = lbs.

Exercise 1:   *Total Weight _____ lbs.   Time _____ mins.   Power Factor _____ lbs./min.   Power Index _____*

■ Exercise: STANDING BARBELL CURL

Weight Reps Sets	Weight Reps Sets	Weight Reps Sets	Weight Reps Sets	Weight Reps Sets	Weight Reps Sets
× ×	× ×	× ×	× ×	× ×	× ×
Subtotal = lbs.	Subtotal = lbs.	Subtotal = lbs.	Subtotal = lbs.	Subtotal = lbs.	Subtotal = lbs.

Exercise 2:   *Total Weight _____ lbs.   Time _____ mins.   Power Factor _____ lbs./min.   Power Index _____*

■ Exercise:

Weight Reps Sets	Weight Reps Sets	Weight Reps Sets	Weight Reps Sets	Weight Reps Sets	Weight Reps Sets
× ×	× ×	× ×	× ×	× ×	× ×
Subtotal = lbs.	Subtotal = lbs.	Subtotal = lbs.	Subtotal = lbs.	Subtotal = lbs.	Subtotal = lbs.

Exercise 3:   *Total Weight _____ lbs.   Time _____ mins.   Power Factor _____ lbs./min.   Power Index _____*

■ Exercise:

Weight Reps Sets	Weight Reps Sets	Weight Reps Sets	Weight Reps Sets	Weight Reps Sets	Weight Reps Sets
× ×	× ×	× ×	× ×	× ×	× ×
Subtotal = lbs.	Subtotal = lbs.	Subtotal = lbs.	Subtotal = lbs.	Subtotal = lbs.	Subtotal = lbs.

Exercise 4:   *Total Weight _____ lbs.   Time _____ mins.   Power Factor _____ lbs./min.   Power Index _____*

■ Exercise:

Weight Reps Sets	Weight Reps Sets	Weight Reps Sets	Weight Reps Sets	Weight Reps Sets	Weight Reps Sets
× ×	× ×	× ×	× ×	× ×	× ×
Subtotal = lbs.	Subtotal = lbs.	Subtotal = lbs.	Subtotal = lbs.	Subtotal = lbs.	Subtotal = lbs.

Exercise 5:   *Total Weight _____ lbs.   Time _____ mins.   Power Factor _____ lbs./min.   Power Index _____*

OVERALL WORKOUT: *Total Weight _____ lbs.   Time _____ mins.   Power Factor _____ lbs./min.   Power Index _____*

Exercise Subtotal = Weight × Reps × Sets   ■ Power Factor = lbs./min.   ■ Power Index = Total Weight × Power Factor ÷ 1,000,000

FOREARM SPECIALIZATION WORKOUT RECORD Date: ___ / ___ / ___

Start Time: _____ Finish Time: _____ Total Time: _____

■ **Exercise: STANDING BARBELL REVERSE CURL**

Weight Reps Sets	Weight Reps Sets	Weight Reps Sets	Weight Reps Sets	Weight Reps Sets	Weight Reps Sets
× ×	× ×	× ×	× ×	× ×	× ×
Subtotal = lbs.	Subtotal = lbs.	Subtotal = lbs.	Subtotal = lbs.	Subtotal = lbs.	Subtotal = lbs.

Exercise 1:   *Total Weight _____ lbs.   Time _____ mins.   Power Factor _____ lbs./min.   Power Index _____*

■ **Exercise: SEATED DUMBBELL REVERSE WRIST CURL**

Weight Reps Sets	Weight Reps Sets	Weight Reps Sets	Weight Reps Sets	Weight Reps Sets	Weight Reps Sets
× ×	× ×	× ×	× ×	× ×	× ×
Subtotal = lbs.	Subtotal = lbs.	Subtotal = lbs.	Subtotal = lbs.	Subtotal = lbs.	Subtotal = lbs.

Exercise 2:   *Total Weight _____ lbs.   Time _____ mins.   Power Factor _____ lbs./min.   Power Index _____*

■ **Exercise: STANDING BARBELL WRIST CURL BEHIND BACK**

Weight Reps Sets	Weight Reps Sets	Weight Reps Sets	Weight Reps Sets	Weight Reps Sets	Weight Reps Sets
× ×	× ×	× ×	× ×	× ×	× ×
Subtotal = lbs.	Subtotal = lbs.	Subtotal = lbs.	Subtotal = lbs.	Subtotal = lbs.	Subtotal = lbs.

Exercise 3:   *Total Weight _____ lbs.   Time _____ mins.   Power Factor _____ lbs./min.   Power Index _____*

■ **Exercise:**

Weight Reps Sets	Weight Reps Sets	Weight Reps Sets	Weight Reps Sets	Weight Reps Sets	Weight Reps Sets
× ×	× ×	× ×	× ×	× ×	× ×
Subtotal = lbs.	Subtotal = lbs.	Subtotal = lbs.	Subtotal = lbs.	Subtotal = lbs.	Subtotal = lbs.

Exercise 4:   *Total Weight _____ lbs.   Time _____ mins.   Power Factor _____ lbs./min.   Power Index _____*

■ **Exercise:**

Weight Reps Sets	Weight Reps Sets	Weight Reps Sets	Weight Reps Sets	Weight Reps Sets	Weight Reps Sets
× ×	× ×	× ×	× ×	× ×	× ×
Subtotal = lbs.	Subtotal = lbs.	Subtotal = lbs.	Subtotal = lbs.	Subtotal = lbs.	Subtotal = lbs.

Exercise 5:   *Total Weight _____ lbs.   Time _____ mins.   Power Factor _____ lbs./min.   Power Index _____*

OVERALL WORKOUT: *Total Weight _____ lbs.   Time _____ mins.   Power Factor _____ lbs./min.   Power Index _____*

Exercise Subtotal = Weight × Reps × Sets   ■ *Power Factor = lbs./min.*   ■ *Power Index = Total Weight × Power Factor ÷ 1,000,000*

FOREARM SPECIALIZATION WORKOUT RECORD Date: ___ / ___ / ___

Start Time: _____ Finish Time: _____ Total Time: _____

■ Exercise: STANDING BARBELL REVERSE CURL

Weight Reps Sets	Weight Reps Sets	Weight Reps Sets	Weight Reps Sets	Weight Reps Sets	Weight Reps Sets
× ×	× ×	× ×	× ×	× ×	× ×
Subtotal = lbs.	Subtotal = lbs.	Subtotal = lbs.	Subtotal = lbs.	Subtotal = lbs.	Subtotal = lbs.

Exercise 1:   *Total Weight* _____ *lbs.*   *Time* _____ *mins.*   *Power Factor* _____ *lbs./min.*   *Power Index* _____

■ Exercise: SEATED DUMBBELL REVERSE WRIST CURL

Weight Reps Sets	Weight Reps Sets	Weight Reps Sets	Weight Reps Sets	Weight Reps Sets	Weight Reps Sets
× ×	× ×	× ×	× ×	× ×	× ×
Subtotal = lbs.	Subtotal = lbs.	Subtotal = lbs.	Subtotal = lbs.	Subtotal = lbs.	Subtotal = lbs.

Exercise 2:   *Total Weight* _____ *lbs.*   *Time* _____ *mins.*   *Power Factor* _____ *lbs./min.*   *Power Index* _____

■ Exercise: STANDING BARBELL WRIST CURL BEHIND BACK

Weight Reps Sets	Weight Reps Sets	Weight Reps Sets	Weight Reps Sets	Weight Reps Sets	Weight Reps Sets
× ×	× ×	× ×	× ×	× ×	× ×
Subtotal = lbs.	Subtotal = lbs.	Subtotal = lbs.	Subtotal = lbs.	Subtotal = lbs.	Subtotal = lbs.

Exercise 3:   *Total Weight* _____ *lbs.*   *Time* _____ *mins.*   *Power Factor* _____ *lbs./min.*   *Power Index* _____

■ Exercise:

Weight Reps Sets	Weight Reps Sets	Weight Reps Sets	Weight Reps Sets	Weight Reps Sets	Weight Reps Sets
× ×	× ×	× ×	× ×	× ×	× ×
Subtotal = lbs.	Subtotal = lbs.	Subtotal = lbs.	Subtotal = lbs.	Subtotal = lbs.	Subtotal = lbs.

Exercise 4:   *Total Weight* _____ *lbs.*   *Time* _____ *mins.*   *Power Factor* _____ *lbs./min.*   *Power Index* _____

■ Exercise:

Weight Reps Sets	Weight Reps Sets	Weight Reps Sets	Weight Reps Sets	Weight Reps Sets	Weight Reps Sets
× ×	× ×	× ×	× ×	× ×	× ×
Subtotal = lbs.	Subtotal = lbs.	Subtotal = lbs.	Subtotal = lbs.	Subtotal = lbs.	Subtotal = lbs.

Exercise 5:   *Total Weight* _____ *lbs.*   *Time* _____ *mins.*   *Power Factor* _____ *lbs./min.*   *Power Index* _____

OVERALL WORKOUT: *Total Weight* _____ *lbs.*   *Time* _____ *mins.*   *Power Factor* _____ *lbs./min.*   *Power Index* _____

Exercise Subtotal = Weight × Reps × Sets   ■ *Power Factor = lbs./min.*   ■ *Power Index = Total Weight × Power Factor ÷ 1,000,000*

FOREARM SPECIALIZATION WORKOUT RECORD Date: ___ / ___ / ___

Start Time: _____   Finish Time: _____   Total Time: _____

■ Exercise: STANDING BARBELL REVERSE CURL

Weight Reps Sets	Weight Reps Sets	Weight Reps Sets	Weight Reps Sets	Weight Reps Sets	Weight Reps Sets
× ×	× ×	× ×	× ×	× ×	× ×
Subtotal = lbs.	Subtotal = lbs.	Subtotal = lbs.	Subtotal = lbs.	Subtotal = lbs.	Subtotal = lbs.

Exercise 1:   *Total Weight* _____ *lbs.*   *Time* _____ *mins.*   *Power Factor* _____ *lbs./min.*   *Power Index* _____

■ Exercise: SEATED DUMBBELL REVERSE WRIST CURL

Weight Reps Sets	Weight Reps Sets	Weight Reps Sets	Weight Reps Sets	Weight Reps Sets	Weight Reps Sets
× ×	× ×	× ×	× ×	× ×	× ×
Subtotal = lbs.	Subtotal = lbs.	Subtotal = lbs.	Subtotal = lbs.	Subtotal = lbs.	Subtotal = lbs.

Exercise 2:   *Total Weight* _____ *lbs.*   *Time* _____ *mins.*   *Power Factor* _____ *lbs./min.*   *Power Index* _____

■ Exercise: STANDING BARBELL WRIST CURL BEHIND BACK

Weight Reps Sets	Weight Reps Sets	Weight Reps Sets	Weight Reps Sets	Weight Reps Sets	Weight Reps Sets
× ×	× ×	× ×	× ×	× ×	× ×
Subtotal = lbs.	Subtotal = lbs.	Subtotal = lbs.	Subtotal = lbs.	Subtotal = lbs.	Subtotal = lbs.

Exercise 3:   *Total Weight* _____ *lbs.*   *Time* _____ *mins.*   *Power Factor* _____ *lbs./min.*   *Power Index* _____

■ Exercise:

Weight Reps Sets	Weight Reps Sets	Weight Reps Sets	Weight Reps Sets	Weight Reps Sets	Weight Reps Sets
× ×	× ×	× ×	× ×	× ×	× ×
Subtotal = lbs.	Subtotal = lbs.	Subtotal = lbs.	Subtotal = lbs.	Subtotal = lbs.	Subtotal = lbs.

Exercise 4:   *Total Weight* _____ *lbs.*   *Time* _____ *mins.*   *Power Factor* _____ *lbs./min.*   *Power Index* _____

■ Exercise:

Weight Reps Sets	Weight Reps Sets	Weight Reps Sets	Weight Reps Sets	Weight Reps Sets	Weight Reps Sets
× ×	× ×	× ×	× ×	× ×	× ×
Subtotal = lbs.	Subtotal = lbs.	Subtotal = lbs.	Subtotal = lbs.	Subtotal = lbs.	Subtotal = lbs.

Exercise 5:   *Total Weight* _____ *lbs.*   *Time* _____ *mins.*   *Power Factor* _____ *lbs./min.*   *Power Index* _____

OVERALL WORKOUT: *Total Weight* _____ *lbs.*   *Time* _____ *mins.*   *Power Factor* _____ *lbs./min.*   *Power Index* _____

Exercise Subtotal = Weight × Reps × Sets   ■ *Power Factor = lbs./min.*   ■ *Power Index = Total Weight × Power Factor ÷ 1,000,000*

FOREARM SPECIALIZATION WORKOUT RECORD Date: ___ / ___ / ___

Start Time: _____ **Finish Time:** _____ **Total Time:** _____

▪ Exercise: STANDING BARBELL REVERSE CURL

Weight Reps Sets	Weight Reps Sets	Weight Reps Sets	Weight Reps Sets	Weight Reps Sets	Weight Reps Sets
× ×	× ×	× ×	× ×	× ×	× ×
Subtotal = lbs.	Subtotal = lbs.	Subtotal = lbs.	Subtotal = lbs.	Subtotal = lbs.	Subtotal = lbs.

Exercise 1: *Total Weight* _____ *lbs.* *Time* _____ *mins.* *Power Factor* _____ *lbs./min.* *Power Index* _____

▪ Exercise: SEATED DUMBBELL REVERSE WRIST CURL

Weight Reps Sets	Weight Reps Sets	Weight Reps Sets	Weight Reps Sets	Weight Reps Sets	Weight Reps Sets
× ×	× ×	× ×	× ×	× ×	× ×
Subtotal = lbs.	Subtotal = lbs.	Subtotal = lbs.	Subtotal = lbs.	Subtotal = lbs.	Subtotal = lbs.

Exercise 2: *Total Weight* _____ *lbs.* *Time* _____ *mins.* *Power Factor* _____ *lbs./min.* *Power Index* _____

▪ Exercise: STANDING BARBELL WRIST CURL BEHIND BACK

Weight Reps Sets	Weight Reps Sets	Weight Reps Sets	Weight Reps Sets	Weight Reps Sets	Weight Reps Sets
× ×	× ×	× ×	× ×	× ×	× ×
Subtotal = lbs.	Subtotal = lbs.	Subtotal = lbs.	Subtotal = lbs.	Subtotal = lbs.	Subtotal = lbs.

Exercise 3: *Total Weight* _____ *lbs.* *Time* _____ *mins.* *Power Factor* _____ *lbs./min.* *Power Index* _____

▪ Exercise:

Weight Reps Sets	Weight Reps Sets	Weight Reps Sets	Weight Reps Sets	Weight Reps Sets	Weight Reps Sets
× ×	× ×	× ×	× ×	× ×	× ×
Subtotal = lbs.	Subtotal = lbs.	Subtotal = lbs.	Subtotal = lbs.	Subtotal = lbs.	Subtotal = lbs.

Exercise 4: *Total Weight* _____ *lbs.* *Time* _____ *mins.* *Power Factor* _____ *lbs./min.* *Power Index* _____

▪ Exercise:

Weight Reps Sets	Weight Reps Sets	Weight Reps Sets	Weight Reps Sets	Weight Reps Sets	Weight Reps Sets
× ×	× ×	× ×	× ×	× ×	× ×
Subtotal = lbs.	Subtotal = lbs.	Subtotal = lbs.	Subtotal = lbs.	Subtotal = lbs.	Subtotal = lbs.

Exercise 5: *Total Weight* _____ *lbs.* *Time* _____ *mins.* *Power Factor* _____ *lbs./min.* *Power Index* _____

OVERALL WORKOUT: *Total Weight* _____ *lbs.* *Time* _____ *mins.* *Power Factor* _____ *lbs./min.* *Power Index* _____

Exercise Subtotal = Weight × Reps × Sets ▪ *Power Factor = lbs./min.* ▪ *Power Index = Total Weight × Power Factor ÷ 1,000,000*

FOREARM SPECIALIZATION WORKOUT RECORD Date: ___ / ___ / ___

Start Time: _____ Finish Time: _____ Total Time: _____

■ **Exercise: STANDING BARBELL REVERSE CURL**

Weight	Reps	Sets	Weight	Reps	Sets	Weight	Reps	Sets	Weight	Reps	Sets	Weight	Reps	Sets	Weight	Reps	Sets
×	×		×	×		×	×		×	×		×	×		×	×	
Subtotal =	lbs.		Subtotal =	lbs.		Subtotal =	lbs.		Subtotal =	lbs.		Subtotal =	lbs.		Subtotal =	lbs.	

Exercise 1:   *Total Weight* _____ *lbs.*   *Time* _____ *mins.*   *Power Factor* _____ *lbs./min.*   *Power Index* _____

■ **Exercise: SEATED DUMBBELL REVERSE WRIST CURL**

Weight	Reps	Sets	Weight	Reps	Sets	Weight	Reps	Sets	Weight	Reps	Sets	Weight	Reps	Sets	Weight	Reps	Sets
×	×		×	×		×	×		×	×		×	×		×	×	
Subtotal =	lbs.		Subtotal =	lbs.		Subtotal =	lbs.		Subtotal =	lbs.		Subtotal =	lbs.		Subtotal =	lbs.	

Exercise 2:   *Total Weight* _____ *lbs.*   *Time* _____ *mins.*   *Power Factor* _____ *lbs./min.*   *Power Index* _____

■ **Exercise: STANDING BARBELL WRIST CURL BEHIND BACK**

Weight	Reps	Sets	Weight	Reps	Sets	Weight	Reps	Sets	Weight	Reps	Sets	Weight	Reps	Sets	Weight	Reps	Sets
×	×		×	×		×	×		×	×		×	×		×	×	
Subtotal =	lbs.		Subtotal =	lbs.		Subtotal =	lbs.		Subtotal =	lbs.		Subtotal =	lbs.		Subtotal =	lbs.	

Exercise 3:   *Total Weight* _____ *lbs.*   *Time* _____ *mins.*   *Power Factor* _____ *lbs./min.*   *Power Index* _____

■ **Exercise:**

Weight	Reps	Sets	Weight	Reps	Sets	Weight	Reps	Sets	Weight	Reps	Sets	Weight	Reps	Sets	Weight	Reps	Sets
×	×		×	×		×	×		×	×		×	×		×	×	
Subtotal =	lbs.		Subtotal =	lbs.		Subtotal =	lbs.		Subtotal =	lbs.		Subtotal =	lbs.		Subtotal =	lbs.	

Exercise 4:   *Total Weight* _____ *lbs.*   *Time* _____ *mins.*   *Power Factor* _____ *lbs./min.*   *Power Index* _____

■ **Exercise:**

Weight	Reps	Sets	Weight	Reps	Sets	Weight	Reps	Sets	Weight	Reps	Sets	Weight	Reps	Sets	Weight	Reps	Sets
×	×		×	×		×	×		×	×		×	×		×	×	
Subtotal =	lbs.		Subtotal =	lbs.		Subtotal =	lbs.		Subtotal =	lbs.		Subtotal =	lbs.		Subtotal =	lbs.	

Exercise 5:   *Total Weight* _____ *lbs.*   *Time* _____ *mins.*   *Power Factor* _____ *lbs./min.*   *Power Index* _____

OVERALL WORKOUT: *Total Weight* _____ *lbs.*   *Time* _____ *mins.*   *Power Factor* _____ *lbs./min.*   *Power Index* _____

Exercise Subtotal = Weight × Reps × Sets   ■ *Power Factor = lbs./min.*   ■ *Power Index = Total Weight × Power Factor ÷ 1,000,000*

FOREARM SPECIALIZATION WORKOUT RECORD Date: ____ / ____ / ____

Start Time: _____ Finish Time: _____ Total Time: _____

■ Exercise: STANDING BARBELL REVERSE CURL

Weight Reps Sets	Weight Reps Sets	Weight Reps Sets	Weight Reps Sets	Weight Reps Sets	Weight Reps Sets
× ×	× ×	× ×	× ×	× ×	× ×
Subtotal = lbs.	Subtotal = lbs.	Subtotal = lbs.	Subtotal = lbs.	Subtotal = lbs.	Subtotal = lbs.

Exercise 1: *Total Weight _____ lbs. Time _____ mins. Power Factor _____ lbs./min. Power Index _____*

■ Exercise: SEATED DUMBBELL REVERSE WRIST CURL

Weight Reps Sets	Weight Reps Sets	Weight Reps Sets	Weight Reps Sets	Weight Reps Sets	Weight Reps Sets
× ×	× ×	× ×	× ×	× ×	× ×
Subtotal = lbs.	Subtotal = lbs.	Subtotal = lbs.	Subtotal = lbs.	Subtotal = lbs.	Subtotal = lbs.

Exercise 2: *Total Weight _____ lbs. Time _____ mins. Power Factor _____ lbs./min. Power Index _____*

■ Exercise: STANDING BARBELL WRIST CURL BEHIND BACK

Weight Reps Sets	Weight Reps Sets	Weight Reps Sets	Weight Reps Sets	Weight Reps Sets	Weight Reps Sets
× ×	× ×	× ×	× ×	× ×	× ×
Subtotal = lbs.	Subtotal = lbs.	Subtotal = lbs.	Subtotal = lbs.	Subtotal = lbs.	Subtotal = lbs.

Exercise 3: *Total Weight _____ lbs. Time _____ mins. Power Factor _____ lbs./min. Power Index _____*

■ Exercise:

Weight Reps Sets	Weight Reps Sets	Weight Reps Sets	Weight Reps Sets	Weight Reps Sets	Weight Reps Sets
× ×	× ×	× ×	× ×	× ×	× ×
Subtotal = lbs.	Subtotal = lbs.	Subtotal = lbs.	Subtotal = lbs.	Subtotal = lbs.	Subtotal = lbs.

Exercise 4: *Total Weight _____ lbs. Time _____ mins. Power Factor _____ lbs./min. Power Index _____*

■ Exercise:

Weight Reps Sets	Weight Reps Sets	Weight Reps Sets	Weight Reps Sets	Weight Reps Sets	Weight Reps Sets
× ×	× ×	× ×	× ×	× ×	× ×
Subtotal = lbs.	Subtotal = lbs.	Subtotal = lbs.	Subtotal = lbs.	Subtotal = lbs.	Subtotal = lbs.

Exercise 5: *Total Weight _____ lbs. Time _____ mins. Power Factor _____ lbs./min. Power Index _____*

OVERALL WORKOUT: *Total Weight _____ lbs. Time _____ mins. Power Factor _____ lbs./min. Power Index _____*

Exercise Subtotal = Weight × Reps × Sets ■ Power Factor = lbs./min. ■ Power Index = Total Weight × Power Factor ÷ 1,000,000

FOREARM SPECIALIZATION WORKOUT RECORD Date: ___ / ___ / ___

Start Time: _____   Finish Time: _____   Total Time: _____

■ **Exercise: STANDING BARBELL REVERSE CURL**

Weight Reps Sets	Weight Reps Sets	Weight Reps Sets	Weight Reps Sets	Weight Reps Sets	Weight Reps Sets
× ×	× ×	× ×	× ×	× ×	× ×
Subtotal = lbs.	Subtotal = lbs.	Subtotal = lbs.	Subtotal = lbs.	Subtotal = lbs.	Subtotal = lbs.

Exercise 1:   *Total Weight _____ lbs.   Time _____ mins.   Power Factor _____ lbs./min.   Power Index _____*

■ **Exercise: SEATED DUMBBELL REVERSE WRIST CURL**

Weight Reps Sets	Weight Reps Sets	Weight Reps Sets	Weight Reps Sets	Weight Reps Sets	Weight Reps Sets
× ×	× ×	× ×	× ×	× ×	× ×
Subtotal = lbs.	Subtotal = lbs.	Subtotal = lbs.	Subtotal = lbs.	Subtotal = lbs.	Subtotal = lbs.

Exercise 2:   *Total Weight _____ lbs.   Time _____ mins.   Power Factor _____ lbs./min.   Power Index _____*

■ **Exercise: STANDING BARBELL WRIST CURL BEHIND BACK**

Weight Reps Sets	Weight Reps Sets	Weight Reps Sets	Weight Reps Sets	Weight Reps Sets	Weight Reps Sets
× ×	× ×	× ×	× ×	× ×	× ×
Subtotal = lbs.	Subtotal = lbs.	Subtotal = lbs.	Subtotal = lbs.	Subtotal = lbs.	Subtotal = lbs.

Exercise 3:   *Total Weight _____ lbs.   Time _____ mins.   Power Factor _____ lbs./min.   Power Index _____*

■ **Exercise:**

Weight Reps Sets	Weight Reps Sets	Weight Reps Sets	Weight Reps Sets	Weight Reps Sets	Weight Reps Sets
× ×	× ×	× ×	× ×	× ×	× ×
Subtotal = lbs.	Subtotal = lbs.	Subtotal = lbs.	Subtotal = lbs.	Subtotal = lbs.	Subtotal = lbs.

Exercise 4:   *Total Weight _____ lbs.   Time _____ mins.   Power Factor _____ lbs./min.   Power Index _____*

■ **Exercise:**

Weight Reps Sets	Weight Reps Sets	Weight Reps Sets	Weight Reps Sets	Weight Reps Sets	Weight Reps Sets
× ×	× ×	× ×	× ×	× ×	× ×
Subtotal = lbs.	Subtotal = lbs.	Subtotal = lbs.	Subtotal = lbs.	Subtotal = lbs.	Subtotal = lbs.

Exercise 5:   *Total Weight _____ lbs.   Time _____ mins.   Power Factor _____ lbs./min.   Power Index _____*

OVERALL WORKOUT: *Total Weight _____ lbs.   Time _____ mins.   Power Factor _____ lbs./min.   Power Index _____*

Exercise Subtotal = Weight × Reps × Sets   ■   *Power Factor = lbs./min.*   ■   *Power Index = Total Weight × Power Factor ÷ 1,000,000*

FOREARM SPECIALIZATION WORKOUT RECORD Date: ___ / ___ / ___

Start Time: _____   **Finish Time:** _____   **Total Time:** _____

■ Exercise: STANDING BARBELL REVERSE CURL

Weight Reps Sets	Weight Reps Sets	Weight Reps Sets	Weight Reps Sets	Weight Reps Sets	Weight Reps Sets
× ×	× ×	× ×	× ×	× ×	× ×
Subtotal = lbs.	Subtotal = lbs.	Subtotal = lbs.	Subtotal = lbs.	Subtotal = lbs.	Subtotal = lbs.

Exercise 1:   *Total Weight* _____ *lbs.   Time* _____ *mins.   Power Factor* _____ *lbs./min.   Power Index* _____

■ Exercise: SEATED DUMBBELL REVERSE WRIST CURL

Weight Reps Sets	Weight Reps Sets	Weight Reps Sets	Weight Reps Sets	Weight Reps Sets	Weight Reps Sets
× ×	× ×	× ×	× ×	× ×	× ×
Subtotal = lbs.	Subtotal = lbs.	Subtotal = lbs.	Subtotal = lbs.	Subtotal = lbs.	Subtotal = lbs.

Exercise 2:   *Total Weight* _____ *lbs.   Time* _____ *mins.   Power Factor* _____ *lbs./min.   Power Index* _____

■ Exercise: STANDING BARBELL WRIST CURL BEHIND BACK

Weight Reps Sets	Weight Reps Sets	Weight Reps Sets	Weight Reps Sets	Weight Reps Sets	Weight Reps Sets
× ×	× ×	× ×	× ×	× ×	× ×
Subtotal = lbs.	Subtotal = lbs.	Subtotal = lbs.	Subtotal = lbs.	Subtotal = lbs.	Subtotal = lbs.

Exercise 3:   *Total Weight* _____ *lbs.   Time* _____ *mins.   Power Factor* _____ *lbs./min.   Power Index* _____

■ Exercise:

Weight Reps Sets	Weight Reps Sets	Weight Reps Sets	Weight Reps Sets	Weight Reps Sets	Weight Reps Sets
× ×	× ×	× ×	× ×	× ×	× ×
Subtotal = lbs.	Subtotal = lbs.	Subtotal = lbs.	Subtotal = lbs.	Subtotal = lbs.	Subtotal = lbs.

Exercise 4:   *Total Weight* _____ *lbs.   Time* _____ *mins.   Power Factor* _____ *lbs./min.   Power Index* _____

■ Exercise:

Weight Reps Sets	Weight Reps Sets	Weight Reps Sets	Weight Reps Sets	Weight Reps Sets	Weight Reps Sets
× ×	× ×	× ×	× ×	× ×	× ×
Subtotal = lbs.	Subtotal = lbs.	Subtotal = lbs.	Subtotal = lbs.	Subtotal = lbs.	Subtotal = lbs.

Exercise 5:   *Total Weight* _____ *lbs.   Time* _____ *mins.   Power Factor* _____ *lbs./min.   Power Index* _____

OVERALL WORKOUT: *Total Weight* _____ *lbs.   Time* _____ *mins.   Power Factor* _____ *lbs./min.   Power Index* _____

Exercise Subtotal = Weight × Reps × Sets   ■ *Power Factor = lbs./min.*   ■ *Power Index = Total Weight × Power Factor ÷ 1,000,000*

FOREARM SPECIALIZATION WORKOUT RECORD Date: ___ / ___ / ___

Start Time: _____ **Finish Time:** _____ **Total Time:** _____

■ **Exercise: STANDING BARBELL REVERSE CURL**

Weight Reps Sets	Weight Reps Sets	Weight Reps Sets	Weight Reps Sets	Weight Reps Sets	Weight Reps Sets
× ×	× ×	× ×	× ×	× ×	× ×
Subtotal = lbs.	Subtotal = lbs.	Subtotal = lbs.	Subtotal = lbs.	Subtotal = lbs.	Subtotal = lbs.

Exercise 1:   *Total Weight _____ lbs.   Time _____ mins.   Power Factor _____ lbs./min.   Power Index _____*

■ **Exercise: SEATED DUMBBELL REVERSE WRIST CURL**

Weight Reps Sets	Weight Reps Sets	Weight Reps Sets	Weight Reps Sets	Weight Reps Sets	Weight Reps Sets
× ×	× ×	× ×	× ×	× ×	× ×
Subtotal = lbs.	Subtotal = lbs.	Subtotal = lbs.	Subtotal = lbs.	Subtotal = lbs.	Subtotal = lbs.

Exercise 2:   *Total Weight _____ lbs.   Time _____ mins.   Power Factor _____ lbs./min.   Power Index _____*

■ **Exercise: STANDING BARBELL WRIST CURL BEHIND BACK**

Weight Reps Sets	Weight Reps Sets	Weight Reps Sets	Weight Reps Sets	Weight Reps Sets	Weight Reps Sets
× ×	× ×	× ×	× ×	× ×	× ×
Subtotal = lbs.	Subtotal = lbs.	Subtotal = lbs.	Subtotal = lbs.	Subtotal = lbs.	Subtotal = lbs.

Exercise 3:   *Total Weight _____ lbs.   Time _____ mins.   Power Factor _____ lbs./min.   Power Index _____*

■ **Exercise:**

Weight Reps Sets	Weight Reps Sets	Weight Reps Sets	Weight Reps Sets	Weight Reps Sets	Weight Reps Sets
× ×	× ×	× ×	× ×	× ×	× ×
Subtotal = lbs.	Subtotal = lbs.	Subtotal = lbs.	Subtotal = lbs.	Subtotal = lbs.	Subtotal = lbs.

Exercise 4:   *Total Weight _____ lbs.   Time _____ mins.   Power Factor _____ lbs./min.   Power Index _____*

■ **Exercise:**

Weight Reps Sets	Weight Reps Sets	Weight Reps Sets	Weight Reps Sets	Weight Reps Sets	Weight Reps Sets
× ×	× ×	× ×	× ×	× ×	× ×
Subtotal = lbs.	Subtotal = lbs.	Subtotal = lbs.	Subtotal = lbs.	Subtotal = lbs.	Subtotal = lbs.

Exercise 5:   *Total Weight _____ lbs.   Time _____ mins.   Power Factor _____ lbs./min.   Power Index _____*

OVERALL WORKOUT: *Total Weight _____ lbs.   Time _____ mins.   Power Factor _____ lbs./min.   Power Index _____*

Exercise Subtotal = Weight × Reps × Sets ■ *Power Factor = lbs./min.* ■ *Power Index = Total Weight × Power Factor ÷ 1,000,000*

FOREARM SPECIALIZATION WORKOUT RECORD Date: ____ / ____ / ____

Start Time: _____   Finish Time: _____   Total Time: _____

■ Exercise: STANDING BARBELL REVERSE CURL

Weight Reps Sets	Weight Reps Sets	Weight Reps Sets	Weight Reps Sets	Weight Reps Sets	Weight Reps Sets
× ×	× ×	× ×	× ×	× ×	× ×
Subtotal = lbs.	Subtotal = lbs.	Subtotal = lbs.	Subtotal = lbs.	Subtotal = lbs.	Subtotal = lbs.

Exercise 1:   *Total Weight _____ lbs.   Time _____ mins.   Power Factor _____ lbs./min.   Power Index _____*

■ Exercise: SEATED DUMBBELL REVERSE WRIST CURL

Weight Reps Sets	Weight Reps Sets	Weight Reps Sets	Weight Reps Sets	Weight Reps Sets	Weight Reps Sets
× ×	× ×	× ×	× ×	× ×	× ×
Subtotal = lbs.	Subtotal = lbs.	Subtotal = lbs.	Subtotal = lbs.	Subtotal = lbs.	Subtotal = lbs.

Exercise 2:   *Total Weight _____ lbs.   Time _____ mins.   Power Factor _____ lbs./min.   Power Index _____*

■ Exercise: STANDING BARBELL WRIST CURL BEHIND BACK

Weight Reps Sets	Weight Reps Sets	Weight Reps Sets	Weight Reps Sets	Weight Reps Sets	Weight Reps Sets
× ×	× ×	× ×	× ×	× ×	× ×
Subtotal = lbs.	Subtotal = lbs.	Subtotal = lbs.	Subtotal = lbs.	Subtotal = lbs.	Subtotal = lbs.

Exercise 3:   *Total Weight _____ lbs.   Time _____ mins.   Power Factor _____ lbs./min.   Power Index _____*

■ Exercise:

Weight Reps Sets	Weight Reps Sets	Weight Reps Sets	Weight Reps Sets	Weight Reps Sets	Weight Reps Sets
× ×	× ×	× ×	× ×	× ×	× ×
Subtotal = lbs.	Subtotal = lbs.	Subtotal = lbs.	Subtotal = lbs.	Subtotal = lbs.	Subtotal = lbs.

Exercise 4:   *Total Weight _____ lbs.   Time _____ mins.   Power Factor _____ lbs./min.   Power Index _____*

■ Exercise:

Weight Reps Sets	Weight Reps Sets	Weight Reps Sets	Weight Reps Sets	Weight Reps Sets	Weight Reps Sets
× ×	× ×	× ×	× ×	× ×	× ×
Subtotal = lbs.	Subtotal = lbs.	Subtotal = lbs.	Subtotal = lbs.	Subtotal = lbs.	Subtotal = lbs.

Exercise 5:   *Total Weight _____ lbs.   Time _____ mins.   Power Factor _____ lbs./min.   Power Index _____*

OVERALL WORKOUT: *Total Weight _____ lbs.   Time _____ mins.   Power Factor _____ lbs./min.   Power Index _____*

Exercise Subtotal = Weight × Reps × Sets   ■ *Power Factor = lbs./min.*   ■ *Power Index = Total Weight × Power Factor ÷ 1,000,000*

FOREARM SPECIALIZATION WORKOUT RECORD Date: ___ / ___ / ___

Start Time: _____   Finish Time: _____   Total Time: _____

■ Exercise: STANDING BARBELL REVERSE CURL

Weight Reps Sets	Weight Reps Sets	Weight Reps Sets	Weight Reps Sets	Weight Reps Sets	Weight Reps Sets
× ×	× ×	× ×	× ×	× ×	× ×
Subtotal = lbs.	Subtotal = lbs.	Subtotal = lbs.	Subtotal = lbs.	Subtotal = lbs.	Subtotal = lbs.

Exercise 1:   *Total Weight* _____ *lbs.*   *Time* _____ *mins.*   *Power Factor* _____ *lbs./min.*   *Power Index* _____

■ Exercise: SEATED DUMBBELL REVERSE WRIST CURL

Weight Reps Sets	Weight Reps Sets	Weight Reps Sets	Weight Reps Sets	Weight Reps Sets	Weight Reps Sets
× ×	× ×	× ×	× ×	× ×	× ×
Subtotal = lbs.	Subtotal = lbs.	Subtotal = lbs.	Subtotal = lbs.	Subtotal = lbs.	Subtotal = lbs.

Exercise 2:   *Total Weight* _____ *lbs.*   *Time* _____ *mins.*   *Power Factor* _____ *lbs./min.*   *Power Index* _____

■ Exercise: STANDING BARBELL WRIST CURL BEHIND BACK

Weight Reps Sets	Weight Reps Sets	Weight Reps Sets	Weight Reps Sets	Weight Reps Sets	Weight Reps Sets
× ×	× ×	× ×	× ×	× ×	× ×
Subtotal = lbs.	Subtotal = lbs.	Subtotal = lbs.	Subtotal = lbs.	Subtotal = lbs.	Subtotal = lbs.

Exercise 3:   *Total Weight* _____ *lbs.*   *Time* _____ *mins.*   *Power Factor* _____ *lbs./min.*   *Power Index* _____

■ Exercise:

Weight Reps Sets	Weight Reps Sets	Weight Reps Sets	Weight Reps Sets	Weight Reps Sets	Weight Reps Sets
× ×	× ×	× ×	× ×	× ×	× ×
Subtotal = lbs.	Subtotal = lbs.	Subtotal = lbs.	Subtotal = lbs.	Subtotal = lbs.	Subtotal = lbs.

Exercise 4:   *Total Weight* _____ *lbs.*   *Time* _____ *mins.*   *Power Factor* _____ *lbs./min.*   *Power Index* _____

■ Exercise:

Weight Reps Sets	Weight Reps Sets	Weight Reps Sets	Weight Reps Sets	Weight Reps Sets	Weight Reps Sets
× ×	× ×	× ×	× ×	× ×	× ×
Subtotal = lbs.	Subtotal = lbs.	Subtotal = lbs.	Subtotal = lbs.	Subtotal = lbs.	Subtotal = lbs.

Exercise 5:   *Total Weight* _____ *lbs.*   *Time* _____ *mins.*   *Power Factor* _____ *lbs./min.*   *Power Index* _____

OVERALL WORKOUT: *Total Weight* _____ *lbs.*   *Time* _____ *mins.*   *Power Factor* _____ *lbs./min.*   *Power Index* _____

Exercise Subtotal = Weight × Reps × Sets   ■ *Power Factor = lbs./min.*   ■ *Power Index = Total Weight × Power Factor ÷ 1,000,000*

FOREARM SPECIALIZATION WORKOUT RECORD Date: ___ / ___ / ___

Start Time: _____ **Finish Time:** _____ **Total Time:** _____

▪ Exercise: STANDING BARBELL REVERSE CURL

Weight Reps Sets	Weight Reps Sets	Weight Reps Sets	Weight Reps Sets	Weight Reps Sets	Weight Reps Sets
× ×	× ×	× ×	× ×	× ×	× ×
Subtotal = lbs.	Subtotal = lbs.	Subtotal = lbs.	Subtotal = lbs.	Subtotal = lbs.	Subtotal = lbs.

Exercise 1: *Total Weight* _____ *lbs.* *Time* _____ *mins.* *Power Factor* _____ *lbs./min.* *Power Index* _____

▪ Exercise: SEATED DUMBBELL REVERSE WRIST CURL

Weight Reps Sets	Weight Reps Sets	Weight Reps Sets	Weight Reps Sets	Weight Reps Sets	Weight Reps Sets
× ×	× ×	× ×	× ×	× ×	× ×
Subtotal = lbs.	Subtotal = lbs.	Subtotal = lbs.	Subtotal = lbs.	Subtotal = lbs.	Subtotal = lbs.

Exercise 2: *Total Weight* _____ *lbs.* *Time* _____ *mins.* *Power Factor* _____ *lbs./min.* *Power Index* _____

▪ Exercise: STANDING BARBELL WRIST CURL BEHIND BACK

Weight Reps Sets	Weight Reps Sets	Weight Reps Sets	Weight Reps Sets	Weight Reps Sets	Weight Reps Sets
× ×	× ×	× ×	× ×	× ×	× ×
Subtotal = lbs.	Subtotal = lbs.	Subtotal = lbs.	Subtotal = lbs.	Subtotal = lbs.	Subtotal = lbs.

Exercise 3: *Total Weight* _____ *lbs.* *Time* _____ *mins.* *Power Factor* _____ *lbs./min.* *Power Index* _____

▪ Exercise:

Weight Reps Sets	Weight Reps Sets	Weight Reps Sets	Weight Reps Sets	Weight Reps Sets	Weight Reps Sets
× ×	× ×	× ×	× ×	× ×	× ×
Subtotal = lbs.	Subtotal = lbs.	Subtotal = lbs.	Subtotal = lbs.	Subtotal = lbs.	Subtotal = lbs.

Exercise 4: *Total Weight* _____ *lbs.* *Time* _____ *mins.* *Power Factor* _____ *lbs./min.* *Power Index* _____

▪ Exercise:

Weight Reps Sets	Weight Reps Sets	Weight Reps Sets	Weight Reps Sets	Weight Reps Sets	Weight Reps Sets
× ×	× ×	× ×	× ×	× ×	× ×
Subtotal = lbs.	Subtotal = lbs.	Subtotal = lbs.	Subtotal = lbs.	Subtotal = lbs.	Subtotal = lbs.

Exercise 5: *Total Weight* _____ *lbs.* *Time* _____ *mins.* *Power Factor* _____ *lbs./min.* *Power Index* _____

OVERALL WORKOUT: *Total Weight* _____ *lbs.* *Time* _____ *mins.* *Power Factor* _____ *lbs./min.* *Power Index* _____

Exercise Subtotal = Weight × Reps × Sets ▪ *Power Factor = lbs./min.* ▪ *Power Index = Total Weight × Power Factor ÷ 1,000,000*

FOREARM SPECIALIZATION WORKOUT RECORD Date: ___ / ___ / ___

Start Time: _____ Finish Time: _____ Total Time: _____

■ Exercise: STANDING BARBELL REVERSE CURL

Weight	Reps	Sets	Weight	Reps	Sets	Weight	Reps	Sets	Weight	Reps	Sets	Weight	Reps	Sets	Weight	Reps	Sets
×	×		×	×		×	×		×	×		×	×		×	×	
Subtotal =		lbs.	Subtotal =		lbs.	Subtotal =		lbs.	Subtotal =		lbs.	Subtotal =		lbs.	Subtotal =		lbs.

Exercise 1: _____ Total Weight _____ lbs. Time _____ mins. Power Factor _____ lbs./min. Power Index _____

■ Exercise: SEATED DUMBBELL REVERSE WRIST CURL

Weight	Reps	Sets	Weight	Reps	Sets	Weight	Reps	Sets	Weight	Reps	Sets	Weight	Reps	Sets	Weight	Reps	Sets
×	×		×	×		×	×		×	×		×	×		×	×	
Subtotal =		lbs.	Subtotal =		lbs.	Subtotal =		lbs.	Subtotal =		lbs.	Subtotal =		lbs.	Subtotal =		lbs.

Exercise 2: _____ Total Weight _____ lbs. Time _____ mins. Power Factor _____ lbs./min. Power Index _____

■ Exercise: STANDING BARBELL WRIST CURL BEHIND BACK

Weight	Reps	Sets	Weight	Reps	Sets	Weight	Reps	Sets	Weight	Reps	Sets	Weight	Reps	Sets	Weight	Reps	Sets
×	×		×	×		×	×		×	×		×	×		×	×	
Subtotal =		lbs.	Subtotal =		lbs.	Subtotal =		lbs.	Subtotal =		lbs.	Subtotal =		lbs.	Subtotal =		lbs.

Exercise 3: _____ Total Weight _____ lbs. Time _____ mins. Power Factor _____ lbs./min. Power Index _____

■ Exercise: _____

Weight	Reps	Sets	Weight	Reps	Sets	Weight	Reps	Sets	Weight	Reps	Sets	Weight	Reps	Sets	Weight	Reps	Sets
×	×		×	×		×	×		×	×		×	×		×	×	
Subtotal =		lbs.	Subtotal =		lbs.	Subtotal =		lbs.	Subtotal =		lbs.	Subtotal =		lbs.	Subtotal =		lbs.

Exercise 4: _____ Total Weight _____ lbs. Time _____ mins. Power Factor _____ lbs./min. Power Index _____

■ Exercise: _____

Weight	Reps	Sets	Weight	Reps	Sets	Weight	Reps	Sets	Weight	Reps	Sets	Weight	Reps	Sets	Weight	Reps	Sets
×	×		×	×		×	×		×	×		×	×		×	×	
Subtotal =		lbs.	Subtotal =		lbs.	Subtotal =		lbs.	Subtotal =		lbs.	Subtotal =		lbs.	Subtotal =		lbs.

Exercise 5: _____ Total Weight _____ lbs. Time _____ mins. Power Factor _____ lbs./min. Power Index _____

OVERALL WORKOUT: Total Weight _____ lbs. Time _____ mins. Power Factor _____ lbs./min. Power Index _____

Exercise Subtotal = Weight × Reps × Sets ■ *Power Factor = lbs./min.* ■ *Power Index = Total Weight × Power Factor ÷ 1,000,000*

FOREARM SPECIALIZATION WORKOUT RECORD Date: ___ / ___ / ___

Start Time: _____   Finish Time: _____   Total Time: _____

▪ Exercise: STANDING BARBELL REVERSE CURL

Weight Reps Sets	Weight Reps Sets	Weight Reps Sets	Weight Reps Sets	Weight Reps Sets	Weight Reps Sets
× ×	× ×	× ×	× ×	× ×	× ×
Subtotal = lbs.	Subtotal = lbs.	Subtotal = lbs.	Subtotal = lbs.	Subtotal = lbs.	Subtotal = lbs.

Exercise 1:   *Total Weight _____ lbs.   Time _____ mins.   Power Factor _____ lbs./min.   Power Index _____*

▪ Exercise: SEATED DUMBBELL REVERSE WRIST CURL

Weight Reps Sets	Weight Reps Sets	Weight Reps Sets	Weight Reps Sets	Weight Reps Sets	Weight Reps Sets
× ×	× ×	× ×	× ×	× ×	× ×
Subtotal = lbs.	Subtotal = lbs.	Subtotal = lbs.	Subtotal = lbs.	Subtotal = lbs.	Subtotal = lbs.

Exercise 2:   *Total Weight _____ lbs.   Time _____ mins.   Power Factor _____ lbs./min.   Power Index _____*

▪ Exercise: STANDING BARBELL WRIST CURL BEHIND BACK

Weight Reps Sets	Weight Reps Sets	Weight Reps Sets	Weight Reps Sets	Weight Reps Sets	Weight Reps Sets
× ×	× ×	× ×	× ×	× ×	× ×
Subtotal = lbs.	Subtotal = lbs.	Subtotal = lbs.	Subtotal = lbs.	Subtotal = lbs.	Subtotal = lbs.

Exercise 3:   *Total Weight _____ lbs.   Time _____ mins.   Power Factor _____ lbs./min.   Power Index _____*

▪ Exercise:

Weight Reps Sets	Weight Reps Sets	Weight Reps Sets	Weight Reps Sets	Weight Reps Sets	Weight Reps Sets
× ×	× ×	× ×	× ×	× ×	× ×
Subtotal = lbs.	Subtotal = lbs.	Subtotal = lbs.	Subtotal = lbs.	Subtotal = lbs.	Subtotal = lbs.

Exercise 4:   *Total Weight _____ lbs.   Time _____ mins.   Power Factor _____ lbs./min.   Power Index _____*

▪ Exercise:

Weight Reps Sets	Weight Reps Sets	Weight Reps Sets	Weight Reps Sets	Weight Reps Sets	Weight Reps Sets
× ×	× ×	× ×	× ×	× ×	× ×
Subtotal = lbs.	Subtotal = lbs.	Subtotal = lbs.	Subtotal = lbs.	Subtotal = lbs.	Subtotal = lbs.

Exercise 5:   *Total Weight _____ lbs.   Time _____ mins.   Power Factor _____ lbs./min.   Power Index _____*

OVERALL WORKOUT: *Total Weight _____ lbs.   Time _____ mins.   Power Factor _____ lbs./min.   Power Index _____*

Exercise Subtotal = Weight × Reps × Sets   ▪ Power Factor = lbs./min.   ▪ Power Index = Total Weight × Power Factor ÷ 1,000,000

FOREARM SPECIALIZATION WORKOUT RECORD Date: ___ / ___ / ___

Start Time: _____   Finish Time: _____   Total Time: _____

■ Exercise: STANDING BARBELL REVERSE CURL

Weight Reps Sets	Weight Reps Sets	Weight Reps Sets	Weight Reps Sets	Weight Reps Sets	Weight Reps Sets
× ×	× ×	× ×	× ×	× ×	× ×
Subtotal = lbs.	Subtotal = lbs.	Subtotal = lbs.	Subtotal = lbs.	Subtotal = lbs.	Subtotal = lbs.

Exercise 1:   *Total Weight _____ lbs.   Time _____ mins.   Power Factor _____ lbs./min.   Power Index _____*

■ Exercise: SEATED DUMBBELL REVERSE WRIST CURL

Weight Reps Sets	Weight Reps Sets	Weight Reps Sets	Weight Reps Sets	Weight Reps Sets	Weight Reps Sets
× ×	× ×	× ×	× ×	× ×	× ×
Subtotal = lbs.	Subtotal = lbs.	Subtotal = lbs.	Subtotal = lbs.	Subtotal = lbs.	Subtotal = lbs.

Exercise 2:   *Total Weight _____ lbs.   Time _____ mins.   Power Factor _____ lbs./min.   Power Index _____*

■ Exercise: STANDING BARBELL WRIST CURL BEHIND BACK

Weight Reps Sets	Weight Reps Sets	Weight Reps Sets	Weight Reps Sets	Weight Reps Sets	Weight Reps Sets
× ×	× ×	× ×	× ×	× ×	× ×
Subtotal = lbs.	Subtotal = lbs.	Subtotal = lbs.	Subtotal = lbs.	Subtotal = lbs.	Subtotal = lbs.

Exercise 3:   *Total Weight _____ lbs.   Time _____ mins.   Power Factor _____ lbs./min.   Power Index _____*

■ Exercise:

Weight Reps Sets	Weight Reps Sets	Weight Reps Sets	Weight Reps Sets	Weight Reps Sets	Weight Reps Sets
× ×	× ×	× ×	× ×	× ×	× ×
Subtotal = lbs.	Subtotal = lbs.	Subtotal = lbs.	Subtotal = lbs.	Subtotal = lbs.	Subtotal = lbs.

Exercise 4:   *Total Weight _____ lbs.   Time _____ mins.   Power Factor _____ lbs./min.   Power Index _____*

■ Exercise:

Weight Reps Sets	Weight Reps Sets	Weight Reps Sets	Weight Reps Sets	Weight Reps Sets	Weight Reps Sets
× ×	× ×	× ×	× ×	× ×	× ×
Subtotal = lbs.	Subtotal = lbs.	Subtotal = lbs.	Subtotal = lbs.	Subtotal = lbs.	Subtotal = lbs.

Exercise 5:   *Total Weight _____ lbs.   Time _____ mins.   Power Factor _____ lbs./min.   Power Index _____*

OVERALL WORKOUT: *Total Weight _____ lbs.   Time _____ mins.   Power Factor _____ lbs./min.   Power Index _____*

Exercise Subtotal = Weight × Reps × Sets   ■ Power Factor = lbs./min.   ■ Power Index = Total Weight × Power Factor ÷ 1,000,000

FOREARM SPECIALIZATION WORKOUT RECORD Date: ___ / ___ / ___

Start Time: _____   Finish Time: _____   Total Time: _____

▪ Exercise: STANDING BARBELL REVERSE CURL

Weight Reps Sets	Weight Reps Sets	Weight Reps Sets	Weight Reps Sets	Weight Reps Sets	Weight Reps Sets
× ×	× ×	× ×	× ×	× ×	× ×
Subtotal = lbs.	Subtotal = lbs.	Subtotal = lbs.	Subtotal = lbs.	Subtotal = lbs.	Subtotal = lbs.

Exercise 1:   *Total Weight _____ lbs.   Time _____ mins.   Power Factor _____ lbs./min.   Power Index _____*

▪ Exercise: SEATED DUMBBELL REVERSE WRIST CURL

Weight Reps Sets	Weight Reps Sets	Weight Reps Sets	Weight Reps Sets	Weight Reps Sets	Weight Reps Sets
× ×	× ×	× ×	× ×	× ×	× ×
Subtotal = lbs.	Subtotal = lbs.	Subtotal = lbs.	Subtotal = lbs.	Subtotal = lbs.	Subtotal = lbs.

Exercise 2:   *Total Weight _____ lbs.   Time _____ mins.   Power Factor _____ lbs./min.   Power Index _____*

▪ Exercise: STANDING BARBELL WRIST CURL BEHIND BACK

Weight Reps Sets	Weight Reps Sets	Weight Reps Sets	Weight Reps Sets	Weight Reps Sets	Weight Reps Sets
× ×	× ×	× ×	× ×	× ×	× ×
Subtotal = lbs.	Subtotal = lbs.	Subtotal = lbs.	Subtotal = lbs.	Subtotal = lbs.	Subtotal = lbs.

Exercise 3:   *Total Weight _____ lbs.   Time _____ mins.   Power Factor _____ lbs./min.   Power Index _____*

▪ Exercise:

Weight Reps Sets	Weight Reps Sets	Weight Reps Sets	Weight Reps Sets	Weight Reps Sets	Weight Reps Sets
× ×	× ×	× ×	× ×	× ×	× ×
Subtotal = lbs.	Subtotal = lbs.	Subtotal = lbs.	Subtotal = lbs.	Subtotal = lbs.	Subtotal = lbs.

Exercise 4:   *Total Weight _____ lbs.   Time _____ mins.   Power Factor _____ lbs./min.   Power Index _____*

▪ Exercise:

Weight Reps Sets	Weight Reps Sets	Weight Reps Sets	Weight Reps Sets	Weight Reps Sets	Weight Reps Sets
× ×	× ×	× ×	× ×	× ×	× ×
Subtotal = lbs.	Subtotal = lbs.	Subtotal = lbs.	Subtotal = lbs.	Subtotal = lbs.	Subtotal = lbs.

Exercise 5:   *Total Weight _____ lbs.   Time _____ mins.   Power Factor _____ lbs./min.   Power Index _____*

OVERALL WORKOUT: *Total Weight _____ lbs.   Time _____ mins.   Power Factor _____ lbs./min.   Power Index _____*

Exercise Subtotal = Weight × Reps × Sets   ▪ *Power Factor = lbs./min.*   ▪ *Power Index = Total Weight × Power Factor ÷ 1,000,000*

FOREARM SPECIALIZATION WORKOUT RECORD Date: ___ / ___ / ___

Start Time: _____   Finish Time: _____   Total Time: _____

■ **Exercise: STANDING BARBELL REVERSE CURL**

Weight Reps Sets	Weight Reps Sets	Weight Reps Sets	Weight Reps Sets	Weight Reps Sets	Weight Reps Sets
× ×	× ×	× ×	× ×	× ×	× ×
Subtotal = lbs.	Subtotal = lbs.	Subtotal = lbs.	Subtotal = lbs.	Subtotal = lbs.	Subtotal = lbs.

Exercise 1: _____   *Total Weight* _____ *lbs.*   *Time* _____ *mins.*   *Power Factor* _____ *lbs./min.*   *Power Index* _____

■ **Exercise: SEATED DUMBBELL REVERSE WRIST CURL**

Weight Reps Sets	Weight Reps Sets	Weight Reps Sets	Weight Reps Sets	Weight Reps Sets	Weight Reps Sets
× ×	× ×	× ×	× ×	× ×	× ×
Subtotal = lbs.	Subtotal = lbs.	Subtotal = lbs.	Subtotal = lbs.	Subtotal = lbs.	Subtotal = lbs.

Exercise 2: _____   *Total Weight* _____ *lbs.*   *Time* _____ *mins.*   *Power Factor* _____ *lbs./min.*   *Power Index* _____

■ **Exercise: STANDING BARBELL WRIST CURL BEHIND BACK**

Weight Reps Sets	Weight Reps Sets	Weight Reps Sets	Weight Reps Sets	Weight Reps Sets	Weight Reps Sets
× ×	× ×	× ×	× ×	× ×	× ×
Subtotal = lbs.	Subtotal = lbs.	Subtotal = lbs.	Subtotal = lbs.	Subtotal = lbs.	Subtotal = lbs.

Exercise 3: _____   *Total Weight* _____ *lbs.*   *Time* _____ *mins.*   *Power Factor* _____ *lbs./min.*   *Power Index* _____

■ **Exercise:**

Weight Reps Sets	Weight Reps Sets	Weight Reps Sets	Weight Reps Sets	Weight Reps Sets	Weight Reps Sets
× ×	× ×	× ×	× ×	× ×	× ×
Subtotal = lbs.	Subtotal = lbs.	Subtotal = lbs.	Subtotal = lbs.	Subtotal = lbs.	Subtotal = lbs.

Exercise 4: _____   *Total Weight* _____ *lbs.*   *Time* _____ *mins.*   *Power Factor* _____ *lbs./min.*   *Power Index* _____

■ **Exercise:**

Weight Reps Sets	Weight Reps Sets	Weight Reps Sets	Weight Reps Sets	Weight Reps Sets	Weight Reps Sets
× ×	× ×	× ×	× ×	× ×	× ×
Subtotal = lbs.	Subtotal = lbs.	Subtotal = lbs.	Subtotal = lbs.	Subtotal = lbs.	Subtotal = lbs.

Exercise 5: _____   *Total Weight* _____ *lbs.*   *Time* _____ *mins.*   *Power Factor* _____ *lbs./min.*   *Power Index* _____

OVERALL WORKOUT: *Total Weight* _____ *lbs.*   *Time* _____ *mins.*   *Power Factor* _____ *lbs./min.*   *Power Index* _____

Exercise Subtotal = Weight × Reps × Sets   ■ *Power Factor = lbs./min.*   ■ *Power Index = Total Weight × Power Factor ÷ 1,000,000*

FOREARM SPECIALIZATION WORKOUT RECORD Date: ___ / ___ / ___

Start Time: _____   Finish Time: _____   Total Time: _____

■ **Exercise:** STANDING BARBELL REVERSE CURL

Weight Reps Sets	Weight Reps Sets	Weight Reps Sets	Weight Reps Sets	Weight Reps Sets	Weight Reps Sets
× ×	× ×	× ×	× ×	× ×	× ×
Subtotal = lbs.	Subtotal = lbs.	Subtotal = lbs.	Subtotal = lbs.	Subtotal = lbs.	Subtotal = lbs.

Exercise 1:   *Total Weight* _____ *lbs.*   *Time* _____ *mins.*   *Power Factor* _____ *lbs./min.*   *Power Index* _____

■ **Exercise:** SEATED DUMBBELL REVERSE WRIST CURL

Weight Reps Sets	Weight Reps Sets	Weight Reps Sets	Weight Reps Sets	Weight Reps Sets	Weight Reps Sets
× ×	× ×	× ×	× ×	× ×	× ×
Subtotal = lbs.	Subtotal = lbs.	Subtotal = lbs.	Subtotal = lbs.	Subtotal = lbs.	Subtotal = lbs.

Exercise 2:   *Total Weight* _____ *lbs.*   *Time* _____ *mins.*   *Power Factor* _____ *lbs./min.*   *Power Index* _____

■ **Exercise:** STANDING BARBELL WRIST CURL BEHIND BACK

Weight Reps Sets	Weight Reps Sets	Weight Reps Sets	Weight Reps Sets	Weight Reps Sets	Weight Reps Sets
× ×	× ×	× ×	× ×	× ×	× ×
Subtotal = lbs.	Subtotal = lbs.	Subtotal = lbs.	Subtotal = lbs.	Subtotal = lbs.	Subtotal = lbs.

Exercise 3:   *Total Weight* _____ *lbs.*   *Time* _____ *mins.*   *Power Factor* _____ *lbs./min.*   *Power Index* _____

■ **Exercise:**

Weight Reps Sets	Weight Reps Sets	Weight Reps Sets	Weight Reps Sets	Weight Reps Sets	Weight Reps Sets
× ×	× ×	× ×	× ×	× ×	× ×
Subtotal = lbs.	Subtotal = lbs.	Subtotal = lbs.	Subtotal = lbs.	Subtotal = lbs.	Subtotal = lbs.

Exercise 4:   *Total Weight* _____ *lbs.*   *Time* _____ *mins.*   *Power Factor* _____ *lbs./min.*   *Power Index* _____

■ **Exercise:**

Weight Reps Sets	Weight Reps Sets	Weight Reps Sets	Weight Reps Sets	Weight Reps Sets	Weight Reps Sets
× ×	× ×	× ×	× ×	× ×	× ×
Subtotal = lbs.	Subtotal = lbs.	Subtotal = lbs.	Subtotal = lbs.	Subtotal = lbs.	Subtotal = lbs.

Exercise 5:   *Total Weight* _____ *lbs.*   *Time* _____ *mins.*   *Power Factor* _____ *lbs./min.*   *Power Index* _____

OVERALL WORKOUT: *Total Weight* _____ *lbs.*   *Time* _____ *mins.*   *Power Factor* _____ *lbs./min.*   *Power Index* _____

Exercise Subtotal = Weight × Reps × Sets   ■ *Power Factor = lbs./min.*   ■ *Power Index = Total Weight × Power Factor ÷ 1,000,000*

FOREARM SPECIALIZATION WORKOUT RECORD Date: ___ / ___ / ___

Start Time: _____   **Finish Time:** _____   **Total Time:** _____

■ **Exercise: STANDING BARBELL REVERSE CURL**

Weight Reps Sets	Weight Reps Sets	Weight Reps Sets	Weight Reps Sets	Weight Reps Sets	Weight Reps Sets
× ×	× ×	× ×	× ×	× ×	× ×
Subtotal = lbs.	Subtotal = lbs.	Subtotal = lbs.	Subtotal = lbs.	Subtotal = lbs.	Subtotal = lbs.

Exercise 1:   *Total Weight* _____ *lbs.*   *Time* _____ *mins.*   *Power Factor* _____ *lbs./min.*   *Power Index* _____

■ **Exercise: SEATED DUMBBELL REVERSE WRIST CURL**

Weight Reps Sets	Weight Reps Sets	Weight Reps Sets	Weight Reps Sets	Weight Reps Sets	Weight Reps Sets
× ×	× ×	× ×	× ×	× ×	× ×
Subtotal = lbs.	Subtotal = lbs.	Subtotal = lbs.	Subtotal = lbs.	Subtotal = lbs.	Subtotal = lbs.

Exercise 2:   *Total Weight* _____ *lbs.*   *Time* _____ *mins.*   *Power Factor* _____ *lbs./min.*   *Power Index* _____

■ **Exercise: STANDING BARBELL WRIST CURL BEHIND BACK**

Weight Reps Sets	Weight Reps Sets	Weight Reps Sets	Weight Reps Sets	Weight Reps Sets	Weight Reps Sets
× ×	× ×	× ×	× ×	× ×	× ×
Subtotal = lbs.	Subtotal = lbs.	Subtotal = lbs.	Subtotal = lbs.	Subtotal = lbs.	Subtotal = lbs.

Exercise 3:   *Total Weight* _____ *lbs.*   *Time* _____ *mins.*   *Power Factor* _____ *lbs./min.*   *Power Index* _____

■ **Exercise:**

Weight Reps Sets	Weight Reps Sets	Weight Reps Sets	Weight Reps Sets	Weight Reps Sets	Weight Reps Sets
× ×	× ×	× ×	× ×	× ×	× ×
Subtotal = lbs.	Subtotal = lbs.	Subtotal = lbs.	Subtotal = lbs.	Subtotal = lbs.	Subtotal = lbs.

Exercise 4:   *Total Weight* _____ *lbs.*   *Time* _____ *mins.*   *Power Factor* _____ *lbs./min.*   *Power Index* _____

■ **Exercise:**

Weight Reps Sets	Weight Reps Sets	Weight Reps Sets	Weight Reps Sets	Weight Reps Sets	Weight Reps Sets
× ×	× ×	× ×	× ×	× ×	× ×
Subtotal = lbs.	Subtotal = lbs.	Subtotal = lbs.	Subtotal = lbs.	Subtotal = lbs.	Subtotal = lbs.

Exercise 5:   *Total Weight* _____ *lbs.*   *Time* _____ *mins.*   *Power Factor* _____ *lbs./min.*   *Power Index* _____

OVERALL WORKOUT: *Total Weight* _____ *lbs.*   *Time* _____ *mins.*   *Power Factor* _____ *lbs./min.*   *Power Index* _____

Exercise Subtotal = Weight × Reps × Sets ■ *Power Factor = lbs./min.* ■ *Power Index = Total Weight × Power Factor ÷ 1,000,000*

FOREARM SPECIALIZATION WORKOUT RECORD Date: ___ / ___ / ___

Start Time: _____   **Finish Time:** _____   **Total Time:** _____

▪ Exercise: STANDING BARBELL REVERSE CURL

Weight Reps Sets	Weight Reps Sets	Weight Reps Sets	Weight Reps Sets	Weight Reps Sets	Weight Reps Sets
× ×	× ×	× ×	× ×	× ×	× ×
Subtotal = lbs.	Subtotal = lbs.	Subtotal = lbs.	Subtotal = lbs.	Subtotal = lbs.	Subtotal = lbs.

Exercise 1:   *Total Weight* _____ *lbs.*   *Time* _____ *mins.*   *Power Factor* _____ *lbs./min.*   *Power Index* _____

▪ Exercise: SEATED DUMBBELL REVERSE WRIST CURL

Weight Reps Sets	Weight Reps Sets	Weight Reps Sets	Weight Reps Sets	Weight Reps Sets	Weight Reps Sets
× ×	× ×	× ×	× ×	× ×	× ×
Subtotal = lbs.	Subtotal = lbs.	Subtotal = lbs.	Subtotal = lbs.	Subtotal = lbs.	Subtotal = lbs.

Exercise 2:   *Total Weight* _____ *lbs.*   *Time* _____ *mins.*   *Power Factor* _____ *lbs./min.*   *Power Index* _____

▪ Exercise: STANDING BARBELL WRIST CURL BEHIND BACK

Weight Reps Sets	Weight Reps Sets	Weight Reps Sets	Weight Reps Sets	Weight Reps Sets	Weight Reps Sets
× ×	× ×	× ×	× ×	× ×	× ×
Subtotal = lbs.	Subtotal = lbs.	Subtotal = lbs.	Subtotal = lbs.	Subtotal = lbs.	Subtotal = lbs.

Exercise 3:   *Total Weight* _____ *lbs.*   *Time* _____ *mins.*   *Power Factor* _____ *lbs./min.*   *Power Index* _____

▪ Exercise:

Weight Reps Sets	Weight Reps Sets	Weight Reps Sets	Weight Reps Sets	Weight Reps Sets	Weight Reps Sets
× ×	× ×	× ×	× ×	× ×	× ×
Subtotal = lbs.	Subtotal = lbs.	Subtotal = lbs.	Subtotal = lbs.	Subtotal = lbs.	Subtotal = lbs.

Exercise 4:   *Total Weight* _____ *lbs.*   *Time* _____ *mins.*   *Power Factor* _____ *lbs./min.*   *Power Index* _____

▪ Exercise:

Weight Reps Sets	Weight Reps Sets	Weight Reps Sets	Weight Reps Sets	Weight Reps Sets	Weight Reps Sets
× ×	× ×	× ×	× ×	× ×	× ×
Subtotal = lbs.	Subtotal = lbs.	Subtotal = lbs.	Subtotal = lbs.	Subtotal = lbs.	Subtotal = lbs.

Exercise 5:   *Total Weight* _____ *lbs.*   *Time* _____ *mins.*   *Power Factor* _____ *lbs./min.*   *Power Index* _____

OVERALL WORKOUT: *Total Weight* _____ *lbs.*   *Time* _____ *mins.*   *Power Factor* _____ *lbs./min.*   *Power Index* _____

Exercise Subtotal = Weight × Reps × Sets   ▪ *Power Factor = lbs./min.*   ▪ *Power Index = Total Weight × Power Factor ÷ 1,000,000*

SHOULDER SPECIALIZATION WORKOUT RECORD Date: ___ / ___ / ___

Start Time: _____   Finish Time: _____   Total Time: _____

■ Exercise: STANDING BARBELL PRESS

Weight Reps Sets	Weight Reps Sets	Weight Reps Sets	Weight Reps Sets	Weight Reps Sets	Weight Reps Sets
× ×	× ×	× ×	× ×	× ×	× ×
Subtotal = lbs.	Subtotal = lbs.	Subtotal = lbs.	Subtotal = lbs.	Subtotal = lbs.	Subtotal = lbs.

Exercise 1:   *Total Weight _____ lbs.   Time _____ mins.   Power Factor _____ lbs./min.   Power Index _____*

■ Exercise: BARBELL SHRUG

Weight Reps Sets	Weight Reps Sets	Weight Reps Sets	Weight Reps Sets	Weight Reps Sets	Weight Reps Sets
× ×	× ×	× ×	× ×	× ×	× ×
Subtotal = lbs.	Subtotal = lbs.	Subtotal = lbs.	Subtotal = lbs.	Subtotal = lbs.	Subtotal = lbs.

Exercise 2:   *Total Weight _____ lbs.   Time _____ mins.   Power Factor _____ lbs./min.   Power Index _____*

■ Exercise: STANDING BENT-OVER DUMBBELL LATERAL

Weight Reps Sets	Weight Reps Sets	Weight Reps Sets	Weight Reps Sets	Weight Reps Sets	Weight Reps Sets
× ×	× ×	× ×	× ×	× ×	× ×
Subtotal = lbs.	Subtotal = lbs.	Subtotal = lbs.	Subtotal = lbs.	Subtotal = lbs.	Subtotal = lbs.

Exercise 3:   *Total Weight _____ lbs.   Time _____ mins.   Power Factor _____ lbs./min.   Power Index _____*

■ Exercise:

Weight Reps Sets	Weight Reps Sets	Weight Reps Sets	Weight Reps Sets	Weight Reps Sets	Weight Reps Sets
× ×	× ×	× ×	× ×	× ×	× ×
Subtotal = lbs.	Subtotal = lbs.	Subtotal = lbs.	Subtotal = lbs.	Subtotal = lbs.	Subtotal = lbs.

Exercise 4:   *Total Weight _____ lbs.   Time _____ mins.   Power Factor _____ lbs./min.   Power Index _____*

■ Exercise:

Weight Reps Sets	Weight Reps Sets	Weight Reps Sets	Weight Reps Sets	Weight Reps Sets	Weight Reps Sets
× ×	× ×	× ×	× ×	× ×	× ×
Subtotal = lbs.	Subtotal = lbs.	Subtotal = lbs.	Subtotal = lbs.	Subtotal = lbs.	Subtotal = lbs.

Exercise 5:   *Total Weight _____ lbs.   Time _____ mins.   Power Factor _____ lbs./min.   Power Index _____*

OVERALL WORKOUT: *Total Weight _____ lbs.   Time _____ mins.   Power Factor _____ lbs./min.   Power Index _____*

Exercise Subtotal = Weight × Reps × Sets   ■ *Power Factor = lbs./min.*   ■ *Power Index = Total Weight × Power Factor ÷ 1,000,000*

SHOULDER SPECIALIZATION WORKOUT RECORD Date: ___ / ___ / ___

Start Time: _____ **Finish Time:** _____ **Total Time:** _____

■ Exercise: STANDING BARBELL PRESS

Weight Reps Sets	Weight Reps Sets	Weight Reps Sets	Weight Reps Sets	Weight Reps Sets	Weight Reps Sets
× ×	× ×	× ×	× ×	× ×	× ×
Subtotal = lbs.	Subtotal = lbs.	Subtotal = lbs.	Subtotal = lbs.	Subtotal = lbs.	Subtotal = lbs.

Exercise 1: *Total Weight* _____ *lbs.* *Time* _____ *mins.* *Power Factor* _____ *lbs./min.* *Power Index* _____

■ Exercise: BARBELL SHRUG

Weight Reps Sets	Weight Reps Sets	Weight Reps Sets	Weight Reps Sets	Weight Reps Sets	Weight Reps Sets
× ×	× ×	× ×	× ×	× ×	× ×
Subtotal = lbs.	Subtotal = lbs.	Subtotal = lbs.	Subtotal = lbs.	Subtotal = lbs.	Subtotal = lbs.

Exercise 2: *Total Weight* _____ *lbs.* *Time* _____ *mins.* *Power Factor* _____ *lbs./min.* *Power Index* _____

■ Exercise: STANDING BENT-OVER DUMBBELL LATERAL

Weight Reps Sets	Weight Reps Sets	Weight Reps Sets	Weight Reps Sets	Weight Reps Sets	Weight Reps Sets
× ×	× ×	× ×	× ×	× ×	× ×
Subtotal = lbs.	Subtotal = lbs.	Subtotal = lbs.	Subtotal = lbs.	Subtotal = lbs.	Subtotal = lbs.

Exercise 3: *Total Weight* _____ *lbs.* *Time* _____ *mins.* *Power Factor* _____ *lbs./min.* *Power Index* _____

■ Exercise:

Weight Reps Sets	Weight Reps Sets	Weight Reps Sets	Weight Reps Sets	Weight Reps Sets	Weight Reps Sets
× ×	× ×	× ×	× ×	× ×	× ×
Subtotal = lbs.	Subtotal = lbs.	Subtotal = lbs.	Subtotal = lbs.	Subtotal = lbs.	Subtotal = lbs.

Exercise 4: *Total Weight* _____ *lbs.* *Time* _____ *mins.* *Power Factor* _____ *lbs./min.* *Power Index* _____

■ Exercise:

Weight Reps Sets	Weight Reps Sets	Weight Reps Sets	Weight Reps Sets	Weight Reps Sets	Weight Reps Sets
× ×	× ×	× ×	× ×	× ×	× ×
Subtotal = lbs.	Subtotal = lbs.	Subtotal = lbs.	Subtotal = lbs.	Subtotal = lbs.	Subtotal = lbs.

Exercise 5: *Total Weight* _____ *lbs.* *Time* _____ *mins.* *Power Factor* _____ *lbs./min.* *Power Index* _____

OVERALL WORKOUT: *Total Weight* _____ *lbs.* *Time* _____ *mins.* *Power Factor* _____ *lbs./min.* *Power Index* _____

Exercise Subtotal = Weight × Reps × Sets ■ *Power Factor = lbs./min.* ■ *Power Index = Total Weight × Power Factor ÷ 1,000,000*

SHOULDER SPECIALIZATION WORKOUT RECORD Date: ___ / ___ / ___

Start Time: _____   Finish Time: _____   Total Time: _____

■ Exercise: STANDING BARBELL PRESS

Weight Reps Sets	Weight Reps Sets	Weight Reps Sets	Weight Reps Sets	Weight Reps Sets	Weight Reps Sets
× ×	× ×	× ×	× ×	× ×	× ×
Subtotal = lbs.	Subtotal = lbs.	Subtotal = lbs.	Subtotal = lbs.	Subtotal = lbs.	Subtotal = lbs.

Exercise 1:   *Total Weight _____ lbs.   Time _____ mins.   Power Factor _____ lbs./min.   Power Index _____*

■ Exercise: BARBELL SHRUG

Weight Reps Sets	Weight Reps Sets	Weight Reps Sets	Weight Reps Sets	Weight Reps Sets	Weight Reps Sets
× ×	× ×	× ×	× ×	× ×	× ×
Subtotal = lbs.	Subtotal = lbs.	Subtotal = lbs.	Subtotal = lbs.	Subtotal = lbs.	Subtotal = lbs.

Exercise 2:   *Total Weight _____ lbs.   Time _____ mins.   Power Factor _____ lbs./min.   Power Index _____*

■ Exercise: STANDING BENT-OVER DUMBBELL LATERAL

Weight Reps Sets	Weight Reps Sets	Weight Reps Sets	Weight Reps Sets	Weight Reps Sets	Weight Reps Sets
× ×	× ×	× ×	× ×	× ×	× ×
Subtotal = lbs.	Subtotal = lbs.	Subtotal = lbs.	Subtotal = lbs.	Subtotal = lbs.	Subtotal = lbs.

Exercise 3:   *Total Weight _____ lbs.   Time _____ mins.   Power Factor _____ lbs./min.   Power Index _____*

■ Exercise:

Weight Reps Sets	Weight Reps Sets	Weight Reps Sets	Weight Reps Sets	Weight Reps Sets	Weight Reps Sets
× ×	× ×	× ×	× ×	× ×	× ×
Subtotal = lbs.	Subtotal = lbs.	Subtotal = lbs.	Subtotal = lbs.	Subtotal = lbs.	Subtotal = lbs.

Exercise 4:   *Total Weight _____ lbs.   Time _____ mins.   Power Factor _____ lbs./min.   Power Index _____*

■ Exercise:

Weight Reps Sets	Weight Reps Sets	Weight Reps Sets	Weight Reps Sets	Weight Reps Sets	Weight Reps Sets
× ×	× ×	× ×	× ×	× ×	× ×
Subtotal = lbs.	Subtotal = lbs.	Subtotal = lbs.	Subtotal = lbs.	Subtotal = lbs.	Subtotal = lbs.

Exercise 5:   *Total Weight _____ lbs.   Time _____ mins.   Power Factor _____ lbs./min.   Power Index _____*

OVERALL WORKOUT: *Total Weight _____ lbs.   Time _____ mins.   Power Factor _____ lbs./min.   Power index _____*

Exercise Subtotal = Weight × Reps × Sets   ■ Power Factor = lbs./min.   ■ Power Index = Total Weight × Power Factor ÷ 1,000,000

SHOULDER SPECIALIZATION WORKOUT RECORD Date: ___ / ___ / ___

Start Time: _____   Finish Time: _____   Total Time: _____

■ Exercise: STANDING BARBELL PRESS

Weight Reps Sets	Weight Reps Sets	Weight Reps Sets	Weight Reps Sets	Weight Reps Sets	Weight Reps Sets
× ×	× ×	× ×	× ×	× ×	× ×
Subtotal = lbs.	Subtotal = lbs.	Subtotal = lbs.	Subtotal = lbs.	Subtotal = lbs.	Subtotal = lbs.

Exercise 1:   *Total Weight _____ lbs.   Time _____ mins.   Power Factor _____ lbs./min.   Power Index _____*

■ Exercise: BARBELL SHRUG

Weight Reps Sets	Weight Reps Sets	Weight Reps Sets	Weight Reps Sets	Weight Reps Sets	Weight Reps Sets
× ×	× ×	× ×	× ×	× ×	× ×
Subtotal = lbs.	Subtotal = lbs.	Subtotal = lbs.	Subtotal = lbs.	Subtotal = lbs.	Subtotal = lbs.

Exercise 2:   *Total Weight _____ lbs.   Time _____ mins.   Power Factor _____ lbs./min.   Power Index _____*

■ Exercise: STANDING BENT-OVER DUMBBELL LATERAL

Weight Reps Sets	Weight Reps Sets	Weight Reps Sets	Weight Reps Sets	Weight Reps Sets	Weight Reps Sets
× ×	× ×	× ×	× ×	× ×	× ×
Subtotal = lbs.	Subtotal = lbs.	Subtotal = lbs.	Subtotal = lbs.	Subtotal = lbs.	Subtotal = lbs.

Exercise 3:   *Total Weight _____ lbs.   Time _____ mins.   Power Factor _____ lbs./min.   Power Index _____*

■ Exercise:

Weight Reps Sets	Weight Reps Sets	Weight Reps Sets	Weight Reps Sets	Weight Reps Sets	Weight Reps Sets
× ×	× ×	× ×	× ×	× ×	× ×
Subtotal = lbs.	Subtotal = lbs.	Subtotal = lbs.	Subtotal = lbs.	Subtotal = lbs.	Subtotal = lbs.

Exercise 4:   *Total Weight _____ lbs.   Time _____ mins.   Power Factor _____ lbs./min.   Power Index _____*

■ Exercise:

Weight Reps Sets	Weight Reps Sets	Weight Reps Sets	Weight Reps Sets	Weight Reps Sets	Weight Reps Sets
× ×	× ×	× ×	× ×	× ×	× ×
Subtotal = lbs.	Subtotal = lbs.	Subtotal = lbs.	Subtotal = lbs.	Subtotal = lbs.	Subtotal = lbs.

Exercise 5:   *Total Weight _____ lbs.   Time _____ mins.   Power Factor _____ lbs./min.   Power Index _____*

OVERALL WORKOUT: *Total Weight _____ lbs.   Time _____ mins.   Power Factor _____ lbs./min.   Power Index _____*

Exercise Subtotal = Weight × Reps × Sets   ■ Power Factor = lbs./min.   ■ Power Index = Total Weight × Power Factor ÷ 1,000,000

SHOULDER SPECIALIZATION WORKOUT RECORD Date: ___ / ___ / ___

Start Time: _____   Finish Time: _____   Total Time: _____

■ Exercise: STANDING BARBELL PRESS

Weight Reps Sets	Weight Reps Sets	Weight Reps Sets	Weight Reps Sets	Weight Reps Sets	Weight Reps Sets
× ×	× ×	× ×	× ×	× ×	× ×
Subtotal = lbs.	Subtotal = lbs.	Subtotal = lbs.	Subtotal = lbs.	Subtotal = lbs.	Subtotal = lbs.

Exercise 1:   *Total Weight* _____ *lbs.*   *Time* _____ *mins.*   *Power Factor* _____ *lbs./min.*   *Power Index* _____

■ Exercise: BARBELL SHRUG

Weight Reps Sets	Weight Reps Sets	Weight Reps Sets	Weight Reps Sets	Weight Reps Sets	Weight Reps Sets
× ×	× ×	× ×	× ×	× ×	× ×
Subtotal = lbs.	Subtotal = lbs.	Subtotal = lbs.	Subtotal = lbs.	Subtotal = lbs.	Subtotal = lbs.

Exercise 2:   *Total Weight* _____ *lbs.*   *Time* _____ *mins.*   *Power Factor* _____ *lbs./min.*   *Power Index* _____

■ Exercise: STANDING BENT-OVER DUMBBELL LATERAL

Weight Reps Sets	Weight Reps Sets	Weight Reps Sets	Weight Reps Sets	Weight Reps Sets	Weight Reps Sets
× ×	× ×	× ×	× ×	× ×	× ×
Subtotal = lbs.	Subtotal = lbs.	Subtotal = lbs.	Subtotal = lbs.	Subtotal = lbs.	Subtotal = lbs.

Exercise 3:   *Total Weight* _____ *lbs.*   *Time* _____ *mins.*   *Power Factor* _____ *lbs./min.*   *Power Index* _____

■ Exercise:

Weight Reps Sets	Weight Reps Sets	Weight Reps Sets	Weight Reps Sets	Weight Reps Sets	Weight Reps Sets
× ×	× ×	× ×	× ×	× ×	× ×
Subtotal = lbs.	Subtotal = lbs.	Subtotal = lbs.	Subtotal = lbs.	Subtotal = lbs.	Subtotal = lbs.

Exercise 4:   *Total Weight* _____ *lbs.*   *Time* _____ *mins.*   *Power Factor* _____ *lbs./min.*   *Power Index* _____

■ Exercise:

Weight Reps Sets	Weight Reps Sets	Weight Reps Sets	Weight Reps Sets	Weight Reps Sets	Weight Reps Sets
× ×	× ×	× ×	× ×	× ×	× ×
Subtotal = lbs.	Subtotal = lbs.	Subtotal = lbs.	Subtotal = lbs.	Subtotal = lbs.	Subtotal = lbs.

Exercise 5:   *Total Weight* _____ *lbs.*   *Time* _____ *mins.*   *Power Factor* _____ *lbs./min.*   *Power Index* _____

OVERALL WORKOUT: *Total Weight* _____ *lbs.*   *Time* _____ *mins.*   *Power Factor* _____ *lbs./min.*   *Power Index* _____

Exercise Subtotal = Weight × Reps × Sets   ■ *Power Factor = lbs./min.*   ■ *Power Index = Total Weight × Power Factor ÷ 1,000,000*

SHOULDER SPECIALIZATION WORKOUT RECORD Date: ___ / ___ / ___

Start Time: _____   Finish Time: _____   Total Time: _____

■ **Exercise: STANDING BARBELL PRESS**

Weight Reps Sets	Weight Reps Sets	Weight Reps Sets	Weight Reps Sets	Weight Reps Sets	Weight Reps Sets
× ×	× ×	× ×	× ×	× ×	× ×
Subtotal = lbs.	Subtotal = lbs.	Subtotal = lbs.	Subtotal = lbs.	Subtotal = lbs.	Subtotal = lbs.

Exercise 1:   *Total Weight _____ lbs.   Time _____ mins.   Power Factor _____ lbs./min.   Power Index _____*

■ **Exercise: BARBELL SHRUG**

Weight Reps Sets	Weight Reps Sets	Weight Reps Sets	Weight Reps Sets	Weight Reps Sets	Weight Reps Sets
× ×	× ×	× ×	× ×	× ×	× ×
Subtotal = lbs.	Subtotal = lbs.	Subtotal = lbs.	Subtotal = lbs.	Subtotal = lbs.	Subtotal = lbs.

Exercise 2:   *Total Weight _____ lbs.   Time _____ mins.   Power Factor _____ lbs./min.   Power Index _____*

■ **Exercise: STANDING BENT-OVER DUMBBELL LATERAL**

Weight Reps Sets	Weight Reps Sets	Weight Reps Sets	Weight Reps Sets	Weight Reps Sets	Weight Reps Sets
× ×	× ×	× ×	× ×	× ×	× ×
Subtotal = lbs.	Subtotal = lbs.	Subtotal = lbs.	Subtotal = lbs.	Subtotal = lbs.	Subtotal = lbs.

Exercise 3:   *Total Weight _____ lbs.   Time _____ mins.   Power Factor _____ lbs./min.   Power Index _____*

■ **Exercise:**

Weight Reps Sets	Weight Reps Sets	Weight Reps Sets	Weight Reps Sets	Weight Reps Sets	Weight Reps Sets
× ×	× ×	× ×	× ×	× ×	× ×
Subtotal = lbs.	Subtotal = lbs.	Subtotal = lbs.	Subtotal = lbs.	Subtotal = lbs.	Subtotal = lbs.

Exercise 4:   *Total Weight _____ lbs.   Time _____ mins.   Power Factor _____ lbs./min.   Power Index _____*

■ **Exercise:**

Weight Reps Sets	Weight Reps Sets	Weight Reps Sets	Weight Reps Sets	Weight Reps Sets	Weight Reps Sets
× ×	× ×	× ×	× ×	× ×	× ×
Subtotal = lbs.	Subtotal = lbs.	Subtotal = lbs.	Subtotal = lbs.	Subtotal = lbs.	Subtotal = lbs.

Exercise 5:   *Total Weight _____ lbs.   Time _____ mins.   Power Factor _____ lbs./min.   Power Index _____*

OVERALL WORKOUT: *Total Weight _____ lbs.   Time _____ mins.   Power Factor _____ lbs./min.   Power Index _____*

Exercise Subtotal = Weight × Reps × Sets   ■ Power Factor = lbs./min.   ■ Power Index = Total Weight × Power Factor ÷ 1,000,000

SHOULDER SPECIALIZATION WORKOUT RECORD   Date: ___ / ___ / ___

Start Time: _____   Finish Time: _____   Total Time: _____

■ Exercise: STANDING BARBELL PRESS

Weight Reps Sets	Weight Reps Sets	Weight Reps Sets	Weight Reps Sets	Weight Reps Sets	Weight Reps Sets
× ×	× ×	× ×	× ×	× ×	× ×
Subtotal = lbs.	Subtotal = lbs.	Subtotal = lbs.	Subtotal = lbs.	Subtotal = lbs.	Subtotal = lbs.

Exercise 1:   *Total Weight* _____ *lbs.*   *Time* _____ *mins.*   *Power Factor* _____ *lbs./min.*   *Power Index* _____

■ Exercise: BARBELL SHRUG

Weight Reps Sets	Weight Reps Sets	Weight Reps Sets	Weight Reps Sets	Weight Reps Sets	Weight Reps Sets
× ×	× ×	× ×	× ×	× ×	× ×
Subtotal = lbs.	Subtotal = lbs.	Subtotal = lbs.	Subtotal = lbs.	Subtotal = lbs.	Subtotal = lbs.

Exercise 2:   *Total Weight* _____ *lbs.*   *Time* _____ *mins.*   *Power Factor* _____ *lbs./min.*   *Power Index* _____

■ Exercise: STANDING BENT-OVER DUMBBELL LATERAL

Weight Reps Sets	Weight Reps Sets	Weight Reps Sets	Weight Reps Sets	Weight Reps Sets	Weight Reps Sets
× ×	× ×	× ×	× ×	× ×	× ×
Subtotal = lbs.	Subtotal = lbs.	Subtotal = lbs.	Subtotal = lbs.	Subtotal = lbs.	Subtotal = lbs.

Exercise 3:   *Total Weight* _____ *lbs.*   *Time* _____ *mins.*   *Power Factor* _____ *lbs./min.*   *Power Index* _____

■ Exercise:

Weight Reps Sets	Weight Reps Sets	Weight Reps Sets	Weight Reps Sets	Weight Reps Sets	Weight Reps Sets
× ×	× ×	× ×	× ×	× ×	× ×
Subtotal = lbs.	Subtotal = lbs.	Subtotal = lbs.	Subtotal = lbs.	Subtotal = lbs.	Subtotal = lbs.

Exercise 4:   *Total Weight* _____ *lbs.*   *Time* _____ *mins.*   *Power Factor* _____ *lbs./min.*   *Power Index* _____

■ Exercise:

Weight Reps Sets	Weight Reps Sets	Weight Reps Sets	Weight Reps Sets	Weight Reps Sets	Weight Reps Sets
× ×	× ×	× ×	× ×	× ×	× ×
Subtotal = lbs.	Subtotal = lbs.	Subtotal = lbs.	Subtotal = lbs.	Subtotal = lbs.	Subtotal = lbs.

Exercise 5:   *Total Weight* _____ *lbs.*   *Time* _____ *mins.*   *Power Factor* _____ *lbs./min.*   *Power Index* _____

OVERALL WORKOUT: *Total Weight* _____ *lbs.*   *Time* _____ *mins.*   *Power Factor* _____ *lbs./min.*   *Power Index* _____

Exercise Subtotal = Weight × Reps × Sets   ■ *Power Factor = lbs./min.*   ■ *Power Index = Total Weight × Power Factor ÷ 1,000,000*

SHOULDER SPECIALIZATION WORKOUT RECORD Date: ___ / ___ / ___

Start Time: _____ **Finish Time:** _____ **Total Time:** _____

▪ Exercise: STANDING BARBELL PRESS

Weight Reps Sets	Weight Reps Sets	Weight Reps Sets	Weight Reps Sets	Weight Reps Sets	Weight Reps Sets
× ×	× ×	× ×	× ×	× ×	× ×
Subtotal = lbs.	Subtotal = lbs.	Subtotal = lbs.	Subtotal = lbs.	Subtotal = lbs.	Subtotal = lbs.

Exercise 1:　　*Total Weight* _____ *lbs.*　*Time* _____ *mins.*　*Power Factor* _____ *lbs./min.*　*Power Index* _____

▪ Exercise: BARBELL SHRUG

Weight Reps Sets	Weight Reps Sets	Weight Reps Sets	Weight Reps Sets	Weight Reps Sets	Weight Reps Sets
× ×	× ×	× ×	× ×	× ×	× ×
Subtotal = lbs.	Subtotal = lbs.	Subtotal = lbs.	Subtotal = lbs.	Subtotal = lbs.	Subtotal = lbs.

Exercise 2:　　*Total Weight* _____ *lbs.*　*Time* _____ *mins.*　*Power Factor* _____ *lbs./min.*　*Power Index* _____

▪ Exercise: STANDING BENT-OVER DUMBBELL LATERAL

Weight Reps Sets	Weight Reps Sets	Weight Reps Sets	Weight Reps Sets	Weight Reps Sets	Weight Reps Sets
× ×	× ×	× ×	× ×	× ×	× ×
Subtotal = lbs.	Subtotal = lbs.	Subtotal = lbs.	Subtotal = lbs.	Subtotal = lbs.	Subtotal = lbs.

Exercise 3:　　*Total Weight* _____ *lbs.*　*Time* _____ *mins.*　*Power Factor* _____ *lbs./min.*　*Power Index* _____

▪ Exercise:

Weight Reps Sets	Weight Reps Sets	Weight Reps Sets	Weight Reps Sets	Weight Reps Sets	Weight Reps Sets
× ×	× ×	× ×	× ×	× ×	× ×
Subtotal = lbs.	Subtotal = lbs.	Subtotal = lbs.	Subtotal = lbs.	Subtotal = lbs.	Subtotal = lbs.

Exercise 4:　　*Total Weight* _____ *lbs.*　*Time* _____ *mins.*　*Power Factor* _____ *lbs./min.*　*Power Index* _____

▪ Exercise:

Weight Reps Sets	Weight Reps Sets	Weight Reps Sets	Weight Reps Sets	Weight Reps Sets	Weight Reps Sets
× ×	× ×	× ×	× ×	× ×	× ×
Subtotal = lbs.	Subtotal = lbs.	Subtotal = lbs.	Subtotal = lbs.	Subtotal = lbs.	Subtotal = lbs.

Exercise 5:　　*Total Weight* _____ *lbs.*　*Time* _____ *mins.*　*Power Factor* _____ *lbs./min.*　*Power Index* _____

OVERALL WORKOUT:　*Total Weight* _____ *lbs.*　*Time* _____ *mins.*　*Power Factor* _____ *lbs./min.*　*Power Index* _____

Exercise Subtotal = Weight × Reps × Sets　▪ *Power Factor = lbs./min.*　▪ *Power Index = Total Weight × Power Factor ÷ 1,000,000*

SHOULDER SPECIALIZATION WORKOUT RECORD Date: ___ / ___ / ___

Start Time: _____   **Finish Time:** _____   **Total Time:** _____

■ **Exercise: STANDING BARBELL PRESS**

Weight Reps Sets	Weight Reps Sets	Weight Reps Sets	Weight Reps Sets	Weight Reps Sets	Weight Reps Sets
× ×	× ×	× ×	× ×	× ×	× ×
Subtotal = lbs.	Subtotal = lbs.	Subtotal = lbs.	Subtotal = lbs.	Subtotal = lbs.	Subtotal = lbs.

Exercise 1:   *Total Weight* _____ *lbs.*   *Time* _____ *mins.*   *Power Factor* _____ *lbs./min.*   *Power Index* _____

■ **Exercise: BARBELL SHRUG**

Weight Reps Sets	Weight Reps Sets	Weight Reps Sets	Weight Reps Sets	Weight Reps Sets	Weight Reps Sets
× ×	× ×	× ×	× ×	× ×	× ×
Subtotal = lbs.	Subtotal = lbs.	Subtotal = lbs.	Subtotal = lbs.	Subtotal = lbs.	Subtotal = lbs.

Exercise 2:   *Total Weight* _____ *lbs.*   *Time* _____ *mins.*   *Power Factor* _____ *lbs./min.*   *Power Index* _____

■ **Exercise: STANDING BENT-OVER DUMBBELL LATERAL**

Weight Reps Sets	Weight Reps Sets	Weight Reps Sets	Weight Reps Sets	Weight Reps Sets	Weight Reps Sets
× ×	× ×	× ×	× ×	× ×	× ×
Subtotal = lbs.	Subtotal = lbs.	Subtotal = lbs.	Subtotal = lbs.	Subtotal = lbs.	Subtotal = lbs.

Exercise 3:   *Total Weight* _____ *lbs.*   *Time* _____ *mins.*   *Power Factor* _____ *lbs./min.*   *Power Index* _____

■ **Exercise:**

Weight Reps Sets	Weight Reps Sets	Weight Reps Sets	Weight Reps Sets	Weight Reps Sets	Weight Reps Sets
× ×	× ×	× ×	× ×	× ×	× ×
Subtotal = lbs.	Subtotal = lbs.	Subtotal = lbs.	Subtotal = lbs.	Subtotal = lbs.	Subtotal = lbs.

Exercise 4:   *Total Weight* _____ *lbs.*   *Time* _____ *mins.*   *Power Factor* _____ *lbs./min.*   *Power Index* _____

■ **Exercise:**

Weight Reps Sets	Weight Reps Sets	Weight Reps Sets	Weight Reps Sets	Weight Reps Sets	Weight Reps Sets
× ×	× ×	× ×	× ×	× ×	× ×
Subtotal = lbs.	Subtotal = lbs.	Subtotal = lbs.	Subtotal = lbs.	Subtotal = lbs.	Subtotal = lbs.

Exercise 5:   *Total Weight* _____ *lbs.*   *Time* _____ *mins.*   *Power Factor* _____ *lbs./min.*   *Power Index* _____

OVERALL WORKOUT: *Total Weight* _____ *lbs.*   *Time* _____ *mins.*   *Power Factor* _____ *lbs./min.*   *Power Index* _____

Exercise Subtotal = Weight × Reps × Sets   ■ *Power Factor = lbs./min.*   ■ *Power Index = Total Weight × Power Factor ÷ 1,000,000*

SHOULDER SPECIALIZATION WORKOUT RECORD Date: ___ / ___ / ___

Start Time: _____   Finish Time: _____   Total Time: _____

▪ Exercise: STANDING BARBELL PRESS

Weight Reps Sets	Weight Reps Sets	Weight Reps Sets	Weight Reps Sets	Weight Reps Sets	Weight Reps Sets
× ×	× ×	× ×	× ×	× ×	× ×
Subtotal = lbs.	Subtotal = lbs.	Subtotal = lbs.	Subtotal = lbs.	Subtotal = lbs.	Subtotal = lbs.

Exercise 1:   *Total Weight* _____ *lbs.*   *Time* _____ *mins.*   *Power Factor* _____ *lbs./min.*   *Power Index* _____

▪ Exercise: BARBELL SHRUG

Weight Reps Sets	Weight Reps Sets	Weight Reps Sets	Weight Reps Sets	Weight Reps Sets	Weight Reps Sets
× ×	× ×	× ×	× ×	× ×	× ×
Subtotal = lbs.	Subtotal = lbs.	Subtotal = lbs.	Subtotal = lbs.	Subtotal = lbs.	Subtotal = lbs.

Exercise 2:   *Total Weight* _____ *lbs.*   *Time* _____ *mins.*   *Power Factor* _____ *lbs./min.*   *Power Index* _____

▪ Exercise: STANDING BENT-OVER DUMBBELL LATERAL

Weight Reps Sets	Weight Reps Sets	Weight Reps Sets	Weight Reps Sets	Weight Reps Sets	Weight Reps Sets
× ×	× ×	× ×	× ×	× ×	× ×
Subtotal = lbs.	Subtotal = lbs.	Subtotal = lbs.	Subtotal = lbs.	Subtotal = lbs.	Subtotal = lbs.

Exercise 3:   *Total Weight* _____ *lbs.*   *Time* _____ *mins.*   *Power Factor* _____ *lbs./min.*   *Power Index* _____

▪ Exercise:

Weight Reps Sets	Weight Reps Sets	Weight Reps Sets	Weight Reps Sets	Weight Reps Sets	Weight Reps Sets
× ×	× ×	× ×	× ×	× ×	× ×
Subtotal = lbs.	Subtotal = lbs.	Subtotal = lbs.	Subtotal = lbs.	Subtotal = lbs.	Subtotal = lbs.

Exercise 4:   *Total Weight* _____ *lbs.*   *Time* _____ *mins.*   *Power Factor* _____ *lbs./min.*   *Power Index* _____

▪ Exercise:

Weight Reps Sets	Weight Reps Sets	Weight Reps Sets	Weight Reps Sets	Weight Reps Sets	Weight Reps Sets
× ×	× ×	× ×	× ×	× ×	× ×
Subtotal = lbs.	Subtotal = lbs.	Subtotal = lbs.	Subtotal = lbs.	Subtotal = lbs.	Subtotal = lbs.

Exercise 5:   *Total Weight* _____ *lbs.*   *Time* _____ *mins.*   *Power Factor* _____ *lbs./min.*   *Power Index* _____

OVERALL WORKOUT: *Total Weight* _____ *lbs.*   *Time* _____ *mins.*   *Power Factor* _____ *lbs./min.*   *Power Index* _____

Exercise Subtotal = Weight × Reps × Sets   ▪ *Power Factor = lbs./min.*   ▪ *Power Index = Total Weight × Power Factor ÷ 1,000,000*

SHOULDER SPECIALIZATION WORKOUT RECORD   Date: ___ / ___ / ___

Start Time: _____   Finish Time: _____   Total Time: _____

■ Exercise: STANDING BARBELL PRESS

Weight Reps Sets	Weight Reps Sets	Weight Reps Sets	Weight Reps Sets	Weight Reps Sets	Weight Reps Sets
× ×	× ×	× ×	× ×	× ×	× ×
Subtotal = lbs.	Subtotal = lbs.	Subtotal = lbs.	Subtotal = lbs.	Subtotal = lbs.	Subtotal = lbs.

Exercise 1:   *Total Weight* _____ *lbs.*   *Time* _____ *mins.*   *Power Factor* _____ *lbs./min.*   *Power Index* _____

■ Exercise: BARBELL SHRUG

Weight Reps Sets	Weight Reps Sets	Weight Reps Sets	Weight Reps Sets	Weight Reps Sets	Weight Reps Sets
× ×	× ×	× ×	× ×	× ×	× ×
Subtotal = lbs.	Subtotal = lbs.	Subtotal = lbs.	Subtotal = lbs.	Subtotal = lbs.	Subtotal = lbs.

Exercise 2:   *Total Weight* _____ *lbs.*   *Time* _____ *mins.*   *Power Factor* _____ *lbs./min.*   *Power Index* _____

■ Exercise: STANDING BENT-OVER DUMBBELL LATERAL

Weight Reps Sets	Weight Reps Sets	Weight Reps Sets	Weight Reps Sets	Weight Reps Sets	Weight Reps Sets
× ×	× ×	× ×	× ×	× ×	× ×
Subtotal = lbs.	Subtotal = lbs.	Subtotal = lbs.	Subtotal = lbs.	Subtotal = lbs.	Subtotal = lbs.

Exercise 3:   *Total Weight* _____ *lbs.*   *Time* _____ *mins.*   *Power Factor* _____ *lbs./min.*   *Power Index* _____

■ Exercise:

Weight Reps Sets	Weight Reps Sets	Weight Reps Sets	Weight Reps Sets	Weight Reps Sets	Weight Reps Sets
× ×	× ×	× ×	× ×	× ×	× ×
Subtotal = lbs.	Subtotal = lbs.	Subtotal = lbs.	Subtotal = lbs.	Subtotal = lbs.	Subtotal = lbs.

Exercise 4:   *Total Weight* _____ *lbs.*   *Time* _____ *mins.*   *Power Factor* _____ *lbs./min.*   *Power Index* _____

■ Exercise:

Weight Reps Sets	Weight Reps Sets	Weight Reps Sets	Weight Reps Sets	Weight Reps Sets	Weight Reps Sets
× ×	× ×	× ×	× ×	× ×	× ×
Subtotal = lbs.	Subtotal = lbs.	Subtotal = lbs.	Subtotal = lbs.	Subtotal = lbs.	Subtotal = lbs.

Exercise 5:   *Total Weight* _____ *lbs.*   *Time* _____ *mins.*   *Power Factor* _____ *lbs./min.*   *Power Index* _____

OVERALL WORKOUT: *Total Weight* _____ *lbs.*   *Time* _____ *mins.*   *Power Factor* _____ *lbs./min.*   *Power Index* _____

Exercise Subtotal = Weight × Reps × Sets   ■ *Power Factor = lbs./min.*   ■ *Power Index = Total Weight × Power Factor ÷ 1,000,000*

SHOULDER SPECIALIZATION WORKOUT RECORD Date: ___ / ___ / ___

Start Time: _____   **Finish Time:** _____   **Total Time:** _____

■ Exercise: STANDING BARBELL PRESS

Weight Reps Sets	Weight Reps Sets	Weight Reps Sets	Weight Reps Sets	Weight Reps Sets	Weight Reps Sets
× ×	× ×	× ×	× ×	× ×	× ×
Subtotal = lbs.	Subtotal = lbs.	Subtotal = lbs.	Subtotal = lbs.	Subtotal = lbs.	Subtotal = lbs.

Exercise 1:   *Total Weight* _____ *lbs.*   *Time* _____ *mins.*   *Power Factor* _____ *lbs./min.*   *Power Index* _____

■ Exercise: BARBELL SHRUG

Weight Reps Sets	Weight Reps Sets	Weight Reps Sets	Weight Reps Sets	Weight Reps Sets	Weight Reps Sets
× ×	× ×	× ×	× ×	× ×	× ×
Subtotal = lbs.	Subtotal = lbs.	Subtotal = lbs.	Subtotal = lbs.	Subtotal = lbs.	Subtotal = lbs.

Exercise 2:   *Total Weight* _____ *lbs.*   *Time* _____ *mins.*   *Power Factor* _____ *lbs./min.*   *Power Index* _____

■ Exercise: STANDING BENT-OVER DUMBBELL LATERAL

Weight Reps Sets	Weight Reps Sets	Weight Reps Sets	Weight Reps Sets	Weight Reps Sets	Weight Reps Sets
× ×	× ×	× ×	× ×	× ×	× ×
Subtotal = lbs.	Subtotal = lbs.	Subtotal = lbs.	Subtotal = lbs.	Subtotal = lbs.	Subtotal = lbs.

Exercise 3:   *Total Weight* _____ *lbs.*   *Time* _____ *mins.*   *Power Factor* _____ *lbs./min.*   *Power Index* _____

■ Exercise:

Weight Reps Sets	Weight Reps Sets	Weight Reps Sets	Weight Reps Sets	Weight Reps Sets	Weight Reps Sets
× ×	× ×	× ×	× ×	× ×	× ×
Subtotal = lbs.	Subtotal = lbs.	Subtotal = lbs.	Subtotal = lbs.	Subtotal = lbs.	Subtotal = lbs.

Exercise 4:   *Total Weight* _____ *lbs.*   *Time* _____ *mins.*   *Power Factor* _____ *lbs./min.*   *Power Index* _____

■ Exercise:

Weight Reps Sets	Weight Reps Sets	Weight Reps Sets	Weight Reps Sets	Weight Reps Sets	Weight Reps Sets
× ×	× ×	× ×	× ×	× ×	× ×
Subtotal = lbs.	Subtotal = lbs.	Subtotal = lbs.	Subtotal = lbs.	Subtotal = lbs.	Subtotal = lbs.

Exercise 5:   *Total Weight* _____ *lbs.*   *Time* _____ *mins.*   *Power Factor* _____ *lbs./min.*   *Power Index* _____

OVERALL WORKOUT: *Total Weight* _____ *lbs.*   *Time* _____ *mins.*   *Power Factor* _____ *lbs./min.*   *Power Index* _____

Exercise Subtotal = Weight × Reps × Sets   ■ *Power Factor = lbs./min.*   ■ *Power Index = Total Weight × Power Factor ÷ 1,000,000*

SHOULDER SPECIALIZATION WORKOUT RECORD Date: ___ / ___ / ___

Start Time: _____   **Finish Time:** _____   **Total Time:** _____

■ Exercise: STANDING BARBELL PRESS

Weight Reps Sets	Weight Reps Sets	Weight Reps Sets	Weight Reps Sets	Weight Reps Sets	Weight Reps Sets
× ×	× ×	× ×	× ×	× ×	× ×
Subtotal = lbs.	Subtotal = lbs.	Subtotal = lbs.	Subtotal = lbs.	Subtotal = lbs.	Subtotal = lbs.

Exercise 1:   *Total Weight* _____ *lbs.*   *Time* _____ *mins.*   *Power Factor* _____ *lbs./min.*   *Power Index* _____

■ Exercise: BARBELL SHRUG

Weight Reps Sets	Weight Reps Sets	Weight Reps Sets	Weight Reps Sets	Weight Reps Sets	Weight Reps Sets
× ×	× ×	× ×	× ×	× ×	× ×
Subtotal = lbs.	Subtotal = lbs.	Subtotal = lbs.	Subtotal = lbs.	Subtotal = lbs.	Subtotal = lbs.

Exercise 2:   *Total Weight* _____ *lbs.*   *Time* _____ *mins.*   *Power Factor* _____ *lbs./min.*   *Power Index* _____

■ Exercise: STANDING BENT-OVER DUMBBELL LATERAL

Weight Reps Sets	Weight Reps Sets	Weight Reps Sets	Weight Reps Sets	Weight Reps Sets	Weight Reps Sets
× ×	× ×	× ×	× ×	× ×	× ×
Subtotal = lbs.	Subtotal = lbs.	Subtotal = lbs.	Subtotal = lbs.	Subtotal = lbs.	Subtotal = lbs.

Exercise 3:   *Total Weight* _____ *lbs.*   *Time* _____ *mins.*   *Power Factor* _____ *lbs./min.*   *Power Index* _____

■ Exercise:

Weight Reps Sets	Weight Reps Sets	Weight Reps Sets	Weight Reps Sets	Weight Reps Sets	Weight Reps Sets
× ×	× ×	× ×	× ×	× ×	× ×
Subtotal = lbs.	Subtotal = lbs.	Subtotal = lbs.	Subtotal = lbs.	Subtotal = lbs.	Subtotal = lbs.

Exercise 4:   *Total Weight* _____ *lbs.*   *Time* _____ *mins.*   *Power Factor* _____ *lbs./min.*   *Power Index* _____

■ Exercise:

Weight Reps Sets	Weight Reps Sets	Weight Reps Sets	Weight Reps Sets	Weight Reps Sets	Weight Reps Sets
× ×	× ×	× ×	× ×	× ×	× ×
Subtotal = lbs.	Subtotal = lbs.	Subtotal = lbs.	Subtotal = lbs.	Subtotal = lbs.	Subtotal = lbs.

Exercise 5:   *Total Weight* _____ *lbs.*   *Time* _____ *mins.*   *Power Factor* _____ *lbs./min.*   *Power Index* _____

OVERALL WORKOUT: *Total Weight* _____ *lbs.*   *Time* _____ *mins.*   *Power Factor* _____ *lbs./min.*   *Power Index* _____

Exercise Subtotal = Weight × Reps × Sets   ■ *Power Factor = lbs./min.*   ■ *Power Index = Total Weight × Power Factor ÷ 1,000,000*

SHOULDER SPECIALIZATION WORKOUT RECORD Date: ___ / ___ / ___

Start Time: _____ Finish Time: _____ Total Time: _____

■ Exercise: STANDING BARBELL PRESS

Weight Reps Sets	Weight Reps Sets	Weight Reps Sets	Weight Reps Sets	Weight Reps Sets	Weight Reps Sets
× ×	× ×	× ×	× ×	× ×	× ×
Subtotal = lbs.	Subtotal = lbs.	Subtotal = lbs.	Subtotal = lbs.	Subtotal = lbs.	Subtotal = lbs.

Exercise 1:   *Total Weight _____ lbs.*   *Time _____ mins.*   *Power Factor _____ lbs./min.*   *Power Index _____*

■ Exercise: BARBELL SHRUG

Weight Reps Sets	Weight Reps Sets	Weight Reps Sets	Weight Reps Sets	Weight Reps Sets	Weight Reps Sets
× ×	× ×	× ×	× ×	× ×	× ×
Subtotal = lbs.	Subtotal = lbs.	Subtotal = lbs.	Subtotal = lbs.	Subtotal = lbs.	Subtotal = lbs.

Exercise 2:   *Total Weight _____ lbs.*   *Time _____ mins.*   *Power Factor _____ lbs./min.*   *Power Index _____*

■ Exercise: STANDING BENT-OVER DUMBBELL LATERAL

Weight Reps Sets	Weight Reps Sets	Weight Reps Sets	Weight Reps Sets	Weight Reps Sets	Weight Reps Sets
× ×	× ×	× ×	× ×	× ×	× ×
Subtotal = lbs.	Subtotal = lbs.	Subtotal = lbs.	Subtotal = lbs.	Subtotal = lbs.	Subtotal = lbs.

Exercise 3:   *Total Weight _____ lbs.*   *Time _____ mins.*   *Power Factor _____ lbs./min.*   *Power Index _____*

■ Exercise:

Weight Reps Sets	Weight Reps Sets	Weight Reps Sets	Weight Reps Sets	Weight Reps Sets	Weight Reps Sets
× ×	× ×	× ×	× ×	× ×	× ×
Subtotal = lbs.	Subtotal = lbs.	Subtotal = lbs.	Subtotal = lbs.	Subtotal = lbs.	Subtotal = lbs.

Exercise 4:   *Total Weight _____ lbs.*   *Time _____ mins.*   *Power Factor _____ lbs./min.*   *Power Index _____*

■ Exercise:

Weight Reps Sets	Weight Reps Sets	Weight Reps Sets	Weight Reps Sets	Weight Reps Sets	Weight Reps Sets
× ×	× ×	× ×	× ×	× ×	× ×
Subtotal = lbs.	Subtotal = lbs.	Subtotal = lbs.	Subtotal = lbs.	Subtotal = lbs.	Subtotal = lbs.

Exercise 5:   *Total Weight _____ lbs.*   *Time _____ mins.*   *Power Factor _____ lbs./min.*   *Power Index _____*

OVERALL WORKOUT: *Total Weight _____ lbs.*   *Time _____ mins.*   *Power Factor _____ lbs./min.*   *Power Index _____*

Exercise Subtotal = Weight × Reps × Sets   ■ *Power Factor = lbs./min.*   ■ *Power Index = Total Weight × Power Factor ÷ 1,000,000*

SHOULDER SPECIALIZATION WORKOUT RECORD Date: ___ / ___ / ___

Start Time: _____   Finish Time: _____   Total Time: _____

■ Exercise: STANDING BARBELL PRESS

Weight Reps Sets	Weight Reps Sets	Weight Reps Sets	Weight Reps Sets	Weight Reps Sets	Weight Reps Sets
× ×	× ×	× ×	× ×	× ×	× ×
Subtotal = lbs.	Subtotal = lbs.	Subtotal = lbs.	Subtotal = lbs.	Subtotal = lbs.	Subtotal = lbs.

Exercise 1:   *Total Weight* _____ *lbs.   Time* _____ *mins.   Power Factor* _____ *lbs./min.   Power Index* _____

■ Exercise: BARBELL SHRUG

Weight Reps Sets	Weight Reps Sets	Weight Reps Sets	Weight Reps Sets	Weight Reps Sets	Weight Reps Sets
× ×	× ×	× ×	× ×	× ×	× ×
Subtotal = lbs.	Subtotal = lbs.	Subtotal = lbs.	Subtotal = lbs.	Subtotal = lbs.	Subtotal = lbs.

Exercise 2:   *Total Weight* _____ *lbs.   Time* _____ *mins.   Power Factor* _____ *lbs./min.   Power Index* _____

■ Exercise: STANDING BENT-OVER DUMBBELL LATERAL

Weight Reps Sets	Weight Reps Sets	Weight Reps Sets	Weight Reps Sets	Weight Reps Sets	Weight Reps Sets
× ×	× ×	× ×	× ×	× ×	× ×
Subtotal = lbs.	Subtotal = lbs.	Subtotal = lbs.	Subtotal = lbs.	Subtotal = lbs.	Subtotal = lbs.

Exercise 3:   *Total Weight* _____ *lbs.   Time* _____ *mins.   Power Factor* _____ *lbs./min.   Power Index* _____

■ Exercise:

Weight Reps Sets	Weight Reps Sets	Weight Reps Sets	Weight Reps Sets	Weight Reps Sets	Weight Reps Sets
× ×	× ×	× ×	× ×	× ×	× ×
Subtotal = lbs.	Subtotal = lbs.	Subtotal = lbs.	Subtotal = lbs.	Subtotal = lbs.	Subtotal = lbs.

Exercise 4:   *Total Weight* _____ *lbs.   Time* _____ *mins.   Power Factor* _____ *lbs./min.   Power Index* _____

■ Exercise:

Weight Reps Sets	Weight Reps Sets	Weight Reps Sets	Weight Reps Sets	Weight Reps Sets	Weight Reps Sets
× ×	× ×	× ×	× ×	× ×	× ×
Subtotal = lbs.	Subtotal = lbs.	Subtotal = lbs.	Subtotal = lbs.	Subtotal = lbs.	Subtotal = lbs.

Exercise 5:   *Total Weight* _____ *lbs.   Time* _____ *mins.   Power Factor* _____ *lbs./min.   Power Index* _____

OVERALL WORKOUT: *Total Weight* _____ *lbs.   Time* _____ *mins.   Power Factor* _____ *lbs./min.   Power Index* _____

Exercise Subtotal = Weight × Reps × Sets   ■ Power Factor = lbs./min.   ■ Power Index = Total Weight × Power Factor ÷ 1,000,000

SHOULDER SPECIALIZATION WORKOUT RECORD Date: ___ / ___ / ___

Start Time: _____ **Finish Time:** _____ **Total Time:** _____

■ Exercise: STANDING BARBELL PRESS

Weight Reps Sets	Weight Reps Sets	Weight Reps Sets	Weight Reps Sets	Weight Reps Sets	Weight Reps Sets
× ×	× ×	× ×	× ×	× ×	× ×
Subtotal = lbs.	Subtotal = lbs.	Subtotal = lbs.	Subtotal = lbs.	Subtotal = lbs.	Subtotal = lbs.

Exercise 1:   *Total Weight _____ lbs.*   *Time _____ mins.*   *Power Factor _____ lbs./min.*   *Power Index _____*

■ Exercise: BARBELL SHRUG

Weight Reps Sets	Weight Reps Sets	Weight Reps Sets	Weight Reps Sets	Weight Reps Sets	Weight Reps Sets
× ×	× ×	× ×	× ×	× ×	× ×
Subtotal = lbs.	Subtotal = lbs.	Subtotal = lbs.	Subtotal = lbs.	Subtotal = lbs.	Subtotal = lbs.

Exercise 2:   *Total Weight _____ lbs.*   *Time _____ mins.*   *Power Factor _____ lbs./min.*   *Power Index _____*

■ Exercise: STANDING BENT-OVER DUMBBELL LATERAL

Weight Reps Sets	Weight Reps Sets	Weight Reps Sets	Weight Reps Sets	Weight Reps Sets	Weight Reps Sets
× ×	× ×	× ×	× ×	× ×	× ×
Subtotal = lbs.	Subtotal = lbs.	Subtotal = lbs.	Subtotal = lbs.	Subtotal = lbs.	Subtotal = lbs.

Exercise 3:   *Total Weight _____ lbs.*   *Time _____ mins.*   *Power Factor _____ lbs./min.*   *Power Index _____*

■ Exercise:

Weight Reps Sets	Weight Reps Sets	Weight Reps Sets	Weight Reps Sets	Weight Reps Sets	Weight Reps Sets
× ×	× ×	× ×	× ×	× ×	× ×
Subtotal = lbs.	Subtotal = lbs.	Subtotal = lbs.	Subtotal = lbs.	Subtotal = lbs.	Subtotal = lbs.

Exercise 4:   *Total Weight _____ lbs.*   *Time _____ mins.*   *Power Factor _____ lbs./min.*   *Power Index _____*

■ Exercise:

Weight Reps Sets	Weight Reps Sets	Weight Reps Sets	Weight Reps Sets	Weight Reps Sets	Weight Reps Sets
× ×	× ×	× ×	× ×	× ×	× ×
Subtotal = lbs.	Subtotal = lbs.	Subtotal = lbs.	Subtotal = lbs.	Subtotal = lbs.	Subtotal = lbs.

Exercise 5:   *Total Weight _____ lbs.*   *Time _____ mins.*   *Power Factor _____ lbs./min.*   *Power Index _____*

OVERALL WORKOUT: *Total Weight _____ lbs.*   *Time _____ mins.*   *Power Factor _____ lbs./min.*   *Power Index _____*

Exercise Subtotal = Weight × Reps × Sets   ■ *Power Factor = lbs./min.*   ■ *Power Index = Total Weight × Power Factor ÷ 1,000,000*

SHOULDER SPECIALIZATION WORKOUT RECORD Date: ___ / ___ / ___

Start Time: _____   Finish Time: _____   Total Time: _____

■ Exercise: STANDING BARBELL PRESS

Weight Reps Sets	Weight Reps Sets	Weight Reps Sets	Weight Reps Sets	Weight Reps Sets	Weight Reps Sets
× ×	× ×	× ×	× ×	× ×	× ×
Subtotal = lbs.	Subtotal = lbs.	Subtotal = lbs.	Subtotal = lbs.	Subtotal = lbs.	Subtotal = lbs.

Exercise 1:   *Total Weight* _____ *lbs.*   *Time* _____ *mins.*   *Power Factor* _____ *lbs./min.*   *Power Index* _____

■ Exercise: BARBELL SHRUG

Weight Reps Sets	Weight Reps Sets	Weight Reps Sets	Weight Reps Sets	Weight Reps Sets	Weight Reps Sets
× ×	× ×	× ×	× ×	× ×	× ×
Subtotal = lbs.	Subtotal = lbs.	Subtotal = lbs.	Subtotal = lbs.	Subtotal = lbs.	Subtotal = lbs.

Exercise 2:   *Total Weight* _____ *lbs.*   *Time* _____ *mins.*   *Power Factor* _____ *lbs./min.*   *Power Index* _____

■ Exercise: STANDING BENT-OVER DUMBBELL LATERAL

Weight Reps Sets	Weight Reps Sets	Weight Reps Sets	Weight Reps Sets	Weight Reps Sets	Weight Reps Sets
× ×	× ×	× ×	× ×	× ×	× ×
Subtotal = lbs.	Subtotal = lbs.	Subtotal = lbs.	Subtotal = lbs.	Subtotal = lbs.	Subtotal = lbs.

Exercise 3:   *Total Weight* _____ *lbs.*   *Time* _____ *mins.*   *Power Factor* _____ *lbs./min.*   *Power Index* _____

■ Exercise:

Weight Reps Sets	Weight Reps Sets	Weight Reps Sets	Weight Reps Sets	Weight Reps Sets	Weight Reps Sets
× ×	× ×	× ×	× ×	× ×	× ×
Subtotal = lbs.	Subtotal = lbs.	Subtotal = lbs.	Subtotal = lbs.	Subtotal = lbs.	Subtotal = lbs.

Exercise 4:   *Total Weight* _____ *lbs.*   *Time* _____ *mins.*   *Power Factor* _____ *lbs./min.*   *Power Index* _____

■ Exercise:

Weight Reps Sets	Weight Reps Sets	Weight Reps Sets	Weight Reps Sets	Weight Reps Sets	Weight Reps Sets
× ×	× ×	× ×	× ×	× ×	× ×
Subtotal = lbs.	Subtotal = lbs.	Subtotal = lbs.	Subtotal = lbs.	Subtotal = lbs.	Subtotal = lbs.

Exercise 5:   *Total Weight* _____ *lbs.*   *Time* _____ *mins.*   *Power Factor* _____ *lbs./min.*   *Power Index* _____

OVERALL WORKOUT: *Total Weight* _____ *lbs.*   *Time* _____ *mins.*   *Power Factor* _____ *lbs./min.*   *Power Index* _____

Exercise Subtotal = Weight × Reps × Sets   ■ *Power Factor = lbs./min.*   ■ *Power Index = Total Weight × Power Factor ÷ 1,000,000*

SHOULDER SPECIALIZATION WORKOUT RECORD Date: ___ / ___ / ___

Start Time: _____   Finish Time: _____   Total Time: _____

■ **Exercise: STANDING BARBELL PRESS**

Weight Reps Sets	Weight Reps Sets	Weight Reps Sets	Weight Reps Sets	Weight Reps Sets	Weight Reps Sets
× ×	× ×	× ×	× ×	× ×	× ×
Subtotal = lbs.	Subtotal = lbs.	Subtotal = lbs.	Subtotal = lbs.	Subtotal = lbs.	Subtotal = lbs.

Exercise 1:   *Total Weight _____ lbs.   Time _____ mins.   Power Factor _____ lbs./min.   Power Index _____*

■ **Exercise: BARBELL SHRUG**

Weight Reps Sets	Weight Reps Sets	Weight Reps Sets	Weight Reps Sets	Weight Reps Sets	Weight Reps Sets
× ×	× ×	× ×	× ×	× ×	× ×
Subtotal = lbs.	Subtotal = lbs.	Subtotal = lbs.	Subtotal = lbs.	Subtotal = lbs.	Subtotal = lbs.

Exercise 2:   *Total Weight _____ lbs.   Time _____ mins.   Power Factor _____ lbs./min.   Power Index _____*

■ **Exercise: STANDING BENT-OVER DUMBBELL LATERAL**

Weight Reps Sets	Weight Reps Sets	Weight Reps Sets	Weight Reps Sets	Weight Reps Sets	Weight Reps Sets
× ×	× ×	× ×	× ×	× ×	× ×
Subtotal = lbs.	Subtotal = lbs.	Subtotal = lbs.	Subtotal = lbs.	Subtotal = lbs.	Subtotal = lbs.

Exercise 3:   *Total Weight _____ lbs.   Time _____ mins.   Power Factor _____ lbs./min.   Power Index _____*

■ **Exercise:**

Weight Reps Sets	Weight Reps Sets	Weight Reps Sets	Weight Reps Sets	Weight Reps Sets	Weight Reps Sets
× ×	× ×	× ×	× ×	× ×	× ×
Subtotal = lbs.	Subtotal = lbs.	Subtotal = lbs.	Subtotal = lbs.	Subtotal = lbs.	Subtotal = lbs.

Exercise 4:   *Total Weight _____ lbs.   Time _____ mins.   Power Factor _____ lbs./min.   Power Index _____*

■ **Exercise:**

Weight Reps Sets	Weight Reps Sets	Weight Reps Sets	Weight Reps Sets	Weight Reps Sets	Weight Reps Sets
× ×	× ×	× ×	× ×	× ×	× ×
Subtotal = lbs.	Subtotal = lbs.	Subtotal = lbs.	Subtotal = lbs.	Subtotal = lbs.	Subtotal = lbs.

Exercise 5:   *Total Weight _____ lbs.   Time _____ mins.   Power Factor _____ lbs./min.   Power Index _____*

OVERALL WORKOUT: *Total Weight _____ lbs.   Time _____ mins.   Power Factor _____ lbs./min.   Power Index _____*

Exercise Subtotal = Weight × Reps × Sets   ■ Power Factor = lbs./min.   ■ Power Index = Total Weight × Power Factor ÷ 1,000,000

SHOULDER SPECIALIZATION WORKOUT RECORD Date: ___ / ___ / ___

Start Time: _____   Finish Time: _____   Total Time: _____

▪ Exercise: STANDING BARBELL PRESS

Weight Reps Sets	Weight Reps Sets	Weight Reps Sets	Weight Reps Sets	Weight Reps Sets	Weight Reps Sets
× ×	× ×	× ×	× ×	× ×	× ×
Subtotal = lbs.	Subtotal = lbs.	Subtotal = lbs.	Subtotal = lbs.	Subtotal = lbs.	Subtotal = lbs.

Exercise 1:   Total Weight _____ lbs.   Time _____ mins.   Power Factor _____ lbs./min.   Power Index _____

▪ Exercise: BARBELL SHRUG

Weight Reps Sets	Weight Reps Sets	Weight Reps Sets	Weight Reps Sets	Weight Reps Sets	Weight Reps Sets
× ×	× ×	× ×	× ×	× ×	× ×
Subtotal = lbs.	Subtotal = lbs.	Subtotal = lbs.	Subtotal = lbs.	Subtotal = lbs.	Subtotal = lbs.

Exercise 2:   Total Weight _____ lbs.   Time _____ mins.   Power Factor _____ lbs./min.   Power Index _____

▪ Exercise: STANDING BENT-OVER DUMBBELL LATERAL

Weight Reps Sets	Weight Reps Sets	Weight Reps Sets	Weight Reps Sets	Weight Reps Sets	Weight Reps Sets
× ×	× ×	× ×	× ×	× ×	× ×
Subtotal = lbs.	Subtotal = lbs.	Subtotal = lbs.	Subtotal = lbs.	Subtotal = lbs.	Subtotal = lbs.

Exercise 3:   Total Weight _____ lbs.   Time _____ mins.   Power Factor _____ lbs./min.   Power Index _____

▪ Exercise:

Weight Reps Sets	Weight Reps Sets	Weight Reps Sets	Weight Reps Sets	Weight Reps Sets	Weight Reps Sets
× ×	× ×	× ×	× ×	× ×	× ×
Subtotal = lbs.	Subtotal = lbs.	Subtotal = lbs.	Subtotal = lbs.	Subtotal = lbs.	Subtotal = lbs.

Exercise 4:   Total Weight _____ lbs.   Time _____ mins.   Power Factor _____ lbs./min.   Power Index _____

▪ Exercise:

Weight Reps Sets	Weight Reps Sets	Weight Reps Sets	Weight Reps Sets	Weight Reps Sets	Weight Reps Sets
× ×	× ×	× ×	× ×	× ×	× ×
Subtotal = lbs.	Subtotal = lbs.	Subtotal = lbs.	Subtotal = lbs.	Subtotal = lbs.	Subtotal = lbs.

Exercise 5:   Total Weight _____ lbs.   Time _____ mins.   Power Factor _____ lbs./min.   Power Index _____

OVERALL WORKOUT: Total Weight _____ lbs.   Time _____ mins.   Power Factor _____ lbs./min.   Power Index _____

Exercise Subtotal = Weight × Reps × Sets   ▪ *Power Factor = lbs./min.*   ▪ *Power Index = Total Weight × Power Factor ÷ 1,000,000*

SHOULDER SPECIALIZATION WORKOUT RECORD Date: ___ / ___ / ___

Start Time: _____   **Finish Time:** _____   **Total Time:** _____

■ Exercise: STANDING BARBELL PRESS

Weight Reps Sets	Weight Reps Sets	Weight Reps Sets	Weight Reps Sets	Weight Reps Sets	Weight Reps Sets
× ×	× ×	× ×	× ×	× ×	× ×
Subtotal = lbs.	Subtotal = lbs.	Subtotal = lbs.	Subtotal = lbs.	Subtotal = lbs.	Subtotal = lbs.

Exercise 1:   *Total Weight* _____ *lbs.*   *Time* _____ *mins.*   *Power Factor* _____ *lbs./min.*   *Power Index* _____

■ Exercise: BARBELL SHRUG

Weight Reps Sets	Weight Reps Sets	Weight Reps Sets	Weight Reps Sets	Weight Reps Sets	Weight Reps Sets
× ×	× ×	× ×	× ×	× ×	× ×
Subtotal = lbs.	Subtotal = lbs.	Subtotal = lbs.	Subtotal = lbs.	Subtotal = lbs.	Subtotal = lbs.

Exercise 2:   *Total Weight* _____ *lbs.*   *Time* _____ *mins.*   *Power Factor* _____ *lbs./min.*   *Power Index* _____

■ Exercise: STANDING BENT-OVER DUMBBELL LATERAL

Weight Reps Sets	Weight Reps Sets	Weight Reps Sets	Weight Reps Sets	Weight Reps Sets	Weight Reps Sets
× ×	× ×	× ×	× ×	× ×	× ×
Subtotal = lbs.	Subtotal = lbs.	Subtotal = lbs.	Subtotal = lbs.	Subtotal = lbs.	Subtotal = lbs.

Exercise 3:   *Total Weight* _____ *lbs.*   *Time* _____ *mins.*   *Power Factor* _____ *lbs./min.*   *Power Index* _____

■ Exercise:

Weight Reps Sets	Weight Reps Sets	Weight Reps Sets	Weight Reps Sets	Weight Reps Sets	Weight Reps Sets
× ×	× ×	× ×	× ×	× ×	× ×
Subtotal = lbs.	Subtotal = lbs.	Subtotal = lbs.	Subtotal = lbs.	Subtotal = lbs.	Subtotal = lbs.

Exercise 4:   *Total Weight* _____ *lbs.*   *Time* _____ *mins.*   *Power Factor* _____ *lbs./min.*   *Power Index* _____

■ Exercise:

Weight Reps Sets	Weight Reps Sets	Weight Reps Sets	Weight Reps Sets	Weight Reps Sets	Weight Reps Sets
× ×	× ×	× ×	× ×	× ×	× ×
Subtotal = lbs.	Subtotal = lbs.	Subtotal = lbs.	Subtotal = lbs.	Subtotal = lbs.	Subtotal = lbs.

Exercise 5:   *Total Weight* _____ *lbs.*   *Time* _____ *mins.*   *Power Factor* _____ *lbs./min.*   *Power Index* _____

OVERALL WORKOUT: *Total Weight* _____ *lbs.*   *Time* _____ *mins.*   *Power Factor* _____ *lbs./min.*   *Power Index* _____

Exercise Subtotal = Weight × Reps × Sets   ■ *Power Factor = lbs./min.*   ■ *Power Index = Total Weight × Power Factor ÷ 1,000,000*

BACK SPECIALIZATION WORKOUT RECORD   Date: ___ / ___ / ___

Start Time: _____   Finish Time: _____   Total Time: _____

■ Exercise: LAT PULLDOWN (OR CLOSE-GRIP UNDERHAND CHIN-UP)

Weight Reps Sets	Weight Reps Sets	Weight Reps Sets	Weight Reps Sets	Weight Reps Sets	Weight Reps Sets
× ×	× ×	× ×	× ×	× ×	× ×
Subtotal = lbs.	Subtotal = lbs.	Subtotal = lbs.	Subtotal = lbs.	Subtotal = lbs.	Subtotal = lbs.

Exercise 1:   Total Weight _____ lbs.   Time _____ mins.   Power Factor _____ lbs./min.   Power Index _____

■ Exercise: DEADLIFT

Weight Reps Sets	Weight Reps Sets	Weight Reps Sets	Weight Reps Sets	Weight Reps Sets	Weight Reps Sets
× ×	× ×	× ×	× ×	× ×	× ×
Subtotal = lbs.	Subtotal = lbs.	Subtotal = lbs.	Subtotal = lbs.	Subtotal = lbs.	Subtotal = lbs.

Exercise 2:   Total Weight _____ lbs.   Time _____ mins.   Power Factor _____ lbs./min.   Power Index _____

■ Exercise:

Weight Reps Sets	Weight Reps Sets	Weight Reps Sets	Weight Reps Sets	Weight Reps Sets	Weight Reps Sets
× ×	× ×	× ×	× ×	× ×	× ×
Subtotal = lbs.	Subtotal = lbs.	Subtotal = lbs.	Subtotal = lbs.	Subtotal = lbs.	Subtotal = lbs.

Exercise 3:   Total Weight _____ lbs.   Time _____ mins.   Power Factor _____ lbs./min.   Power Index _____

■ Exercise:

Weight Reps Sets	Weight Reps Sets	Weight Reps Sets	Weight Reps Sets	Weight Reps Sets	Weight Reps Sets
× ×	× ×	× ×	× ×	× ×	× ×
Subtotal = lbs.	Subtotal = lbs.	Subtotal = lbs.	Subtotal = lbs.	Subtotal = lbs.	Subtotal = lbs.

Exercise 4:   Total Weight _____ lbs.   Time _____ mins.   Power Factor _____ lbs./min.   Power Index _____

■ Exercise:

Weight Reps Sets	Weight Reps Sets	Weight Reps Sets	Weight Reps Sets	Weight Reps Sets	Weight Reps Sets
× ×	× ×	× ×	× ×	× ×	× ×
Subtotal = lbs.	Subtotal = lbs.	Subtotal = lbs.	Subtotal = lbs.	Subtotal = lbs.	Subtotal = lbs.

Exercise 5:   Total Weight _____ lbs.   Time _____ mins.   Power Factor _____ lbs./min.   Power Index _____

OVERALL WORKOUT: Total Weight _____ lbs.   Time _____ mins.   Power Factor _____ lbs./min.   Power Index _____

Exercise Subtotal = Weight × Reps × Sets   ■ *Power Factor = lbs./min.*   ■ *Power Index = Total Weight × Power Factor ÷ 1,000,000*

BACK SPECIALIZATION WORKOUT RECORD   Date: ___ / ___ / ___

Start Time: _____   Finish Time: _____   Total Time: _____

▪ Exercise: LAT PULLDOWN (OR CLOSE-GRIP UNDERHAND CHIN-UP)

Weight Reps Sets	Weight Reps Sets	Weight Reps Sets	Weight Reps Sets	Weight Reps Sets	Weight Reps Sets
× ×	× ×	× ×	× ×	× ×	× ×
Subtotal = lbs.	Subtotal = lbs.	Subtotal = lbs.	Subtotal = lbs.	Subtotal = lbs.	Subtotal = lbs.

Exercise 1:   *Total Weight* _____ *lbs.*   *Time* _____ *mins.*   *Power Factor* _____ *lbs./min.*   *Power Index* _____

▪ Exercise: DEADLIFT

Weight Reps Sets	Weight Reps Sets	Weight Reps Sets	Weight Reps Sets	Weight Reps Sets	Weight Reps Sets
× ×	× ×	× ×	× ×	× ×	× ×
Subtotal = lbs.	Subtotal = lbs.	Subtotal = lbs.	Subtotal = lbs.	Subtotal = lbs.	Subtotal = lbs.

Exercise 2:   *Total Weight* _____ *lbs.*   *Time* _____ *mins.*   *Power Factor* _____ *lbs./min.*   *Power Index* _____

▪ Exercise:

Weight Reps Sets	Weight Reps Sets	Weight Reps Sets	Weight Reps Sets	Weight Reps Sets	Weight Reps Sets
× ×	× ×	× ×	× ×	× ×	× ×
Subtotal = lbs.	Subtotal = lbs.	Subtotal = lbs.	Subtotal = lbs.	Subtotal = lbs.	Subtotal = lbs.

Exercise 3:   *Total Weight* _____ *lbs.*   *Time* _____ *mins.*   *Power Factor* _____ *lbs./min.*   *Power Index* _____

▪ Exercise:

Weight Reps Sets	Weight Reps Sets	Weight Reps Sets	Weight Reps Sets	Weight Reps Sets	Weight Reps Sets
× ×	× ×	× ×	× ×	× ×	× ×
Subtotal = lbs.	Subtotal = lbs.	Subtotal = lbs.	Subtotal = lbs.	Subtotal = lbs.	Subtotal = lbs.

Exercise 4:   *Total Weight* _____ *lbs.*   *Time* _____ *mins.*   *Power Factor* _____ *lbs./min.*   *Power Index* _____

▪ Exercise:

Weight Reps Sets	Weight Reps Sets	Weight Reps Sets	Weight Reps Sets	Weight Reps Sets	Weight Reps Sets
× ×	× ×	× ×	× ×	× ×	× ×
Subtotal = lbs.	Subtotal = lbs.	Subtotal = lbs.	Subtotal = lbs.	Subtotal = lbs.	Subtotal = lbs.

Exercise 5:   *Total Weight* _____ *lbs.*   *Time* _____ *mins.*   *Power Factor* _____ *lbs./min.*   *Power Index* _____

OVERALL WORKOUT: *Total Weight* _____ *lbs.*   *Time* _____ *mins.*   *Power Factor* _____ *lbs./min.*   *Power Index* _____

Exercise Subtotal = Weight × Reps × Sets   ▪ *Power Factor = lbs./min.*   ▪ *Power Index = Total Weight × Power Factor ÷ 1,000,000*

BACK SPECIALIZATION WORKOUT RECORD   Date: ___ / ___ / ___

Start Time: _____   **Finish Time:** _____   **Total Time:** _____

■ Exercise: LAT PULLDOWN (OR CLOSE-GRIP UNDERHAND CHIN-UP)

Weight Reps Sets	Weight Reps Sets	Weight Reps Sets	Weight Reps Sets	Weight Reps Sets	Weight Reps Sets
× ×	× ×	× ×	× ×	× ×	× ×
Subtotal = lbs.	Subtotal = lbs.	Subtotal = lbs.	Subtotal = lbs.	Subtotal = lbs.	Subtotal = lbs.

Exercise 1:   *Total Weight* _____ *lbs.   Time* _____ *mins.   Power Factor* _____ *lbs./min.   Power Index* _____

■ Exercise: DEADLIFT

Weight Reps Sets	Weight Reps Sets	Weight Reps Sets	Weight Reps Sets	Weight Reps Sets	Weight Reps Sets
× ×	× ×	× ×	× ×	× ×	× ×
Subtotal = lbs.	Subtotal = lbs.	Subtotal = lbs.	Subtotal = lbs.	Subtotal = lbs.	Subtotal = lbs.

Exercise 2:   *Total Weight* _____ *lbs.   Time* _____ *mins.   Power Factor* _____ *lbs./min.   Power Index* _____

■ Exercise:

Weight Reps Sets	Weight Reps Sets	Weight Reps Sets	Weight Reps Sets	Weight Reps Sets	Weight Reps Sets
× ×	× ×	× ×	× ×	× ×	× ×
Subtotal = lbs.	Subtotal = lbs.	Subtotal = lbs.	Subtotal = lbs.	Subtotal = lbs.	Subtotal = lbs.

Exercise 3:   *Total Weight* _____ *lbs.   Time* _____ *mins.   Power Factor* _____ *lbs./min.   Power Index* _____

■ Exercise:

Weight Reps Sets	Weight Reps Sets	Weight Reps Sets	Weight Reps Sets	Weight Reps Sets	Weight Reps Sets
× ×	× ×	× ×	× ×	× ×	× ×
Subtotal = lbs.	Subtotal = lbs.	Subtotal = lbs.	Subtotal = lbs.	Subtotal = lbs.	Subtotal = lbs.

Exercise 4:   *Total Weight* _____ *lbs.   Time* _____ *mins.   Power Factor* _____ *lbs./min.   Power Index* _____

■ Exercise:

Weight Reps Sets	Weight Reps Sets	Weight Reps Sets	Weight Reps Sets	Weight Reps Sets	Weight Reps Sets
× ×	× ×	× ×	× ×	× ×	× ×
Subtotal = lbs.	Subtotal = lbs.	Subtotal = lbs.	Subtotal = lbs.	Subtotal = lbs.	Subtotal = lbs.

Exercise 5:   *Total Weight* _____ *lbs.   Time* _____ *mins.   Power Factor* _____ *lbs./min.   Power Index* _____

OVERALL WORKOUT: *Total Weight* _____ *lbs.   Time* _____ *mins.   Power Factor* _____ *lbs./min.   Power Index* _____

Exercise Subtotal = Weight × Reps × Sets   ■ *Power Factor = lbs./min.*   ■ *Power Index = Total Weight × Power Factor ÷ 1,000,000*

BACK SPECIALIZATION WORKOUT RECORD   Date: ___ / ___ / ___

Start Time: _____   **Finish Time:** _____   **Total Time:** _____

▪ Exercise: LAT PULLDOWN (OR CLOSE-GRIP UNDERHAND CHIN-UP)

Weight Reps Sets	Weight Reps Sets	Weight Reps Sets	Weight Reps Sets	Weight Reps Sets	Weight Reps Sets
× ×	× ×	× ×	× ×	× ×	× ×
Subtotal = lbs.	Subtotal = ·lbs.	Subtotal = lbs.	Subtotal = lbs.	Subtotal = lbs.	Subtotal = lbs.

Exercise 1:   *Total Weight* _____ *lbs.*   *Time* _____ *mins.*   *Power Factor* _____ *lbs./min.*   *Power Index* _____

▪ Exercise: DEADLIFT

Weight Reps Sets	Weight Reps Sets	Weight Reps Sets	Weight Reps Sets	Weight Reps Sets	Weight Reps Sets
× ×	× ×	× ×	× ×	× ×	× ×
Subtotal = lbs.	Subtotal = lbs.	Subtotal = lbs.	Subtotal = lbs.	Subtotal = lbs.	Subtotal = lbs.

Exercise 2:   *Total Weight* _____ *lbs.*   *Time* _____ *mins.*   *Power Factor* _____ *lbs./min.*   *Power Index* _____

▪ Exercise:

Weight Reps Sets	Weight Reps Sets	Weight Reps Sets	Weight Reps Sets	Weight Reps Sets	Weight Reps Sets
× ×	× ×	× ×	× ×	× ×	× ×
Subtotal = lbs.	Subtotal = lbs.	Subtotal = lbs.	Subtotal = lbs.	Subtotal = lbs.	Subtotal = lbs.

Exercise 3:   *Total Weight* _____ *lbs.*   *Time* _____ *mins.*   *Power Factor* _____ *lbs./min.*   *Power Index* _____

▪ Exercise:

Weight Reps Sets	Weight Reps Sets	Weight Reps Sets	Weight Reps Sets	Weight Reps Sets	Weight Reps Sets
× ×	× ×	× ×	× ×	× ×	× ×
Subtotal = lbs.	Subtotal = lbs.	Subtotal = lbs.	Subtotal = lbs.	Subtotal = lbs.	Subtotal = lbs.

Exercise 4:   *Total Weight* _____ *lbs.*   *Time* _____ *mins.*   *Power Factor* _____ *lbs./min.*   *Power Index* _____

▪ Exercise:

Weight Reps Sets	Weight Reps Sets	Weight Reps Sets	Weight Reps Sets	Weight Reps Sets	Weight Reps Sets
× ×	× ×	× ×	× ×	× ×	× ×
Subtotal = lbs.	Subtotal = lbs.	Subtotal = lbs.	Subtotal = lbs.	Subtotal = lbs.	Subtotal = lbs.

Exercise 5:   *Total Weight* _____ *lbs.*   *Time* _____ *mins.*   *Power Factor* _____ *lbs./min.*   *Power Index* _____

OVERALL WORKOUT: *Total Weight* _____ *lbs.*   *Time* _____ *mins.*   *Power Factor* _____ *lbs./min.*   *Power Index* _____

Exercise Subtotal = Weight × Reps × Sets   ▪ *Power Factor = lbs./min.*   ▪ *Power Index = Total Weight × Power Factor ÷ 1,000,000*

BACK SPECIALIZATION WORKOUT RECORD   Date: ___ / ___ / ___

Start Time: _____   Finish Time: _____   Total Time: _____

▪ Exercise: LAT PULLDOWN (OR CLOSE-GRIP UNDERHAND CHIN-UP)

Weight Reps Sets	Weight Reps Sets	Weight Reps Sets	Weight Reps Sets	Weight Reps Sets	Weight Reps Sets
× ×	× ×	× ×	× ×	× ×	× ×
Subtotal = lbs.	Subtotal = lbs.	Subtotal = lbs.	Subtotal = lbs.	Subtotal = lbs.	Subtotal = lbs.

Exercise 1:   *Total Weight _____ lbs.   Time _____ mins.   Power Factor _____ lbs./min.   Power Index _____*

▪ Exercise: DEADLIFT

Weight Reps Sets	Weight Reps Sets	Weight Reps Sets	Weight Reps Sets	Weight Reps Sets	Weight Reps Sets
× ×	× ×	× ×	× ×	× ×	× ×
Subtotal = lbs.	Subtotal = lbs.	Subtotal = lbs.	Subtotal = lbs.	Subtotal = lbs.	Subtotal = lbs.

Exercise 2:   *Total Weight _____ lbs.   Time _____ mins.   Power Factor _____ lbs./min.   Power Index _____*

▪ Exercise:

Weight Reps Sets	Weight Reps Sets	Weight Reps Sets	Weight Reps Sets	Weight Reps Sets	Weight Reps Sets
× ×	× ×	× ×	× ×	× ×	× ×
Subtotal = lbs.	Subtotal = lbs.	Subtotal = lbs.	Subtotal = lbs.	Subtotal = lbs.	Subtotal = lbs.

Exercise 3:   *Total Weight _____ lbs.   Time _____ mins.   Power Factor _____ lbs./min.   Power Index _____*

▪ Exercise:

Weight Reps Sets	Weight Reps Sets	Weight Reps Sets	Weight Reps Sets	Weight Reps Sets	Weight Reps Sets
× ×	× ×	× ×	× ×	× ×	× ×
Subtotal = lbs.	Subtotal = lbs.	Subtotal = lbs.	Subtotal = lbs.	Subtotal = lbs.	Subtotal = lbs.

Exercise 4:   *Total Weight _____ lbs.   Time _____ mins.   Power Factor _____ lbs./min.   Power Index _____*

▪ Exercise:

Weight Reps Sets	Weight Reps Sets	Weight Reps Sets	Weight Reps Sets	Weight Reps Sets	Weight Reps Sets
× ×	× ×	× ×	× ×	× ×	× ×
Subtotal = lbs.	Subtotal = lbs.	Subtotal = lbs.	Subtotal = lbs.	Subtotal = lbs.	Subtotal = lbs.

Exercise 5:   *Total Weight _____ lbs.   Time _____ mins.   Power Factor _____ lbs./min.   Power Index _____*

OVERALL WORKOUT: *Total Weight _____ lbs.   Time _____ mins.   Power Factor _____ lbs./min.   Power Index _____*

Exercise Subtotal = Weight × Reps × Sets   ▪ Power Factor = lbs./min.   ▪ Power Index = Total Weight × Power Factor ÷ 1,000,000

BACK SPECIALIZATION WORKOUT RECORD   Date: ___ / ___ / ___

Start Time: _____   Finish Time: _____   Total Time: _____

▪ Exercise: LAT PULLDOWN (OR CLOSE-GRIP UNDERHAND CHIN-UP)

Weight Reps Sets	Weight Reps Sets	Weight Reps Sets	Weight Reps Sets	Weight Reps Sets	Weight Reps Sets
× ×	× ×	× ×	× ×	× ×	× ×
Subtotal = lbs.	Subtotal = lbs.	Subtotal = lbs.	Subtotal = lbs.	Subtotal = lbs.	Subtotal = lbs.

Exercise 1:   *Total Weight* _____ *lbs.*   *Time* _____ *mins.*   *Power Factor* _____ *lbs./min.*   *Power Index* _____

▪ Exercise: DEADLIFT

Weight Reps Sets	Weight Reps Sets	Weight Reps Sets	Weight Reps Sets	Weight Reps Sets	Weight Reps Sets
× ×	× ×	× ×	× ×	× ×	× ×
Subtotal = lbs.	Subtotal = lbs.	Subtotal = lbs.	Subtotal = lbs.	Subtotal = lbs.	Subtotal = lbs.

Exercise 2:   *Total Weight* _____ *lbs.*   *Time* _____ *mins.*   *Power Factor* _____ *lbs./min.*   *Power Index* _____

▪ Exercise:

Weight Reps Sets	Weight Reps Sets	Weight Reps Sets	Weight Reps Sets	Weight Reps Sets	Weight Reps Sets
× ×	× ×	× ×	× ×	× ×	× ×
Subtotal = lbs.	Subtotal = lbs.	Subtotal = lbs.	Subtotal = lbs.	Subtotal = lbs.	Subtotal = lbs.

Exercise 3:   *Total Weight* _____ *lbs.*   *Time* _____ *mins.*   *Power Factor* _____ *lbs./min.*   *Power Index* _____

▪ Exercise:

Weight Reps Sets	Weight Reps Sets	Weight Reps Sets	Weight Reps Sets	Weight Reps Sets	Weight Reps Sets
× ×	× ×	× ×	× ×	× ×	× ×
Subtotal = lbs.	Subtotal = lbs.	Subtotal = lbs.	Subtotal = lbs.	Subtotal = lbs.	Subtotal = lbs.

Exercise 4:   *Total Weight* _____ *lbs.*   *Time* _____ *mins.*   *Power Factor* _____ *lbs./min.*   *Power Index* _____

▪ Exercise:

Weight Reps Sets	Weight Reps Sets	Weight Reps Sets	Weight Reps Sets	Weight Reps Sets	Weight Reps Sets
× ×	× ×	× ×	× ×	× ×	× ×
Subtotal = lbs.	Subtotal = lbs.	Subtotal = lbs.	Subtotal = lbs.	Subtotal = lbs.	Subtotal = lbs.

Exercise 5:   *Total Weight* _____ *lbs.*   *Time* _____ *mins.*   *Power Factor* _____ *lbs./min.*   *Power Index* _____

OVERALL WORKOUT: *Total Weight* _____ *lbs.*   *Time* _____ *mins.*   *Power Factor* _____ *lbs./min.*   *Power Index* _____

Exercise Subtotal = Weight × Reps × Sets   ▪ *Power Factor = lbs./min.*   ▪ *Power Index = Total Weight × Power Factor ÷ 1,000,000*

BACK SPECIALIZATION WORKOUT RECORD   Date: ___ / ___ / ___

Start Time: _____   Finish Time: _____   Total Time: _____

▪ Exercise: LAT PULLDOWN (OR CLOSE-GRIP UNDERHAND CHIN-UP)

Weight Reps Sets	Weight Reps Sets	Weight Reps Sets	Weight Reps Sets	Weight Reps Sets	Weight Reps Sets
× ×	× ×	× ×	× ×	× ×	× ×
Subtotal = lbs.	Subtotal = lbs.	Subtotal = lbs.	Subtotal = lbs.	Subtotal = lbs.	Subtotal = lbs.

Exercise 1:   *Total Weight _____ lbs.   Time _____ mins.   Power Factor _____ lbs./min.   Power Index _____*

▪ Exercise: DEADLIFT

Weight Reps Sets	Weight Reps Sets	Weight Reps Sets	Weight Reps Sets	Weight Reps Sets	Weight Reps Sets
× ×	× ×	× ×	× ×	× ×	× ×
Subtotal = lbs.	Subtotal = lbs.	Subtotal = lbs.	Subtotal = lbs.	Subtotal = lbs.	Subtotal = lbs.

Exercise 2:   *Total Weight _____ lbs.   Time _____ mins.   Power Factor _____ lbs./min.   Power Index _____*

▪ Exercise:

Weight Reps Sets	Weight Reps Sets	Weight Reps Sets	Weight Reps Sets	Weight Reps Sets	Weight Reps Sets
× ×	× ×	× ×	× ×	× ×	× ×
Subtotal = lbs.	Subtotal = lbs.	Subtotal = lbs.	Subtotal = lbs.	Subtotal = lbs.	Subtotal = lbs.

Exercise 3:   *Total Weight _____ lbs.   Time _____ mins.   Power Factor _____ lbs./min.   Power Index _____*

▪ Exercise:

Weight Reps Sets	Weight Reps Sets	Weight Reps Sets	Weight Reps Sets	Weight Reps Sets	Weight Reps Sets
× ×	× ×	× ×	× ×	× ×	× ×
Subtotal = lbs.	Subtotal = lbs.	Subtotal = lbs.	Subtotal = lbs.	Subtotal = lbs.	Subtotal = lbs.

Exercise 4:   *Total Weight _____ lbs.   Time _____ mins.   Power Factor _____ lbs./min.   Power Index _____*

▪ Exercise:

Weight Reps Sets	Weight Reps Sets	Weight Reps Sets	Weight Reps Sets	Weight Reps Sets	Weight Reps Sets
× ×	× ×	× ×	× ×	× ×	× ×
Subtotal = lbs.	Subtotal = lbs.	Subtotal = lbs.	Subtotal = lbs.	Subtotal = lbs.	Subtotal = lbs.

Exercise 5:   *Total Weight _____ lbs.   Time _____ mins.   Power Factor _____ lbs./min.   Power Index _____*

OVERALL WORKOUT: *Total Weight _____ lbs.   Time _____ mins.   Power Factor _____ lbs./min.   Power Index _____*

Exercise Subtotal = Weight × Reps × Sets   ▪ Power Factor = lbs./min.   ▪ Power Index = Total Weight × Power Factor ÷ 1,000,000

BACK SPECIALIZATION WORKOUT RECORD   Date: ____ / ____ / ____

Start Time: _____   Finish Time: _____   Total Time: _____

■ Exercise: LAT PULLDOWN (OR CLOSE-GRIP UNDERHAND CHIN-UP)

Weight Reps Sets	Weight Reps Sets	Weight Reps Sets	Weight Reps Sets	Weight Reps Sets	Weight Reps Sets
× ×	× ×	× ×	× ×	× ×	× ×
Subtotal = lbs.	Subtotal = lbs.	Subtotal = lbs.	Subtotal = lbs.	Subtotal = lbs.	Subtotal = lbs.

Exercise 1:   *Total Weight* _____ *lbs.*   *Time* _____ *mins.*   *Power Factor* _____ *lbs./min.*   *Power Index* _____

■ Exercise: DEADLIFT

Weight Reps Sets	Weight Reps Sets	Weight Reps Sets	Weight Reps Sets	Weight Reps Sets	Weight Reps Sets
× ×	× ×	× ×	× ×	× ×	× ×
Subtotal = lbs.	Subtotal = lbs.	Subtotal = lbs.	Subtotal = lbs.	Subtotal = lbs.	Subtotal = lbs.

Exercise 2:   *Total Weight* _____ *lbs.*   *Time* _____ *mins.*   *Power Factor* _____ *lbs./min.*   *Power Index* _____

■ Exercise:

Weight Reps Sets	Weight Reps Sets	Weight Reps Sets	Weight Reps Sets	Weight Reps Sets	Weight Reps Sets
× ×	× ×	× ×	× ×	× ×	× ×
Subtotal = lbs.	Subtotal = lbs.	Subtotal = lbs.	Subtotal = lbs.	Subtotal = lbs.	Subtotal = lbs.

Exercise 3:   *Total Weight* _____ *lbs.*   *Time* _____ *mins.*   *Power Factor* _____ *lbs./min.*   *Power Index* _____

■ Exercise:

Weight Reps Sets	Weight Reps Sets	Weight Reps Sets	Weight Reps Sets	Weight Reps Sets	Weight Reps Sets
× ×	× ×	× ×	× ×	× ×	× ×
Subtotal = lbs.	Subtotal = lbs.	Subtotal = lbs.	Subtotal = lbs.	Subtotal = lbs.	Subtotal = lbs.

Exercise 4:   *Total Weight* _____ *lbs.*   *Time* _____ *mins.*   *Power Factor* _____ *lbs./min.*   *Power Index* _____

■ Exercise:

Weight Reps Sets	Weight Reps Sets	Weight Reps Sets	Weight Reps Sets	Weight Reps Sets	Weight Reps Sets
× ×	× ×	× ×	× ×	× ×	× ×
Subtotal = lbs.	Subtotal = lbs.	Subtotal = lbs.	Subtotal = lbs.	Subtotal = lbs.	Subtotal = lbs.

Exercise 5:   *Total Weight* _____ *lbs.*   *Time* _____ *mins.*   *Power Factor* _____ *lbs./min.*   *Power Index* _____

OVERALL WORKOUT: *Total Weight* _____ *lbs.*   *Time* _____ *mins.*   *Power Factor* _____ *lbs./min.*   *Power Index* _____

Exercise Subtotal = Weight × Reps × Sets   ■ *Power Factor = lbs./min.*   ■ *Power Index = Total Weight × Power Factor ÷ 1,000,000*

BACK SPECIALIZATION WORKOUT RECORD   Date: ___ / ___ / ___

Start Time: _____   Finish Time: _____   Total Time: _____

■ **Exercise: LAT PULLDOWN (OR CLOSE-GRIP UNDERHAND CHIN-UP)**

Weight Reps Sets	Weight Reps Sets	Weight Reps Sets	Weight Reps Sets	Weight Reps Sets	Weight Reps Sets
× ×	× ×	× ×	× ×	× ×	× ×
Subtotal = lbs.	Subtotal = lbs.	Subtotal = lbs.	Subtotal = lbs.	Subtotal = lbs.	Subtotal = lbs.

Exercise 1:   *Total Weight* _____ *lbs.*   *Time* _____ *mins.*   *Power Factor* _____ *lbs./min.*   *Power Index* _____

■ **Exercise: DEADLIFT**

Weight Reps Sets	Weight Reps Sets	Weight Reps Sets	Weight Reps Sets	Weight Reps Sets	Weight Reps Sets
× ×	× ×	× ×	× ×	× ×	× ×
Subtotal = lbs.	Subtotal = lbs.	Subtotal = lbs.	Subtotal = lbs.	Subtotal = lbs.	Subtotal = lbs.

Exercise 2:   *Total Weight* _____ *lbs.*   *Time* _____ *mins.*   *Power Factor* _____ *lbs./min.*   *Power Index* _____

■ **Exercise:**

Weight Reps Sets	Weight Reps Sets	Weight Reps Sets	Weight Reps Sets	Weight Reps Sets	Weight Reps Sets
× ×	× ×	× ×	× ×	× ×	× ×
Subtotal = lbs.	Subtotal = lbs.	Subtotal = lbs.	Subtotal = lbs.	Subtotal = lbs.	Subtotal = lbs.

Exercise 3:   *Total Weight* _____ *lbs.*   *Time* _____ *mins.*   *Power Factor* _____ *lbs./min.*   *Power Index* _____

■ **Exercise:**

Weight Reps Sets	Weight Reps Sets	Weight Reps Sets	Weight Reps Sets	Weight Reps Sets	Weight Reps Sets
× ×	× ×	× ×	× ×	× ×	× ×
Subtotal = lbs.	Subtotal = lbs.	Subtotal = lbs.	Subtotal = lbs.	Subtotal = lbs.	Subtotal = lbs.

Exercise 4:   *Total Weight* _____ *lbs.*   *Time* _____ *mins.*   *Power Factor* _____ *lbs./min.*   *Power Index* _____

■ **Exercise:**

Weight Reps Sets	Weight Reps Sets	Weight Reps Sets	Weight Reps Sets	Weight Reps Sets	Weight Reps Sets
× ×	× ×	× ×	× ×	× ×	× ×
Subtotal = lbs.	Subtotal = lbs.	Subtotal = lbs.	Subtotal = lbs.	Subtotal = lbs.	Subtotal = lbs.

Exercise 5:   *Total Weight* _____ *lbs.*   *Time* _____ *mins.*   *Power Factor* _____ *lbs./min.*   *Power Index* _____

OVERALL WORKOUT: *Total Weight* _____ *lbs.*   *Time* _____ *mins.*   *Power Factor* _____ *lbs./min.*   *Power Index* _____

Exercise Subtotal = Weight × Reps × Sets   ■   *Power Factor = lbs./min.*   ■   *Power Index = Total Weight × Power Factor ÷ 1,000,000*

BACK SPECIALIZATION WORKOUT RECORD   Date: ___ / ___ / ___

Start Time: _____   Finish Time: _____   Total Time: _____

■ Exercise: LAT PULLDOWN (OR CLOSE-GRIP UNDERHAND CHIN-UP)

Weight Reps Sets	Weight Reps Sets	Weight Reps Sets	Weight Reps Sets	Weight Reps Sets	Weight Reps Sets
× ×	× ×	× ×	× ×	× ×	× ×
Subtotal = lbs.	Subtotal = lbs.	Subtotal = lbs.	Subtotal = lbs.	Subtotal = lbs.	Subtotal = lbs.

Exercise 1:   *Total Weight _____ lbs.   Time _____ mins.   Power Factor _____ lbs./min.   Power Index _____*

■ Exercise: DEADLIFT

Weight Reps Sets	Weight Reps Sets	Weight Reps Sets	Weight Reps Sets	Weight Reps Sets	Weight Reps Sets
× ×	× ×	× ×	× ×	× ×	× ×
Subtotal = lbs.	Subtotal = lbs.	Subtotal = lbs.	Subtotal = lbs.	Subtotal = lbs.	Subtotal = lbs.

Exercise 2:   *Total Weight _____ lbs.   Time _____ mins.   Power Factor _____ lbs./min.   Power Index _____*

■ Exercise:

Weight Reps Sets	Weight Reps Sets	Weight Reps Sets	Weight Reps Sets	Weight Reps Sets	Weight Reps Sets
× ×	× ×	× ×	× ×	× ×	× ×
Subtotal = lbs.	Subtotal = lbs.	Subtotal = lbs.	Subtotal = lbs.	Subtotal = lbs.	Subtotal = lbs.

Exercise 3:   *Total Weight _____ lbs.   Time _____ mins.   Power Factor _____ lbs./min.   Power Index _____*

■ Exercise:

Weight Reps Sets	Weight Reps Sets	Weight Reps Sets	Weight Reps Sets	Weight Reps Sets	Weight Reps Sets
× ×	× ×	× ×	× ×	× ×	× ×
Subtotal = lbs.	Subtotal = lbs.	Subtotal = lbs.	Subtotal = lbs.	Subtotal = lbs.	Subtotal = lbs.

Exercise 4:   *Total Weight _____ lbs.   Time _____ mins.   Power Factor _____ lbs./min.   Power Index _____*

■ Exercise:

Weight Reps Sets	Weight Reps Sets	Weight Reps Sets	Weight Reps Sets	Weight Reps Sets	Weight Reps Sets
× ×	× ×	× ×	× ×	× ×	× ×
Subtotal = lbs.	Subtotal = lbs.	Subtotal = lbs.	Subtotal = lbs.	Subtotal = lbs.	Subtotal = lbs.

Exercise 5:   *Total Weight _____ lbs.   Time _____ mins.   Power Factor _____ lbs./min.   Power Index _____*

OVERALL WORKOUT: *Total Weight _____ lbs.   Time _____ mins.   Power Factor _____ lbs./min.   Power Index _____*

Exercise Subtotal = Weight × Reps × Sets   ■ Power Factor = lbs./min.   ■ Power Index = Total Weight × Power Factor ÷ 1,000,000

BACK SPECIALIZATION WORKOUT RECORD   Date: ___ / ___ / ___

Start Time: _____   **Finish Time:** _____   **Total Time:** _____

■ **Exercise: LAT PULLDOWN (OR CLOSE-GRIP UNDERHAND CHIN-UP)**

Weight Reps Sets	Weight Reps Sets	Weight Reps Sets	Weight Reps Sets	Weight Reps Sets	Weight Reps Sets
× ×	× ×	× ×	× ×	× ×	× ×
Subtotal = lbs.	Subtotal = lbs.	Subtotal = lbs.	Subtotal = lbs.	Subtotal = lbs.	Subtotal = lbs.

Exercise 1:   *Total Weight* _____ *lbs.*   *Time* _____ *mins.*   *Power Factor* _____ *lbs./min.*   *Power Index* _____

■ **Exercise: DEADLIFT**

Weight Reps Sets	Weight Reps Sets	Weight Reps Sets	Weight Reps Sets	Weight Reps Sets	Weight Reps Sets
× ×	× ×	× ×	× ×	× ×	× ×
Subtotal = lbs.	Subtotal = lbs.	Subtotal = lbs.	Subtotal = lbs.	Subtotal = lbs.	Subtotal = lbs.

Exercise 2:   *Total Weight* _____ *lbs.*   *Time* _____ *mins.*   *Power Factor* _____ *lbs./min.*   *Power Index* _____

■ **Exercise:**

Weight Reps Sets	Weight Reps Sets	Weight Reps Sets	Weight Reps Sets	Weight Reps Sets	Weight Reps Sets
× ×	× ×	× ×	× ×	× ×	× ×
Subtotal = lbs.	Subtotal = lbs.	Subtotal = lbs.	Subtotal = lbs.	Subtotal = lbs.	Subtotal = lbs.

Exercise 3:   *Total Weight* _____ *lbs.*   *Time* _____ *mins.*   *Power Factor* _____ *lbs./min.*   *Power Index* _____

■ **Exercise:**

Weight Reps Sets	Weight Reps Sets	Weight Reps Sets	Weight Reps Sets	Weight Reps Sets	Weight Reps Sets
× ×	× ×	× ×	× ×	× ×	× ×
Subtotal = lbs.	Subtotal = lbs.	Subtotal = lbs.	Subtotal = lbs.	Subtotal = lbs.	Subtotal = lbs.

Exercise 4:   *Total Weight* _____ *lbs.*   *Time* _____ *mins.*   *Power Factor* _____ *lbs./min.*   *Power Index* _____

■ **Exercise:**

Weight Reps Sets	Weight Reps Sets	Weight Reps Sets	Weight Reps Sets	Weight Reps Sets	Weight Reps Sets
× ×	× ×	× ×	× ×	× ×	× ×
Subtotal = lbs.	Subtotal = lbs.	Subtotal = lbs.	Subtotal = lbs.	Subtotal = lbs.	Subtotal = lbs.

Exercise 5:   *Total Weight* _____ *lbs.*   *Time* _____ *mins.*   *Power Factor* _____ *lbs./min.*   *Power Index* _____

OVERALL WORKOUT: *Total Weight* _____ *lbs.*   *Time* _____ *mins.*   *Power Factor* _____ *lbs./min.*   *Power Index* _____

Exercise Subtotal = Weight × Reps × Sets   ■ *Power Factor = lbs./min.*   ■ *Power Index = Total Weight × Power Factor ÷ 1,000,000*

BACK SPECIALIZATION WORKOUT RECORD   Date: ____ / ____ / ____

Start Time: _____   Finish Time: _____   Total Time: _____

▪ Exercise: LAT PULLDOWN (OR CLOSE-GRIP UNDERHAND CHIN-UP)

Weight Reps Sets	Weight Reps Sets	Weight Reps Sets	Weight Reps Sets	Weight Reps Sets	Weight Reps Sets
× ×	× ×	× ×	× ×	× ×	× ×
Subtotal = lbs.	Subtotal = lbs.	Subtotal = lbs.	Subtotal = lbs.	Subtotal = lbs.	Subtotal = lbs.

Exercise 1:   Total Weight _____ lbs.   Time _____ mins.   Power Factor _____ lbs./min.   Power Index _____

▪ Exercise: DEADLIFT

Weight Reps Sets	Weight Reps Sets	Weight Reps Sets	Weight Reps Sets	Weight Reps Sets	Weight Reps Sets
× ×	× ×	× ×	× ×	× ×	× ×
Subtotal = lbs.	Subtotal = lbs.	Subtotal = lbs.	Subtotal = lbs.	Subtotal = lbs.	Subtotal = lbs.

Exercise 2:   Total Weight _____ lbs.   Time _____ mins.   Power Factor _____ lbs./min.   Power Index _____

▪ Exercise:

Weight Reps Sets	Weight Reps Sets	Weight Reps Sets	Weight Reps Sets	Weight Reps Sets	Weight Reps Sets
× ×	× ×	× ×	× ×	× ×	× ×
Subtotal = lbs.	Subtotal = lbs.	Subtotal = lbs.	Subtotal = lbs.	Subtotal = lbs.	Subtotal = lbs.

Exercise 3:   Total Weight _____ lbs.   Time _____ mins.   Power Factor _____ lbs./min.   Power Index _____

▪ Exercise:

Weight Reps Sets	Weight Reps Sets	Weight Reps Sets	Weight Reps Sets	Weight Reps Sets	Weight Reps Sets
× ×	× ×	× ×	× ×	× ×	× ×
Subtotal = lbs.	Subtotal = lbs.	Subtotal = lbs.	Subtotal = lbs.	Subtotal = lbs.	Subtotal = lbs.

Exercise 4:   Total Weight _____ lbs.   Time _____ mins.   Power Factor _____ lbs./min.   Power Index _____

▪ Exercise:

Weight Reps Sets	Weight Reps Sets	Weight Reps Sets	Weight Reps Sets	Weight Reps Sets	Weight Reps Sets
× ×	× ×	× ×	× ×	× ×	× ×
Subtotal = lbs.	Subtotal = lbs.	Subtotal = lbs.	Subtotal = lbs.	Subtotal = lbs.	Subtotal = lbs.

Exercise 5:   Total Weight _____ lbs.   Time _____ mins.   Power Factor _____ lbs./min.   Power Index _____

OVERALL WORKOUT: *Total Weight* _____ *lbs.*   *Time* _____ *mins.*   *Power Factor* _____ *lbs./min.*   *Power Index* _____

Exercise Subtotal = Weight × Reps × Sets   ▪ *Power Factor = lbs./min.*   ▪ *Power Index = Total Weight × Power Factor ÷ 1,000,000*

BACK SPECIALIZATION WORKOUT RECORD   Date: ___ / ___ / ___

Start Time: _____   Finish Time: _____   Total Time: _____

■ Exercise: LAT PULLDOWN (OR CLOSE-GRIP UNDERHAND CHIN-UP)

Weight Reps Sets	Weight Reps Sets	Weight Reps Sets	Weight Reps Sets	Weight Reps Sets	Weight Reps Sets
× ×	× ×	× ×	× ×	× ×	× ×
Subtotal = lbs.	Subtotal = lbs.	Subtotal = lbs.	Subtotal = lbs.	Subtotal = lbs.	Subtotal = lbs.

Exercise 1:   *Total Weight* _____ *lbs.*   *Time* _____ *mins.*   *Power Factor* _____ *lbs./min.*   *Power Index* _____

■ Exercise: DEADLIFT

Weight Reps Sets	Weight Reps Sets	Weight Reps Sets	Weight Reps Sets	Weight Reps Sets	Weight Reps Sets
× ×	× ×	× ×	× ×	× ×	× ×
Subtotal = lbs.	Subtotal = lbs.	Subtotal = lbs.	Subtotal = lbs.	Subtotal = lbs.	Subtotal = lbs.

Exercise 2:   *Total Weight* _____ *lbs.*   *Time* _____ *mins.*   *Power Factor* _____ *lbs./min.*   *Power Index* _____

■ Exercise:

Weight Reps Sets	Weight Reps Sets	Weight Reps Sets	Weight Reps Sets	Weight Reps Sets	Weight Reps Sets
× ×	× ×	× ×	× ×	× ×	× ×
Subtotal = lbs.	Subtotal = lbs.	Subtotal = lbs.	Subtotal = lbs.	Subtotal = lbs.	Subtotal = lbs.

Exercise 3:   *Total Weight* _____ *lbs.*   *Time* _____ *mins.*   *Power Factor* _____ *lbs./min.*   *Power Index* _____

■ Exercise:

Weight Reps Sets	Weight Reps Sets	Weight Reps Sets	Weight Reps Sets	Weight Reps Sets	Weight Reps Sets
× ×	× ×	× ×	× ×	× ×	× ×
Subtotal = lbs.	Subtotal = lbs.	Subtotal = lbs.	Subtotal = lbs.	Subtotal = lbs.	Subtotal = lbs.

Exercise 4:   *Total Weight* _____ *lbs.*   *Time* _____ *mins.*   *Power Factor* _____ *lbs./min.*   *Power Index* _____

■ Exercise:

Weight Reps Sets	Weight Reps Sets	Weight Reps Sets	Weight Reps Sets	Weight Reps Sets	Weight Reps Sets
× ×	× ×	× ×	× ×	× ×	× ×
Subtotal = lbs.	Subtotal = lbs.	Subtotal = lbs.	Subtotal = lbs.	Subtotal = lbs.	Subtotal = lbs.

Exercise 5:   *Total Weight* _____ *lbs.*   *Time* _____ *mins.*   *Power Factor* _____ *lbs./min.*   *Power Index* _____

OVERALL WORKOUT: *Total Weight* _____ *lbs.*   *Time* _____ *mins.*   *Power Factor* _____ *lbs./min.*   *Power Index* _____

Exercise Subtotal = Weight × Reps × Sets   ■ *Power Factor = lbs./min.*   ■ *Power Index = Total Weight × Power Factor ÷ 1,000,000*

BACK SPECIALIZATION WORKOUT RECORD   Date: ____ / ____ / ____

Start Time: _____   **Finish Time:** _____   **Total Time:** _____

■ **Exercise: LAT PULLDOWN (OR CLOSE-GRIP UNDERHAND CHIN-UP)**

Weight Reps Sets	Weight Reps Sets	Weight Reps Sets	Weight Reps Sets	Weight Reps Sets	Weight Reps Sets
× ×	× ×	× ×	× ×	× ×	× ×
Subtotal = lbs.	Subtotal = lbs.	Subtotal = lbs.	Subtotal = lbs.	Subtotal = lbs.	Subtotal = lbs.

Exercise 1:   *Total Weight* _____ *lbs.*   *Time* _____ *mins.*   *Power Factor* _____ *lbs./min.*   *Power Index* _____

■ **Exercise: DEADLIFT**

Weight Reps Sets	Weight Reps Sets	Weight Reps Sets	Weight Reps Sets	Weight Reps Sets	Weight Reps Sets
× ×	× ×	× ×	× ×	× ×	× ×
Subtotal = lbs.	Subtotal = lbs.	Subtotal = lbs.	Subtotal = lbs.	Subtotal = lbs.	Subtotal = lbs.

Exercise 2:   *Total Weight* _____ *lbs.*   *Time* _____ *mins.*   *Power Factor* _____ *lbs./min.*   *Power Index* _____

■ **Exercise:**

Weight Reps Sets	Weight Reps Sets	Weight Reps Sets	Weight Reps Sets	Weight Reps Sets	Weight Reps Sets
× ×	× ×	× ×	× ×	× ×	× ×
Subtotal = lbs.	Subtotal = lbs.	Subtotal = lbs.	Subtotal = lbs.	Subtotal = lbs.	Subtotal = lbs.

Exercise 3:   *Total Weight* _____ *lbs.*   *Time* _____ *mins.*   *Power Factor* _____ *lbs./min.*   *Power Index* _____

■ **Exercise:**

Weight Reps Sets	Weight Reps Sets	Weight Reps Sets	Weight Reps Sets	Weight Reps Sets	Weight Reps Sets
× ×	× ×	× ×	× ×	× ×	× ×
Subtotal = lbs.	Subtotal = lbs.	Subtotal = lbs.	Subtotal = lbs.	Subtotal = lbs.	Subtotal = lbs.

Exercise 4:   *Total Weight* _____ *lbs.*   *Time* _____ *mins.*   *Power Factor* _____ *lbs./min.*   *Power Index* _____

■ **Exercise:**

Weight Reps Sets	Weight Reps Sets	Weight Reps Sets	Weight Reps Sets	Weight Reps Sets	Weight Reps Sets
× ×	× ×	× ×	× ×	× ×	× ×
Subtotal = lbs.	Subtotal = lbs.	Subtotal = lbs.	Subtotal = lbs.	Subtotal = lbs.	Subtotal = lbs.

Exercise 5:   *Total Weight* _____ *lbs.*   *Time* _____ *mins.*   *Power Factor* _____ *lbs./min.*   *Power Index* _____

OVERALL WORKOUT: *Total Weight* _____ *lbs.*   *Time* _____ *mins.*   *Power Factor* _____ *lbs./min.*   *Power Index* _____

Exercise Subtotal = Weight × Reps × Sets   ■   *Power Factor = lbs./min.*   ■   *Power Index = Total Weight × Power Factor ÷ 1,000,000*

BACK SPECIALIZATION WORKOUT RECORD   Date: ___ / ___ / ___

Start Time: _____   Finish Time: _____   Total Time: _____

■ Exercise: LAT PULLDOWN (OR CLOSE-GRIP UNDERHAND CHIN-UP)

Weight Reps Sets	Weight Reps Sets	Weight Reps Sets	Weight Reps Sets	Weight Reps Sets	Weight Reps Sets
× ×	× ×	× ×	× ×	× ×	× ×
Subtotal = lbs.	Subtotal = lbs.	Subtotal = lbs.	Subtotal = lbs.	Subtotal = lbs.	Subtotal = lbs.

Exercise 1:   *Total Weight _____ lbs.   Time _____ mins.   Power Factor _____ lbs./min.   Power Index _____*

■ Exercise: DEADLIFT

Weight Reps Sets	Weight Reps Sets	Weight Reps Sets	Weight Reps Sets	Weight Reps Sets	Weight Reps Sets
× ×	× ×	× ×	× ×	× ×	× ×
Subtotal = lbs.	Subtotal = lbs.	Subtotal = lbs.	Subtotal = lbs.	Subtotal = lbs.	Subtotal = lbs.

Exercise 2:   *Total Weight _____ lbs.   Time _____ mins.   Power Factor _____ lbs./min.   Power Index _____*

■ Exercise:

Weight Reps Sets	Weight Reps Sets	Weight Reps Sets	Weight Reps Sets	Weight Reps Sets	Weight Reps Sets
× ×	× ×	× ×	× ×	× ×	× ×
Subtotal = lbs.	Subtotal = lbs.	Subtotal = lbs.	Subtotal = lbs.	Subtotal = lbs.	Subtotal = lbs.

Exercise 3:   *Total Weight _____ lbs.   Time _____ mins.   Power Factor _____ lbs./min.   Power Index _____*

■ Exercise:

Weight Reps Sets	Weight Reps Sets	Weight Reps Sets	Weight Reps Sets	Weight Reps Sets	Weight Reps Sets
× ×	× ×	× ×	× ×	× ×	× ×
Subtotal = lbs.	Subtotal = lbs.	Subtotal = lbs.	Subtotal = lbs.	Subtotal = lbs.	Subtotal = lbs.

Exercise 4:   *Total Weight _____ lbs.   Time _____ mins.   Power Factor _____ lbs./min.   Power Index _____*

■ Exercise:

Weight Reps Sets	Weight Reps Sets	Weight Reps Sets	Weight Reps Sets	Weight Reps Sets	Weight Reps Sets
× ×	× ×	× ×	× ×	× ×	× ×
Subtotal = lbs.	Subtotal = lbs.	Subtotal = lbs.	Subtotal = lbs.	Subtotal = lbs.	Subtotal = lbs.

Exercise 5:   *Total Weight _____ lbs.   Time _____ mins.   Power Factor _____ lbs./min.   Power Index _____*

OVERALL WORKOUT: *Total Weight _____ lbs.   Time _____ mins.   Power Factor _____ lbs./min.   Power Index _____*

Exercise Subtotal = Weight × Reps × Sets   ■ Power Factor = lbs./min.   ■ Power Index = Total Weight × Power Factor ÷ 1,000,000

BACK SPECIALIZATION WORKOUT RECORD   Date: ___ / ___ / ___

Start Time: _____   Finish Time: _____   Total Time: _____

■ Exercise: LAT PULLDOWN (OR CLOSE-GRIP UNDERHAND CHIN-UP)

Weight Reps Sets	Weight Reps Sets	Weight Reps Sets	Weight Reps Sets	Weight Reps Sets	Weight Reps Sets
× ×	× ×	× ×	× ×	× ×	× ×
Subtotal = lbs.	Subtotal = lbs.	Subtotal = lbs.	Subtotal = lbs.	Subtotal = lbs.	Subtotal = lbs.

Exercise 1:   *Total Weight* _____ *lbs.*   *Time* _____ *mins.*   *Power Factor* _____ *lbs./min.*   *Power Index* _____

■ Exercise: DEADLIFT

Weight Reps Sets	Weight Reps Sets	Weight Reps Sets	Weight Reps Sets	Weight Reps Sets	Weight Reps Sets
× ×	× ×	× ×	× ×	× ×	× ×
Subtotal = lbs.	Subtotal = lbs.	Subtotal = lbs.	Subtotal = lbs.	Subtotal = lbs.	Subtotal = lbs.

Exercise 2:   *Total Weight* _____ *lbs.*   *Time* _____ *mins.*   *Power Factor* _____ *lbs./min.*   *Power Index* _____

■ Exercise:

Weight Reps Sets	Weight Reps Sets	Weight Reps Sets	Weight Reps Sets	Weight Reps Sets	Weight Reps Sets
× ×	× ×	× ×	× ×	× ×	× ×
Subtotal = lbs.	Subtotal = lbs.	Subtotal = lbs.	Subtotal = lbs.	Subtotal = lbs.	Subtotal = lbs.

Exercise 3:   *Total Weight* _____ *lbs.*   *Time* _____ *mins.*   *Power Factor* _____ *lbs./min.*   *Power Index* _____

■ Exercise:

Weight Reps Sets	Weight Reps Sets	Weight Reps Sets	Weight Reps Sets	Weight Reps Sets	Weight Reps Sets
× ×	× ×	× ×	× ×	× ×	× ×
Subtotal = lbs.	Subtotal = lbs.	Subtotal = lbs.	Subtotal = lbs.	Subtotal = lbs.	Subtotal = lbs.

Exercise 4:   *Total Weight* _____ *lbs.*   *Time* _____ *mins.*   *Power Factor* _____ *lbs./min.*   *Power Index* _____

■ Exercise:

Weight Reps Sets	Weight Reps Sets	Weight Reps Sets	Weight Reps Sets	Weight Reps Sets	Weight Reps Sets
× ×	× ×	× ×	× ×	× ×	× ×
Subtotal = lbs.	Subtotal = lbs.	Subtotal = lbs.	Subtotal = lbs.	Subtotal = lbs.	Subtotal = lbs.

Exercise 5:   *Total Weight* _____ *lbs.*   *Time* _____ *mins.*   *Power Factor* _____ *lbs./min.*   *Power Index* _____

OVERALL WORKOUT: *Total Weight* _____ *lbs.*   *Time* _____ *mins.*   *Power Factor* _____ *lbs./min.*   *Power Index* _____

Exercise Subtotal = Weight × Reps × Sets   ■ *Power Factor = lbs./min.*   ■ *Power Index = Total Weight × Power Factor ÷ 1,000,000*

BACK SPECIALIZATION WORKOUT RECORD   Date: ____ / ____ / ____

Start Time: _____   **Finish Time:** _____   **Total Time:** _____

■ **Exercise: LAT PULLDOWN (OR CLOSE-GRIP UNDERHAND CHIN-UP)**

Weight Reps Sets	Weight Reps Sets	Weight Reps Sets	Weight Reps Sets	Weight Reps Sets	Weight Reps Sets
× ×	× ×	× ×	× ×	× ×	× ×
Subtotal = lbs.	Subtotal = lbs.	Subtotal = lbs.	Subtotal = lbs.	Subtotal = lbs.	Subtotal = lbs.

Exercise 1:   *Total Weight* _____ *lbs.*   *Time* _____ *mins.*   *Power Factor* _____ *lbs./min.*   *Power Index* _____

■ **Exercise: DEADLIFT**

Weight Reps Sets	Weight Reps Sets	Weight Reps Sets	Weight Reps Sets	Weight Reps Sets	Weight Reps Sets
× ×	× ×	× ×	× ×	× ×	× ×
Subtotal = lbs.	Subtotal = lbs.	Subtotal = lbs.	Subtotal = lbs.	Subtotal = lbs.	Subtotal = lbs.

Exercise 2:   *Total Weight* _____ *lbs.*   *Time* _____ *mins.*   *Power Factor* _____ *lbs./min.*   *Power Index* _____

■ **Exercise:**

Weight Reps Sets	Weight Reps Sets	Weight Reps Sets	Weight Reps Sets	Weight Reps Sets	Weight Reps Sets
× ×	× ×	× ×	× ×	× ×	× ×
Subtotal = lbs.	Subtotal = lbs.	Subtotal = lbs.	Subtotal = lbs.	Subtotal = lbs.	Subtotal = lbs.

Exercise 3:   *Total Weight* _____ *lbs.*   *Time* _____ *mins.*   *Power Factor* _____ *lbs./min.*   *Power Index* _____

■ **Exercise:**

Weight Reps Sets	Weight Reps Sets	Weight Reps Sets	Weight Reps Sets	Weight Reps Sets	Weight Reps Sets
× ×	× ×	× ×	× ×	× ×	× ×
Subtotal = lbs.	Subtotal = lbs.	Subtotal = lbs.	Subtotal = lbs.	Subtotal = lbs.	Subtotal = lbs.

Exercise 4:   *Total Weight* _____ *lbs.*   *Time* _____ *mins.*   *Power Factor* _____ *lbs./min.*   *Power Index* _____

■ **Exercise:**

Weight Reps Sets	Weight Reps Sets	Weight Reps Sets	Weight Reps Sets	Weight Reps Sets	Weight Reps Sets
× ×	× ×	× ×	× ×	× ×	× ×
Subtotal = lbs.	Subtotal = lbs.	Subtotal = lbs.	Subtotal = lbs.	Subtotal = lbs.	Subtotal = lbs.

Exercise 5:   *Total Weight* _____ *lbs.*   *Time* _____ *mins.*   *Power Factor* _____ *lbs./min.*   *Power Index* _____

OVERALL WORKOUT: *Total Weight* _____ *lbs.*   *Time* _____ *mins.*   *Power Factor* _____ *lbs./min.*   *Power Index* _____

Exercise Subtotal = Weight × Reps × Sets   ■ *Power Factor = lbs./min.*   ■ *Power Index = Total Weight × Power Factor ÷ 1,000,000*

BACK SPECIALIZATION WORKOUT RECORD   Date: ___ / ___ / ___

Start Time: _____   Finish Time: _____   Total Time: _____

■ Exercise: LAT PULLDOWN (OR CLOSE-GRIP UNDERHAND CHIN-UP)

Weight Reps Sets	Weight Reps Sets	Weight Reps Sets	Weight Reps Sets	Weight Reps Sets	Weight Reps Sets
✕ ✕	✕ ✕	✕ ✕	✕ ✕	✕ ✕	✕ ✕
Subtotal = lbs.	Subtotal = lbs.	Subtotal = lbs.	Subtotal = lbs.	Subtotal = lbs.	Subtotal = lbs.

Exercise 1:   *Total Weight* _____ *lbs.*   *Time* _____ *mins.*   *Power Factor* _____ *lbs./min.*   *Power Index* _____

■ Exercise: DEADLIFT

Weight Reps Sets	Weight Reps Sets	Weight Reps Sets	Weight Reps Sets	Weight Reps Sets	Weight Reps Sets
✕ ✕	✕ ✕	✕ ✕	✕ ✕	✕ ✕	✕ ✕
Subtotal = lbs.	Subtotal = lbs.	Subtotal = lbs.	Subtotal = lbs.	Subtotal = lbs.	Subtotal = lbs.

Exercise 2:   *Total Weight* _____ *lbs.*   *Time* _____ *mins.*   *Power Factor* _____ *lbs./min.*   *Power Index* _____

■ Exercise:

Weight Reps Sets	Weight Reps Sets	Weight Reps Sets	Weight Reps Sets	Weight Reps Sets	Weight Reps Sets
✕ ✕	✕ ✕	✕ ✕	✕ ✕	✕ ✕	✕ ✕
Subtotal = lbs.	Subtotal = lbs.	Subtotal = lbs.	Subtotal = lbs.	Subtotal = lbs.	Subtotal = lbs.

Exercise 3:   *Total Weight* _____ *lbs.*   *Time* _____ *mins.*   *Power Factor* _____ *lbs./min.*   *Power Index* _____

■ Exercise:

Weight Reps Sets	Weight Reps Sets	Weight Reps Sets	Weight Reps Sets	Weight Reps Sets	Weight Reps Sets
✕ ✕	✕ ✕	✕ ✕	✕ ✕	✕ ✕	✕ ✕
Subtotal = lbs.	Subtotal = lbs.	Subtotal = lbs.	Subtotal = lbs.	Subtotal = lbs.	Subtotal = lbs.

Exercise 4:   *Total Weight* _____ *lbs.*   *Time* _____ *mins.*   *Power Factor* _____ *lbs./min.*   *Power Index* _____

■ Exercise:

Weight Reps Sets	Weight Reps Sets	Weight Reps Sets	Weight Reps Sets	Weight Reps Sets	Weight Reps Sets
✕ ✕	✕ ✕	✕ ✕	✕ ✕	✕ ✕	✕ ✕
Subtotal = lbs.	Subtotal = lbs.	Subtotal = lbs.	Subtotal = lbs.	Subtotal = lbs.	Subtotal = lbs.

Exercise 5:   *Total Weight* _____ *lbs.*   *Time* _____ *mins.*   *Power Factor* _____ *lbs./min.*   *Power Index* _____

OVERALL WORKOUT: *Total Weight* _____ *lbs.*   *Time* _____ *mins.*   *Power Factor* _____ *lbs./min.*   *Power Index* _____

Exercise Subtotal = Weight ✕ Reps ✕ Sets   ■ *Power Factor = lbs./min.*   ■ *Power Index = Total Weight ✕ Power Factor ÷ 1,000,000*

BACK SPECIALIZATION WORKOUT RECORD   Date: ____ / ____ / ____

Start Time: _____   **Finish Time:** _____   **Total Time:** _____

■ **Exercise: LAT PULLDOWN (OR CLOSE-GRIP UNDERHAND CHIN-UP)**

Weight Reps Sets	Weight Reps Sets	Weight Reps Sets	Weight Reps Sets	Weight Reps Sets	Weight Reps Sets
× ×	× ×	× ×	× ×	× ×	× ×
Subtotal = lbs.	Subtotal = lbs.	Subtotal = lbs.	Subtotal = lbs.	Subtotal = lbs.	Subtotal = lbs.

Exercise 1:   *Total Weight* _____ *lbs.*   *Time* _____ *mins.*   *Power Factor* _____ *lbs./min.*   *Power Index* _____

■ **Exercise: DEADLIFT**

Weight Reps Sets	Weight Reps Sets	Weight Reps Sets	Weight Reps Sets	Weight Reps Sets	Weight Reps Sets
× ×	× ×	× ×	× ×	× ×	× ×
Subtotal = lbs.	Subtotal = lbs.	Subtotal = lbs.	Subtotal = lbs.	Subtotal = lbs.	Subtotal = lbs.

Exercise 2:   *Total Weight* _____ *lbs.*   *Time* _____ *mins.*   *Power Factor* _____ *lbs./min.*   *Power Index* _____

■ **Exercise:**

Weight Reps Sets	Weight Reps Sets	Weight Reps Sets	Weight Reps Sets	Weight Reps Sets	Weight Reps Sets
× ×	× ×	× ×	× ×	× ×	× ×
Subtotal = lbs.	Subtotal = lbs.	Subtotal = lbs.	Subtotal = lbs.	Subtotal = lbs.	Subtotal = lbs.

Exercise 3:   *Total Weight* _____ *lbs.*   *Time* _____ *mins.*   *Power Factor* _____ *lbs./min.*   *Power Index* _____

■ **Exercise:**

Weight Reps Sets	Weight Reps Sets	Weight Reps Sets	Weight Reps Sets	Weight Reps Sets	Weight Reps Sets
× ×	× ×	× ×	× ×	× ×	× ×
Subtotal = lbs.	Subtotal = lbs.	Subtotal = lbs.	Subtotal = lbs.	Subtotal = lbs.	Subtotal = lbs.

Exercise 4:   *Total Weight* _____ *lbs.*   *Time* _____ *mins.*   *Power Factor* _____ *lbs./min.*   *Power Index* _____

■ **Exercise:**

Weight Reps Sets	Weight Reps Sets	Weight Reps Sets	Weight Reps Sets	Weight Reps Sets	Weight Reps Sets
× ×	× ×	× ×	× ×	× ×	× ×
Subtotal = lbs.	Subtotal = lbs.	Subtotal = lbs.	Subtotal = lbs.	Subtotal = lbs.	Subtotal = lbs.

Exercise 5:   *Total Weight* _____ *lbs.*   *Time* _____ *mins.*   *Power Factor* _____ *lbs./min.*   *Power Index* _____

OVERALL WORKOUT: *Total Weight* _____ *lbs.*   *Time* _____ *mins.*   *Power Factor* _____ *lbs./min.*   *Power Index* _____

Exercise Subtotal = Weight × Reps × Sets   ■   *Power Factor = lbs./min.*   ■   *Power Index = Total Weight × Power Factor ÷ 1,000,000*

BACK SPECIALIZATION WORKOUT RECORD Date: ___ / ___ / ___

Start Time: _____ Finish Time: _____ Total Time: _____

■ Exercise: LAT PULLDOWN (OR CLOSE-GRIP UNDERHAND CHIN-UP)

Weight Reps Sets	Weight Reps Sets	Weight Reps Sets	Weight Reps Sets	Weight Reps Sets	Weight Reps Sets
× ×	× ×	× ×	× ×	× ×	× ×
Subtotal = lbs.	Subtotal = lbs.	Subtotal = lbs.	Subtotal = lbs.	Subtotal = lbs.	Subtotal = lbs.

Exercise 1:   *Total Weight _____ lbs.*   *Time _____ mins.*   *Power Factor _____ lbs./min.*   *Power Index _____*

■ Exercise: DEADLIFT

Weight Reps Sets	Weight Reps Sets	Weight Reps Sets	Weight Reps Sets	Weight Reps Sets	Weight Reps Sets
× ×	× ×	× ×	× ×	× ×	× ×
Subtotal = lbs.	Subtotal = lbs.	Subtotal = lbs.	Subtotal = lbs.	Subtotal = lbs.	Subtotal = lbs.

Exercise 2:   *Total Weight _____ lbs.*   *Time _____ mins.*   *Power Factor _____ lbs./min.*   *Power Index _____*

■ Exercise:

Weight Reps Sets	Weight Reps Sets	Weight Reps Sets	Weight Reps Sets	Weight Reps Sets	Weight Reps Sets
× ×	× ×	× ×	× ×	× ×	× ×
Subtotal = lbs.	Subtotal = lbs.	Subtotal = lbs.	Subtotal = lbs.	Subtotal = lbs.	Subtotal = lbs.

Exercise 3:   *Total Weight _____ lbs.*   *Time _____ mins.*   *Power Factor _____ lbs./min.*   *Power Index _____*

■ Exercise:

Weight Reps Sets	Weight Reps Sets	Weight Reps Sets	Weight Reps Sets	Weight Reps Sets	Weight Reps Sets
× ×	× ×	× ×	× ×	× ×	× ×
Subtotal = lbs.	Subtotal = lbs.	Subtotal = lbs.	Subtotal = lbs.	Subtotal = lbs.	Subtotal = lbs.

Exercise 4:   *Total Weight _____ lbs.*   *Time _____ mins.*   *Power Factor _____ lbs./min.*   *Power Index _____*

■ Exercise:

Weight Reps Sets	Weight Reps Sets	Weight Reps Sets	Weight Reps Sets	Weight Reps Sets	Weight Reps Sets
× ×	× ×	× ×	× ×	× ×	× ×
Subtotal = lbs.	Subtotal = lbs.	Subtotal = lbs.	Subtotal = lbs.	Subtotal = lbs.	Subtotal = lbs.

Exercise 5:   *Total Weight _____ lbs.*   *Time _____ mins.*   *Power Factor _____ lbs./min.*   *Power Index _____*

OVERALL WORKOUT: *Total Weight _____ lbs.*   *Time _____ mins.*   *Power Factor _____ lbs./min.*   *Power Index _____*

Exercise Subtotal = Weight × Reps × Sets ■ *Power Factor = lbs./min.* ■ *Power Index = Total Weight × Power Factor ÷ 1,000,000*

LEG SPECIALIZATION WORKOUT RECORD   Date: ___ / ___ / ___

Start Time: _____   Finish Time: _____   Total Time: _____

■ Exercise: TOE-UP ON LEG CURL MACHINE

Weight Reps Sets	Weight Reps Sets	Weight Reps Sets	Weight Reps Sets	Weight Reps Sets	Weight Reps Sets
× ×	× ×	× ×	× ×	× ×	× ×
Subtotal = lbs.	Subtotal = lbs.	Subtotal = lbs.	Subtotal = lbs.	Subtotal = lbs.	Subtotal = lbs.

Exercise 1:   *Total Weight _____ lbs.   Time _____ mins.   Power Factor _____ lbs./min.   Power Index _____*

■ Exercise: STANDING CALF RAISE (OR TOE PRESS ON LEG PRESS MACHINE)

Weight Reps Sets	Weight Reps Sets	Weight Reps Sets	Weight Reps Sets	Weight Reps Sets	Weight Reps Sets
× ×	× ×	× ×	× ×	× ×	× ×
Subtotal = lbs.	Subtotal = lbs.	Subtotal = lbs.	Subtotal = lbs.	Subtotal = lbs.	Subtotal = lbs.

Exercise 2:   *Total Weight _____ lbs.   Time _____ mins.   Power Factor _____ lbs./min.   Power Index _____*

■ Exercise:

Weight Reps Sets	Weight Reps Sets	Weight Reps Sets	Weight Reps Sets	Weight Reps Sets	Weight Reps Sets
× ×	× ×	× ×	× ×	× ×	× ×
Subtotal = lbs.	Subtotal = lbs.	Subtotal = lbs.	Subtotal = lbs.	Subtotal = lbs.	Subtotal = lbs.

Exercise 3:   *Total Weight _____ lbs.   Time _____ mins.   Power Factor _____ lbs./min.   Power Index _____*

■ Exercise:

Weight Reps Sets	Weight Reps Sets	Weight Reps Sets	Weight Reps Sets	Weight Reps Sets	Weight Reps Sets
× ×	× ×	× ×	× ×	× ×	× ×
Subtotal = lbs.	Subtotal = lbs.	Subtotal = lbs.	Subtotal = lbs.	Subtotal = lbs.	Subtotal = lbs.

Exercise 4:   *Total Weight _____ lbs.   Time _____ mins.   Power Factor _____ lbs./min.   Power Index _____*

■ Exercise:

Weight Reps Sets	Weight Reps Sets	Weight Reps Sets	Weight Reps Sets	Weight Reps Sets	Weight Reps Sets
× ×	× ×	× ×	× ×	× ×	× ×
Subtotal = lbs.	Subtotal = lbs.	Subtotal = lbs.	Subtotal = lbs.	Subtotal = lbs.	Subtotal = lbs.

Exercise 5:   *Total Weight _____ lbs.   Time _____ mins.   Power Factor _____ lbs./min.   Power Index _____*

OVERALL WORKOUT: *Total Weight _____ lbs.   Time _____ mins.   Power Factor _____ lbs./min.   Power Index _____*

Exercise Subtotal = Weight × Reps × Sets   ■ Power Factor = lbs./min.   ■ Power Index = Total Weight × Power Factor ÷ 1,000,000

LEG SPECIALIZATION WORKOUT RECORD   Date: ___ / ___ / ___

Start Time: _____   **Finish Time:** _____   **Total Time:** _____

▪ Exercise: TOE-UP ON LEG CURL MACHINE

Weight Reps Sets	Weight Reps Sets	Weight Reps Sets	Weight Reps Sets	Weight Reps Sets	Weight Reps Sets
× ×	× ×	× ×	× ×	× ×	× ×
Subtotal = lbs.	Subtotal = lbs.	Subtotal = lbs.	Subtotal = lbs.	Subtotal = lbs.	Subtotal = lbs.

Exercise 1:   *Total Weight _____ lbs.   Time _____ mins.   Power Factor _____ lbs./min.   Power Index _____*

▪ Exercise: STANDING CALF RAISE (OR TOE PRESS ON LEG PRESS MACHINE)

Weight Reps Sets	Weight Reps Sets	Weight Reps Sets	Weight Reps Sets	Weight Reps Sets	Weight Reps Sets
× ×	× ×	× ×	× ×	× ×	× ×
Subtotal = lbs.	Subtotal = lbs.	Subtotal = lbs.	Subtotal = lbs.	Subtotal = lbs.	Subtotal = lbs.

Exercise 2:   *Total Weight _____ lbs.   Time _____ mins.   Power Factor _____ lbs./min.   Power Index _____*

▪ Exercise:

Weight Reps Sets	Weight Reps Sets	Weight Reps Sets	Weight Reps Sets	Weight Reps Sets	Weight Reps Sets
× ×	× ×	× ×	× ×	× ×	× ×
Subtotal = lbs.	Subtotal = lbs.	Subtotal = lbs.	Subtotal = lbs.	Subtotal = lbs.	Subtotal = lbs.

Exercise 3:   *Total Weight _____ lbs.   Time _____ mins.   Power Factor _____ lbs./min.   Power Index _____*

▪ Exercise:

Weight Reps Sets	Weight Reps Sets	Weight Reps Sets	Weight Reps Sets	Weight Reps Sets	Weight Reps Sets
× ×	× ×	× ×	× ×	× ×	× ×
Subtotal = lbs.	Subtotal = lbs.	Subtotal = lbs.	Subtotal = lbs.	Subtotal = lbs.	Subtotal = lbs.

Exercise 4:   *Total Weight _____ lbs.   Time _____ mins.   Power Factor _____ lbs./min.   Power Index _____*

▪ Exercise:

Weight Reps Sets	Weight Reps Sets	Weight Reps Sets	Weight Reps Sets	Weight Reps Sets	Weight Reps Sets
× ×	× ×	× ×	× ×	× ×	× ×
Subtotal = lbs.	Subtotal = lbs.	Subtotal = lbs.	Subtotal = lbs.	Subtotal = lbs.	Subtotal = lbs.

Exercise 5:   *Total Weight _____ lbs.   Time _____ mins.   Power Factor _____ lbs./min.   Power Index _____*

OVERALL WORKOUT: *Total Weight _____ lbs.   Time _____ mins.   Power Factor _____ lbs./min.   Power Index _____*

Exercise Subtotal = Weight × Reps × Sets   ▪ Power Factor = lbs./min.   ▪ Power Index = Total Weight × Power Factor ÷ 1,000,000

LEG SPECIALIZATION WORKOUT RECORD   Date: ___ / ___ / ___

Start Time: _____   **Finish Time:** _____   **Total Time:** _____

■ Exercise: TOE-UP ON LEG CURL MACHINE

Weight	Reps	Sets	Weight	Reps	Sets	Weight	Reps	Sets	Weight	Reps	Sets	Weight	Reps	Sets	Weight	Reps	Sets
×	×		×	×		×	×		×	×		×	×		×	×	
Subtotal =		lbs.	Subtotal =		lbs.	Subtotal =		lbs.	Subtotal =		lbs.	Subtotal =		lbs.	Subtotal =		lbs.

Exercise 1:   *Total Weight* _____ *lbs.   Time* _____ *mins.   Power Factor* _____ *lbs./min.   Power Index* _____

■ Exercise: STANDING CALF RAISE (OR TOE PRESS ON LEG PRESS MACHINE)

Weight	Reps	Sets	Weight	Reps	Sets	Weight	Reps	Sets	Weight	Reps	Sets	Weight	Reps	Sets	Weight	Reps	Sets
×	×		×	×		×	×		×	×		×	×		×	×	
Subtotal =		lbs.	Subtotal =		lbs.	Subtotal =		lbs.	Subtotal =		lbs.	Subtotal =		lbs.	Subtotal =		lbs.

Exercise 2:   *Total Weight* _____ *lbs.   Time* _____ *mins.   Power Factor* _____ *lbs./min.   Power Index* _____

■ Exercise:

Weight	Reps	Sets	Weight	Reps	Sets	Weight	Reps	Sets	Weight	Reps	Sets	Weight	Reps	Sets	Weight	Reps	Sets
×	×		×	×		×	×		×	×		×	×		×	×	
Subtotal =		lbs.	Subtotal =		lbs.	Subtotal =		lbs.	Subtotal =		lbs.	Subtotal =		lbs.	Subtotal =		lbs.

Exercise 3:   *Total Weight* _____ *lbs.   Time* _____ *mins.   Power Factor* _____ *lbs./min.   Power Index* _____

■ Exercise:

Weight	Reps	Sets	Weight	Reps	Sets	Weight	Reps	Sets	Weight	Reps	Sets	Weight	Reps	Sets	Weight	Reps	Sets
×	×		×	×		×	×		×	×		×	×		×	×	
Subtotal =		lbs.	Subtotal =		lbs.	Subtotal =		lbs.	Subtotal =		lbs.	Subtotal =		lbs.	Subtotal =		lbs.

Exercise 4:   *Total Weight* _____ *lbs.   Time* _____ *mins.   Power Factor* _____ *lbs./min.   Power Index* _____

■ Exercise:

Weight	Reps	Sets	Weight	Reps	Sets	Weight	Reps	Sets	Weight	Reps	Sets	Weight	Reps	Sets	Weight	Reps	Sets
×	×		×	×		×	×		×	×		×	×		×	×	
Subtotal =		lbs.	Subtotal =		lbs.	Subtotal =		lbs.	Subtotal =		lbs.	Subtotal =		lbs.	Subtotal =		lbs.

Exercise 5:   *Total Weight* _____ *lbs.   Time* _____ *mins.   Power Factor* _____ *lbs./min.   Power Index* _____

OVERALL WORKOUT: *Total Weight* _____ *lbs.   Time* _____ *mins.   Power Factor* _____ *lbs./min.   Power Index* _____

Exercise Subtotal = Weight × Reps × Sets   ■ Power Factor = lbs./min.   ■ Power Index = Total Weight × Power Factor ÷ 1,000,000

LEG SPECIALIZATION WORKOUT RECORD   Date: ____ / ____ / ____

Start Time: _____   Finish Time: _____   Total Time: _____

■ Exercise: TOE-UP ON LEG CURL MACHINE

Weight	Reps	Sets	Weight	Reps	Sets	Weight	Reps	Sets	Weight	Reps	Sets	Weight	Reps	Sets	Weight	Reps	Sets
×	×		×	×		×	×		×	×		×	×		×	×	
Subtotal =		lbs.	Subtotal =		lbs.	Subtotal =		lbs.	Subtotal =		lbs.	Subtotal =		lbs.	Subtotal =		lbs.

Exercise 1:   *Total Weight* _____ *lbs.*   *Time* _____ *mins.*   *Power Factor* _____ *lbs./min.*   *Power Index* _____

■ Exercise: STANDING CALF RAISE (OR TOE PRESS ON LEG PRESS MACHINE)

Weight	Reps	Sets	Weight	Reps	Sets	Weight	Reps	Sets	Weight	Reps	Sets	Weight	Reps	Sets	Weight	Reps	Sets
×	×		×	×		×	×		×	×		×	×		×	×	
Subtotal =		lbs.	Subtotal =		lbs.	Subtotal =		lbs.	Subtotal =		lbs.	Subtotal =		lbs.	Subtotal =		lbs.

Exercise 2:   *Total Weight* _____ *lbs.*   *Time* _____ *mins.*   *Power Factor* _____ *lbs./min.*   *Power Index* _____

■ Exercise:

Weight	Reps	Sets	Weight	Reps	Sets	Weight	Reps	Sets	Weight	Reps	Sets	Weight	Reps	Sets	Weight	Reps	Sets
×	×		×	×		×	×		×	×		×	×		×	×	
Subtotal =		lbs.	Subtotal =		lbs.	Subtotal =		lbs.	Subtotal =		lbs.	Subtotal =		lbs.	Subtotal =		lbs.

Exercise 3:   *Total Weight* _____ *lbs.*   *Time* _____ *mins.*   *Power Factor* _____ *lbs./min.*   *Power Index* _____

■ Exercise:

Weight	Reps	Sets	Weight	Reps	Sets	Weight	Reps	Sets	Weight	Reps	Sets	Weight	Reps	Sets	Weight	Reps	Sets
×	×		×	×		×	×		×	×		×	×		×	×	
Subtotal =		lbs.	Subtotal =		lbs.	Subtotal =		lbs.	Subtotal =		lbs.	Subtotal =		lbs.	Subtotal =		lbs.

Exercise 4:   *Total Weight* _____ *lbs.*   *Time* _____ *mins.*   *Power Factor* _____ *lbs./min.*   *Power Index* _____

■ Exercise:

Weight	Reps	Sets	Weight	Reps	Sets	Weight	Reps	Sets	Weight	Reps	Sets	Weight	Reps	Sets	Weight	Reps	Sets
×	×		×	×		×	×		×	×		×	×		×	×	
Subtotal =		lbs.	Subtotal =		lbs.	Subtotal =		lbs.	Subtotal =		lbs.	Subtotal =		lbs.	Subtotal =		lbs.

Exercise 5:   *Total Weight* _____ *lbs.*   *Time* _____ *mins.*   *Power Factor* _____ *lbs./min.*   *Power Index* _____

OVERALL WORKOUT: *Total Weight* _____ *lbs.*   *Time* _____ *mins.*   *Power Factor* _____ *lbs./min.*   *Power Index* _____

Exercise Subtotal = Weight × Reps × Sets   ■ *Power Factor = lbs./min.*   ■ *Power Index = Total Weight × Power Factor ÷ 1,000,000*

LEG SPECIALIZATION WORKOUT RECORD   Date: ____ / ____ / ____

Start Time: _____   Finish Time: _____   Total Time: _____

■ **Exercise: TOE-UP ON LEG CURL MACHINE**

Weight Reps Sets	Weight Reps Sets	Weight Reps Sets	Weight Reps Sets	Weight Reps Sets	Weight Reps Sets
× ×	× ×	× ×	× ×	× ×	× ×
Subtotal = lbs.	Subtotal = lbs.	Subtotal = lbs.	Subtotal = lbs.	Subtotal = lbs.	Subtotal = lbs.

Exercise 1:   *Total Weight _____ lbs.   Time _____ mins.   Power Factor _____ lbs./min.   Power Index _____*

■ **Exercise: STANDING CALF RAISE (OR TOE PRESS ON LEG PRESS MACHINE)**

Weight Reps Sets	Weight Reps Sets	Weight Reps Sets	Weight Reps Sets	Weight Reps Sets	Weight Reps Sets
× ×	× ×	× ×	× ×	× ×	× ×
Subtotal = lbs.	Subtotal = lbs.	Subtotal = lbs.	Subtotal = lbs.	Subtotal = lbs.	Subtotal = lbs.

Exercise 2:   *Total Weight _____ lbs.   Time _____ mins.   Power Factor _____ lbs./min.   Power Index _____*

■ **Exercise:**

Weight Reps Sets	Weight Reps Sets	Weight Reps Sets	Weight Reps Sets	Weight Reps Sets	Weight Reps Sets
× ×	× ×	× ×	× ×	× ×	× ×
Subtotal = lbs.	Subtotal = lbs.	Subtotal = lbs.	Subtotal = lbs.	Subtotal = lbs.	Subtotal = lbs.

Exercise 3:   *Total Weight _____ lbs.   Time _____ mins.   Power Factor _____ lbs./min.   Power Index _____*

■ **Exercise:**

Weight Reps Sets	Weight Reps Sets	Weight Reps Sets	Weight Reps Sets	Weight Reps Sets	Weight Reps Sets
× ×	× ×	× ×	× ×	× ×	× ×
Subtotal = lbs.	Subtotal = lbs.	Subtotal = lbs.	Subtotal = lbs.	Subtotal = lbs.	Subtotal = lbs.

Exercise 4:   *Total Weight _____ lbs.   Time _____ mins.   Power Factor _____ lbs./min.   Power Index _____*

■ **Exercise:**

Weight Reps Sets	Weight Reps Sets	Weight Reps Sets	Weight Reps Sets	Weight Reps Sets	Weight Reps Sets
× ×	× ×	× ×	× ×	× ×	× ×
Subtotal = lbs.	Subtotal = lbs.	Subtotal = lbs.	Subtotal = lbs.	Subtotal = lbs.	Subtotal = lbs.

Exercise 5:   *Total Weight _____ lbs.   Time _____ mins.   Power Factor _____ lbs./min.   Power Index _____*

OVERALL WORKOUT: *Total Weight _____ lbs.   Time _____ mins.   Power Factor _____ lbs./min.   Power Index _____*

Exercise Subtotal = Weight × Reps × Sets   ■ *Power Factor = lbs./min.*   ■ *Power Index = Total Weight × Power Factor ÷ 1,000,000*

LEG SPECIALIZATION WORKOUT RECORD   Date: ___ / ___ / ___

Start Time: _____   Finish Time: _____   Total Time: _____

■ Exercise: TOE-UP ON LEG CURL MACHINE

Weight Reps Sets	Weight Reps Sets	Weight Reps Sets	Weight Reps Sets	Weight Reps Sets	Weight Reps Sets
× ×	× ×	× ×	× ×	× ×	× ×
Subtotal = lbs.	Subtotal = lbs.	Subtotal = lbs.	Subtotal = lbs.	Subtotal = lbs.	Subtotal = lbs.

Exercise 1:   *Total Weight _____ lbs.   Time _____ mins.   Power Factor _____ lbs./min.   Power Index _____*

■ Exercise: STANDING CALF RAISE (OR TOE PRESS ON LEG PRESS MACHINE)

Weight Reps Sets	Weight Reps Sets	Weight Reps Sets	Weight Reps Sets	Weight Reps Sets	Weight Reps Sets
× ×	× ×	× ×	× ×	× ×	× ×
Subtotal = lbs.	Subtotal = lbs.	Subtotal = lbs.	Subtotal = lbs.	Subtotal = lbs.	Subtotal = lbs.

Exercise 2:   *Total Weight _____ lbs.   Time _____ mins.   Power Factor _____ lbs./min.   Power Index _____*

■ Exercise:

Weight Reps Sets	Weight Reps Sets	Weight Reps Sets	Weight Reps Sets	Weight Reps Sets	Weight Reps Sets
× ×	× ×	× ×	× ×	× ×	× ×
Subtotal = lbs.	Subtotal = lbs.	Subtotal = lbs.	Subtotal = lbs.	Subtotal = lbs.	Subtotal = lbs.

Exercise 3:   *Total Weight _____ lbs.   Time _____ mins.   Power Factor _____ lbs./min.   Power Index _____*

■ Exercise:

Weight Reps Sets	Weight Reps Sets	Weight Reps Sets	Weight Reps Sets	Weight Reps Sets	Weight Reps Sets
× ×	× ×	× ×	× ×	× ×	× ×
Subtotal = lbs.	Subtotal = lbs.	Subtotal = lbs.	Subtotal = lbs.	Subtotal = lbs.	Subtotal = lbs.

Exercise 4:   *Total Weight _____ lbs.   Time _____ mins.   Power Factor _____ lbs./min.   Power Index _____*

■ Exercise:

Weight Reps Sets	Weight Reps Sets	Weight Reps Sets	Weight Reps Sets	Weight Reps Sets	Weight Reps Sets
× ×	× ×	× ×	× ×	× ×	× ×
Subtotal = lbs.	Subtotal = lbs.	Subtotal = lbs.	Subtotal = lbs.	Subtotal = lbs.	Subtotal = lbs.

Exercise 5:   *Total Weight _____ lbs.   Time _____ mins.   Power Factor _____ lbs./min.   Power Index _____*

OVERALL WORKOUT: *Total Weight _____ lbs.   Time _____ mins.   Power Factor _____ lbs./min.   Power Index _____*

Exercise Subtotal = Weight × Reps × Sets ■ *Power Factor = lbs./min.* ■ *Power Index = Total Weight × Power Factor ÷ 1,000,000*

LEG SPECIALIZATION WORKOUT RECORD   Date: ___ / ___ / ___

Start Time: _____   **Finish Time:** _____   **Total Time:** _____

■ Exercise: TOE-UP ON LEG CURL MACHINE

Weight Reps Sets	Weight Reps Sets	Weight Reps Sets	Weight Reps Sets	Weight Reps Sets	Weight Reps Sets
× ×	× ×	× ×	× ×	× ×	× ×
Subtotal = lbs.	Subtotal = lbs.	Subtotal = lbs.	Subtotal = lbs.	Subtotal = lbs.	Subtotal = lbs.

Exercise 1:   *Total Weight* _____ *lbs.*   *Time* _____ *mins.*   *Power Factor* _____ *lbs./min.*   *Power Index* _____

■ Exercise: STANDING CALF RAISE (OR TOE PRESS ON LEG PRESS MACHINE)

Weight Reps Sets	Weight Reps Sets	Weight Reps Sets	Weight Reps Sets	Weight Reps Sets	Weight Reps Sets
× ×	× ×	× ×	× ×	× ×	× ×
Subtotal = lbs.	Subtotal = lbs.	Subtotal = lbs.	Subtotal = lbs.	Subtotal = lbs.	Subtotal = lbs.

Exercise 2:   *Total Weight* _____ *lbs.*   *Time* _____ *mins.*   *Power Factor* _____ *lbs./min.*   *Power Index* _____

■ Exercise:

Weight Reps Sets	Weight Reps Sets	Weight Reps Sets	Weight Reps Sets	Weight Reps Sets	Weight Reps Sets
× ×	× ×	× ×	× ×	× ×	× ×
Subtotal = lbs.	Subtotal = lbs.	Subtotal = lbs.	Subtotal = lbs.	Subtotal = lbs.	Subtotal = lbs.

Exercise 3:   *Total Weight* _____ *lbs.*   *Time* _____ *mins.*   *Power Factor* _____ *lbs./min.*   *Power Index* _____

■ Exercise:

Weight Reps Sets	Weight Reps Sets	Weight Reps Sets	Weight Reps Sets	Weight Reps Sets	Weight Reps Sets
× ×	× ×	× ×	× ×	× ×	× ×
Subtotal = lbs.	Subtotal = lbs.	Subtotal = lbs.	Subtotal = lbs.	Subtotal = lbs.	Subtotal = lbs.

Exercise 4:   *Total Weight* _____ *lbs.*   *Time* _____ *mins.*   *Power Factor* _____ *lbs./min.*   *Power Index* _____

■ Exercise:

Weight Reps Sets	Weight Reps Sets	Weight Reps Sets	Weight Reps Sets	Weight Reps Sets	Weight Reps Sets
× ×	× ×	× ×	× ×	× ×	× ×
Subtotal = lbs.	Subtotal = lbs.	Subtotal = lbs.	Subtotal = lbs.	Subtotal = lbs.	Subtotal = lbs.

Exercise 5:   *Total Weight* _____ *lbs.*   *Time* _____ *mins.*   *Power Factor* _____ *lbs./min.*   *Power Index* _____

OVERALL WORKOUT: *Total Weight* _____ *lbs.*   *Time* _____ *mins.*   *Power Factor* _____ *lbs./min.*   *Power Index* _____

Exercise Subtotal = Weight × Reps × Sets   ■ *Power Factor = lbs./min.*   ■ *Power Index = Total Weight × Power Factor ÷ 1,000,000*

LEG SPECIALIZATION WORKOUT RECORD   Date: ___ / ___ / ___

Start Time: _____   Finish Time: _____   Total Time: _____

▪ Exercise: TOE-UP ON LEG CURL MACHINE

Weight Reps Sets	Weight Reps Sets	Weight Reps Sets	Weight Reps Sets	Weight Reps Sets	Weight Reps Sets
× ×	× ×	× ×	× ×	× ×	× ×
Subtotal = lbs.	Subtotal = lbs.	Subtotal = lbs.	Subtotal = lbs.	Subtotal = lbs.	Subtotal = lbs.

Exercise 1:   *Total Weight* _____ *lbs.*   *Time* _____ *mins.*   *Power Factor* _____ *lbs./min.*   *Power Index* _____

▪ Exercise: STANDING CALF RAISE (OR TOE PRESS ON LEG PRESS MACHINE)

Weight Reps Sets	Weight Reps Sets	Weight Reps Sets	Weight Reps Sets	Weight Reps Sets	Weight Reps Sets
× ×	× ×	× ×	× ×	× ×	× ×
Subtotal = lbs.	Subtotal = lbs.	Subtotal = lbs.	Subtotal = lbs.	Subtotal = lbs.	Subtotal = lbs.

Exercise 2:   *Total Weight* _____ *lbs.*   *Time* _____ *mins.*   *Power Factor* _____ *lbs./min.*   *Power Index* _____

▪ Exercise:

Weight Reps Sets	Weight Reps Sets	Weight Reps Sets	Weight Reps Sets	Weight Reps Sets	Weight Reps Sets
× ×	× ×	× ×	× ×	× ×	× ×
Subtotal = lbs.	Subtotal = lbs.	Subtotal = lbs.	Subtotal = lbs.	Subtotal = lbs.	Subtotal = lbs.

Exercise 3:   *Total Weight* _____ *lbs.*   *Time* _____ *mins.*   *Power Factor* _____ *lbs./min.*   *Power Index* _____

▪ Exercise:

Weight Reps Sets	Weight Reps Sets	Weight Reps Sets	Weight Reps Sets	Weight Reps Sets	Weight Reps Sets
× ×	× ×	× ×	× ×	× ×	× ×
Subtotal = lbs.	Subtotal = lbs.	Subtotal = lbs.	Subtotal = lbs.	Subtotal = lbs.	Subtotal = lbs.

Exercise 4:   *Total Weight* _____ *lbs.*   *Time* _____ *mins.*   *Power Factor* _____ *lbs./min.*   *Power Index* _____

▪ Exercise:

Weight Reps Sets	Weight Reps Sets	Weight Reps Sets	Weight Reps Sets	Weight Reps Sets	Weight Reps Sets
× ×	× ×	× ×	× ×	× ×	× ×
Subtotal = lbs.	Subtotal = lbs.	Subtotal = lbs.	Subtotal = lbs.	Subtotal = lbs.	Subtotal = lbs.

Exercise 5:   *Total Weight* _____ *lbs.*   *Time* _____ *mins.*   *Power Factor* _____ *lbs./min.*   *Power Index* _____

OVERALL WORKOUT: *Total Weight* _____ *lbs.*   *Time* _____ *mins.*   *Power Factor* _____ *lbs./min.*   *Power Index* _____

Exercise Subtotal = Weight × Reps × Sets   ▪ *Power Factor = lbs./min.*   ▪ *Power Index = Total Weight × Power Factor ÷ 1,000,000*

LEG SPECIALIZATION WORKOUT RECORD   Date: ___ / ___ / ___

Start Time: _____   **Finish Time:** _____   **Total Time:** _____

■ Exercise: TOE-UP ON LEG CURL MACHINE

Weight Reps Sets	Weight Reps Sets	Weight Reps Sets	Weight Reps Sets	Weight Reps Sets	Weight Reps Sets
× ×	× ×	× ×	× ×	× ×	× ×
Subtotal = lbs.	Subtotal = lbs.	Subtotal = lbs.	Subtotal = lbs.	Subtotal = lbs.	Subtotal = lbs.

Exercise 1:   *Total Weight* _____ *lbs.*   *Time* _____ *mins.*   *Power Factor* _____ *lbs./min.*   *Power Index* _____

■ Exercise: STANDING CALF RAISE (OR TOE PRESS ON LEG PRESS MACHINE)

Weight Reps Sets	Weight Reps Sets	Weight Reps Sets	Weight Reps Sets	Weight Reps Sets	Weight Reps Sets
× ×	× ×	× ×	× ×	× ×	× ×
Subtotal = lbs.	Subtotal = lbs.	Subtotal = lbs.	Subtotal = lbs.	Subtotal = lbs.	Subtotal = lbs.

Exercise 2:   *Total Weight* _____ *lbs.*   *Time* _____ *mins.*   *Power Factor* _____ *lbs./min.*   *Power Index* _____

■ Exercise:

Weight Reps Sets	Weight Reps Sets	Weight Reps Sets	Weight Reps Sets	Weight Reps Sets	Weight Reps Sets
× ×	× ×	× ×	× ×	× ×	× ×
Subtotal = lbs.	Subtotal = lbs.	Subtotal = lbs.	Subtotal = lbs.	Subtotal = lbs.	Subtotal = lbs.

Exercise 3:   *Total Weight* _____ *lbs.*   *Time* _____ *mins.*   *Power Factor* _____ *lbs./min.*   *Power Index* _____

■ Exercise:

Weight Reps Sets	Weight Reps Sets	Weight Reps Sets	Weight Reps Sets	Weight Reps Sets	Weight Reps Sets
× ×	× ×	× ×	× ×	× ×	× ×
Subtotal = lbs.	Subtotal = lbs.	Subtotal = lbs.	Subtotal = lbs.	Subtotal = lbs.	Subtotal = lbs.

Exercise 4:   *Total Weight* _____ *lbs.*   *Time* _____ *mins.*   *Power Factor* _____ *lbs./min.*   *Power Index* _____

■ Exercise:

Weight Reps Sets	Weight Reps Sets	Weight Reps Sets	Weight Reps Sets	Weight Reps Sets	Weight Reps Sets
× ×	× ×	× ×	× ×	× ×	× ×
Subtotal = lbs.	Subtotal = lbs.	Subtotal = lbs.	Subtotal = lbs.	Subtotal = lbs.	Subtotal = lbs.

Exercise 5:   *Total Weight* _____ *lbs.*   *Time* _____ *mins.*   *Power Factor* _____ *lbs./min.*   *Power Index* _____

OVERALL WORKOUT: *Total Weight* _____ *lbs.*   *Time* _____ *mins.*   *Power Factor* _____ *lbs./min.*   *Power Index* _____

Exercise Subtotal = Weight × Reps × Sets   ■ *Power Factor = lbs./min.*   ■ *Power Index = Total Weight × Power Factor ÷ 1,000,000*

LEG SPECIALIZATION WORKOUT RECORD   Date: ____ / ____ / ____

Start Time: _____   Finish Time: _____   Total Time: _____

▪ Exercise: TOE-UP ON LEG CURL MACHINE

Weight Reps Sets	Weight Reps Sets	Weight Reps Sets	Weight Reps Sets	Weight Reps Sets	Weight Reps Sets
× ×	× ×	× ×	× ×	× ×	× ×
Subtotal = lbs.	Subtotal = lbs.	Subtotal = lbs.	Subtotal = lbs.	Subtotal = lbs.	Subtotal = lbs.

Exercise 1:   *Total Weight* _____ *lbs.*   *Time* _____ *mins.*   *Power Factor* _____ *lbs./min.*   *Power Index* _____

▪ Exercise: STANDING CALF RAISE (OR TOE PRESS ON LEG PRESS MACHINE)

Weight Reps Sets	Weight Reps Sets	Weight Reps Sets	Weight Reps Sets	Weight Reps Sets	Weight Reps Sets
× ×	× ×	× ×	× ×	× ×	× ×
Subtotal = lbs.	Subtotal = lbs.	Subtotal = lbs.	Subtotal = lbs.	Subtotal = lbs.	Subtotal = lbs.

Exercise 2:   *Total Weight* _____ *lbs.*   *Time* _____ *mins.*   *Power Factor* _____ *lbs./min.*   *Power Index* _____

▪ Exercise:

Weight Reps Sets	Weight Reps Sets	Weight Reps Sets	Weight Reps Sets	Weight Reps Sets	Weight Reps Sets
× ×	× ×	× ×	× ×	× ×	× ×
Subtotal = lbs.	Subtotal = lbs.	Subtotal = lbs.	Subtotal = lbs.	Subtotal = lbs.	Subtotal = lbs.

Exercise 3:   *Total Weight* _____ *lbs.*   *Time* _____ *mins.*   *Power Factor* _____ *lbs./min.*   *Power Index* _____

▪ Exercise:

Weight Reps Sets	Weight Reps Sets	Weight Reps Sets	Weight Reps Sets	Weight Reps Sets	Weight Reps Sets
× ×	× ×	× ×	× ×	× ×	× ×
Subtotal = lbs.	Subtotal = lbs.	Subtotal = lbs.	Subtotal = lbs.	Subtotal = lbs.	Subtotal = lbs.

Exercise 4:   *Total Weight* _____ *lbs.*   *Time* _____ *mins.*   *Power Factor* _____ *lbs./min.*   *Power Index* _____

▪ Exercise:

Weight Reps Sets	Weight Reps Sets	Weight Reps Sets	Weight Reps Sets	Weight Reps Sets	Weight Reps Sets
× ×	× ×	× ×	× ×	× ×	× ×
Subtotal = lbs.	Subtotal = lbs.	Subtotal = lbs.	Subtotal = lbs.	Subtotal = lbs.	Subtotal = lbs.

Exercise 5:   *Total Weight* _____ *lbs.*   *Time* _____ *mins.*   *Power Factor* _____ *lbs./min.*   *Power Index* _____

OVERALL WORKOUT: *Total Weight* _____ *lbs.*   *Time* _____ *mins.*   *Power Factor* _____ *lbs./min.*   *Power Index* _____

Exercise Subtotal = Weight × Reps × Sets   ▪ *Power Factor = lbs./min.*   ▪ *Power Index = Total Weight × Power Factor ÷ 1,000,000*

LEG SPECIALIZATION WORKOUT RECORD   Date: ___ / ___ / ___

Start Time: _____   Finish Time: _____   Total Time: _____

■ **Exercise: TOE-UP ON LEG CURL MACHINE**

Weight Reps Sets	Weight Reps Sets	Weight Reps Sets	Weight Reps Sets	Weight Reps Sets	Weight Reps Sets
× ×	× ×	× ×	× ×	× ×	× ×
Subtotal = lbs.	Subtotal = lbs.	Subtotal = lbs.	Subtotal = lbs.	Subtotal = lbs.	Subtotal = lbs.

Exercise 1: _____ *Total Weight* _____ *lbs.* *Time* _____ *mins.* *Power Factor* _____ *lbs./min.* *Power Index* _____

■ **Exercise: STANDING CALF RAISE (OR TOE PRESS ON LEG PRESS MACHINE)**

Weight Reps Sets	Weight Reps Sets	Weight Reps Sets	Weight Reps Sets	Weight Reps Sets	Weight Reps Sets
× ×	× ×	× ×	× ×	× ×	× ×
Subtotal = lbs.	Subtotal = lbs.	Subtotal = lbs.	Subtotal = lbs.	Subtotal = lbs.	Subtotal = lbs.

Exercise 2: _____ *Total Weight* _____ *lbs.* *Time* _____ *mins.* *Power Factor* _____ *lbs./min.* *Power Index* _____

■ **Exercise:**

Weight Reps Sets	Weight Reps Sets	Weight Reps Sets	Weight Reps Sets	Weight Reps Sets	Weight Reps Sets
× ×	× ×	× ×	× ×	× ×	× ×
Subtotal = lbs.	Subtotal = lbs.	Subtotal = lbs.	Subtotal = lbs.	Subtotal = lbs.	Subtotal = lbs.

Exercise 3: _____ *Total Weight* _____ *lbs.* *Time* _____ *mins.* *Power Factor* _____ *lbs./min.* *Power Index* _____

■ **Exercise:**

Weight Reps Sets	Weight Reps Sets	Weight Reps Sets	Weight Reps Sets	Weight Reps Sets	Weight Reps Sets
× ×	× ×	× ×	× ×	× ×	× ×
Subtotal = lbs.	Subtotal = lbs.	Subtotal = lbs.	Subtotal = lbs.	Subtotal = lbs.	Subtotal = lbs.

Exercise 4: _____ *Total Weight* _____ *lbs.* *Time* _____ *mins.* *Power Factor* _____ *lbs./min.* *Power Index* _____

■ **Exercise:**

Weight Reps Sets	Weight Reps Sets	Weight Reps Sets	Weight Reps Sets	Weight Reps Sets	Weight Reps Sets
× ×	× ×	× ×	× ×	× ×	× ×
Subtotal = lbs.	Subtotal = lbs.	Subtotal = lbs.	Subtotal = lbs.	Subtotal = lbs.	Subtotal = lbs.

Exercise 5: _____ *Total Weight* _____ *lbs.* *Time* _____ *mins.* *Power Factor* _____ *lbs./min.* *Power Index* _____

OVERALL WORKOUT: *Total Weight* _____ *lbs.* *Time* _____ *mins.* *Power Factor* _____ *lbs./min.* *Power Index* _____

Exercise Subtotal = Weight × Reps × Sets   ■ *Power Factor = lbs./min.*   ■ *Power Index = Total Weight × Power Factor ÷ 1,000,000*

LEG SPECIALIZATION WORKOUT RECORD   Date: ____ / ____ / ____

Start Time: _____   **Finish Time:** _____   **Total Time:** _____

■ Exercise: TOE-UP ON LEG CURL MACHINE

Weight Reps Sets	Weight Reps Sets	Weight Reps Sets	Weight Reps Sets	Weight Reps Sets	Weight Reps Sets
× ×	× ×	× ×	× ×	× ×	× ×
Subtotal = lbs.	Subtotal = lbs.	Subtotal = lbs.	Subtotal = lbs.	Subtotal = lbs.	Subtotal = lbs.

Exercise 1:   *Total Weight* _____ *lbs.*   *Time* _____ *mins.*   *Power Factor* _____ *lbs./min.*   *Power Index* _____

■ Exercise: STANDING CALF RAISE (OR TOE PRESS ON LEG PRESS MACHINE)

Weight Reps Sets	Weight Reps Sets	Weight Reps Sets	Weight Reps Sets	Weight Reps Sets	Weight Reps Sets
× ×	× ×	× ×	× ×	× ×	× ×
Subtotal = lbs.	Subtotal = lbs.	Subtotal = lbs.	Subtotal = lbs.	Subtotal = lbs.	Subtotal = lbs.

Exercise 2:   *Total Weight* _____ *lbs.*   *Time* _____ *mins.*   *Power Factor* _____ *lbs./min.*   *Power Index* _____

■ Exercise:

Weight Reps Sets	Weight Reps Sets	Weight Reps Sets	Weight Reps Sets	Weight Reps Sets	Weight Reps Sets
× ×	× ×	× ×	× ×	× ×	× ×
Subtotal = lbs.	Subtotal = lbs.	Subtotal = lbs.	Subtotal = lbs.	Subtotal = lbs.	Subtotal = lbs.

Exercise 3:   *Total Weight* _____ *lbs.*   *Time* _____ *mins.*   *Power Factor* _____ *lbs./min.*   *Power Index* _____

■ Exercise:

Weight Reps Sets	Weight Reps Sets	Weight Reps Sets	Weight Reps Sets	Weight Reps Sets	Weight Reps Sets
× ×	× ×	× ×	× ×	× ×	× ×
Subtotal = lbs.	Subtotal = lbs.	Subtotal = lbs.	Subtotal = lbs.	Subtotal = lbs.	Subtotal = lbs.

Exercise 4:   *Total Weight* _____ *lbs.*   *Time* _____ *mins.*   *Power Factor* _____ *lbs./min.*   *Power Index* _____

■ Exercise:

Weight Reps Sets	Weight Reps Sets	Weight Reps Sets	Weight Reps Sets	Weight Reps Sets	Weight Reps Sets
× ×	× ×	× ×	× ×	× ×	× ×
Subtotal = lbs.	Subtotal = lbs.	Subtotal = lbs.	Subtotal = lbs.	Subtotal = lbs.	Subtotal = lbs.

Exercise 5:   *Total Weight* _____ *lbs.*   *Time* _____ *mins.*   *Power Factor* _____ *lbs./min.*   *Power Index* _____

OVERALL WORKOUT: *Total Weight* _____ *lbs.*   *Time* _____ *mins.*   *Power Factor* _____ *lbs./min.*   *Power Index* _____

Exercise Subtotal = Weight × Reps × Sets   ■ *Power Factor = lbs./min.*   ■ *Power Index = Total Weight × Power Factor ÷ 1,000,000*

LEG SPECIALIZATION WORKOUT RECORD   Date: ____ / ____ / ____

Start Time: _____   Finish Time: _____   Total Time: _____

■ Exercise: TOE-UP ON LEG CURL MACHINE

Weight Reps Sets	Weight Reps Sets	Weight Reps Sets	Weight Reps Sets	Weight Reps Sets	Weight Reps Sets
× ×	× ×	× ×	× ×	× ×	× ×
Subtotal = lbs.	Subtotal = lbs.	Subtotal = lbs.	Subtotal = lbs.	Subtotal = lbs.	Subtotal = lbs.

Exercise 1:   *Total Weight* _____ *lbs.*   *Time* _____ *mins.*   *Power Factor* _____ *lbs./min.*   *Power Index* _____

■ Exercise: STANDING CALF RAISE (OR TOE PRESS ON LEG PRESS MACHINE)

Weight Reps Sets	Weight Reps Sets	Weight Reps Sets	Weight Reps Sets	Weight Reps Sets	Weight Reps Sets
× ×	× ×	× ×	× ×	× ×	× ×
Subtotal = lbs.	Subtotal = lbs.	Subtotal = lbs.	Subtotal = lbs.	Subtotal = lbs.	Subtotal = lbs.

Exercise 2:   *Total Weight* _____ *lbs.*   *Time* _____ *mins.*   *Power Factor* _____ *lbs./min.*   *Power Index* _____

■ Exercise:

Weight Reps Sets	Weight Reps Sets	Weight Reps Sets	Weight Reps Sets	Weight Reps Sets	Weight Reps Sets
× ×	× ×	× ×	× ×	× ×	× ×
Subtotal = lbs.	Subtotal = lbs.	Subtotal = lbs.	Subtotal = lbs.	Subtotal = lbs.	Subtotal = lbs.

Exercise 3:   *Total Weight* _____ *lbs.*   *Time* _____ *mins.*   *Power Factor* _____ *lbs./min.*   *Power Index* _____

■ Exercise:

Weight Reps Sets	Weight Reps Sets	Weight Reps Sets	Weight Reps Sets	Weight Reps Sets	Weight Reps Sets
× ×	× ×	× ×	× ×	× ×	× ×
Subtotal = lbs.	Subtotal = lbs.	Subtotal = lbs.	Subtotal = lbs.	Subtotal = lbs.	Subtotal = lbs.

Exercise 4:   *Total Weight* _____ *lbs.*   *Time* _____ *mins.*   *Power Factor* _____ *lbs./min.*   *Power Index* _____

■ Exercise:

Weight Reps Sets	Weight Reps Sets	Weight Reps Sets	Weight Reps Sets	Weight Reps Sets	Weight Reps Sets
× ×	× ×	× ×	× ×	× ×	× ×
Subtotal = lbs.	Subtotal = lbs.	Subtotal = lbs.	Subtotal = lbs.	Subtotal = lbs.	Subtotal = lbs.

Exercise 5:   *Total Weight* _____ *lbs.*   *Time* _____ *mins.*   *Power Factor* _____ *lbs./min.*   *Power Index* _____

OVERALL WORKOUT: *Total Weight* _____ *lbs.*   *Time* _____ *mins.*   *Power Factor* _____ *lbs./min.*   *Power Index* _____

Exercise Subtotal = Weight × Reps × Sets   ■ *Power Factor = lbs./min.*   ■ *Power Index = Total Weight × Power Factor ÷ 1,000,000*

LEG SPECIALIZATION WORKOUT RECORD   Date: ___ / ___ / ___

Start Time: _____   Finish Time: _____   Total Time: _____

■ Exercise: TOE-UP ON LEG CURL MACHINE

Weight Reps Sets	Weight Reps Sets	Weight Reps Sets	Weight Reps Sets	Weight Reps Sets	Weight Reps Sets
× ×	× ×	× ×	× ×	× ×	× ×
Subtotal = lbs.	Subtotal = lbs.	Subtotal = lbs.	Subtotal = lbs.	Subtotal = lbs.	Subtotal = lbs.

Exercise 1:   *Total Weight* _____ *lbs.*   *Time* _____ *mins.*   *Power Factor* _____ *lbs./min.*   *Power Index* _____

■ Exercise: STANDING CALF RAISE (OR TOE PRESS ON LEG PRESS MACHINE)

Weight Reps Sets	Weight Reps Sets	Weight Reps Sets	Weight Reps Sets	Weight Reps Sets	Weight Reps Sets
× ×	× ×	× ×	× ×	× ×	× ×
Subtotal = lbs.	Subtotal = lbs.	Subtotal = lbs.	Subtotal = lbs.	Subtotal = lbs.	Subtotal = lbs.

Exercise 2:   *Total Weight* _____ *lbs.*   *Time* _____ *mins.*   *Power Factor* _____ *lbs./min.*   *Power Index* _____

■ Exercise:

Weight Reps Sets	Weight Reps Sets	Weight Reps Sets	Weight Reps Sets	Weight Reps Sets	Weight Reps Sets
× ×	× ×	× ×	× ×	× ×	× ×
Subtotal = lbs.	Subtotal = lbs.	Subtotal = lbs.	Subtotal = lbs.	Subtotal = lbs.	Subtotal = lbs.

Exercise 3:   *Total Weight* _____ *lbs.*   *Time* _____ *mins.*   *Power Factor* _____ *lbs./min.*   *Power Index* _____

■ Exercise:

Weight Reps Sets	Weight Reps Sets	Weight Reps Sets	Weight Reps Sets	Weight Reps Sets	Weight Reps Sets
× ×	× ×	× ×	× ×	× ×	× ×
Subtotal = lbs.	Subtotal = lbs.	Subtotal = lbs.	Subtotal = lbs.	Subtotal = lbs.	Subtotal = lbs.

Exercise 4:   *Total Weight* _____ *lbs.*   *Time* _____ *mins.*   *Power Factor* _____ *lbs./min.*   *Power Index* _____

■ Exercise:

Weight Reps Sets	Weight Reps Sets	Weight Reps Sets	Weight Reps Sets	Weight Reps Sets	Weight Reps Sets
× ×	× ×	× ×	× ×	× ×	× ×
Subtotal = lbs.	Subtotal = lbs.	Subtotal = lbs.	Subtotal = lbs.	Subtotal = lbs.	Subtotal = lbs.

Exercise 5:   *Total Weight* _____ *lbs.*   *Time* _____ *mins.*   *Power Factor* _____ *lbs./min.*   *Power Index* _____

OVERALL WORKOUT: *Total Weight* _____ *lbs.*   *Time* _____ *mins.*   *Power Factor* _____ *lbs./min.*   *Power Index* _____

Exercise Subtotal = Weight × Reps × Sets   ■ *Power Factor = lbs./min.*   ■ *Power Index = Total Weight × Power Factor ÷ 1,000,000*

LEG SPECIALIZATION WORKOUT RECORD   Date: ___ / ___ / ___

Start Time: _____   Finish Time: _____   Total Time: _____

■ Exercise: TOE-UP ON LEG CURL MACHINE

Weight Reps Sets	Weight Reps Sets	Weight Reps Sets	Weight Reps Sets	Weight Reps Sets	Weight Reps Sets
× ×	× ×	× ×	× ×	× ×	× ×
Subtotal = lbs.	Subtotal = lbs.	Subtotal = lbs.	Subtotal = lbs.	Subtotal = lbs.	Subtotal = lbs.

Exercise 1:   Total Weight _____ lbs.   Time _____ mins.   Power Factor _____ lbs./min.   Power Index _____

■ Exercise: STANDING CALF RAISE (OR TOE PRESS ON LEG PRESS MACHINE)

Weight Reps Sets	Weight Reps Sets	Weight Reps Sets	Weight Reps Sets	Weight Reps Sets	Weight Reps Sets
× ×	× ×	× ×	× ×	× ×	× ×
Subtotal = lbs.	Subtotal = lbs.	Subtotal = lbs.	Subtotal = lbs.	Subtotal = lbs.	Subtotal = lbs.

Exercise 2:   Total Weight _____ lbs.   Time _____ mins.   Power Factor _____ lbs./min.   Power Index _____

■ Exercise:

Weight Reps Sets	Weight Reps Sets	Weight Reps Sets	Weight Reps Sets	Weight Reps Sets	Weight Reps Sets
× ×	× ×	× ×	× ×	× ×	× ×
Subtotal = lbs.	Subtotal = lbs.	Subtotal = lbs.	Subtotal = lbs.	Subtotal = lbs.	Subtotal = lbs.

Exercise 3:   Total Weight _____ lbs.   Time _____ mins.   Power Factor _____ lbs./min.   Power Index _____

■ Exercise:

Weight Reps Sets	Weight Reps Sets	Weight Reps Sets	Weight Reps Sets	Weight Reps Sets	Weight Reps Sets
× ×	× ×	× ×	× ×	× ×	× ×
Subtotal = lbs.	Subtotal = lbs.	Subtotal = lbs.	Subtotal = lbs.	Subtotal = lbs.	Subtotal = lbs.

Exercise 4:   Total Weight _____ lbs.   Time _____ mins.   Power Factor _____ lbs./min.   Power Index _____

■ Exercise:

Weight Reps Sets	Weight Reps Sets	Weight Reps Sets	Weight Reps Sets	Weight Reps Sets	Weight Reps Sets
× ×	× ×	× ×	× ×	× ×	× ×
Subtotal = lbs.	Subtotal = lbs.	Subtotal = lbs.	Subtotal = lbs.	Subtotal = lbs.	Subtotal = lbs.

Exercise 5:   Total Weight _____ lbs.   Time _____ mins.   Power Factor _____ lbs./min.   Power Index _____

OVERALL WORKOUT: *Total Weight _____ lbs.   Time _____ mins.   Power Factor _____ lbs./min.   Power Index _____*

Exercise Subtotal = Weight × Reps × Sets   ■ *Power Factor = lbs./min.*   ■ *Power Index = Total Weight × Power Factor ÷ 1,000,000*

LEG SPECIALIZATION WORKOUT RECORD   Date: ___ / ___ / ___

Start Time: _____   **Finish Time:** _____   **Total Time:** _____

▪ Exercise: TOE-UP ON LEG CURL MACHINE

Weight Reps Sets	Weight Reps Sets	Weight Reps Sets	Weight Reps Sets	Weight Reps Sets	Weight Reps Sets
× ×	× ×	× ×	× ×	× ×	× ×
Subtotal = lbs.	Subtotal = lbs.	Subtotal = lbs.	Subtotal = lbs.	Subtotal = lbs.	Subtotal = lbs.

Exercise 1:   *Total Weight* _____ *lbs.*   *Time* _____ *mins.*   *Power Factor* _____ *lbs./min.*   *Power Index* _____

▪ Exercise: STANDING CALF RAISE (OR TOE PRESS ON LEG PRESS MACHINE)

Weight Reps Sets	Weight Reps Sets	Weight Reps Sets	Weight Reps Sets	Weight Reps Sets	Weight Reps Sets
× ×	× ×	× ×	× ×	× ×	× ×
Subtotal = lbs.	Subtotal = lbs.	Subtotal = lbs.	Subtotal = lbs.	Subtotal = lbs.	Subtotal = lbs.

Exercise 2:   *Total Weight* _____ *lbs.*   *Time* _____ *mins.*   *Power Factor* _____ *lbs./min.*   *Power Index* _____

▪ Exercise:

Weight Reps Sets	Weight Reps Sets	Weight Reps Sets	Weight Reps Sets	Weight Reps Sets	Weight Reps Sets
× ×	× ×	× ×	× ×	× ×	× ×
Subtotal = lbs.	Subtotal = lbs.	Subtotal = lbs.	Subtotal = lbs.	Subtotal = lbs.	Subtotal = lbs.

Exercise 3:   *Total Weight* _____ *lbs.*   *Time* _____ *mins.*   *Power Factor* _____ *lbs./min.*   *Power Index* _____

▪ Exercise:

Weight Reps Sets	Weight Reps Sets	Weight Reps Sets	Weight Reps Sets	Weight Reps Sets	Weight Reps Sets
× ×	× ×	× ×	× ×	× ×	× ×
Subtotal = lbs.	Subtotal = lbs.	Subtotal = lbs.	Subtotal = lbs.	Subtotal = lbs.	Subtotal = lbs.

Exercise 4:   *Total Weight* _____ *lbs.*   *Time* _____ *mins.*   *Power Factor* _____ *lbs./min.*   *Power Index* _____

▪ Exercise:

Weight Reps Sets	Weight Reps Sets	Weight Reps Sets	Weight Reps Sets	Weight Reps Sets	Weight Reps Sets
× ×	× ×	× ×	× ×	× ×	× ×
Subtotal = lbs.	Subtotal = lbs.	Subtotal = lbs.	Subtotal = lbs.	Subtotal = lbs.	Subtotal = lbs.

Exercise 5:   *Total Weight* _____ *lbs.*   *Time* _____ *mins.*   *Power Factor* _____ *lbs./min.*   *Power Index* _____

OVERALL WORKOUT: *Total Weight* _____ *lbs.*   *Time* _____ *mins.*   *Power Factor* _____ *lbs./min.*   *Power Index* _____

Exercise Subtotal = Weight × Reps × Sets   ▪ *Power Factor = lbs./min.*   ▪ *Power Index = Total Weight × Power Factor ÷ 1,000,000*

LEG SPECIALIZATION WORKOUT RECORD   Date: ___ / ___ / ___

Start Time: _____   Finish Time: _____   Total Time: _____

■ **Exercise: TOE-UP ON LEG CURL MACHINE**

Weight Reps Sets	Weight Reps Sets	Weight Reps Sets	Weight Reps Sets	Weight Reps Sets	Weight Reps Sets
× ×	× ×	× ×	× ×	× ×	× ×
Subtotal = lbs.	Subtotal = lbs.	Subtotal = lbs.	Subtotal = lbs.	Subtotal = lbs.	Subtotal = lbs.

Exercise 1:   *Total Weight* _____ *lbs.   Time* _____ *mins.   Power Factor* _____ *lbs./min.   Power Index* _____

■ **Exercise: STANDING CALF RAISE (OR TOE PRESS ON LEG PRESS MACHINE)**

Weight Reps Sets	Weight Reps Sets	Weight Reps Sets	Weight Reps Sets	Weight Reps Sets	Weight Reps Sets
× ×	× ×	× ×	× ×	× ×	× ×
Subtotal = lbs.	Subtotal = lbs.	Subtotal = lbs.	Subtotal = lbs.	Subtotal = lbs.	Subtotal = lbs.

Exercise 2:   *Total Weight* _____ *lbs.   Time* _____ *mins.   Power Factor* _____ *lbs./min.   Power Index* _____

■ **Exercise:**

Weight Reps Sets	Weight Reps Sets	Weight Reps Sets	Weight Reps Sets	Weight Reps Sets	Weight Reps Sets
× ×	× ×	× ×	× ×	× ×	× ×
Subtotal = lbs.	Subtotal = lbs.	Subtotal = lbs.	Subtotal = lbs.	Subtotal = lbs.	Subtotal = lbs.

Exercise 3:   *Total Weight* _____ *lbs.   Time* _____ *mins.   Power Factor* _____ *lbs./min.   Power Index* _____

■ **Exercise:**

Weight Reps Sets	Weight Reps Sets	Weight Reps Sets	Weight Reps Sets	Weight Reps Sets	Weight Reps Sets
× ×	× ×	× ×	× ×	× ×	× ×
Subtotal = lbs.	Subtotal = lbs.	Subtotal = lbs.	Subtotal = lbs.	Subtotal = lbs.	Subtotal = lbs.

Exercise 4:   *Total Weight* _____ *lbs.   Time* _____ *mins.   Power Factor* _____ *lbs./min.   Power Index* _____

■ **Exercise:**

Weight Reps Sets	Weight Reps Sets	Weight Reps Sets	Weight Reps Sets	Weight Reps Sets	Weight Reps Sets
× ×	× ×	× ×	× ×	× ×	× ×
Subtotal = lbs.	Subtotal = lbs.	Subtotal = lbs.	Subtotal = lbs.	Subtotal = lbs.	Subtotal = lbs.

Exercise 5:   *Total Weight* _____ *lbs.   Time* _____ *mins.   Power Factor* _____ *lbs./min.   Power Index* _____

OVERALL WORKOUT: *Total Weight* _____ *lbs.   Time* _____ *mins.   Power Factor* _____ *lbs./min.   Power Index* _____

Exercise Subtotal = Weight × Reps × Sets   ■ *Power Factor = lbs./min.*   ■ *Power Index = Total Weight × Power Factor ÷ 1,000,000*

LEG SPECIALIZATION WORKOUT RECORD   Date: ____ / ____ / ____

Start Time: _____   Finish Time: _____   Total Time: _____

■ **Exercise: TOE-UP ON LEG CURL MACHINE**

Weight Reps Sets	Weight Reps Sets	Weight Reps Sets	Weight Reps Sets	Weight Reps Sets	Weight Reps Sets
× ×	× ×	× ×	× ×	× ×	× ×
Subtotal = ___ lbs.	Subtotal = ___ lbs.	Subtotal = ___ lbs.	Subtotal = ___ lbs.	Subtotal = ___ lbs.	Subtotal = ___ lbs.

Exercise 1:   *Total Weight* _____ *lbs.*   *Time* _____ *mins.*   *Power Factor* _____ *lbs./min.*   *Power Index* _____

■ **Exercise: STANDING CALF RAISE (OR TOE PRESS ON LEG PRESS MACHINE)**

Weight Reps Sets	Weight Reps Sets	Weight Reps Sets	Weight Reps Sets	Weight Reps Sets	Weight Reps Sets
× ×	× ×	× ×	× ×	× ×	× ×
Subtotal = ___ lbs.	Subtotal = ___ lbs.	Subtotal = ___ lbs.	Subtotal = ___ lbs.	Subtotal = ___ lbs.	Subtotal = ___ lbs.

Exercise 2:   *Total Weight* _____ *lbs.*   *Time* _____ *mins.*   *Power Factor* _____ *lbs./min.*   *Power Index* _____

■ **Exercise:**

Weight Reps Sets	Weight Reps Sets	Weight Reps Sets	Weight Reps Sets	Weight Reps Sets	Weight Reps Sets
× ×	× ×	× ×	× ×	× ×	× ×
Subtotal = ___ lbs.	Subtotal = ___ lbs.	Subtotal = ___ lbs.	Subtotal = ___ lbs.	Subtotal = ___ lbs.	Subtotal = ___ lbs.

Exercise 3:   *Total Weight* _____ *lbs.*   *Time* _____ *mins.*   *Power Factor* _____ *lbs./min.*   *Power Index* _____

■ **Exercise:**

Weight Reps Sets	Weight Reps Sets	Weight Reps Sets	Weight Reps Sets	Weight Reps Sets	Weight Reps Sets
× ×	× ×	× ×	× ×	× ×	× ×
Subtotal = ___ lbs.	Subtotal = ___ lbs.	Subtotal = ___ lbs.	Subtotal = ___ lbs.	Subtotal = ___ lbs.	Subtotal = ___ lbs.

Exercise 4:   *Total Weight* _____ *lbs.*   *Time* _____ *mins.*   *Power Factor* _____ *lbs./min.*   *Power Index* _____

■ **Exercise:**

Weight Reps Sets	Weight Reps Sets	Weight Reps Sets	Weight Reps Sets	Weight Reps Sets	Weight Reps Sets
× ×	× ×	× ×	× ×	× ×	× ×
Subtotal = ___ lbs.	Subtotal = ___ lbs.	Subtotal = ___ lbs.	Subtotal = ___ lbs.	Subtotal = ___ lbs.	Subtotal = ___ lbs.

Exercise 5:   *Total Weight* _____ *lbs.*   *Time* _____ *mins.*   *Power Factor* _____ *lbs./min.*   *Power Index* _____

OVERALL WORKOUT: *Total Weight* _____ *lbs.*   *Time* _____ *mins.*   *Power Factor* _____ *lbs./min.*   *Power Index* _____

Exercise Subtotal = Weight × Reps × Sets   ■ *Power Factor = lbs./min.*   ■ *Power Index = Total Weight × Power Factor ÷ 1,000,000*

LEG SPECIALIZATION WORKOUT RECORD   Date: ____ / ____ / ____

Start Time: _____   **Finish Time:** _____   **Total Time:** _____

■ Exercise: TOE-UP ON LEG CURL MACHINE

Weight Reps Sets	Weight Reps Sets	Weight Reps Sets	Weight Reps Sets	Weight Reps Sets	Weight Reps Sets
× ×	× ×	× ×	× ×	× ×	× ×
Subtotal = lbs.	Subtotal = lbs.	Subtotal = lbs.	Subtotal = lbs.	Subtotal = lbs.	Subtotal = lbs.

Exercise 1:   *Total Weight _____ lbs.   Time _____ mins.   Power Factor _____ lbs./min.   Power Index _____*

■ Exercise: STANDING CALF RAISE (OR TOE PRESS ON LEG PRESS MACHINE)

Weight Reps Sets	Weight Reps Sets	Weight Reps Sets	Weight Reps Sets	Weight Reps Sets	Weight Reps Sets
× ×	× ×	× ×	× ×	× ×	× ×
Subtotal = lbs.	Subtotal = lbs.	Subtotal = lbs.	Subtotal = lbs.	Subtotal = lbs.	Subtotal = lbs.

Exercise 2:   *Total Weight _____ lbs.   Time _____ mins.   Power Factor _____ lbs./min.   Power Index _____*

■ Exercise:

Weight Reps Sets	Weight Reps Sets	Weight Reps Sets	Weight Reps Sets	Weight Reps Sets	Weight Reps Sets
× ×	× ×	× ×	× ×	× ×	× ×
Subtotal = lbs.	Subtotal = lbs.	Subtotal = lbs.	Subtotal = lbs.	Subtotal = lbs.	Subtotal = lbs.

Exercise 3:   *Total Weight _____ lbs.   Time _____ mins.   Power Factor _____ lbs./min.   Power Index _____*

■ Exercise:

Weight Reps Sets	Weight Reps Sets	Weight Reps Sets	Weight Reps Sets	Weight Reps Sets	Weight Reps Sets
× ×	× ×	× ×	× ×	× ×	× ×
Subtotal = lbs.	Subtotal = lbs.	Subtotal = lbs.	Subtotal = lbs.	Subtotal = lbs.	Subtotal = lbs.

Exercise 4:   *Total Weight _____ lbs.   Time _____ mins.   Power Factor _____ lbs./min.   Power Index _____*

■ Exercise:

Weight Reps Sets	Weight Reps Sets	Weight Reps Sets	Weight Reps Sets	Weight Reps Sets	Weight Reps Sets
× ×	× ×	× ×	× ×	× ×	× ×
Subtotal = lbs.	Subtotal = lbs.	Subtotal = lbs.	Subtotal = lbs.	Subtotal = lbs.	Subtotal = lbs.

Exercise 5:   *Total Weight _____ lbs.   Time _____ mins.   Power Factor _____ lbs./min.   Power Index _____*

OVERALL WORKOUT: *Total Weight _____ lbs.   Time _____ mins.   Power Factor _____ lbs./min.   Power Index _____*

Exercise Subtotal = Weight × Reps × Sets   ■ Power Factor = lbs./min.   ■ Power Index = Total Weight × Power Factor ÷ 1,000,000

LEG SPECIALIZATION WORKOUT RECORD   Date: ___ / ___ / ___

Start Time: _____   Finish Time: _____   Total Time: _____

■ Exercise: TOE-UP ON LEG CURL MACHINE

Weight Reps Sets	Weight Reps Sets	Weight Reps Sets	Weight Reps Sets	Weight Reps Sets	Weight Reps Sets
× ×	× ×	× ×	× ×	× ×	× ×
Subtotal = lbs.	Subtotal = lbs.	Subtotal = lbs.	Subtotal = lbs.	Subtotal = lbs.	Subtotal = lbs.

Exercise 1:　　*Total Weight _____ lbs.　Time _____ mins.　Power Factor _____ lbs./min.　Power Index _____*

■ Exercise: STANDING CALF RAISE (OR TOE PRESS ON LEG PRESS MACHINE)

Weight Reps Sets	Weight Reps Sets	Weight Reps Sets	Weight Reps Sets	Weight Reps Sets	Weight Reps Sets
× ×	× ×	× ×	× ×	× ×	× ×
Subtotal = lbs.	Subtotal = lbs.	Subtotal = lbs.	Subtotal = lbs.	Subtotal = lbs.	Subtotal = lbs.

Exercise 2:　　*Total Weight _____ lbs.　Time _____ mins.　Power Factor _____ lbs./min.　Power Index _____*

■ Exercise:

Weight Reps Sets	Weight Reps Sets	Weight Reps Sets	Weight Reps Sets	Weight Reps Sets	Weight Reps Sets
× ×	× ×	× ×	× ×	× ×	× ×
Subtotal = lbs.	Subtotal = lbs.	Subtotal = lbs.	Subtotal = lbs.	Subtotal = lbs.	Subtotal = lbs.

Exercise 3:　　*Total Weight _____ lbs.　Time _____ mins.　Power Factor _____ lbs./min.　Power Index _____*

■ Exercise:

Weight Reps Sets	Weight Reps Sets	Weight Reps Sets	Weight Reps Sets	Weight Reps Sets	Weight Reps Sets
× ×	× ×	× ×	× ×	× ×	× ×
Subtotal = lbs.	Subtotal = lbs.	Subtotal = lbs.	Subtotal = lbs.	Subtotal = lbs.	Subtotal = lbs.

Exercise 4:　　*Total Weight _____ lbs.　Time _____ mins.　Power Factor _____ lbs./min.　Power Index _____*

■ Exercise:

Weight Reps Sets	Weight Reps Sets	Weight Reps Sets	Weight Reps Sets	Weight Reps Sets	Weight Reps Sets
× ×	× ×	× ×	× ×	× ×	× ×
Subtotal = lbs.	Subtotal = lbs.	Subtotal = lbs.	Subtotal = lbs.	Subtotal = lbs.	Subtotal = lbs.

Exercise 5:　　*Total Weight _____ lbs.　Time _____ mins.　Power Factor _____ lbs./min.　Power Index _____*

OVERALL WORKOUT:　*Total Weight _____ lbs.　Time _____ mins.　Power Factor _____ lbs./min.　Power Index _____*

Exercise Subtotal = Weight × Reps × Sets　■ *Power Factor = lbs./min.*　■ *Power Index = Total Weight × Power Factor ÷ 1,000,000*

ABDOMINAL SPECIALIZATION WORKOUT RECORD   Date: ___ / ___ / ___

Start Time: _____   Finish Time: _____   Total Time: _____

▪ Exercise: DUMBBELL SIDE BEND

Weight Reps Sets	Weight Reps Sets	Weight Reps Sets	Weight Reps Sets	Weight Reps Sets	Weight Reps Sets
× ×	× ×	× ×	× ×	× ×	× ×
Subtotal = lbs.	Subtotal = lbs.	Subtotal = lbs.	Subtotal = lbs.	Subtotal = lbs.	Subtotal = lbs.

Exercise 1:   *Total Weight* _____ *lbs.*   *Time* _____ *mins.*   *Power Factor* _____ *lbs./min.*   *Power Index* _____

▪ Exercise: WEIGHTED CRUNCH

Weight Reps Sets	Weight Reps Sets	Weight Reps Sets	Weight Reps Sets	Weight Reps Sets	Weight Reps Sets
× ×	× ×	× ×	× ×	× ×	× ×
Subtotal = lbs.	Subtotal = lbs.	Subtotal = lbs.	Subtotal = lbs.	Subtotal = lbs.	Subtotal = lbs.

Exercise 2:   *Total Weight* _____ *lbs.*   *Time* _____ *mins.*   *Power Factor* _____ *lbs./min.*   *Power Index* _____

▪ Exercise:

Weight Reps Sets	Weight Reps Sets	Weight Reps Sets	Weight Reps Sets	Weight Reps Sets	Weight Reps Sets
× ×	× ×	× ×	× ×	× ×	× ×
Subtotal = lbs.	Subtotal = lbs.	Subtotal = lbs.	Subtotal = lbs.	Subtotal = lbs.	Subtotal = lbs.

Exercise 3:   *Total Weight* _____ *lbs.*   *Time* _____ *mins.*   *Power Factor* _____ *lbs./min.*   *Power Index* _____

▪ Exercise:

Weight Reps Sets	Weight Reps Sets	Weight Reps Sets	Weight Reps Sets	Weight Reps Sets	Weight Reps Sets
× ×	× ×	× ×	× ×	× ×	× ×
Subtotal = lbs.	Subtotal = lbs.	Subtotal = lbs.	Subtotal = lbs.	Subtotal = lbs.	Subtotal = lbs.

Exercise 4:   *Total Weight* _____ *lbs.*   *Time* _____ *mins.*   *Power Factor* _____ *lbs./min.*   *Power Index* _____

▪ Exercise:

Weight Reps Sets	Weight Reps Sets	Weight Reps Sets	Weight Reps Sets	Weight Reps Sets	Weight Reps Sets
× ×	× ×	× ×	× ×	× ×	× ×
Subtotal = lbs.	Subtotal = lbs.	Subtotal = lbs.	Subtotal = lbs.	Subtotal = lbs.	Subtotal = lbs.

Exercise 5:   *Total Weight* _____ *lbs.*   *Time* _____ *mins.*   *Power Factor* _____ *lbs./min.*   *Power Index* _____

OVERALL WORKOUT: *Total Weight* _____ *lbs.*   *Time* _____ *mins.*   *Power Factor* _____ *lbs./min.*   *Power Index* _____

Exercise Subtotal = Weight × Reps × Sets   ▪ *Power Factor = lbs./min.*   ▪ *Power Index = Total Weight × Power Factor ÷ 1,000,000*

ABDOMINAL SPECIALIZATION WORKOUT RECORD   Date: ___ / ___ / ___

Start Time: _____   **Finish Time:** _____   **Total Time:** _____

■ Exercise: DUMBBELL SIDE BEND

Weight Reps Sets	Weight Reps Sets	Weight Reps Sets	Weight Reps Sets	Weight Reps Sets	Weight Reps Sets
× ×	× ×	× ×	× ×	× ×	× ×
Subtotal = lbs.	Subtotal = lbs.	Subtotal = lbs.	Subtotal = lbs.	Subtotal = lbs.	Subtotal = lbs.

Exercise 1:   *Total Weight _____ lbs.   Time _____ mins.   Power Factor _____ lbs./min.   Power Index _____*

■ Exercise: WEIGHTED CRUNCH

Weight Reps Sets	Weight Reps Sets	Weight Reps Sets	Weight Reps Sets	Weight Reps Sets	Weight Reps Sets
× ×	× ×	× ×	× ×	× ×	× ×
Subtotal = lbs.	Subtotal = lbs.	Subtotal = lbs.	Subtotal = lbs.	Subtotal = lbs.	Subtotal = lbs.

Exercise 2:   *Total Weight _____ lbs.   Time _____ mins.   Power Factor _____ lbs./min.   Power Index _____*

■ Exercise:

Weight Reps Sets	Weight Reps Sets	Weight Reps Sets	Weight Reps Sets	Weight Reps Sets	Weight Reps Sets
× ×	× ×	× ×	× ×	× ×	× ×
Subtotal = lbs.	Subtotal = lbs.	Subtotal = lbs.	Subtotal = lbs.	Subtotal = lbs.	Subtotal = lbs.

Exercise 3:   *Total Weight _____ lbs.   Time _____ mins.   Power Factor _____ lbs./min.   Power Index _____*

■ Exercise:

Weight Reps Sets	Weight Reps Sets	Weight Reps Sets	Weight Reps Sets	Weight Reps Sets	Weight Reps Sets
× ×	× ×	× ×	× ×	× ×	× ×
Subtotal = lbs.	Subtotal = lbs.	Subtotal = lbs.	Subtotal = lbs.	Subtotal = lbs.	Subtotal = lbs.

Exercise 4:   *Total Weight _____ lbs.   Time _____ mins.   Power Factor _____ lbs./min.   Power Index _____*

■ Exercise:

Weight Reps Sets	Weight Reps Sets	Weight Reps Sets	Weight Reps Sets	Weight Reps Sets	Weight Reps Sets
× ×	× ×	× ×	× ×	× ×	× ×
Subtotal = lbs.	Subtotal = lbs.	Subtotal = lbs.	Subtotal = lbs.	Subtotal = lbs.	Subtotal = lbs.

Exercise 5:   *Total Weight _____ lbs.   Time _____ mins.   Power Factor _____ lbs./min.   Power Index _____*

OVERALL WORKOUT: *Total Weight _____ lbs.   Time _____ mins.   Power Factor _____ lbs./min.   Power Index _____*

Exercise Subtotal = Weight × Reps × Sets   ■ Power Factor = lbs./min.   ■ Power Index = Total Weight × Power Factor ÷ 1,000,000

ABDOMINAL SPECIALIZATION WORKOUT RECORD   Date: ___ / ___ / ___

Start Time: _____   **Finish Time:** _____   **Total Time:** _____

■ Exercise: DUMBBELL SIDE BEND

Weight Reps Sets	Weight Reps Sets	Weight Reps Sets	Weight Reps Sets	Weight Reps Sets	Weight Reps Sets
× ×	× ×	× ×	× ×	× ×	× ×
Subtotal = lbs.	Subtotal = lbs.	Subtotal = lbs.	Subtotal = lbs.	Subtotal = lbs.	Subtotal = lbs.

Exercise 1:   Total Weight _____ lbs.   Time _____ mins.   Power Factor _____ lbs./min.   Power Index _____

■ Exercise: WEIGHTED CRUNCH

Weight Reps Sets	Weight Reps Sets	Weight Reps Sets	Weight Reps Sets	Weight Reps Sets	Weight Reps Sets
× ×	× ×	× ×	× ×	× ×	× ×
Subtotal = lbs.	Subtotal = lbs.	Subtotal = lbs.	Subtotal = lbs.	Subtotal = lbs.	Subtotal = lbs.

Exercise 2:   Total Weight _____ lbs.   Time _____ mins.   Power Factor _____ lbs./min.   Power Index _____

■ Exercise:

Weight Reps Sets	Weight Reps Sets	Weight Reps Sets	Weight Reps Sets	Weight Reps Sets	Weight Reps Sets
× ×	× ×	× ×	× ×	× ×	× ×
Subtotal = lbs.	Subtotal = lbs.	Subtotal = lbs.	Subtotal = lbs.	Subtotal = lbs.	Subtotal = lbs.

Exercise 3:   Total Weight _____ lbs.   Time _____ mins.   Power Factor _____ lbs./min.   Power Index _____

■ Exercise:

Weight Reps Sets	Weight Reps Sets	Weight Reps Sets	Weight Reps Sets	Weight Reps Sets	Weight Reps Sets
× ×	× ×	× ×	× ×	× ×	× ×
Subtotal = lbs.	Subtotal = lbs.	Subtotal = lbs.	Subtotal = lbs.	Subtotal = lbs.	Subtotal = lbs.

Exercise 4:   Total Weight _____ lbs.   Time _____ mins.   Power Factor _____ lbs./min.   Power Index _____

■ Exercise:

Weight Reps Sets	Weight Reps Sets	Weight Reps Sets	Weight Reps Sets	Weight Reps Sets	Weight Reps Sets
× ×	× ×	× ×	× ×	× ×	× ×
Subtotal = lbs.	Subtotal = lbs.	Subtotal = lbs.	Subtotal = lbs.	Subtotal = lbs.	Subtotal = lbs.

Exercise 5:   Total Weight _____ lbs.   Time _____ mins.   Power Factor _____ lbs./min.   Power Index _____

OVERALL WORKOUT: Total Weight _____ lbs.   Time _____ mins.   Power Factor _____ lbs./min.   Power Index _____

Exercise Subtotal = Weight × Reps × Sets   ■ *Power Factor = lbs./min.*   ■ *Power Index = Total Weight × Power Factor ÷ 1,000,000*

ABDOMINAL SPECIALIZATION WORKOUT RECORD   Date: ___ / ___ / ___

Start Time: _____   **Finish Time:** _____   **Total Time:** _____

▪ Exercise: DUMBBELL SIDE BEND

Weight Reps Sets	Weight Reps Sets	Weight Reps Sets	Weight Reps Sets	Weight Reps Sets	Weight Reps Sets
× ×	× ×	× ×	× ×	× ×	× ×
Subtotal = lbs.	Subtotal = lbs.	Subtotal = lbs.	Subtotal = lbs.	Subtotal = lbs.	Subtotal = lbs.

Exercise 1:   *Total Weight* _____ *lbs.*   *Time* _____ *mins.*   *Power Factor* _____ *lbs./min.*   *Power Index* _____

▪ Exercise: WEIGHTED CRUNCH

Weight Reps Sets	Weight Reps Sets	Weight Reps Sets	Weight Reps Sets	Weight Reps Sets	Weight Reps Sets
× ×	× ×	× ×	× ×	× ×	× ×
Subtotal = lbs.	Subtotal = lbs.	Subtotal = lbs.	Subtotal = lbs.	Subtotal = lbs.	Subtotal = lbs.

Exercise 2:   *Total Weight* _____ *lbs.*   *Time* _____ *mins.*   *Power Factor* _____ *lbs./min.*   *Power Index* _____

▪ Exercise:

Weight Reps Sets	Weight Reps Sets	Weight Reps Sets	Weight Reps Sets	Weight Reps Sets	Weight Reps Sets
× ×	× ×	× ×	× ×	× ×	× ×
Subtotal = lbs.	Subtotal = lbs.	Subtotal = lbs.	Subtotal = lbs.	Subtotal = lbs.	Subtotal = lbs.

Exercise 3:   *Total Weight* _____ *lbs.*   *Time* _____ *mins.*   *Power Factor* _____ *lbs./min.*   *Power Index* _____

▪ Exercise:

Weight Reps Sets	Weight Reps Sets	Weight Reps Sets	Weight Reps Sets	Weight Reps Sets	Weight Reps Sets
× ×	× ×	× ×	× ×	× ×	× ×
Subtotal = lbs.	Subtotal = lbs.	Subtotal = lbs.	Subtotal = lbs.	Subtotal = lbs.	Subtotal = lbs.

Exercise 4:   *Total Weight* _____ *lbs.*   *Time* _____ *mins.*   *Power Factor* _____ *lbs./min.*   *Power Index* _____

▪ Exercise:

Weight Reps Sets	Weight Reps Sets	Weight Reps Sets	Weight Reps Sets	Weight Reps Sets	Weight Reps Sets
× ×	× ×	× ×	× ×	× ×	× ×
Subtotal = lbs.	Subtotal = lbs.	Subtotal = lbs.	Subtotal = lbs.	Subtotal = lbs.	Subtotal = lbs.

Exercise 5:   *Total Weight* _____ *lbs.*   *Time* _____ *mins.*   *Power Factor* _____ *lbs./min.*   *Power Index* _____

OVERALL WORKOUT: *Total Weight* _____ *lbs.*   *Time* _____ *mins.*   *Power Factor* _____ *lbs./min.*   *Power Index* _____

Exercise Subtotal = Weight × Reps × Sets   ▪ *Power Factor = lbs./min.*   ▪ *Power Index = Total Weight × Power Factor ÷ 1,000,000*

ABDOMINAL SPECIALIZATION WORKOUT RECORD   Date: ___ / ___ / ___

Start Time: _____   **Finish Time:** _____   **Total Time:** _____

■ **Exercise: DUMBBELL SIDE BEND**

Weight Reps Sets	Weight Reps Sets	Weight Reps Sets	Weight Reps Sets	Weight Reps Sets	Weight Reps Sets
× ×	× ×	× ×	× ×	× ×	× ×
Subtotal = lbs.	Subtotal = lbs.	Subtotal = lbs.	Subtotal = lbs.	Subtotal = lbs.	Subtotal = lbs.

Exercise 1:   *Total Weight* _____ *lbs.*   *Time* _____ *mins.*   *Power Factor* _____ *lbs./min.*   *Power Index* _____

■ **Exercise: WEIGHTED CRUNCH**

Weight Reps Sets	Weight Reps Sets	Weight Reps Sets	Weight Reps Sets	Weight Reps Sets	Weight Reps Sets
× ×	× ×	× ×	× ×	× ×	× ×
Subtotal = lbs.	Subtotal = lbs.	Subtotal = lbs.	Subtotal = lbs.	Subtotal = lbs.	Subtotal = lbs.

Exercise 2:   *Total Weight* _____ *lbs.*   *Time* _____ *mins.*   *Power Factor* _____ *lbs./min.*   *Power Index* _____

■ **Exercise:**

Weight Reps Sets	Weight Reps Sets	Weight Reps Sets	Weight Reps Sets	Weight Reps Sets	Weight Reps Sets
× ×	× ×	× ×	× ×	× ×	× ×
Subtotal = lbs.	Subtotal = lbs.	Subtotal = lbs.	Subtotal = lbs.	Subtotal = lbs.	Subtotal = lbs.

Exercise 3:   *Total Weight* _____ *lbs.*   *Time* _____ *mins.*   *Power Factor* _____ *lbs./min.*   *Power Index* _____

■ **Exercise:**

Weight Reps Sets	Weight Reps Sets	Weight Reps Sets	Weight Reps Sets	Weight Reps Sets	Weight Reps Sets
× ×	× ×	× ×	× ×	× ×	× ×
Subtotal = lbs.	Subtotal = lbs.	Subtotal = lbs.	Subtotal = lbs.	Subtotal = lbs.	Subtotal = lbs.

Exercise 4:   *Total Weight* _____ *lbs.*   *Time* _____ *mins.*   *Power Factor* _____ *lbs./min.*   *Power Index* _____

■ **Exercise:**

Weight Reps Sets	Weight Reps Sets	Weight Reps Sets	Weight Reps Sets	Weight Reps Sets	Weight Reps Sets
× ×	× ×	× ×	× ×	× ×	× ×
Subtotal = lbs.	Subtotal = lbs.	Subtotal = lbs.	Subtotal = lbs.	Subtotal = lbs.	Subtotal = lbs.

Exercise 5:   *Total Weight* _____ *lbs.*   *Time* _____ *mins.*   *Power Factor* _____ *lbs./min.*   *Power Index* _____

OVERALL WORKOUT: *Total Weight* _____ *lbs.*   *Time* _____ *mins.*   *Power Factor* _____ *lbs./min.*   *Power Index* _____

Exercise Subtotal = Weight × Reps × Sets   ■ *Power Factor = lbs./min.*   ■ *Power Index = Total Weight × Power Factor ÷ 1,000,000*

ABDOMINAL SPECIALIZATION WORKOUT RECORD Date: ___ / ___ / ___

Start Time: _____ **Finish Time:** _____ **Total Time:** _____

■ Exercise: DUMBBELL SIDE BEND

Weight Reps Sets	Weight Reps Sets	Weight Reps Sets	Weight Reps Sets	Weight Reps Sets	Weight Reps Sets
× ×	× ×	× ×	× ×	× ×	× ×
Subtotal = lbs.	Subtotal = lbs.	Subtotal = lbs.	Subtotal = lbs.	Subtotal = lbs.	Subtotal = lbs.

Exercise 1: *Total Weight _____ lbs.* *Time _____ mins.* *Power Factor _____ lbs./min.* *Power Index _____*

■ Exercise: WEIGHTED CRUNCH

Weight Reps Sets	Weight Reps Sets	Weight Reps Sets	Weight Reps Sets	Weight Reps Sets	Weight Reps Sets
× ×	× ×	× ×	× ×	× ×	× ×
Subtotal = lbs.	Subtotal = lbs.	Subtotal = lbs.	Subtotal = lbs.	Subtotal = lbs.	Subtotal = lbs.

Exercise 2: *Total Weight _____ lbs.* *Time _____ mins.* *Power Factor _____ lbs./min.* *Power Index _____*

■ Exercise:

Weight Reps Sets	Weight Reps Sets	Weight Reps Sets	Weight Reps Sets	Weight Reps Sets	Weight Reps Sets
× ×	× ×	× ×	× ×	× ×	× ×
Subtotal = lbs.	Subtotal = lbs.	Subtotal = lbs.	Subtotal = lbs.	Subtotal = lbs.	Subtotal = lbs.

Exercise 3: *Total Weight _____ lbs.* *Time _____ mins.* *Power Factor _____ lbs./min.* *Power Index _____*

■ Exercise:

Weight Reps Sets	Weight Reps Sets	Weight Reps Sets	Weight Reps Sets	Weight Reps Sets	Weight Reps Sets
× ×	× ×	× ×	× ×	× ×	× ×
Subtotal = lbs.	Subtotal = lbs.	Subtotal = lbs.	Subtotal = lbs.	Subtotal = lbs.	Subtotal = lbs.

Exercise 4: *Total Weight _____ lbs.* *Time _____ mins.* *Power Factor _____ lbs./min.* *Power Index _____*

■ Exercise:

Weight Reps Sets	Weight Reps Sets	Weight Reps Sets	Weight Reps Sets	Weight Reps Sets	Weight Reps Sets
× ×	× ×	× ×	× ×	× ×	× ×
Subtotal = lbs.	Subtotal = lbs.	Subtotal = lbs.	Subtotal = lbs.	Subtotal = lbs.	Subtotal = lbs.

Exercise 5: *Total Weight _____ lbs.* *Time _____ mins.* *Power Factor _____ lbs./min.* *Power Index _____*

OVERALL WORKOUT: *Total Weight _____ lbs.* *Time _____ mins.* *Power Factor _____ lbs./min.* *Power Index _____*

Exercise Subtotal = Weight × Reps × Sets ■ *Power Factor = lbs./min.* ■ *Power Index = Total Weight × Power Factor ÷ 1,000,000*

ABDOMINAL SPECIALIZATION WORKOUT RECORD   Date: ___ / ___ / ___

Start Time: _____   Finish Time: _____   Total Time: _____

■ **Exercise: DUMBBELL SIDE BEND**

Weight Reps Sets	Weight Reps Sets	Weight Reps Sets	Weight Reps Sets	Weight Reps Sets	Weight Reps Sets
× ×	× ×	× ×	× ×	× ×	× ×
Subtotal = lbs.	Subtotal = lbs.	Subtotal = lbs.	Subtotal = lbs.	Subtotal = lbs.	Subtotal = lbs.

Exercise 1:   *Total Weight* _____ *lbs.*   *Time* _____ *mins.*   *Power Factor* _____ *lbs./min.*   *Power Index* _____

■ **Exercise: WEIGHTED CRUNCH**

Weight Reps Sets	Weight Reps Sets	Weight Reps Sets	Weight Reps Sets	Weight Reps Sets	Weight Reps Sets
× ×	× ×	× ×	× ×	× ×	× ×
Subtotal = lbs.	Subtotal = lbs.	Subtotal = lbs.	Subtotal = lbs.	Subtotal = lbs.	Subtotal = lbs.

Exercise 2:   *Total Weight* _____ *lbs.*   *Time* _____ *mins.*   *Power Factor* _____ *lbs./min.*   *Power Index* _____

■ **Exercise:**

Weight Reps Sets	Weight Reps Sets	Weight Reps Sets	Weight Reps Sets	Weight Reps Sets	Weight Reps Sets
× ×	× ×	× ×	× ×	× ×	× ×
Subtotal = lbs.	Subtotal = lbs.	Subtotal = lbs.	Subtotal = lbs.	Subtotal = lbs.	Subtotal = lbs.

Exercise 3:   *Total Weight* _____ *lbs.*   *Time* _____ *mins.*   *Power Factor* _____ *lbs./min.*   *Power Index* _____

■ **Exercise:**

Weight Reps Sets	Weight Reps Sets	Weight Reps Sets	Weight Reps Sets	Weight Reps Sets	Weight Reps Sets
× ×	× ×	× ×	× ×	× ×	× ×
Subtotal = lbs.	Subtotal = lbs.	Subtotal = lbs.	Subtotal = lbs.	Subtotal = lbs.	Subtotal = lbs.

Exercise 4:   *Total Weight* _____ *lbs.*   *Time* _____ *mins.*   *Power Factor* _____ *lbs./min.*   *Power Index* _____

■ **Exercise:**

Weight Reps Sets	Weight Reps Sets	Weight Reps Sets	Weight Reps Sets	Weight Reps Sets	Weight Reps Sets
× ×	× ×	× ×	× ×	× ×	× ×
Subtotal = lbs.	Subtotal = lbs.	Subtotal = lbs.	Subtotal = lbs.	Subtotal = lbs.	Subtotal = lbs.

Exercise 5:   *Total Weight* _____ *lbs.*   *Time* _____ *mins.*   *Power Factor* _____ *lbs./min.*   *Power Index* _____

OVERALL WORKOUT: *Total Weight* _____ *lbs.*   *Time* _____ *mins.*   *Power Factor* _____ *lbs./min.*   *Power Index* _____

Exercise Subtotal = Weight × Reps × Sets   ■ *Power Factor = lbs./min.*   ■ *Power Index = Total Weight × Power Factor ÷ 1,000,000*

ABDOMINAL SPECIALIZATION WORKOUT RECORD   Date: ___ / ___ / ___

Start Time: _____   **Finish Time:** _____   **Total Time:** _____

■ Exercise: DUMBBELL SIDE BEND

Weight Reps Sets	Weight Reps Sets	Weight Reps Sets	Weight Reps Sets	Weight Reps Sets	Weight Reps Sets
× ×	× ×	× ×	× ×	× ×	× ×
Subtotal = ___ lbs.	Subtotal = ___ lbs.	Subtotal = ___ lbs.	Subtotal = ___ lbs.	Subtotal = ___ lbs.	Subtotal = ___ lbs.

Exercise 1:   *Total Weight* _____ *lbs.*   *Time* _____ *mins.*   *Power Factor* _____ *lbs./min.*   *Power Index* _____

■ Exercise: WEIGHTED CRUNCH

Weight Reps Sets	Weight Reps Sets	Weight Reps Sets	Weight Reps Sets	Weight Reps Sets	Weight Reps Sets
× ×	× ×	× ×	× ×	× ×	× ×
Subtotal = ___ lbs.	Subtotal = ___ lbs.	Subtotal = ___ lbs.	Subtotal = ___ lbs.	Subtotal = ___ lbs.	Subtotal = ___ lbs.

Exercise 2:   *Total Weight* _____ *lbs.*   *Time* _____ *mins.*   *Power Factor* _____ *lbs./min.*   *Power Index* _____

■ Exercise:

Weight Reps Sets	Weight Reps Sets	Weight Reps Sets	Weight Reps Sets	Weight Reps Sets	Weight Reps Sets
× ×	× ×	× ×	× ×	× ×	× ×
Subtotal = ___ lbs.	Subtotal = ___ lbs.	Subtotal = ___ lbs.	Subtotal = ___ lbs.	Subtotal = ___ lbs.	Subtotal = ___ lbs.

Exercise 3:   *Total Weight* _____ *lbs.*   *Time* _____ *mins.*   *Power Factor* _____ *lbs./min.*   *Power Index* _____

■ Exercise:

Weight Reps Sets	Weight Reps Sets	Weight Reps Sets	Weight Reps Sets	Weight Reps Sets	Weight Reps Sets
× ×	× ×	× ×	× ×	× ×	× ×
Subtotal = ___ lbs.	Subtotal = ___ lbs.	Subtotal = ___ lbs.	Subtotal = ___ lbs.	Subtotal = ___ lbs.	Subtotal = ___ lbs.

Exercise 4:   *Total Weight* _____ *lbs.*   *Time* _____ *mins.*   *Power Factor* _____ *lbs./min.*   *Power Index* _____

■ Exercise:

Weight Reps Sets	Weight Reps Sets	Weight Reps Sets	Weight Reps Sets	Weight Reps Sets	Weight Reps Sets
× ×	× ×	× ×	× ×	× ×	× ×
Subtotal = ___ lbs.	Subtotal = ___ lbs.	Subtotal = ___ lbs.	Subtotal = ___ lbs.	Subtotal = ___ lbs.	Subtotal = ___ lbs.

Exercise 5:   *Total Weight* _____ *lbs.*   *Time* _____ *mins.*   *Power Factor* _____ *lbs./min.*   *Power Index* _____

OVERALL WORKOUT: *Total Weight* _____ *lbs.*   *Time* _____ *mins.*   *Power Factor* _____ *lbs./min.*   *Power Index* _____

Exercise Subtotal = Weight × Reps × Sets   ■ *Power Factor = lbs./min.*   ■ *Power Index = Total Weight × Power Factor ÷ 1,000,000*

ABDOMINAL SPECIALIZATION WORKOUT RECORD   Date: ___ / ___ / ___

Start Time: _____   Finish Time: _____   Total Time: _____

■ Exercise: DUMBBELL SIDE BEND

Weight Reps Sets	Weight Reps Sets	Weight Reps Sets	Weight Reps Sets	Weight Reps Sets	Weight Reps Sets
× ×	× ×	× ×	× ×	× ×	× ×
Subtotal = lbs.	Subtotal = lbs.	Subtotal = lbs.	Subtotal = lbs.	Subtotal = lbs.	Subtotal = lbs.

Exercise 1:   *Total Weight* _____ *lbs.*   *Time* _____ *mins.*   *Power Factor* _____ *lbs./min.*   *Power Index* _____

■ Exercise: WEIGHTED CRUNCH

Weight Reps Sets	Weight Reps Sets	Weight Reps Sets	Weight Reps Sets	Weight Reps Sets	Weight Reps Sets
× ×	× ×	× ×	× ×	× ×	× ×
Subtotal = lbs.	Subtotal = lbs.	Subtotal = lbs.	Subtotal = lbs.	Subtotal = lbs.	Subtotal = lbs.

Exercise 2:   *Total Weight* _____ *lbs.*   *Time* _____ *mins.*   *Power Factor* _____ *lbs./min.*   *Power Index* _____

■ Exercise:

Weight Reps Sets	Weight Reps Sets	Weight Reps Sets	Weight Reps Sets	Weight Reps Sets	Weight Reps Sets
× ×	× ×	× ×	× ×	× ×	× ×
Subtotal = lbs.	Subtotal = lbs.	Subtotal = lbs.	Subtotal = lbs.	Subtotal = lbs.	Subtotal = lbs.

Exercise 3:   *Total Weight* _____ *lbs.*   *Time* _____ *mins.*   *Power Factor* _____ *lbs./min.*   *Power Index* _____

■ Exercise:

Weight Reps Sets	Weight Reps Sets	Weight Reps Sets	Weight Reps Sets	Weight Reps Sets	Weight Reps Sets
× ×	× ×	× ×	× ×	× ×	× ×
Subtotal = lbs.	Subtotal = lbs.	Subtotal = lbs.	Subtotal = lbs.	Subtotal = lbs.	Subtotal = lbs.

Exercise 4:   *Total Weight* _____ *lbs.*   *Time* _____ *mins.*   *Power Factor* _____ *lbs./min.*   *Power Index* _____

■ Exercise:

Weight Reps Sets	Weight Reps Sets	Weight Reps Sets	Weight Reps Sets	Weight Reps Sets	Weight Reps Sets
× ×	× ×	× ×	× ×	× ×	× ×
Subtotal = lbs.	Subtotal = lbs.	Subtotal = lbs.	Subtotal = lbs.	Subtotal = lbs.	Subtotal = lbs.

Exercise 5:   *Total Weight* _____ *lbs.*   *Time* _____ *mins.*   *Power Factor* _____ *lbs./min.*   *Power Index* _____

OVERALL WORKOUT: *Total Weight* _____ *lbs.*   *Time* _____ *mins.*   *Power Factor* _____ *lbs./min.*   *Power Index* _____

Exercise Subtotal = Weight × Reps × Sets   ■ *Power Factor = lbs./min.*   ■ *Power Index = Total Weight × Power Factor ÷ 1,000,000*

ABDOMINAL SPECIALIZATION WORKOUT RECORD   Date: ___ / ___ / ___

Start Time: _____   **Finish Time:** _____   **Total Time:** _____

■ Exercise: DUMBBELL SIDE BEND

Weight Reps Sets	Weight Reps Sets	Weight Reps Sets	Weight Reps Sets	Weight Reps Sets	Weight Reps Sets
× ×	× ×	× ×	× ×	× ×	× ×
Subtotal = lbs.	Subtotal = lbs.	Subtotal = lbs.	Subtotal = lbs.	Subtotal = lbs.	Subtotal = lbs.

Exercise 1:   *Total Weight* _____ *lbs.*   *Time* _____ *mins.*   *Power Factor* _____ *lbs./min.*   *Power Index* _____

■ Exercise: WEIGHTED CRUNCH

Weight Reps Sets	Weight Reps Sets	Weight Reps Sets	Weight Reps Sets	Weight Reps Sets	Weight Reps Sets
× ×	× ×	× ×	× ×	× ×	× ×
Subtotal = lbs.	Subtotal = lbs.	Subtotal = lbs.	Subtotal = lbs.	Subtotal = lbs.	Subtotal = lbs.

Exercise 2:   *Total Weight* _____ *lbs.*   *Time* _____ *mins.*   *Power Factor* _____ *lbs./min.*   *Power Index* _____

■ Exercise:

Weight Reps Sets	Weight Reps Sets	Weight Reps Sets	Weight Reps Sets	Weight Reps Sets	Weight Reps Sets
× ×	× ×	× ×	× ×	× ×	× ×
Subtotal = lbs.	Subtotal = lbs.	Subtotal = lbs.	Subtotal = lbs.	Subtotal = lbs.	Subtotal = lbs.

Exercise 3:   *Total Weight* _____ *lbs.*   *Time* _____ *mins.*   *Power Factor* _____ *lbs./min.*   *Power Index* _____

■ Exercise:

Weight Reps Sets	Weight Reps Sets	Weight Reps Sets	Weight Reps Sets	Weight Reps Sets	Weight Reps Sets
× ×	× ×	× ×	× ×	× ×	× ×
Subtotal = lbs.	Subtotal = lbs.	Subtotal = lbs.	Subtotal = lbs.	Subtotal = lbs.	Subtotal = lbs.

Exercise 4:   *Total Weight* _____ *lbs.*   *Time* _____ *mins.*   *Power Factor* _____ *lbs./min.*   *Power Index* _____

■ Exercise:

Weight Reps Sets	Weight Reps Sets	Weight Reps Sets	Weight Reps Sets	Weight Reps Sets	Weight Reps Sets
× ×	× ×	× ×	× ×	× ×	× ×
Subtotal = lbs.	Subtotal = lbs.	Subtotal = lbs.	Subtotal = lbs.	Subtotal = lbs.	Subtotal = lbs.

Exercise 5:   *Total Weight* _____ *lbs.*   *Time* _____ *mins.*   *Power Factor* _____ *lbs./min.*   *Power Index* _____

OVERALL WORKOUT: *Total Weight* _____ *lbs.*   *Time* _____ *mins.*   *Power Factor* _____ *lbs./min.*   *Power Index* _____

Exercise Subtotal = Weight × Reps × Sets   ■ *Power Factor = lbs./min.*   ■ *Power Index = Total Weight × Power Factor ÷ 1,000,000*

ABDOMINAL SPECIALIZATION WORKOUT RECORD   Date: ___ / ___ / ___

Start Time: _____   **Finish Time:** _____   **Total Time:** _____

▪ Exercise: DUMBBELL SIDE BEND

Weight Reps Sets	Weight Reps Sets	Weight Reps Sets	Weight Reps Sets	Weight Reps Sets	Weight Reps Sets
× ×	× ×	× ×	× ×	× ×	× ×
Subtotal = lbs.	Subtotal = lbs.	Subtotal = lbs.	Subtotal = lbs.	Subtotal = lbs.	Subtotal = lbs.

Exercise 1: _____ Total Weight _____ lbs.   Time _____ mins.   Power Factor _____ lbs./min.   Power Index _____

▪ Exercise: WEIGHTED CRUNCH

Weight Reps Sets	Weight Reps Sets	Weight Reps Sets	Weight Reps Sets	Weight Reps Sets	Weight Reps Sets
× ×	× ×	× ×	× ×	× ×	× ×
Subtotal = lbs.	Subtotal = lbs.	Subtotal = lbs.	Subtotal = lbs.	Subtotal = lbs.	Subtotal = lbs.

Exercise 2: _____ Total Weight _____ lbs.   Time _____ mins.   Power Factor _____ lbs./min.   Power Index _____

▪ Exercise:

Weight Reps Sets	Weight Reps Sets	Weight Reps Sets	Weight Reps Sets	Weight Reps Sets	Weight Reps Sets
× ×	× ×	× ×	× ×	× ×	× ×
Subtotal = lbs.	Subtotal = lbs.	Subtotal = lbs.	Subtotal = lbs.	Subtotal = lbs.	Subtotal = lbs.

Exercise 3: _____ Total Weight _____ lbs.   Time _____ mins.   Power Factor _____ lbs./min.   Power Index _____

▪ Exercise:

Weight Reps Sets	Weight Reps Sets	Weight Reps Sets	Weight Reps Sets	Weight Reps Sets	Weight Reps Sets
× ×	× ×	× ×	× ×	× ×	× ×
Subtotal = lbs.	Subtotal = lbs.	Subtotal = lbs.	Subtotal = lbs.	Subtotal = lbs.	Subtotal = lbs.

Exercise 4: _____ Total Weight _____ lbs.   Time _____ mins.   Power Factor _____ lbs./min.   Power Index _____

▪ Exercise:

Weight Reps Sets	Weight Reps Sets	Weight Reps Sets	Weight Reps Sets	Weight Reps Sets	Weight Reps Sets
× ×	× ×	× ×	× ×	× ×	× ×
Subtotal = lbs.	Subtotal = lbs.	Subtotal = lbs.	Subtotal = lbs.	Subtotal = lbs.	Subtotal = lbs.

Exercise 5: _____ Total Weight _____ lbs.   Time _____ mins.   Power Factor _____ lbs./min.   Power Index _____

OVERALL WORKOUT: *Total Weight* _____ lbs.   *Time* _____ mins.   *Power Factor* _____ lbs./min.   *Power Index* _____

Exercise Subtotal = Weight × Reps × Sets   ▪ *Power Factor = lbs./min.*   ▪ *Power Index = Total Weight × Power Factor ÷ 1,000,000*

ABDOMINAL SPECIALIZATION WORKOUT RECORD   Date: ___ / ___ / ___

Start Time: _____   **Finish Time:** _____   **Total Time:** _____

▪ Exercise: DUMBBELL SIDE BEND

Weight Reps Sets	Weight Reps Sets	Weight Reps Sets	Weight Reps Sets	Weight Reps Sets	Weight Reps Sets
× ×	× ×	× ×	× ×	× ×	× ×
Subtotal = lbs.	Subtotal = lbs.	Subtotal = lbs.	Subtotal = lbs.	Subtotal = lbs.	Subtotal = lbs.

Exercise 1:   *Total Weight* _____ *lbs.*   *Time* _____ *mins.*   *Power Factor* _____ *lbs./min.*   *Power Index* _____

▪ Exercise: WEIGHTED CRUNCH

Weight Reps Sets	Weight Reps Sets	Weight Reps Sets	Weight Reps Sets	Weight Reps Sets	Weight Reps Sets
× ×	× ×	× ×	× ×	× ×	× ×
Subtotal = lbs.	Subtotal = lbs.	Subtotal = lbs.	Subtotal = lbs.	Subtotal = lbs.	Subtotal = lbs.

Exercise 2:   *Total Weight* _____ *lbs.*   *Time* _____ *mins.*   *Power Factor* _____ *lbs./min.*   *Power Index* _____

▪ Exercise:

Weight Reps Sets	Weight Reps Sets	Weight Reps Sets	Weight Reps Sets	Weight Reps Sets	Weight Reps Sets
× ×	× ×	× ×	× ×	× ×	× ×
Subtotal = lbs.	Subtotal = lbs.	Subtotal = lbs.	Subtotal = lbs.	Subtotal = lbs.	Subtotal = lbs.

Exercise 3:   *Total Weight* _____ *lbs.*   *Time* _____ *mins.*   *Power Factor* _____ *lbs./min.*   *Power Index* _____

▪ Exercise:

Weight Reps Sets	Weight Reps Sets	Weight Reps Sets	Weight Reps Sets	Weight Reps Sets	Weight Reps Sets
× ×	× ×	× ×	× ×	× ×	× ×
Subtotal = lbs.	Subtotal = lbs.	Subtotal = lbs.	Subtotal = lbs.	Subtotal = lbs.	Subtotal = lbs.

Exercise 4:   *Total Weight* _____ *lbs.*   *Time* _____ *mins.*   *Power Factor* _____ *lbs./min.*   *Power Index* _____

▪ Exercise:

Weight Reps Sets	Weight Reps Sets	Weight Reps Sets	Weight Reps Sets	Weight Reps Sets	Weight Reps Sets
× ×	× ×	× ×	× ×	× ×	× ×
Subtotal = lbs.	Subtotal = lbs.	Subtotal = lbs.	Subtotal = lbs.	Subtotal = lbs.	Subtotal = lbs.

Exercise 5:   *Total Weight* _____ *lbs.*   *Time* _____ *mins.*   *Power Factor* _____ *lbs./min.*   *Power Index* _____

OVERALL WORKOUT: *Total Weight* _____ *lbs.*   *Time* _____ *mins.*   *Power Factor* _____ *lbs./min.*   *Power Index* _____

Exercise Subtotal = Weight × Reps × Sets   ▪ *Power Factor = lbs./min.*   ▪ *Power Index = Total Weight × Power Factor ÷ 1,000,000*

ABDOMINAL SPECIALIZATION WORKOUT RECORD   Date: ___ / ___ / ___

Start Time: _____   Finish Time: _____   Total Time: _____

▪ Exercise: DUMBBELL SIDE BEND

Weight Reps Sets	Weight Reps Sets	Weight Reps Sets	Weight Reps Sets	Weight Reps Sets	Weight Reps Sets
× ×	× ×	× ×	× ×	× ×	× ×
Subtotal = lbs.	Subtotal = lbs.	Subtotal = lbs.	Subtotal = lbs.	Subtotal = lbs.	Subtotal = lbs.

Exercise 1:   *Total Weight* _____ *lbs.*   *Time* _____ *mins.*   *Power Factor* _____ *lbs./min.*   *Power Index* _____

▪ Exercise: WEIGHTED CRUNCH

Weight Reps Sets	Weight Reps Sets	Weight Reps Sets	Weight Reps Sets	Weight Reps Sets	Weight Reps Sets
× ×	× ×	× ×	× ×	× ×	× ×
Subtotal = lbs.	Subtotal = lbs.	Subtotal = lbs.	Subtotal = lbs.	Subtotal = lbs.	Subtotal = lbs.

Exercise 2:   *Total Weight* _____ *lbs.*   *Time* _____ *mins.*   *Power Factor* _____ *lbs./min.*   *Power Index* _____

▪ Exercise:

Weight Reps Sets	Weight Reps Sets	Weight Reps Sets	Weight Reps Sets	Weight Reps Sets	Weight Reps Sets
× ×	× ×	× ×	× ×	× ×	× ×
Subtotal = lbs.	Subtotal = lbs.	Subtotal = lbs.	Subtotal = lbs.	Subtotal = lbs.	Subtotal = lbs.

Exercise 3:   *Total Weight* _____ *lbs.*   *Time* _____ *mins.*   *Power Factor* _____ *lbs./min.*   *Power Index* _____

▪ Exercise:

Weight Reps Sets	Weight Reps Sets	Weight Reps Sets	Weight Reps Sets	Weight Reps Sets	Weight Reps Sets
× ×	× ×	× ×	× ×	× ×	× ×
Subtotal = lbs.	Subtotal = lbs.	Subtotal = lbs.	Subtotal = lbs.	Subtotal = lbs.	Subtotal = lbs.

Exercise 4:   *Total Weight* _____ *lbs.*   *Time* _____ *mins.*   *Power Factor* _____ *lbs./min.*   *Power Index* _____

▪ Exercise:

Weight Reps Sets	Weight Reps Sets	Weight Reps Sets	Weight Reps Sets	Weight Reps Sets	Weight Reps Sets
× ×	× ×	× ×	× ×	× ×	× ×
Subtotal = lbs.	Subtotal = lbs.	Subtotal = lbs.	Subtotal = lbs.	Subtotal = lbs.	Subtotal = lbs.

Exercise 5:   *Total Weight* _____ *lbs.*   *Time* _____ *mins.*   *Power Factor* _____ *lbs./min.*   *Power Index* _____

OVERALL WORKOUT: *Total Weight* _____ *lbs.*   *Time* _____ *mins.*   *Power Factor* _____ *lbs./min.*   *Power Index* _____

Exercise Subtotal = Weight × Reps × Sets   ▪ *Power Factor = lbs./min.*   ▪ *Power Index = Total Weight × Power Factor ÷ 1,000,000*

ABDOMINAL SPECIALIZATION WORKOUT RECORD   Date: ___ / ___ / ___

Start Time: _____   **Finish Time:** _____   **Total Time:** _____

▪ Exercise: DUMBBELL SIDE BEND

Weight Reps Sets	Weight Reps Sets	Weight Reps Sets	Weight Reps Sets	Weight Reps Sets	Weight Reps Sets
× ×	× ×	× ×	× ×	× ×	× ×
Subtotal = lbs.	Subtotal = lbs.	Subtotal = lbs.	Subtotal = lbs.	Subtotal = lbs.	Subtotal = lbs.

Exercise 1:   *Total Weight* _____ *lbs.*   *Time* _____ *mins.*   *Power Factor* _____ *lbs./min.*   *Power Index* _____

▪ Exercise: WEIGHTED CRUNCH

Weight Reps Sets	Weight Reps Sets	Weight Reps Sets	Weight Reps Sets	Weight Reps Sets	Weight Reps Sets
× ×	× ×	× ×	× ×	× ×	× ×
Subtotal = lbs.	Subtotal = lbs.	Subtotal = lbs.	Subtotal = lbs.	Subtotal = lbs.	Subtotal = lbs.

Exercise 2:   *Total Weight* _____ *lbs.*   *Time* _____ *mins.*   *Power Factor* _____ *lbs./min.*   *Power Index* _____

▪ Exercise:

Weight Reps Sets	Weight Reps Sets	Weight Reps Sets	Weight Reps Sets	Weight Reps Sets	Weight Reps Sets
× ×	× ×	× ×	× ×	× ×	× ×
Subtotal = lbs.	Subtotal = lbs.	Subtotal = lbs.	Subtotal = lbs.	Subtotal = lbs.	Subtotal = lbs.

Exercise 3:   *Total Weight* _____ *lbs.*   *Time* _____ *mins.*   *Power Factor* _____ *lbs./min.*   *Power Index* _____

▪ Exercise:

Weight Reps Sets	Weight Reps Sets	Weight Reps Sets	Weight Reps Sets	Weight Reps Sets	Weight Reps Sets
× ×	× ×	× ×	× ×	× ×	× ×
Subtotal = lbs.	Subtotal = lbs.	Subtotal = lbs.	Subtotal = lbs.	Subtotal = lbs.	Subtotal = lbs.

Exercise 4:   *Total Weight* _____ *lbs.*   *Time* _____ *mins.*   *Power Factor* _____ *lbs./min.*   *Power Index* _____

▪ Exercise:

Weight Reps Sets	Weight Reps Sets	Weight Reps Sets	Weight Reps Sets	Weight Reps Sets	Weight Reps Sets
× ×	× ×	× ×	× ×	× ×	× ×
Subtotal = lbs.	Subtotal = lbs.	Subtotal = lbs.	Subtotal = lbs.	Subtotal = lbs.	Subtotal = lbs.

Exercise 5:   *Total Weight* _____ *lbs.*   *Time* _____ *mins.*   *Power Factor* _____ *lbs./min.*   *Power Index* _____

OVERALL WORKOUT: *Total Weight* _____ *lbs.*   *Time* _____ *mins.*   *Power Factor* _____ *lbs./min.*   *Power Index* _____

Exercise Subtotal = Weight × Reps × Sets   ▪ *Power Factor = lbs./min.*   ▪ *Power Index = Total Weight × Power Factor ÷ 1,000,000*

ABDOMINAL SPECIALIZATION WORKOUT RECORD   Date: ___ / ___ / ___

Start Time: _____   **Finish Time:** _____   **Total Time:** _____

■ Exercise: DUMBBELL SIDE BEND

Weight Reps Sets	Weight Reps Sets	Weight Reps Sets	Weight Reps Sets	Weight Reps Sets	Weight Reps Sets
× ×	× ×	× ×	× ×	× ×	× ×
Subtotal = lbs.	Subtotal = lbs.	Subtotal = lbs.	Subtotal = lbs.	Subtotal = lbs.	Subtotal = lbs.

Exercise 1:   *Total Weight* _____ *lbs.*   *Time* _____ *mins.*   *Power Factor* _____ *lbs./min.*   *Power Index* _____

■ Exercise: WEIGHTED CRUNCH

Weight Reps Sets	Weight Reps Sets	Weight Reps Sets	Weight Reps Sets	Weight Reps Sets	Weight Reps Sets
× ×	× ×	× ×	× ×	× ×	× ×
Subtotal = lbs.	Subtotal = lbs.	Subtotal = lbs.	Subtotal = lbs.	Subtotal = lbs.	Subtotal = lbs.

Exercise 2:   *Total Weight* _____ *lbs.*   *Time* _____ *mins.*   *Power Factor* _____ *lbs./min.*   *Power Index* _____

■ Exercise:

Weight Reps Sets	Weight Reps Sets	Weight Reps Sets	Weight Reps Sets	Weight Reps Sets	Weight Reps Sets
× ×	× ×	× ×	× ×	× ×	× ×
Subtotal = lbs.	Subtotal = lbs.	Subtotal = lbs.	Subtotal = lbs.	Subtotal = lbs.	Subtotal = lbs.

Exercise 3:   *Total Weight* _____ *lbs.*   *Time* _____ *mins.*   *Power Factor* _____ *lbs./min.*   *Power Index* _____

■ Exercise:

Weight Reps Sets	Weight Reps Sets	Weight Reps Sets	Weight Reps Sets	Weight Reps Sets	Weight Reps Sets
× ×	× ×	× ×	× ×	× ×	× ×
Subtotal = lbs.	Subtotal = lbs.	Subtotal = lbs.	Subtotal = lbs.	Subtotal = lbs.	Subtotal = lbs.

Exercise 4:   *Total Weight* _____ *lbs.*   *Time* _____ *mins.*   *Power Factor* _____ *lbs./min.*   *Power Index* _____

■ Exercise:

Weight Reps Sets	Weight Reps Sets	Weight Reps Sets	Weight Reps Sets	Weight Reps Sets	Weight Reps Sets
× ×	× ×	× ×	× ×	× ×	× ×
Subtotal = lbs.	Subtotal = lbs.	Subtotal = lbs.	Subtotal = lbs.	Subtotal = lbs.	Subtotal = lbs.

Exercise 5:   *Total Weight* _____ *lbs.*   *Time* _____ *mins.*   *Power Factor* _____ *lbs./min.*   *Power Index* _____

OVERALL WORKOUT: *Total Weight* _____ *lbs.*   *Time* _____ *mins.*   *Power Factor* _____ *lbs./min.*   *Power Index* _____

Exercise Subtotal = Weight × Reps × Sets   ■ *Power Factor = lbs./min.*   ■ *Power Index = Total Weight × Power Factor ÷ 1,000,000*

ABDOMINAL SPECIALIZATION WORKOUT RECORD Date: ___ / ___ / ___

Start Time: _____ Finish Time: _____ Total Time: _____

■ Exercise: DUMBBELL SIDE BEND

Weight Reps Sets	Weight Reps Sets	Weight Reps Sets	Weight Reps Sets	Weight Reps Sets	Weight Reps Sets
× ×	× ×	× ×	× ×	× ×	× ×
Subtotal = lbs.	Subtotal = lbs.	Subtotal = lbs.	Subtotal = lbs.	Subtotal = lbs.	Subtotal = lbs.

Exercise 1:   *Total Weight* _____ *lbs.*   *Time* _____ *mins.*   *Power Factor* _____ *lbs./min.*   *Power Index* _____

■ Exercise: WEIGHTED CRUNCH

Weight Reps Sets	Weight Reps Sets	Weight Reps Sets	Weight Reps Sets	Weight Reps Sets	Weight Reps Sets
× ×	× ×	× ×	× ×	× ×	× ×
Subtotal = lbs.	Subtotal = lbs.	Subtotal = lbs.	Subtotal = lbs.	Subtotal = lbs.	Subtotal = lbs.

Exercise 2:   *Total Weight* _____ *lbs.*   *Time* _____ *mins.*   *Power Factor* _____ *lbs./min.*   *Power Index* _____

■ Exercise:

Weight Reps Sets	Weight Reps Sets	Weight Reps Sets	Weight Reps Sets	Weight Reps Sets	Weight Reps Sets
× ×	× ×	× ×	× ×	× ×	× ×
Subtotal = lbs.	Subtotal = lbs.	Subtotal = lbs.	Subtotal = lbs.	Subtotal = lbs.	Subtotal = lbs.

Exercise 3:   *Total Weight* _____ *lbs.*   *Time* _____ *mins.*   *Power Factor* _____ *lbs./min.*   *Power Index* _____

■ Exercise:

Weight Reps Sets	Weight Reps Sets	Weight Reps Sets	Weight Reps Sets	Weight Reps Sets	Weight Reps Sets
× ×	× ×	× ×	× ×	× ×	× ×
Subtotal = lbs.	Subtotal = lbs.	Subtotal = lbs.	Subtotal = lbs.	Subtotal = lbs.	Subtotal = lbs.

Exercise 4:   *Total Weight* _____ *lbs.*   *Time* _____ *mins.*   *Power Factor* _____ *lbs./min.*   *Power Index* _____

■ Exercise:

Weight Reps Sets	Weight Reps Sets	Weight Reps Sets	Weight Reps Sets	Weight Reps Sets	Weight Reps Sets
× ×	× ×	× ×	× ×	× ×	× ×
Subtotal = lbs.	Subtotal = lbs.	Subtotal = lbs.	Subtotal = lbs.	Subtotal = lbs.	Subtotal = lbs.

Exercise 5:   *Total Weight* _____ *lbs.*   *Time* _____ *mins.*   *Power Factor* _____ *lbs./min.*   *Power Index* _____

OVERALL WORKOUT: *Total Weight* _____ *lbs.*   *Time* _____ *mins.*   *Power Factor* _____ *lbs./min.*   *Power Index* _____

Exercise Subtotal = Weight × Reps × Sets ■ *Power Factor = lbs./min.* ■ *Power Index = Total Weight × Power Factor ÷ 1,000,000*

ABDOMINAL SPECIALIZATION WORKOUT RECORD   Date: ___ / ___ / ___

Start Time: _____   **Finish Time:** _____   **Total Time:** _____

■ Exercise: DUMBBELL SIDE BEND

Weight Reps Sets	Weight Reps Sets	Weight Reps Sets	Weight Reps Sets	Weight Reps Sets	Weight Reps Sets
× ×	× ×	× ×	× ×	× ×	× ×
Subtotal = lbs.	Subtotal = lbs.	Subtotal = lbs.	Subtotal = lbs.	Subtotal = lbs.	Subtotal = lbs.

Exercise 1:   *Total Weight* _____ *lbs.*   *Time* _____ *mins.*   *Power Factor* _____ *lbs./min.*   *Power Index* _____

■ Exercise: WEIGHTED CRUNCH

Weight Reps Sets	Weight Reps Sets	Weight Reps Sets	Weight Reps Sets	Weight Reps Sets	Weight Reps Sets
× ×	× ×	× ×	× ×	× ×	× ×
Subtotal = lbs.	Subtotal = lbs.	Subtotal = lbs.	Subtotal = lbs.	Subtotal = lbs.	Subtotal = lbs.

Exercise 2:   *Total Weight* _____ *lbs.*   *Time* _____ *mins.*   *Power Factor* _____ *lbs./min.*   *Power Index* _____

■ Exercise:

Weight Reps Sets	Weight Reps Sets	Weight Reps Sets	Weight Reps Sets	Weight Reps Sets	Weight Reps Sets
× ×	× ×	× ×	× ×	× ×	× ×
Subtotal = lbs.	Subtotal = lbs.	Subtotal = lbs.	Subtotal = lbs.	Subtotal = lbs.	Subtotal = lbs.

Exercise 3:   *Total Weight* _____ *lbs.*   *Time* _____ *mins.*   *Power Factor* _____ *lbs./min.*   *Power Index* _____

■ Exercise:

Weight Reps Sets	Weight Reps Sets	Weight Reps Sets	Weight Reps Sets	Weight Reps Sets	Weight Reps Sets
× ×	× ×	× ×	× ×	× ×	× ×
Subtotal = lbs.	Subtotal = lbs.	Subtotal = lbs.	Subtotal = lbs.	Subtotal = lbs.	Subtotal = lbs.

Exercise 4:   *Total Weight* _____ *lbs.*   *Time* _____ *mins.*   *Power Factor* _____ *lbs./min.*   *Power Index* _____

■ Exercise:

Weight Reps Sets	Weight Reps Sets	Weight Reps Sets	Weight Reps Sets	Weight Reps Sets	Weight Reps Sets
× ×	× ×	× ×	× ×	× ×	× ×
Subtotal = lbs.	Subtotal = lbs.	Subtotal = lbs.	Subtotal = lbs.	Subtotal = lbs.	Subtotal = lbs.

Exercise 5:   *Total Weight* _____ *lbs.*   *Time* _____ *mins.*   *Power Factor* _____ *lbs./min.*   *Power Index* _____

OVERALL WORKOUT: *Total Weight* _____ *lbs.*   *Time* _____ *mins.*   *Power Factor* _____ *lbs./min.*   *Power Index* _____

Exercise Subtotal = Weight × Reps × Sets   ■ *Power Factor = lbs./min.*   ■ *Power Index = Total Weight × Power Factor ÷ 1,000,000*

ABDOMINAL SPECIALIZATION WORKOUT RECORD　Date: ___ / ___ / ___

Start Time: _____　Finish Time: _____　Total Time: _____

■ **Exercise:　DUMBBELL SIDE BEND**

Weight Reps Sets	Weight Reps Sets	Weight Reps Sets	Weight Reps Sets	Weight Reps Sets	Weight Reps Sets
× ×	× ×	× ×	× ×	× ×	× ×
Subtotal = lbs.	Subtotal = lbs.	Subtotal = lbs.	Subtotal = lbs.	Subtotal = lbs.	Subtotal = lbs.

Exercise 1:　*Total Weight* _____ *lbs.*　*Time* _____ *mins.*　*Power Factor* _____ *lbs./min.*　*Power Index* _____

■ **Exercise:　WEIGHTED CRUNCH**

Weight Reps Sets	Weight Reps Sets	Weight Reps Sets	Weight Reps Sets	Weight Reps Sets	Weight Reps Sets
× ×	× ×	× ×	× ×	× ×	× ×
Subtotal = lbs.	Subtotal = lbs.	Subtotal = lbs.	Subtotal = lbs.	Subtotal = lbs.	Subtotal = lbs.

Exercise 2:　*Total Weight* _____ *lbs.*　*Time* _____ *mins.*　*Power Factor* _____ *lbs./min.*　*Power Index* _____

■ **Exercise:**

Weight Reps Sets	Weight Reps Sets	Weight Reps Sets	Weight Reps Sets	Weight Reps Sets	Weight Reps Sets
× ×	× ×	× ×	× ×	× ×	× ×
Subtotal = lbs.	Subtotal = lbs.	Subtotal = lbs.	Subtotal = lbs.	Subtotal = lbs.	Subtotal = lbs.

Exercise 3:　*Total Weight* _____ *lbs.*　*Time* _____ *mins.*　*Power Factor* _____ *lbs./min.*　*Power Index* _____

■ **Exercise:**

Weight Reps Sets	Weight Reps Sets	Weight Reps Sets	Weight Reps Sets	Weight Reps Sets	Weight Reps Sets
× ×	× ×	× ×	× ×	× ×	× ×
Subtotal = lbs.	Subtotal = lbs.	Subtotal = lbs.	Subtotal = lbs.	Subtotal = lbs.	Subtotal = lbs.

Exercise 4:　*Total Weight* _____ *lbs.*　*Time* _____ *mins.*　*Power Factor* _____ *lbs./min.*　*Power Index* _____

■ **Exercise:**

Weight Reps Sets	Weight Reps Sets	Weight Reps Sets	Weight Reps Sets	Weight Reps Sets	Weight Reps Sets
× ×	× ×	× ×	× ×	× ×	× ×
Subtotal = lbs.	Subtotal = lbs.	Subtotal = lbs.	Subtotal = lbs.	Subtotal = lbs.	Subtotal = lbs.

Exercise 5:　*Total Weight* _____ *lbs.*　*Time* _____ *mins.*　*Power Factor* _____ *lbs./min.*　*Power Index* _____

OVERALL WORKOUT:　*Total Weight* _____ *lbs.*　*Time* _____ *mins.*　*Power Factor* _____ *lbs./min.*　*Power Index* _____

Exercise Subtotal = Weight × Reps × Sets　■ *Power Factor = lbs./min.*　■ *Power Index = Total Weight × Power Factor ÷ 1,000,000*

ABDOMINAL SPECIALIZATION WORKOUT RECORD Date: ___ / ___ / ___

Start Time: _____   **Finish Time:** _____   **Total Time:** _____

▪ Exercise: DUMBBELL SIDE BEND

Weight Reps Sets	Weight Reps Sets	Weight Reps Sets	Weight Reps Sets	Weight Reps Sets	Weight Reps Sets
× ×	× ×	× ×	× ×	× ×	× ×
Subtotal = lbs.	Subtotal = lbs.	Subtotal = lbs.	Subtotal = lbs.	Subtotal = lbs.	Subtotal = lbs.

Exercise 1:   *Total Weight _____ lbs.   Time _____ mins.   Power Factor _____ lbs./min.   Power Index _____*

▪ Exercise: WEIGHTED CRUNCH

Weight Reps Sets	Weight Reps Sets	Weight Reps Sets	Weight Reps Sets	Weight Reps Sets	Weight Reps Sets
× ×	× ×	× ×	× ×	× ×	× ×
Subtotal = lbs.	Subtotal = lbs.	Subtotal = lbs.	Subtotal = lbs.	Subtotal = lbs.	Subtotal = lbs.

Exercise 2:   *Total Weight _____ lbs.   Time _____ mins.   Power Factor _____ lbs./min.   Power Index _____*

▪ Exercise:

Weight Reps Sets	Weight Reps Sets	Weight Reps Sets	Weight Reps Sets	Weight Reps Sets	Weight Reps Sets
× ×	× ×	× ×	× ×	× ×	× ×
Subtotal = lbs.	Subtotal = lbs.	Subtotal = lbs.	Subtotal = lbs.	Subtotal = lbs.	Subtotal = lbs.

Exercise 3:   *Total Weight _____ lbs.   Time _____ mins.   Power Factor _____ lbs./min.   Power Index _____*

▪ Exercise:

Weight Reps Sets	Weight Reps Sets	Weight Reps Sets	Weight Reps Sets	Weight Reps Sets	Weight Reps Sets
× ×	× ×	× ×	× ×	× ×	× ×
Subtotal = lbs.	Subtotal = lbs.	Subtotal = lbs.	Subtotal = lbs.	Subtotal = lbs.	Subtotal = lbs.

Exercise 4:   *Total Weight _____ lbs.   Time _____ mins.   Power Factor _____ lbs./min.   Power Index _____*

▪ Exercise:

Weight Reps Sets	Weight Reps Sets	Weight Reps Sets	Weight Reps Sets	Weight Reps Sets	Weight Reps Sets
× ×	× ×	× ×	× ×	× ×	× ×
Subtotal = lbs.	Subtotal = lbs.	Subtotal = lbs.	Subtotal = lbs.	Subtotal = lbs.	Subtotal = lbs.

Exercise 5:   *Total Weight _____ lbs.   Time _____ mins.   Power Factor _____ lbs./min.   Power Index _____*

OVERALL WORKOUT: *Total Weight _____ lbs.   Time _____ mins.   Power Factor _____ lbs./min.   Power Index _____*

Exercise Subtotal = Weight × Reps × Sets   ▪ Power Factor = lbs./min.   ▪ Power Index = Total Weight × Power Factor ÷ 1,000,000

ABDOMINAL SPECIALIZATION WORKOUT RECORD   Date: ___ / ___ / ___

Start Time: _____   **Finish Time:** _____   **Total Time:** _____

■ Exercise: DUMBBELL SIDE BEND

Weight Reps Sets	Weight Reps Sets	Weight Reps Sets	Weight Reps Sets	Weight Reps Sets	Weight Reps Sets
× ×	× ×	× ×	× ×	× ×	× ×
Subtotal = lbs.	Subtotal = lbs.	Subtotal = lbs.	Subtotal = lbs.	Subtotal = lbs.	Subtotal = lbs.

Exercise 1:   Total Weight _____ lbs.   Time _____ mins.   Power Factor _____ lbs./min.   Power Index _____

■ Exercise: WEIGHTED CRUNCH

Weight Reps Sets	Weight Reps Sets	Weight Reps Sets	Weight Reps Sets	Weight Reps Sets	Weight Reps Sets
× ×	× ×	× ×	× ×	× ×	× ×
Subtotal = lbs.	Subtotal = lbs.	Subtotal = lbs.	Subtotal = lbs.	Subtotal = lbs.	Subtotal = lbs.

Exercise 2:   Total Weight _____ lbs.   Time _____ mins.   Power Factor _____ lbs./min.   Power Index _____

■ Exercise:

Weight Reps Sets	Weight Reps Sets	Weight Reps Sets	Weight Reps Sets	Weight Reps Sets	Weight Reps Sets
× ×	× ×	× ×	× ×	× ×	× ×
Subtotal = lbs.	Subtotal = lbs.	Subtotal = lbs.	Subtotal = lbs.	Subtotal = lbs.	Subtotal = lbs.

Exercise 3:   Total Weight _____ lbs.   Time _____ mins.   Power Factor _____ lbs./min.   Power Index _____

■ Exercise:

Weight Reps Sets	Weight Reps Sets	Weight Reps Sets	Weight Reps Sets	Weight Reps Sets	Weight Reps Sets
× ×	× ×	× ×	× ×	× ×	× ×
Subtotal = lbs.	Subtotal = lbs.	Subtotal = lbs.	Subtotal = lbs.	Subtotal = lbs.	Subtotal = lbs.

Exercise 4:   Total Weight _____ lbs.   Time _____ mins.   Power Factor _____ lbs./min.   Power Index _____

■ Exercise:

Weight Reps Sets	Weight Reps Sets	Weight Reps Sets	Weight Reps Sets	Weight Reps Sets	Weight Reps Sets
× ×	× ×	× ×	× ×	× ×	× ×
Subtotal = lbs.	Subtotal = lbs.	Subtotal = lbs.	Subtotal = lbs.	Subtotal = lbs.	Subtotal = lbs.

Exercise 5:   Total Weight _____ lbs.   Time _____ mins.   Power Factor _____ lbs./min.   Power Index _____

OVERALL WORKOUT: *Total Weight* _____ *lbs.*   *Time* _____ *mins.*   *Power Factor* _____ *lbs./min.*   *Power Index* _____

Exercise Subtotal = Weight × Reps × Sets   ■   *Power Factor = lbs./min.*   ■   *Power Index = Total Weight × Power Factor ÷ 1,000,000*

APPENDIX C: Exercise/Workout Performance Records

These forms are used to record the performance of every workout and individual exercise that you do. Using the instructions provided on pages 24 to 28, you can calculate the percentage change from workout to workout and determine at a glance whether your efforts were productive.

The Power Factor and Power Index numbers from these forms are plotted on the graphs in Appendix D.

This level of precision and sophistication provides Power Factor trainees with the tools to engineer every workout to obtain maximum results. This is truly the *science* of bodybuilding.

WORKOUT A PERFORMANCE RECORD

Date	Total Weight	% Change	Power Factor	% Change	Power Index	+ or − Change

WORKOUT B PERFORMANCE RECORD

Date	Total Weight	% Change	Power Factor	% Change	Power Index	+ or − Change

STANDING BARBELL PRESS PERFORMANCE RECORD

Date	Total Weight	% Change	Power Factor	% Change	Power Index	+ or − Change

BARBELL SHRUG PERFORMANCE RECORD

Date	Total Weight	% Change	Power Factor	% Change	Power Index	+ or − Change

CLOSE-GRIP BENCH PRESS PERFORMANCE RECORD

Date	Total Weight	% Change	Power Factor	% Change	Power Index	+ or − Change

PREACHER CURL PERFORMANCE RECORD

Date	Total Weight	% Change	Power Factor	% Change	Power Index	+ or − Change

WEIGHTED CRUNCH PERFORMANCE RECORD

Date	Total Weight	% Change	Power Factor	% Change	Power Index	+ or − Change

DEADLIFT PERFORMANCE RECORD

Date	Total Weight	% Change	Power Factor	% Change	Power Index	+ or − Change

BENCH PRESS PERFORMANCE RECORD

Date	Total Weight	% Change	Power Factor	% Change	Power Index	+ or − Change

LAT PULLDOWN PERFORMANCE RECORD

Date	Total Weight	% Change	Power Factor	% Change	Power Index	+ or − Change

LEG PRESS PERFORMANCE RECORD

Date	Total Weight	% Change	Power Factor	% Change	Power Index	+ or − Change

TOE PRESS PERFORMANCE RECORD

Date	Total Weight	% Change	Power Factor	% Change	Power Index	+ or − Change

BARBELL DECLINE BENCH PRESS PERFORMANCE RECORD

Date	Total Weight	% Change	Power Factor	% Change	Power Index	+ or − Change

HIGH-PULLEY CABLE CROSSOVER PERFORMANCE RECORD

Date	Total Weight	% Change	Power Factor	% Change	Power Index	+ or − Change

DIP PERFORMANCE RECORD

Date	Total Weight	% Change	Power Factor	% Change	Power Index	+ or − Change

SEATED BARBELL TRICEPS EXTENSION PERFORMANCE RECORD

Date	Total Weight	% Change	Power Factor	% Change	Power Index	+ or − Change

SEATED BARBELL CURL PERFORMANCE RECORD

Date	Total Weight	% Change	Power Factor	% Change	Power Index	+ or − Change

STANDING BARBELL CURL PERFORMANCE RECORD

Date	Total Weight	% Change	Power Factor	% Change	Power Index	+ or − Change

STANDING BARBELL REVERSE CURL PERFORMANCE RECORD

Date	Total Weight	% Change	Power Factor	% Change	Power Index	+ or − Change

SEATED DUMBBELL REVERSE WRIST CURL PERFORMANCE RECORD

Date	Total Weight	% Change	Power Factor	% Change	Power Index	+ or − Change

STANDING BARBELL WRIST CURL BEHIND BACK PERFORMANCE RECORD

Date	Total Weight	% Change	Power Factor	% Change	Power Index	+ or − Change

STANDING BENT-OVER DUMBBELL LATERAL PERFORMANCE RECORD

Date	Total Weight	% Change	Power Factor	% Change	Power Index	+ or − Change

LAT PULLDOWN PERFORMANCE RECORD

Date	Total Weight	% Change	Power Factor	% Change	Power Index	+ or − Change

TOE-UP ON LEG CURL MACHINE PERFORMANCE RECORD

Date	Total Weight	% Change	Power Factor	% Change	Power Index	+ or − Change

STANDING CALF RAISE PERFORMANCE RECORD

Date	Total Weight	% Change	Power Factor	% Change	Power Index	+ or − Change

DUMBBELL SIDE BEND PERFORMANCE RECORD

Date	Total Weight	% Change	Power Factor	% Change	Power Index	+ or − Change

CLOSE-GRIP UNDERHAND CHIN-UP PERFORMANCE RECORD

Date	Total Weight	% Change	Power Factor	% Change	Power Index	+ or − Change

CHEST SPECIALIZATION WORKOUT PERFORMANCE RECORD

Date	Total Weight	% Change	Power Factor	% Change	Power Index	+ or − Change

TRICEPS SPECIALIZATION WORKOUT PERFORMANCE RECORD

Date	Total Weight	% Change	Power Factor	% Change	Power Index	+ or − Change

BICEPS SPECIALIZATION WORKOUT PERFORMANCE RECORD

Date	Total Weight	% Change	Power Factor	% Change	Power Index	+ or − Change

FOREARM SPECIALIZATION WORKOUT PERFORMANCE RECORD

Date	Total Weight	% Change	Power Factor	% Change	Power Index	+ or − Change

SHOULDER SPECIALIZATION WORKOUT PERFORMANCE RECORD

Date	Total Weight	% Change	Power Factor	% Change	Power Index	+ or − Change

BACK SPECIALIZATION WORKOUT PERFORMANCE RECORD

Date	Total Weight	% Change	Power Factor	% Change	Power Index	+ or − Change

LEG SPECIALIZATION WORKOUT PERFORMANCE RECORD

Date	Total Weight	% Change	Power Factor	% Change	Power Index	+ or − Change

ABDOMINAL SPECIALIZATION WORKOUT PERFORMANCE RECORD

Date	Total Weight	% Change	Power Factor	% Change	Power Index	+ or − Change

APPENDIX D: Progress Graphs

The graphs that follow are used to display the information in the Exercise/ Workout Performance Records. By graphing your Power Factor and Power Index, you'll be able to see at a glance the rate of progress you are achieving. Also, plateaus and declines due to overtraining (or improper training) will be impossible to ignore. These graphs will provide all the evidence that you, or any skeptic in the gym, will need to verify your tangible, objectively measured progress. The sample Progress Graph on page 272 accurately depicts the results from the sample Performance Record on page 25.

Note that the Power Factor number is plotted on the left y-axis (vertical axis) and the Power Index number is plotted on the right y-axis. Note also that the Power Index scale is logarithmic.

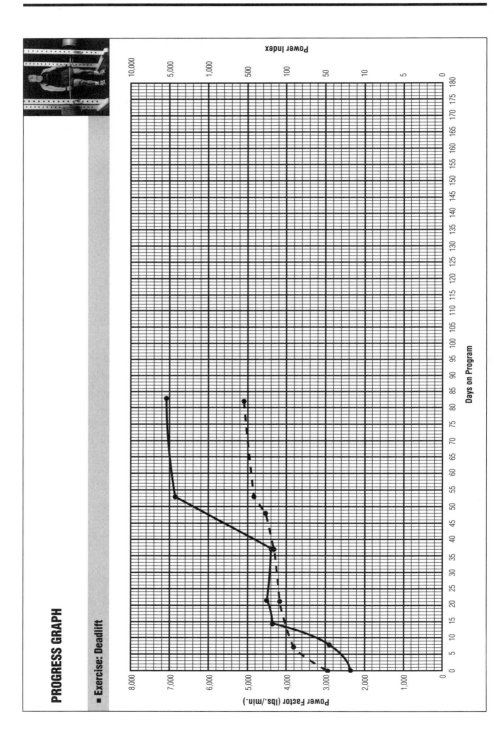

PROGRESS GRAPH

■ Exercise: Deadlift

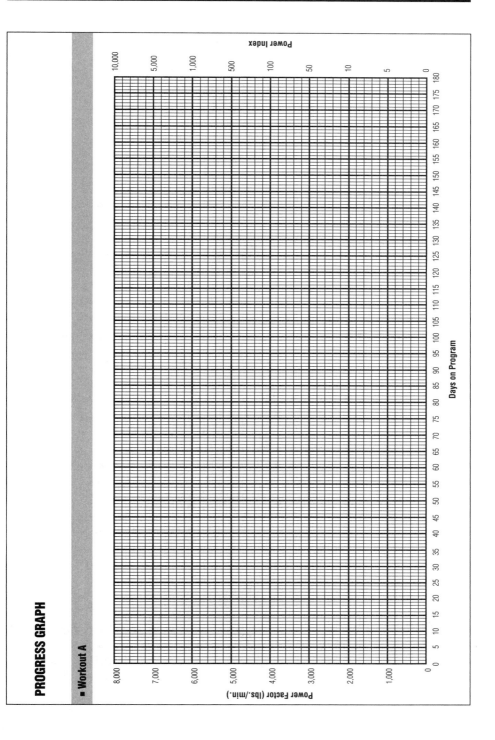

PROGRESS GRAPH

■ Workout A

PROGRESS GRAPH

■ Workout A

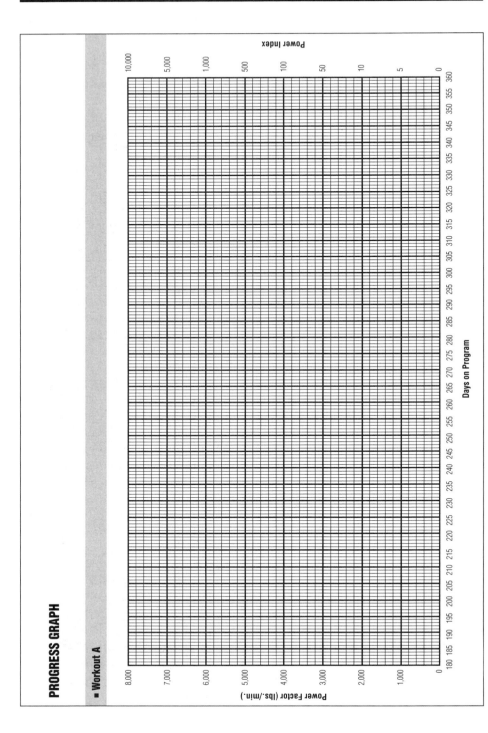

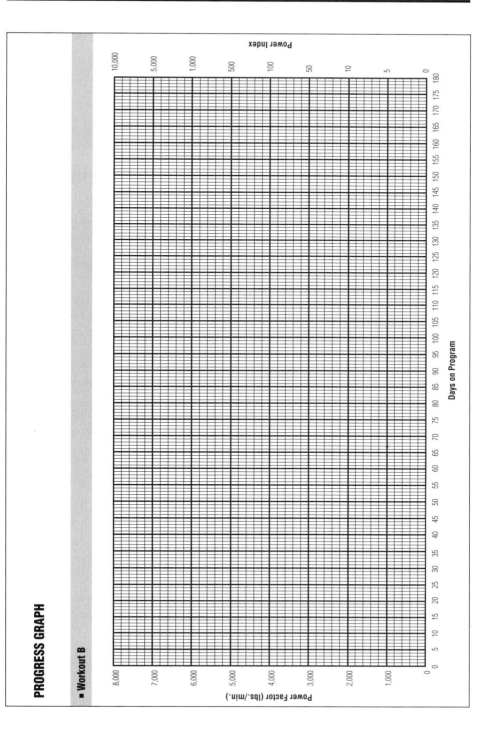

PROGRESS GRAPH

■ Workout B

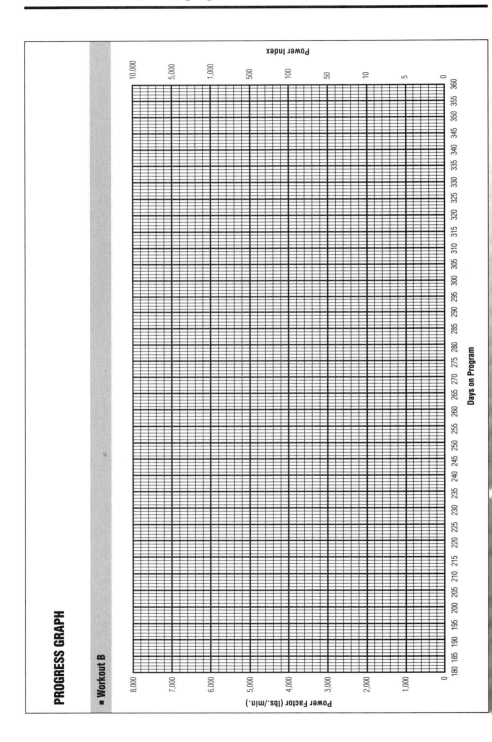

PROGRESS GRAPH

■ **Workout B**

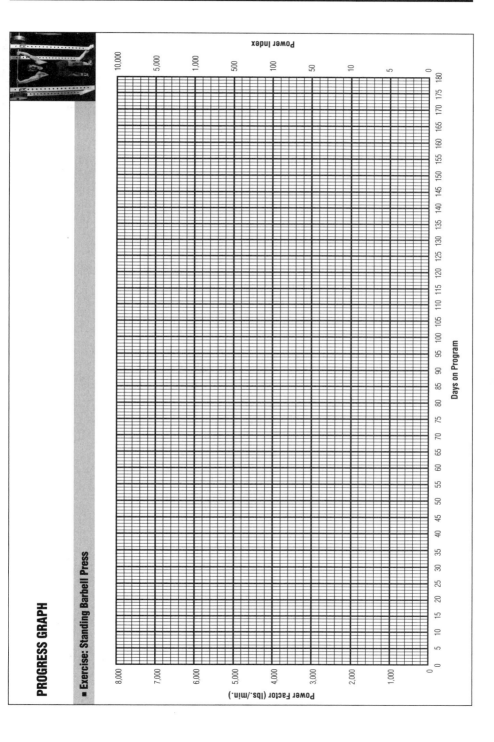

PROGRESS GRAPH

■ Exercise: Standing Barbell Press

PROGRESS GRAPH

■ **Exercise: Barbell Shrug**

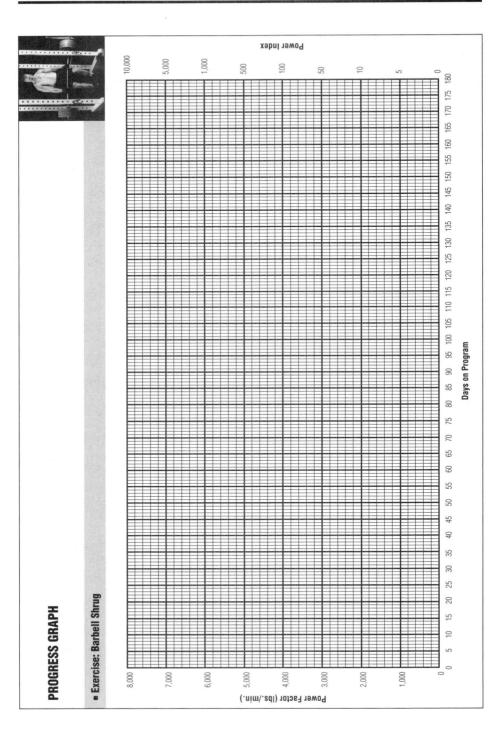

PROGRESS GRAPH

■ **Exercise: Close-Grip Bench Press**

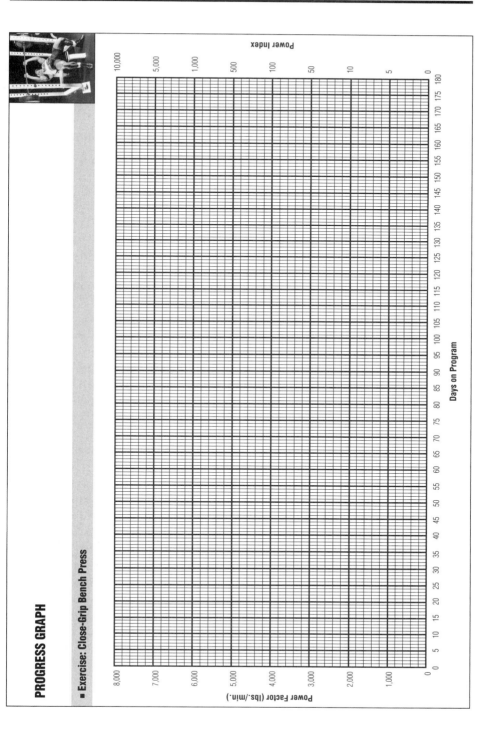

Power Index

Days on Program

Power Factor (lbs./min.)

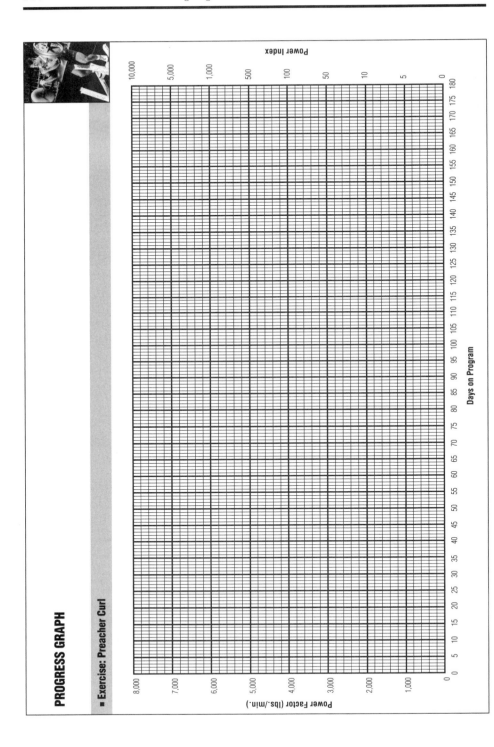

PROGRESS GRAPH

■ **Exercise: Preacher Curl**

Power Index

Power Factor (lbs./min.)

Days on Program

PROGRESS GRAPH

■ Exercise: Weighted Crunch

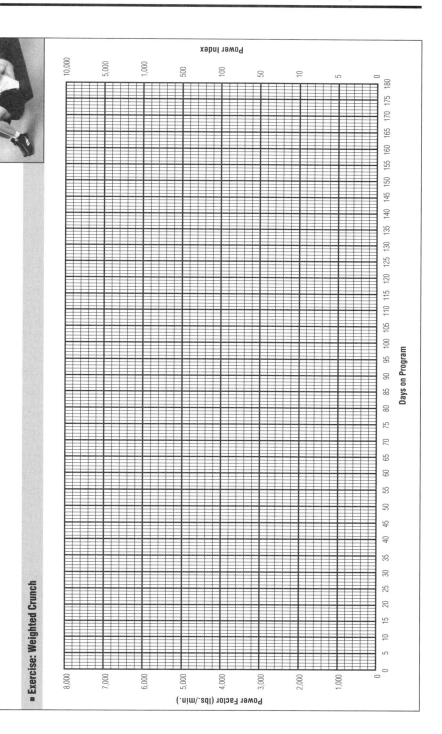

Power Index

10,000 — 5,000 — 1,000 — 500 — 100 — 50 — 10 — 5 — 0

Power Factor (lbs./min.)

8,000 — 7,000 — 6,000 — 5,000 — 4,000 — 3,000 — 2,000 — 1,000 — 0

Days on Program

0 5 10 15 20 25 30 35 40 45 50 55 60 65 70 75 80 85 90 95 100 105 110 115 120 125 130 135 140 145 150 155 160 165 170 175 180

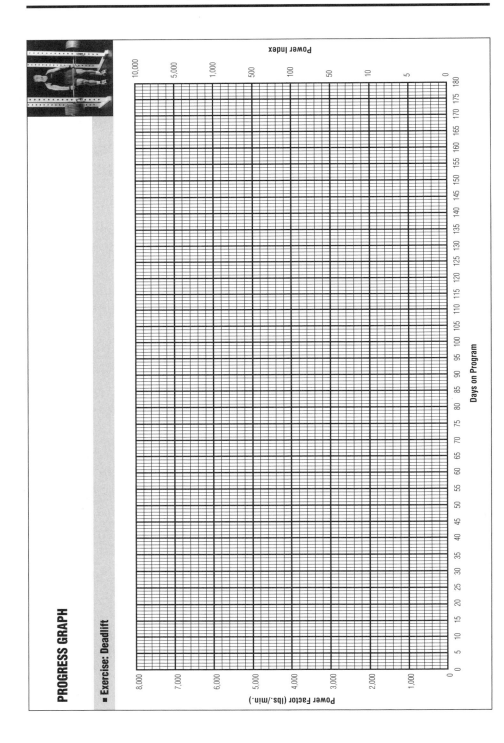

PROGRESS GRAPH

■ Exercise: Deadlift

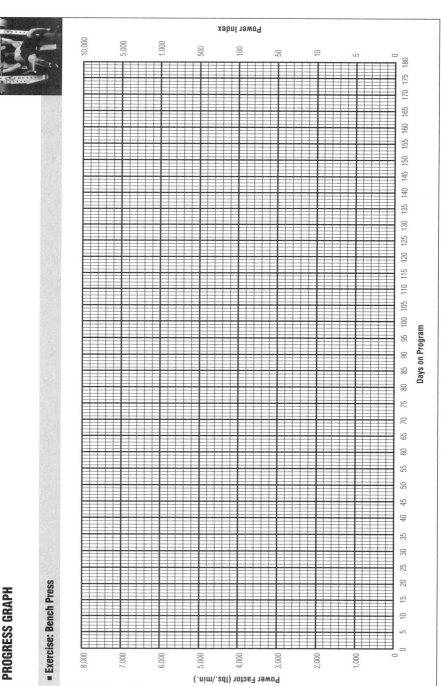

PROGRESS GRAPH

■ **Exercise: Bench Press**

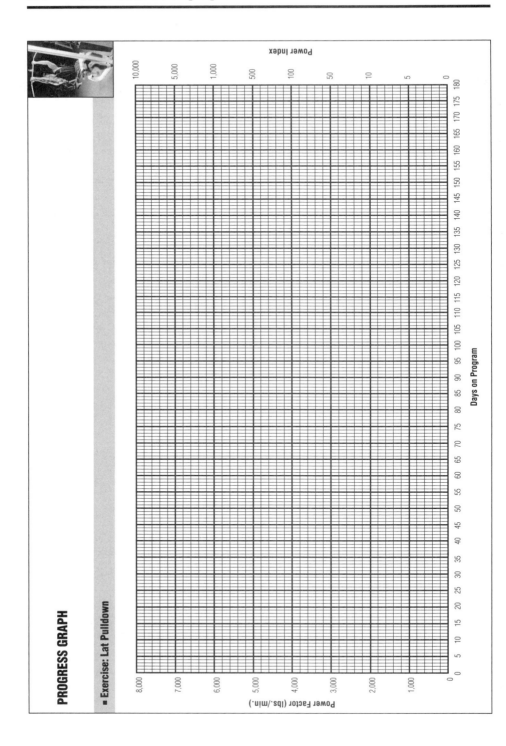

PROGRESS GRAPH

■ Exercise: Lat Pulldown

PROGRESS GRAPH

■ **Exercise: Leg Press**

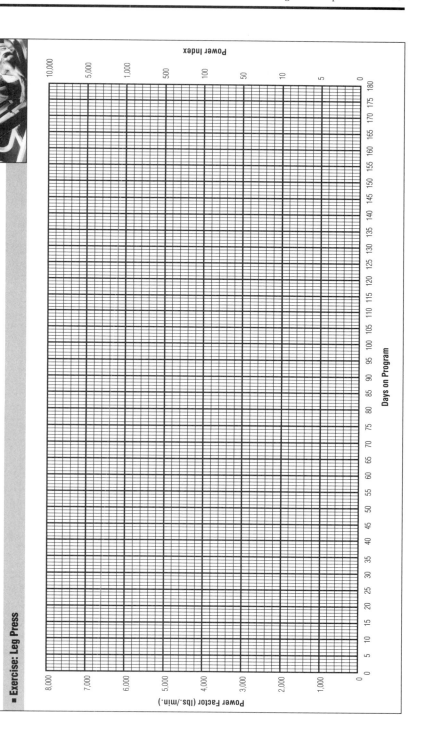

PROGRESS GRAPH

■ Exercise: Toe Press

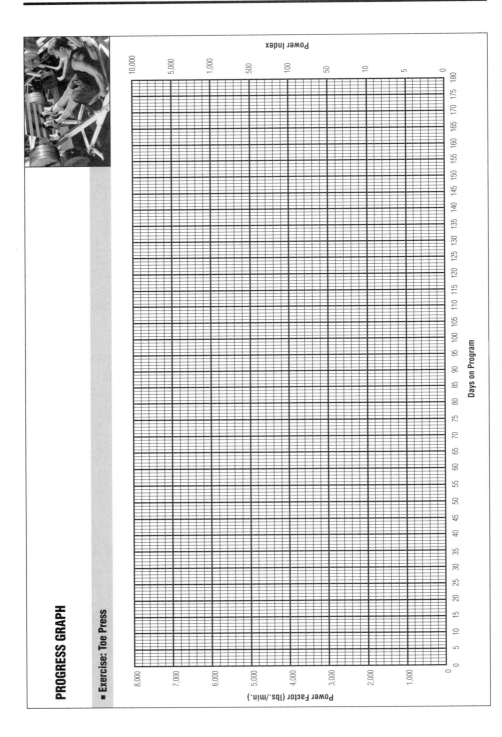

PROGRESS GRAPH

■ **Exercise: Barbell Decline Bench Press**

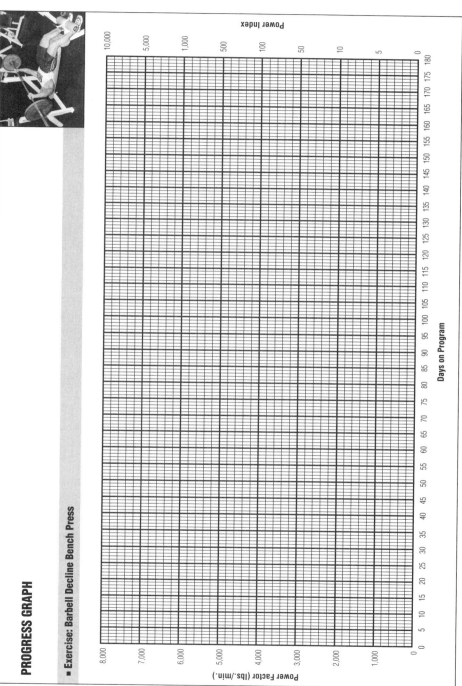

Power Index

Power Factor (lbs./min.)

Days on Program

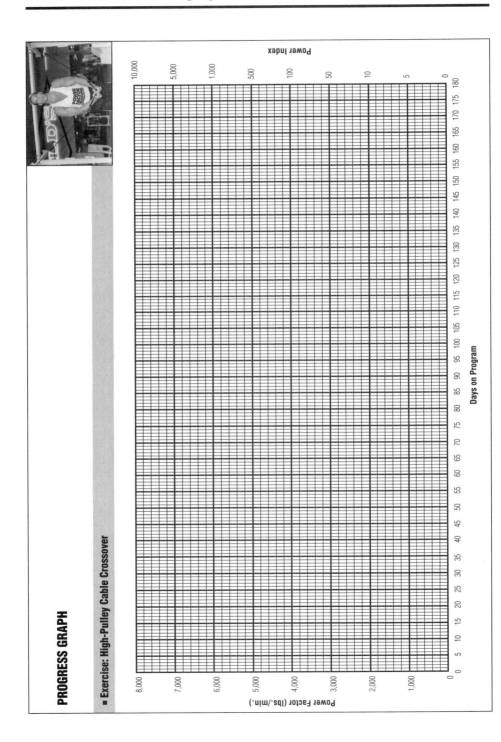

PROGRESS GRAPH

▪ **Exercise: High-Pulley Cable Crossover**

PROGRESS GRAPH

■ **Exercise: Dip**

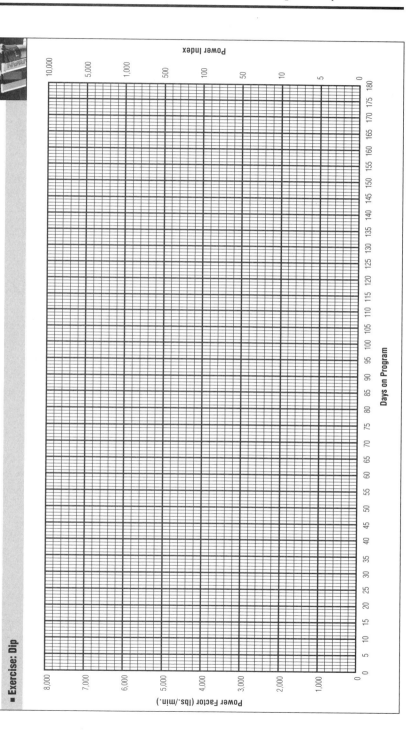

PROGRESS GRAPH

■ **Exercise: Seated Barbell Triceps Extension**

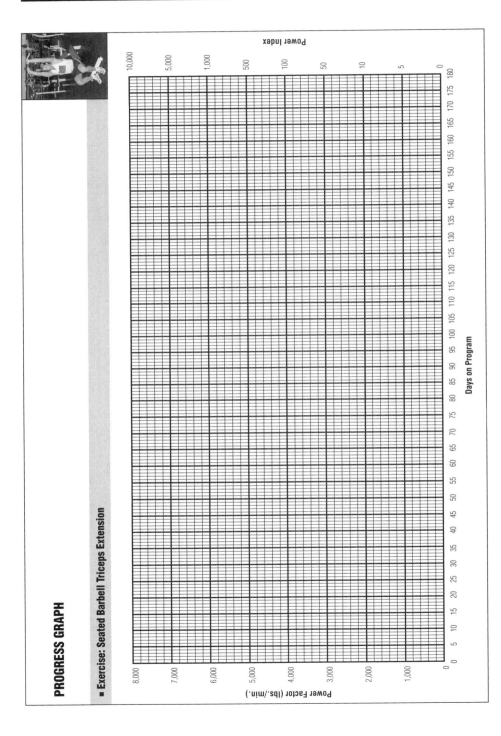

Power Index

Power Factor (lbs./min.)

Days on Program

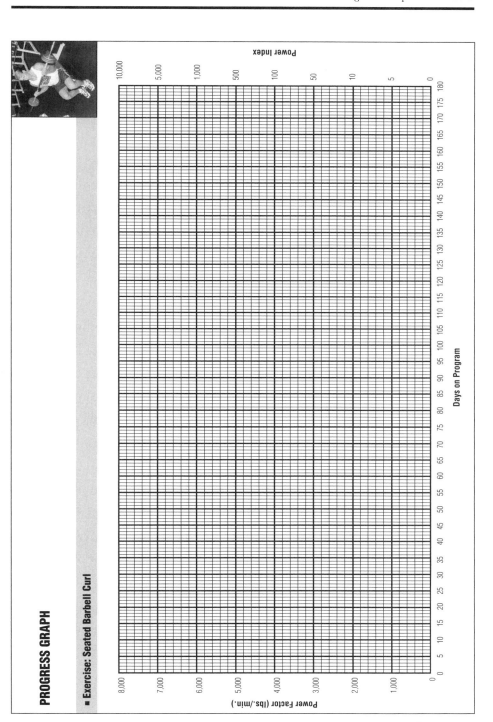

PROGRESS GRAPH

■ Exercise: Seated Barbell Curl

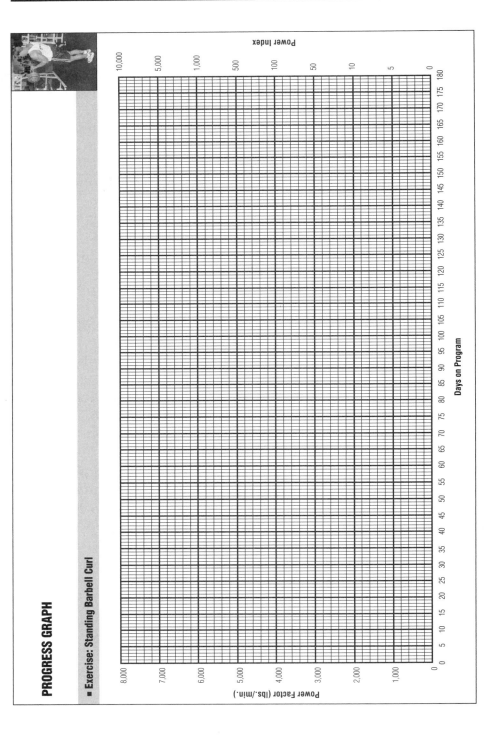

PROGRESS GRAPH

■ **Exercise: Standing Barbell Curl**

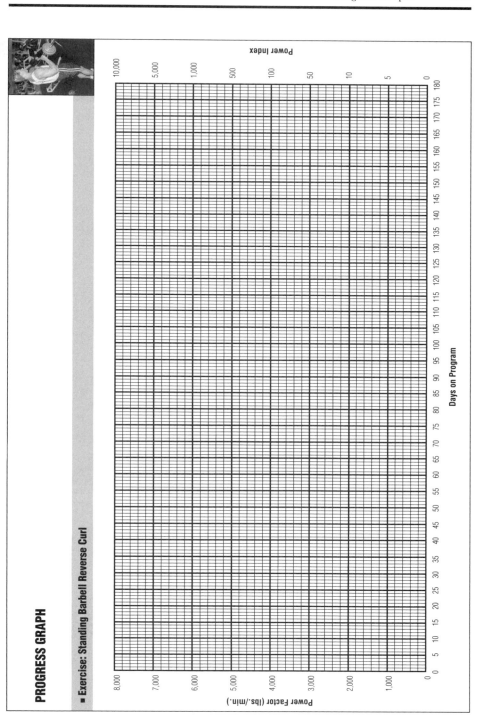

PROGRESS GRAPH

■ **Exercise: Standing Barbell Reverse Curl**

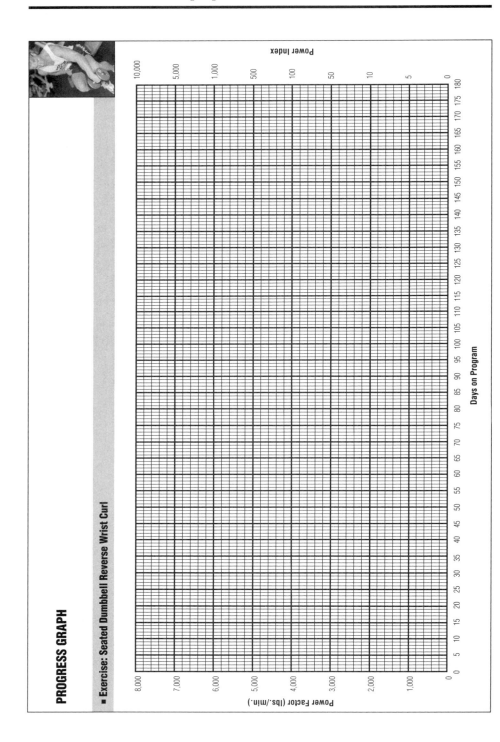

PROGRESS GRAPH

■ Exercise: Seated Dumbbell Reverse Wrist Curl

Power Index

Power Factor (lbs./min.)

Days on Program

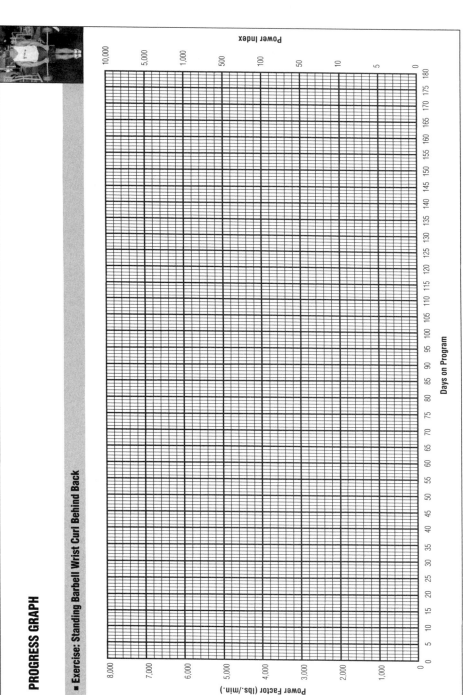

PROGRESS GRAPH

■ Exercise: Standing Barbell Wrist Curl Behind Back

PROGRESS GRAPH

■ Exercise: Standing Bent-Over Dumbbell Lateral

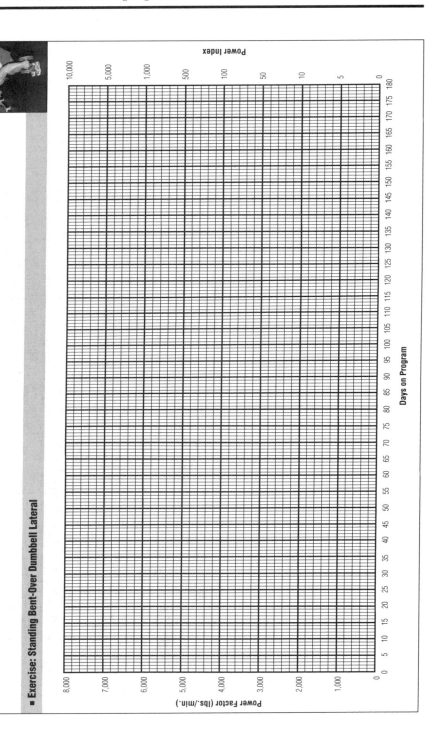

PROGRESS GRAPH

■ **Exercise: Lat Pulldown**

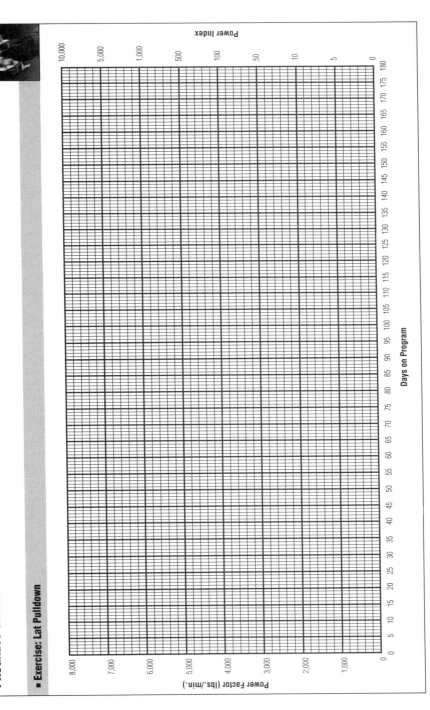

PROGRESS GRAPH

■ Exercise: Toe-Up on Leg Curl Machine

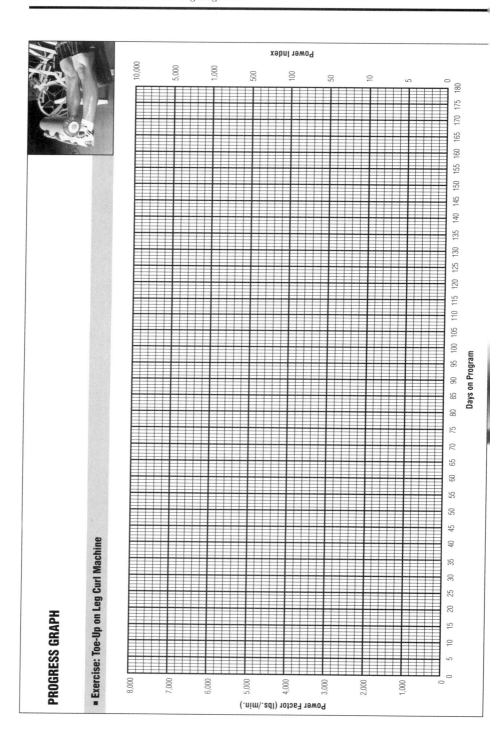

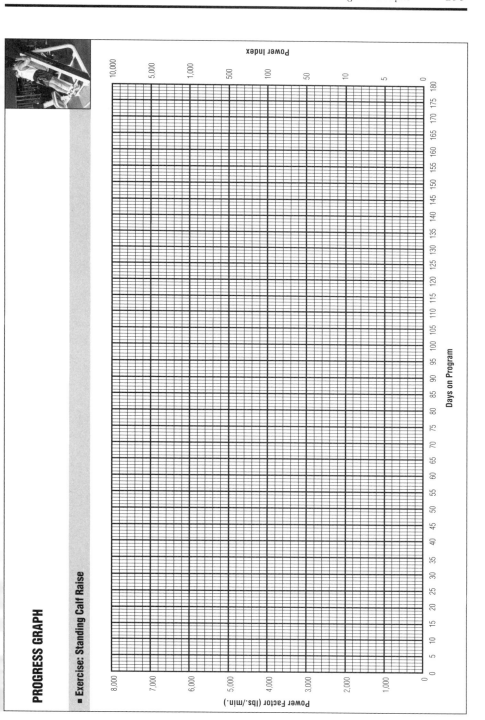

PROGRESS GRAPH

■ **Exercise: Standing Calf Raise**

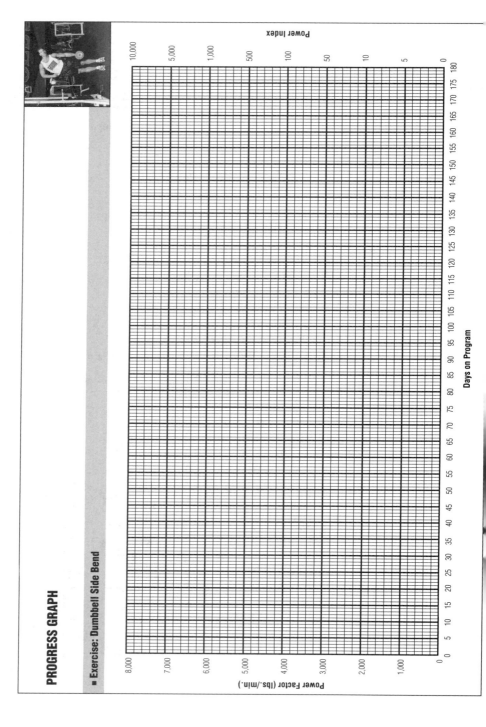

PROGRESS GRAPH

■ **Exercise: Dumbbell Side Bend**

PROGRESS GRAPH

■ Exercise: Close-Grip Underhand Chin-Up

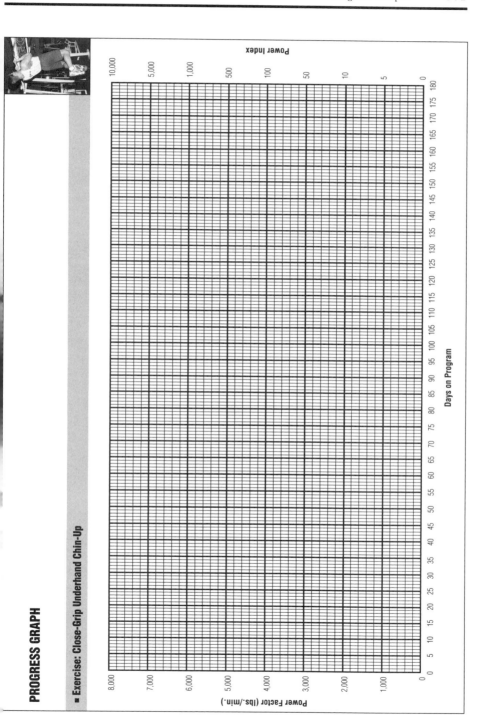

PROGRESS GRAPH

Chest Specialization Workout

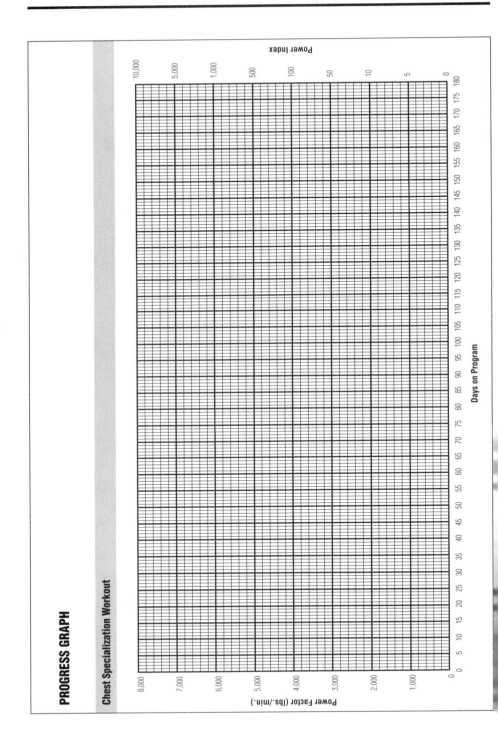

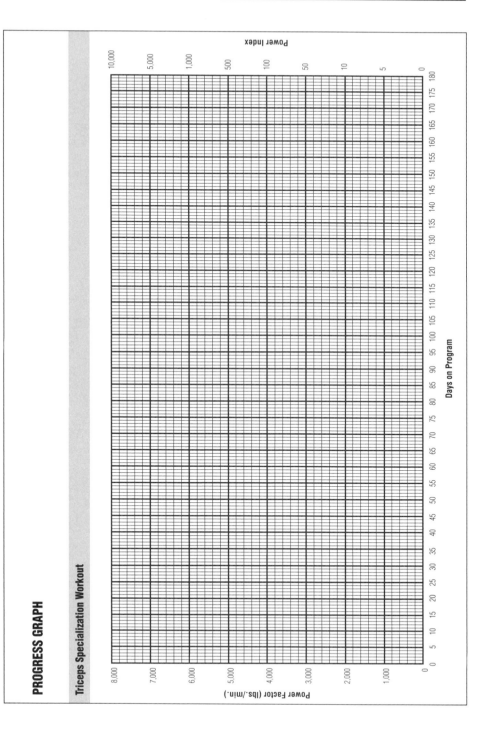

PROGRESS GRAPH

Triceps Specialization Workout

Power Index

Power Factor (lbs./min.)

Days on Program

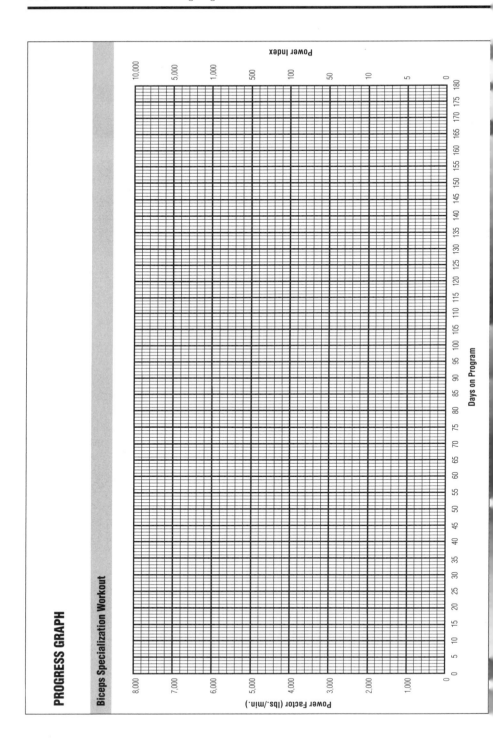

PROGRESS GRAPH

Biceps Specialization Workout

Power Index

Power Factor (lbs./min.)

Days on Program

PROGRESS GRAPH

Forearm Specialization Workout

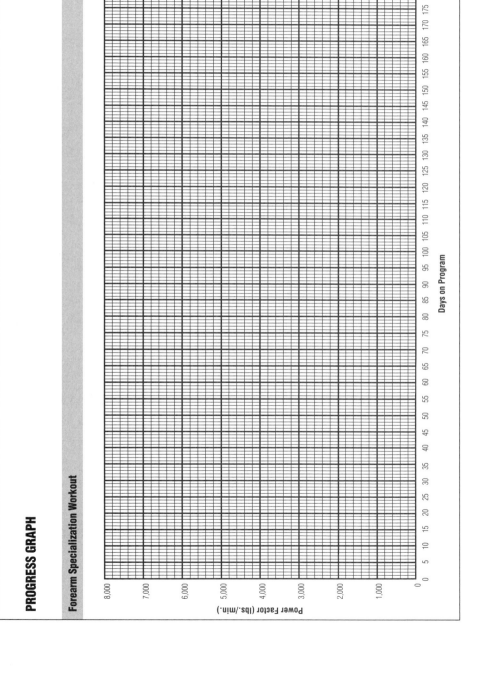

Power Index

Power Factor (lbs./min.)

Days on Program

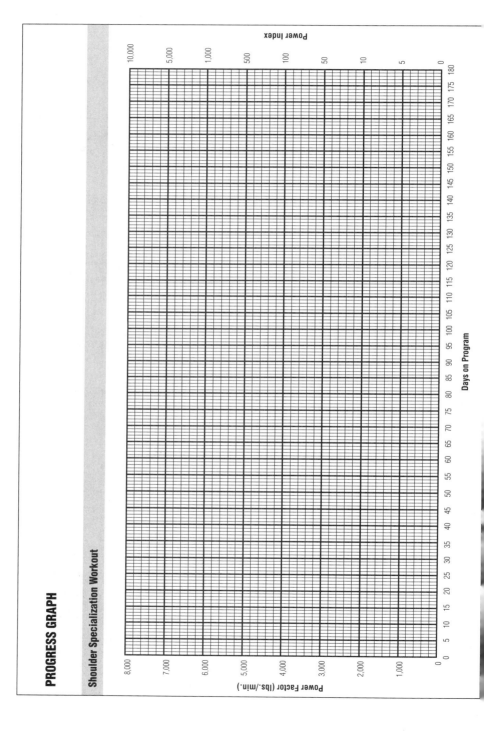

PROGRESS GRAPH

Back Specialization Workout

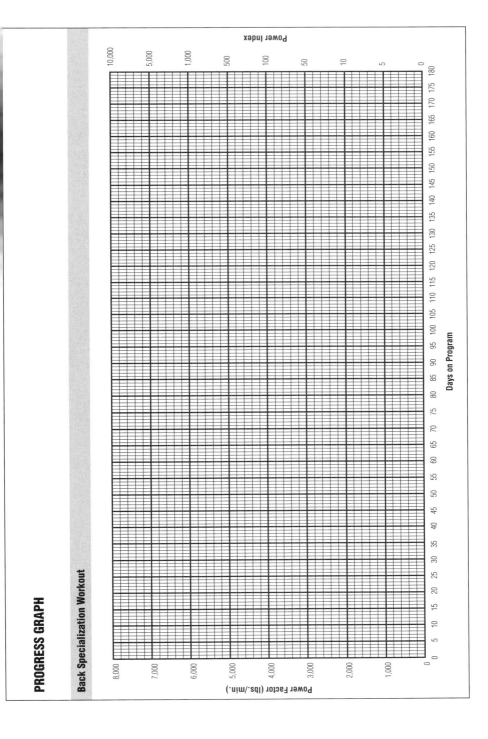

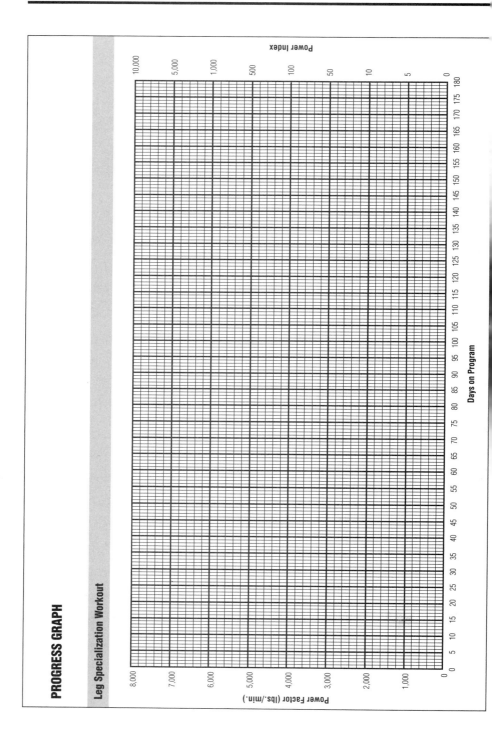

PROGRESS GRAPH

Leg Specialization Workout

Power Index

Power Factor (lbs./min.)

Days on Program

PROGRESS GRAPH

Abdominal Specialization Workout

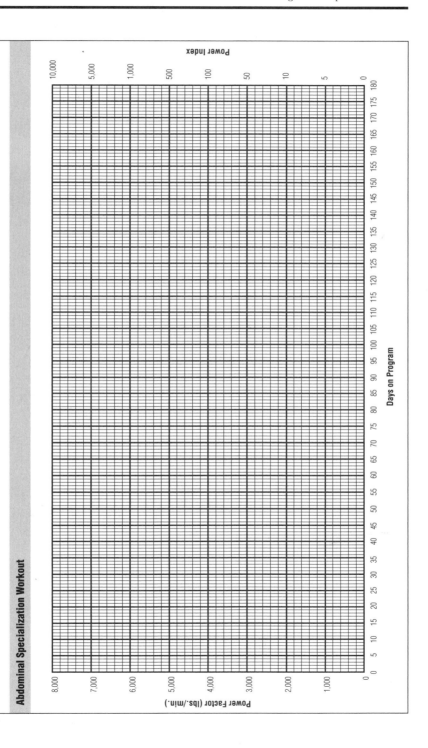